HIMALAYA, KARAKORAM
AND
HINDU KUSH

PAKISTAN
TREKKING GUIDE

HIMALAYA, KARAKORAM
AND
HINDU KUSH

ISOBEL SHAW AND BEN SHAW

Hong Kong

Distribution in the United Kingdom, Ireland, Europe and certain Commonwealth countries by Hodder & Stoughton, Mill Road, Dunton Green, Sevenoaks, Kent TW13 2YA

British Library Cataloguing-in-Publication Data
A catalogue record for this book is available from the British Library

Editor: Peter Fredenburg
Series Editor: Anna Claridge
Design: De•Style Studio
Map Design: Bai Yiliang
Cover Photograph: Isobel Shaw

Production by Twin Age Limited, Hong Kong
Printed in China

TABLE OF CONTENTS

MAP LIST AND LEGEND

Map legend

●	principal towns	6252	altitude in metres
•	smaller towns or villages	≍	pass
·	summer settlements or camp sites	～	river
——	surfaced road	⌁	glacier
——	jeep road	·⊢·⊢·	national boundary
– – –	footpath or trekking route	·▬·▬·	ceasefire line/line of control
▲	mountain	⁼⁼⁼	provincial/district boundary

FOREWORD

We (mother Isobel and son Ben) started trekking in earnest in northern Pakistan in July 1987. In five years we have covered most of the main treks in each region, but this just scratches the surface of the many possibilities. We also asked everyone we could find with an interest in trekking in this area for their comments and experiences, and all were enthusiastic and helpful in sharing their knowledge with us. Without them this book would have been less complete. The styles, observations and timings in the treks differ reflecting the contributors' idiosyncrasies and interests, and credit is given to each at the end of his or her contribution.

Our most invaluable informant is André Roch, who shared his excellent mountain library, answered our almost-daily telephone calls with patience and encouragement, and was an endless source of information on the most obscure facts. At the age of 84, he even accompanied us up the Baltoro Glacier to Concordia, telling stories of all the mountains along the way. Elisabeth Gardner, an inexhaustible trekker, shared all her precise notes and timings of Pakistani treks and has read and edited the entire manuscript. She also spent several months trekking with us in 1987, 1990 and 1991. Hermann Kreutzmann, who spent years in Hunza studying for his doctorate, has been most generous with his time and information, and has checked the sections on Gilgit and Hunza for us.

Many others have helped in the research. Ashraf Aman organised our more difficult expeditions and escorted us over the Hispar Pass. Muhammad Ali Chengezi was always ready to answer questions and spend hours pouring over maps. Nazir Sabir gave ideas on which treks to include and information on how to deal with troublesome porters. Sajid Uwais Agha shared his detailed knowledge of Kohistan, and Vaqar Zakaria took us step by step on the map through Azad Kashmir and over the Dadarili Pass. Babu Muhammad, a specialist on Chitral, corrected my notes on the Phargam and Kachikhani passes, and Steve Razzetti, Gordon Thomson, Christian Dupré, Steve Reich and David Watt all gave information on Shimshal. Steve Venables helped with the Biafo and Khurdopin glaciers, and Mike Searle with the Braldu Glacier. Kent Obee, Larry True, Linda Brown and Cynthia Brown shared their experiences on the Masherbrum Pass. Philip Astley described the Basho Valley, and Beverly Barnett and Philip Parnell checked the Hushe section. Musarat Wali Khan, Joe Brennan and Steve Harvatt described parts of the Rakaposhi Range we have not visited, and Raja Ali Ahmad Jan told us stories of his native Nagar. Siraj and Ghazala ul-Mulk added two treks in Chitral, their uncle

Major Khush Ahmed ul-Mulk and his son Maqsood described some remote valleys round Tirich Mir, and Colonel Khushwaqt ul-Mulk filled us in on the history of his ancestors. Alfred Tissières recounted tales of trekking in the Chalt region and his attempt on Rakaposhi in 1954, and Professor K Haserodt shared his research findings in Chitral. Lastly, John King's excellent book on the Karakoram Highway told us several details we had overlooked.

Our sincere thanks also go to our various trekking companions, whose company, if only for a few days, made the research more fun: Katie Shaw, Sue O'Beirne, Suzanne Staples, Jewell Price, Paul Dekkers, Fergus Donaldson, Claude and Frédérique Viret, Elisabeth Gardner, Peter Allison, John Elliott, Khush Ahmed ul-Mulk, Catriona Prebble, Sue Farrington, Annelène Balk, Amanda Edwards and Andy Stevens, Jorge Jäkel, John and Debbie Shephard and, of course, André Roch.

Extra thanks go to those who helped actually write the book: to Tom Roberts for taking the time to go over our sections on flora and fauna, and for his expert help with the birds; to John Shephard, an experienced expedition doctor, for his section on expedition medicine; and to his wife, Debbie, for her help on expedition cooking. We have never eaten so well as when Debbie was with us; being a vegetarian, she has had a lifetime of practice at making palatable dishes out of Pakistani staples like lentils and chickpeas. Thanks also to our friends Sally Alderson and Sheila Schleinitz, who helped by reading and editing parts of the typescript. Most of all, thanks to Peter Fredenburg for his expert and patient work as our editor at The Guidebook Company.

We would also like to thank the trekking companies who lent us equipment each summer: Adventure Tours Pakistan, Karakoram Tours, Mountain Movers, Walji's Adventure Pakistan and Sitara Travel.

All who have struggled with Pakistani red tape know that what you need most is the right contact. Musarrat and Shoaib Sultan Khan have been that invaluable contact for us, opening closed doors, advising, encouraging and helping in every way, from obtaining permits to giving useful introductions and offering transport. Best of all, they gave us their friendship and always welcomed us with traditional Pakistani warmth and generosity such as you seldom find in the West. We can never thank them enough or repay all they have done for us.

We also owe thanks to others who have opened their homes to us, fed and nursed us when we were tired, and generally gave us shelter and encouragement: Jeremy and Patsy Ainslie of the British Embassy in Islamabad, Stephen and Zebu Rasmussen, Major Khush Ahmed ul-Mulk of Chitral and Raja Ali Ahmad Jan of Nagar.

The information in this book comes from first-hand information (if we sometimes slide into first-person singular, it reflects one author's experience). It must never be forgotten, though, that mountains slide and glaciers move, and that conditions are different at different times of year. In many areas there are winter paths and summer paths depending on the snow cover and the height of the rivers. Old paths are buried, new ones are made and bridges get washed out and relocated, so trail information changes from season to season and year to year. By the time this book is available, the jeep roads will stretch a few more miles up many of the valleys. The accuracy of future editions of this book can be improved by you, the users. If you find any descriptions misleading or inaccurate, please send us the details care of the publisher, The Guidebook Company Ltd, 20 Hollywood Road, Central, Hong Kong. Your suggestions and corrections, with credit to you, will be included in the next edition.

Finally we give love and thanks to Robert, our long-suffering husband and father, who with infinite patience finances our summer adventures each year (guidebook writing is not lucrative, especially when it takes five years).

Ben and Isobel Shaw
Geneva, November 1992

INTRODUCTION

Take nothing but photos, leave nothing but footprints.

We pray we do not come to regret having written this book. The information here opens up all of the valleys of Pakistan to trekkers; it invites them to discover for themselves the joys of the unspoiled, unvisited, remoter areas of a beautiful country. We wrote this book with love, sharing our experiences and respect for Pakistan and its people. We hope you will travel here with love and sensitivity and leave the valleys unchanged.

Trekking in northern Pakistan excites the imagination. It is one of the most rugged and isolated places on earth, only recently explored and mapped. Here, strategically close to the heart of Central Asia, is the hub of the world's greatest mountain chains. The Karakoram, the Himalaya, the Hindu Kush and the Pamir radiate out from this centre like spokes on a wheel.

These mountains are the walls that form Pakistan's long and carefully guarded frontiers with China, India and Afghanistan—and, across the narrow Wakhan Corridor, the former Soviet Union. In no other part of the world is there such a large number of high mountains in such a confined space (five peaks over 8,000 metres and 108 higher than 7,000). And nowhere outside of the polar regions has longer or more spectacular glaciers (seven over 40 kilometres long).

Hidden amid this network of snow-capped peaks and striated glaciers are narrow mountain valleys, housing a resilient and hospitable people who call their home *bam-i-dunia*, the roof of the world. These valleys were so cut off that, until recently, they each formed a separate little kingdom, ruled by a raja or mir, each speaking its own isolated language. In the past 20 years, these kingdoms have been absorbed into Pakistan, and jeep tracks are creeping up the valleys, giving access to the outside world.

The combination of hospitable people, isolation and magnificent mountain scenery makes this a perfect place to trek, provided that you have a thirst for adventure, a love of nature and the strength to enjoy challenging walking.

Of the four mountain ranges, the Karakoram is the most remote and wild. The area is a mountain desert whose few inhabitants live by irrigating small oases of terraced land along the rivers—small green patchworks of fields sewn onto the grey valley walls. Were it not for the glacial melt waters, all would be barren. Even today, these mountains are less well explored and mapped than other comparable mountain regions, and many peaks over 6,000 metres remain unnamed and unclimbed.

The Karakoram glaciers are stupendous—huge expanses of tortured ice covered in a blanket of boulders and gravel. Along their lower edges, though, are alpine meadows watered by the melting ice and shaded by willow and juniper trees. These draw the shepherds and their flocks up from the villages for the summer months. These summer pastures, carpeted in edelweiss, gentians and primulas, with banks of orchids along the glacial streams, wild roses and honeysuckle scattered amid the rocks, all surrounded by towering jagged peaks and tumbling cascades of ice, are the reward for the determined trekker.

Trekking in this region is unique—unlike anything in the Americas, Europe or even elsewhere in Asia. The trekking paths follow the animal trails from the last village in a valley to the snout of the glacier, usually around 3,000 metres in altitude. Shepherds' tracks continue along the lower glaciers, giving access to the summer pastures and winter hunting grounds above.

For the first couple of days of your trek, you usually follow these paths, alternating between the ablation valley (the gully between the glacier and the mountain), lateral moraine (the mound of stones left by the glacier along its side) and the edge of the glacier itself. Every few kilometres you come to a shepherds' summer settlement, a collection of stone huts of varying designs depending on the local traditions and available building materials, where you can observe the life of the shepherds: milking, making cheese and guarding the flocks. At some point you may have to cross the glacier—an exciting experience as you learn a new, tentative way of walking, stepping gingerly from boulder to boulder with knees bent, testing to see which way the rock will turn, and scrambling and sliding up and down melting ice slopes.

After about a week, depending on the trek, you reach the pass, usually between 4,000 and 5,000 metres high, and start your descent into the next valley, which may have a completely different culture, with different clothes, houses and language—and even following a different sect of Islam.

Apart from the well-known areas around K2 (the highest mountain in the Karakoram and the second highest in the world) and Nanga Parbat (the western-most peak of the Himalayan Range and the world's ninth highest), you are likely to meet few fellow trekkers; in the more remote areas it is possible to walk for days along glaciers and over passes without meeting another human being, let alone another Westerner. You can still find remote valleys where the locals have not seen a foreigner for decades—we have been to several settlements where they have never seen a Western woman before. These remoter areas have not yet suffered too much from the clashes with modern culture. Here isolation has preserved a way of life that elsewhere has disappeared.

***

We have written this book both for healthy walkers who have never trekked before and know nothing about Pakistan and for experienced Himalayan explorers looking for new adventures. It describes in detail everything you need to know. Old hands may find it says too much and accuse us of spoiling the exciting adventure of exploring one of the last great wildernesses. Let us whisper—we have not described our favourite valleys, and there is still more for others to discover. Experienced trekkers already know most of what is suggested here and have their own preferences regarding equipment and styles of trekking, so we beg their patience. Our aim is to explain what trekking is like in Pakistan, from the easy walkabouts in the main valleys to difficult mountaineering across glaciated passes. The main rule for the trekker is to know where you are going and your own capabilities, and not to take yourself or your porters to an area for which you are not equipped or prepared.

The first chapters of this book deal mostly with the planning and preparation of your trekking holiday, including also sections on background history, flora and fauna, and how to get from your home country to the beginning of your chosen trek. The later chapters offer descriptions of the valleys of northern Pakistan, stressing each one's individual history, culture, language, dress and customs, pointing out most of the possible treks in each valley, but giving a detailed, stage-by-stage description of only those treks— some long, some short—for which our information is most complete. We have graded the treks as 'easy', 'strenuous', 'very strenuous' or 'technical'. 'Easy' treks involve long days and easy glacier crossings; 'strenuous' treks are harder, involving long days one after another, up to an altitude of 5,000 metres; 'very strenuous' treks are difficult and long and require the use of rope for dangerous glacier crossings; and 'technical' treks require mountaineering and climbing skills.

We feel that trekking can be enjoyed by everyone who is healthy and fit and has a taste for the mountains and outdoor life. Age is no barrier; we have travelled with our three children and various friends of all ages. Ben started as a six-week-old baby on a grand tour of the East African game parks; at three he sulked round India and, at five, enjoyed his first trek in Kashmir (mostly on a pony). At the other end of a lifetime, André Roch escorted us to K2 Base Camp at the age of 84.

The success of any trip depends on you. Hike at home first, go camping with family and friends, and be sure you enjoy living in tents and cooking on a campfire in the rain before you set off for an adventure in Pakistan. You need to be able to walk long distances for many days in a row and, sometimes, in very hot or cold weather. Remember that, if you have walked for a week from the end of the jeep track, it will take you a week to walk back again—a fact you may not appreciate until an emergency.

Above all, you must enjoy walking and being a stranger in a strange land. If so, you should come away from Pakistan not only with memories of a fantastic holiday, but also a profound admiration for the kindhearted and friendly people who wring a livelihood out of the valleys and mountains of northern Pakistan.

LAND AND PEOPLE

> Here the present is so simple and satisfying . . . and so full of peace and
> beauty— that one is more than willing to pretend nothing else ever existed
> or ever can exist. Each day I seem to feel more deeply content and inwardly
> stronger, as though the uncomplicated joy of travelling through these moun-
> tains were a form of nourishment.
>
> Dervla Murphy, *Where the Indus Is Young*

The Himalaya and Karakoram are the world's newest mountains. About 55 million years
ago, the Indian geological plate drifted northwards and collided with the Asian plate,
its northern edge nosing under and pushing up the mountains. The Indian plate is still
driving northwards at about five centimetres a year, causing the mountains to rise about
seven millimetres annually.

In northern Pakistan the mountains are divided into four ranges. The northernmost
tip if the country is the hub of the system. Radiating out to the west, on the border
with Afghanistan, lie the Hindu Kush, whose eastern boundary is marked by the Ishkoman
and Karumbar rivers in Gilgit District. (Most maps mark the eastern end of this range
as the Hindu Raj—a name that means 'Hindu rule' and has therefore fallen out of favour
in Muslim Pakistan.) Flowing north from these, the Pamirs run up into the former Soviet
Union. Spreading from the centre to the northeast, along the border with China, lie
the Karakoram—the main block of mountains in Pakistan, 250 kilometres long and 150
kilometres wide. Finally, in the southeast corner, separated from the Karakoram by the
Indus River, the western tip of the Himalaya Range lies along the disputed border with
India. Within the mountains of northern Pakistan are four main valleys—Indus, Gilgit,
Hunza and Chitral, all within the Indus drainage system.

The Indus existed before the mountains formed, and the mighty river was able to
maintain its course as the mountains rose. It enters Pakistan flowing northwestwards
into Baltistan, having already travelled nearly 1,000 kilometres from its source in Tibet,
passing through Ladakh in northern India along the way.

Politically, Pakistan is divided into four provinces: Sindh, Baluchistan, Punjab and
the North-West Frontier Province (NWFP). In addition, there are two other regions,
the Northern Areas and Azad (Free) Kashmir, which were won from India in 1948.
India and Pakistan still dispute these two areas, along with the portion of Muslim Kashmir
held by India. The United Nations-monitored ceasefire line separates the two sides.

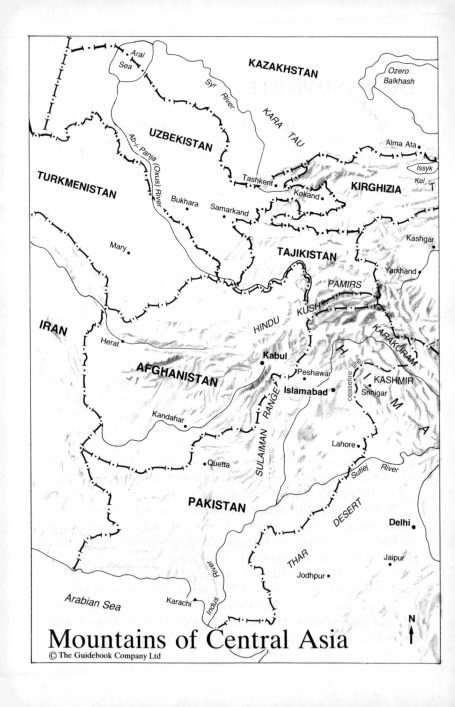

Mountains of Central Asia

© The Guidebook Company Ltd

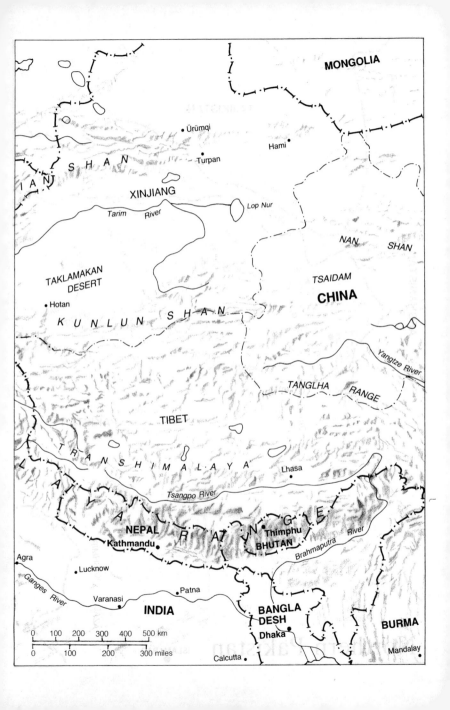

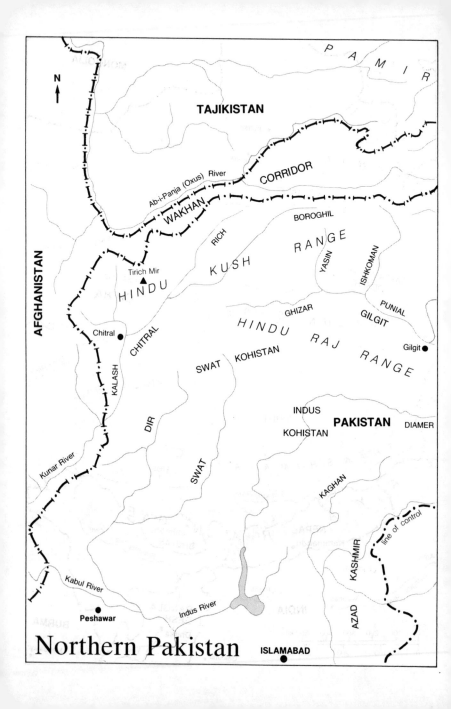

Northern Pakistan

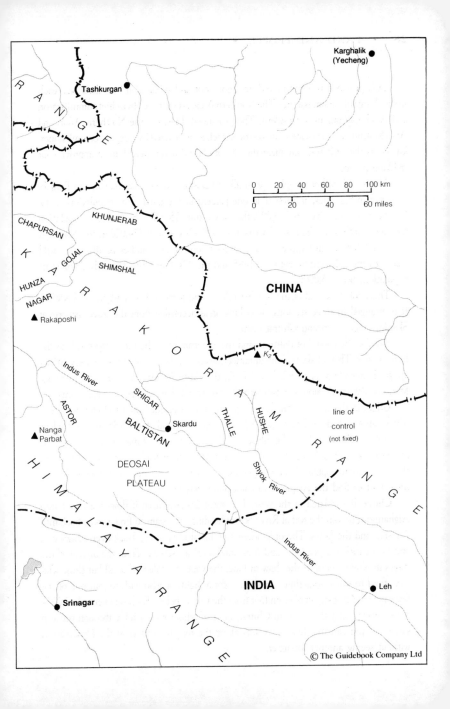

Each province is administered by a governor and subdivided into divisions, each in the charge of a commissioner. The Northern Areas is controlled by a chief administrator, and Azad Kashmir by a president. The provincial divisions, the Northern Areas and Azad Kashmir are subdivided into districts, each administered by a deputy commissioner, known as the DC. You may meet the DC of Chitral if you need him to approve your trekking permit.

About 110 million people live in all of Pakistan—more than half in the Punjab, a quarter in big cities, and less than one percent in the north. The population of the Northern Areas is given as 999,000; that of Chitral 275,000. The northern population has almost trebled in the past 50 years, from a 1940s count of 334,000 in the Northern Areas and 105,000 in Chitral, creating pressure on the land and especially on its wild fauna. In the half century between 1895 and the 40s, Chitral had already doubled its population, from 55,000.

This book covers all of the Northern Areas and parts of Azad Kashmir and NWFP. It is arranged in three sections, describing areas accessible from the three airports at Skardu, Gilgit town and Chitral town.

Skardu, the capital of Baltistan and the easternmost of the three airports, is in the Indus Valley. This is Pakistan's mountaineering centre, the starting point for expeditions up the Baltoro Glacier to K2, Broad Peak, the Gasherbrums and other famous peaks. Many of Pakistan's most spectacular treks are to the base camps of these giants.

Gilgit, in the centre, is the starting point for trips up the Gilgit and Hunza valleys, which run west and north respectively, and lies on the Karakoram Highway, the modern road following a branch of the fabled Silk Route between China and the West. You can also trek south to Nanga Parbat, Kaghan and Swat from here. Compared to Baltistan, this area is more populated and prosperous, the scenery is greener and more gentle, and some visitors find the people kinder and more hospitable.

Chitral lies isolated in the west. The water draining from it flows southwest into Afghanistan to join the Kabul River before heading east again to find its way back into Pakistan and the Indus. The only access to Chitral is by a jeep track over a high pass and by a weather-dependent (and thus unreliable) air service. From the arrival of the snows in November until the thaw in June, the valley is sealed off to all but those who can afford to wait—sometimes for weeks—for a flight, or who wish to join one of the few caravans bringing supplies on foot from the valleys below. Each summer only 2,000–3,000 tourists find their way to Chitral, most of whom pass quickly through on jeep safaris, so you can trek here for weeks along the remoter valleys of the Hindu Kush without seeing another foreigner.

CLIMATE AND TREKKING SEASONS

Pakistan is dry. A quarter of the country has less than 120 millimetres of rain per year, and over three-quarters of Pakistan has less than 250 millimetres. Only on seven percent of the land, mostly in the narrow belt of the Punjab from Lahore to Islamabad, and on the mountain slopes north of Islamabad, does the rainfall exceed 500 millimetres per year. These are the only areas reached by the monsoon, which blows across the northern Punjab from India, causing heavy summer storms from mid-July to mid-September. Further north, the high mountains block all but the most determined clouds, so relatively little rain falls in the main trekking area in the north.

The Swat and Kaghan valleys and the southern side of Nanga Parbat are just inside the monsoon belt, but upper Chitral, Gilgit, Hunza and the upper Indus Valley are all far enough north to offer mostly sunny weather all through the summer. In this region, precipitation comes mostly in the form of snow from mid-November to mid-March.

July is the hottest month, with mid-day temperatures in the 40°C range in most places. Islamabad and Rawalpindi, which you transit on your way north, can be extremely hot and humid—we once landed there in June to find a temperature of 47°C. Naturally, it is cooler at higher altitudes, but it can still be very hot in summer along the dry northern valleys of the Indus and Gilgit rivers, where the heat radiates off the bare mountains. Getting out of the main valleys and up to the summer pastures is the only way to escape the heat.

Above 2,500 metres it is usually pleasant during the day and cool at night. But at such altitudes, the sun is deceptive. With less atmosphere and no pollution to protect you, the rays of the sun are powerful indeed, and on the reflecting surface of a glacier both skin and eyes must be well protected. When the sun goes down, the thin atmosphere fails to retain the heat of the land, and the temperature plummets to near freezing (or below freezing at heights above 4,500 metres). This large temperature difference requires an equally large range of clothing, from light cottons to winter thermals (see page 61). Lower Chitral and the Himalayan foothills are further south and closer to the monsoon belt, making them wetter and so less given to extremes of temperature.

The time of year that you trek is dictated by how high you plan to go. The weather is hospitable between mid-March and mid-November, and walks in the main valleys during spring and autumn are very pleasant. From the end of March the apricot trees are in flower, and the villages are carpeted in pink and white. In October the poplars and birches change colour and paint the valley in myriad reds, oranges and browns. However, the mountain pastures are under snow until the beginning of July, as are some of the higher passes until mid or late August (the permanent snow-line is at about 5,000 metres). By the end of September the weather is becoming cold again, and the first snowfall usually comes at the start of October. The peak of the season is the month of August, and almost all trekking takes place between mid-July and mid-September.

ISLAM

Except for about 3,000 Kalash tribal people in Chitral (see page 309), all of the people of northern Pakistan are Muslim. They are divided in roughly equal numbers by the religion's three sects: Sunni, Shia and Ismaili.

In few countries does religion play as important a part in the lives of its people as in Pakistan, which was created in 1947 specifically to provide the Muslims of British India with a state of their own. Islam pervades every facet of society. Reminders of the devotion and religious fervour of the Pakistanis are many: the muezzin's call to prayer from the minarets of the mosques; men bowed in prayer in fields, shops and airports; Qibbla (Urdu for 'the direction of Mecca') marked in many hotel bedrooms; the veiled women in the streets.

The word Islam is Arabic for 'submission to God'. The religion was founded by the Prophet Muhammad, who was born in the Arabian city of Mecca in the year 570 and died in nearby Medina in 632. As a prophet, Muhammad's message was that there was but one God and that there should be one community of believers; as a statesman, Muhammad possessed an unparalleled power to unify the Arab nation. In his dual roles, he remains a towering figure of history.

Muhammad preached a universal brotherhood in which all men were equal in the sight of God. The masses of the Middle East had exhausted themselves with a long series of wars and were ready to accept Muhammad's new monotheistic religion. The Islamic Empire expanded rapidly, within a century stretching from Spain to India. Islam now claims more than a billion adherents worldwide, ranking the religion second in numbers only to Christianity, with its 1.75 billion.

Islamic dogma holds that the teachings of Islam were first revealed at Creation and that prophets have been sent from time to time to reconvey God's word. These divinely inspired prophets are the Hebrew patriarchs, such as Abraham and Moses, and Jesus, who Muslims revere as a great prophet, though not divine in himself. Muslims call those who follow the prophets—Jews and Christians as well as Muslims—ahl-e-kitab, or 'people of revealed books'.

Muslims believe that, despite the teachings of the early prophets, man has continually erred, and the prophecy has become obscured and overladen with false interpretations. Muhammad was sent to restore purity and bring to mankind the true word of God. He was the last prophet, to be followed only by the Messiah.

Each Muslim has five fundamental religious duties, called the Pillars of Islam. He must recite the creed, *'La illaha illa 'llah Muhammad Rasulu 'llah'* ('There is no god but Allah, and Muhammad is his prophet'). He must also pray five times a day, fast during the month of Ramazan (pronounced 'Ramadan' in other Muslim countries) and give alms (*zakat*) for distribution among the poor. Finally, when all other worldly obligations are fulfilled, he must, if possible, make a pilgrimage to Mecca. The pilgrimage takes place only during a couple of weeks each year and, owing to lack of space, each country has a quota of how many pilgrims may go.

The Koran, the holy book of Islam, is a distillation of the written and oral records compiled during Muhammad's lifetime and in the decades following his death. It lays down the philosophy of Islam and its moral code. As the exact word of God as revealed through Muhammad, the Koran is infallible; it is the supreme authority to which a Muslim looks for guidance.

Islam suffered a major split almost from its beginning. Muhammad died without clearly naming a successor, and there followed a struggle for power, with the result that most of the early leaders of Islam suffered violent deaths. Two main sects emerged; the larger sect, the Sunnis, followed elected leaders called *caliphs* (*khalifa* is Arabic for 'representative' or 'deputy'); the smaller sect, the Shias (or Shi'ites), followed a line of hereditary leaders called *imams*, who were descended directly from Muhammad through his daughter Fatima and his son-in-law and cousin Ali. The twelfth imam, the last Shia imam to date, disappeared in the ninth century.

The Ismailis, the followers of the Aga Khan, are an offshoot of the Shias, who broke away in the eighth century to follow a brother of the Shia imam called Ismail—hence their name. His Highness Prince Karim Aga Khan, the present Ismaili imam, is the forty-ninth in line since the prophet Muhammad.

The people of northern Pakistan are fairly equally divided among the three sects, each influenced by different missionaries. Ismaili missionaries converted parts of Chitral in the tenth century, Pathan Sunni missionaries came up the Indus from Swat in about the sixteenth century and Shia Muslims spread into Baltistan from Kashmir before the seventeenth century. Finally, early in the nineteenth century, Hunza was converted from Shia to Ismaili, the influence coming in from Badakhshan in Afghanistan. Despite being almost 99.6 percent Muslim, the people of northern Pakistan still hold a strong belief in fairies, witches and *jinns* (wizards), and vestiges of planting and harvesting ceremonies survive from pre-Muslim times.

The Islamic principle that is likely to affect many holiday makers in Pakistan most strongly is the ban on the purchase and consumption of alcohol except by permit-holding non-Muslims. Another result of Islam you will notice is the almost total lack of beggars, because the government collects the *zakat* (the welfare tax prescribed by Islam) and distributes it to the poor. The tradition that the rich should give freely to the poor means that you will be expected to give generous tips to your porters, guide and anyone else who works for you.

LANGUAGES

Of the 14 languages spoken in northern Pakistan, at least half are indigenous, the others being spoken by traders coming in from the surrounding districts. A further complication is the multiplicity of dialects that tribal populations have evolved in isolated valleys. Balti, spoken in Baltistan, is archaic Tibetan; the Shina you hear in Gilgit is Dardic (or Indic) in origin; the Burushaski of central Hunza is an aboriginal language unrelated to any other, with different dialects spoken in Nagar and Yasin. In northern Hunza you hear Wakhi, an archaic Iranian dialect. South of Gilgit along the Indus, they speak Kohistani; in Kaghan the language is Hinko; to the west of Gilgit you hear Khowar. About 80 percent of Chitralis speak Khowar, but the non-Muslim Kalash use their own Kalashi, and the Gujar herders speak Gujar. School children are taught in Urdu, and traders wandering throughout northern Pakistan speak Punjabi, Pushto, Kashmiri and, of course, English.

In the appendices, we have included glossaries of Urdu, Balti, Burushaski and Khowar.

ECONOMY

Although farming is the main occupation of the people of northern Pakistan, about half the households have one or two men working outside of agriculture. About 40 percent of these earn a regular wage from factories down country in Pakistan or in the Gulf states, as members of the army or government or in hotels. Another 35 percent earn day wages as porters or agricultural workers, and about a third have a man working in the village as a craftsman: carpenter, builder, weaver, tailor or blacksmith.

There is some small industry in northern Pakistan: marble is quarried, antimony and such gems as rubies, emeralds and garnets are mined, and Gilgit has a small jam factory. Every village has a few shopkeepers and other merchants. Since the opening of the Karakoram Highway, commerce has grown between Gilgit and the rest of Pakistan and China.

THE AGA KHAN DEVELOPMENT NETWORK

The work of the Aga Khan, the spiritual leader of the Ismaili sect, is conspicuous in northern Pakistan. The Aga Khan Development Network, with its headquarters in France, has been active since the 1940s mostly in East Africa, India, Bangladesh, Pakistan and Sardinia, managing programmes in health, education, housing, rural development and tourism. Signs announcing the various programmes—Aga Khan Health Services, Aga Khan Education Services, Aga Khan Tourism Promotion Services (including the Serena Hotels), Aga Khan Housing Board and Aga Khan Rural Support Programme or AKRSP—are noticeable in many villages.

To trekkers, the AKRSP is particularly conspicuous, and the programme has been a resounding success in northern Pakistan. Since 1982 it has been helping villages in various countries to organise themselves and develop their own self-sustaining projects. It offers advice, loans, technical assistance and training, but the villagers themselves choose their own projects and do the actual work of construction and maintenance. In northern Pakistan about 60 percent of all villages take part in the programme, building new water channels, roads and protective dikes. Villagers, both men and women, have joined training courses in a variety of useful skills such as improved farming methods, village accounting, livestock protection and management, poultry breeding, fruit and vegetable farming and marketing. Some of the Aga Khan signs mention the foreign donors who have given aid to the various projects, such as Canadian, Dutch, British, German and European Economic Community agencies.

The Serena Lodge in Gilgit has a couple of videos about the AKRSP, *Valleys in Transition* and *First Harvest*. Ask at the front desk.

AGRICULTURE

Most people in northern Pakistan are peasant farmers. The average household has eight members sharing half a hectare of land. As most of northern Pakistan is a mountain desert, with 20–200 millimetres of rain a year depending on the area, agriculture is possible only by irrigation. Fragile irrigation channels—miracles of village engineering sometimes more than ten kilometres long—feed the water from small mountain streams flowing from the glaciers to any little patch of flat land. Water cannot be taken from the main rivers, as in summer, swelled by melting snow, they rise many metres and become raging torrents that would submerge and tear away any delicate canal headworks.

Shortage of water is the constant concern of most villages, and the channels are patrolled 24 hours a day to maintain the flow, regulate the complicated system of water distribution and guard against water theft. You often meet a guard, spade on shoulder, striding along a channel, opening or closing wooden sluice gates and repairing the bank. The channels also supply the water used in most village households, so be careful not to damage or pollute them, even by washing your hands in them.

The **crops** grown vary from valley to valley, depending on altitude and local customs and preferences. In Baltit, in central Hunza, farmers usually rotate their crops, planting winter wheat in November, harvesting it in July and immediately planting maize, which is harvested in mid-October. The second year the same field is planted in early April with barley, which is harvested in July, then planted with millet, which is harvested in early October. Higher fields may be under maize or barley from late May to August, then buckwheat (*Fagopyrum sagittatum*), which is not left to ripen, but harvested for fodder early in October.

In lower Chitral a first crop of barley is usually followed by rice. This is a cultural preference and perhaps shows a difference in background, as Aryans traditionally eat wheat rather than rice.

Potatoes were introduced to the mountain areas by the British late in the nineteenth century. They are sown in April and harvested in October. The usual vegetables are peas, broad beans, haricot beans, lentils, onions, spinach, tomatoes, carrots, cucumbers, courgettes, cabbage, cauliflower, turnips and okra (ladies' fingers). Tobacco, poppy and cannabis are also grown, mostly in Chitral. Fields of lucerne are planted for fodder.

Throughout the mountains, **fruit** is an important part of the local diet. Most important of all is the apricot. In Baltit alone there are more than 20 varieties, which make an unforgettable display when they blossom at the beginning of April. No part of the apricot is wasted: besides eating the fruit, the people use the shell for fuel, pound the nut for oil and use the pulp as animal feed. As some species grow at 3,000 metres, you find apricots even in the highest villages. The harvest runs from early June at 1,000 metres, to September at 3,000 metres. In Baltit, the average family harvests 300 kilograms of fruit from ten to 12 trees, which can be up to 200 years old.

The fruit is split and spread out to dry, creating golden carpets on rooftops and large rocks. It is eaten throughout the winter and especially in the lean spring months, when food stocks are running low. Little is eaten raw because of its purgative effect.

(Be warned: these apricots taste so good that they are hard to resist. We try to limit ourselves to no more than 20 per day.)

Other popular fruit trees are apple, cherry, pear, plum and peach, with Baltit families owning about three trees of each variety. Then there are huge mulberry trees, whose fruit is eaten fresh or dried—and, in Hunza, is also made into brandy (*arak*). Enormous walnut trees, which can be over 20 metres high, need space as their thick shade means nothing can grow beneath them. The walnut harvest is in September and October.

Giant grapevines climb trees and festoon terrace walls. The grapes are eaten fresh or dried and, in Hunza and in the Kalash areas of Chitral, made into wine (referred to as 'Hunza water' in Hunza). The wine does not keep, so is drunk quickly or sold at high prices to 'safe' tourists (as the sale of alcohol is forbidden). The only samples we have tried have not encouraged us to go back for more.

Tall, straight poplars grow along the edges of terraces and water channels. These create little shade, so do not interfere with the growth of crops beneath them. They are used for building; the flat mud roofs of the houses are held up on poplar poles, and windows, doors, cupboards and beds are also of poplar wood. The small branches are cropped for firewood, and the leaves are given as fodder to animals.

The usual **domestic animals** are sheep, goats, yaks, cattle and the various yak-cow crosses, which are called dzos, dzomos and yakmos depending on sex and parentage. Full-blooded yaks appear only at high altitude, as they are not happy below 3,000 metres. Yaks are used as pack animals, while the cattle and crosses are used for milk, meat and pulling the plough. They are small and thin and produce little milk, meaning that there is seldom enough to sell. A few villages have donkeys, but only the rich keep a horse for playing polo.

The distribution of the animals varies in the different villages and valleys. In Baltit, each family owns between ten and 50 sheep and goats, and one or two cows, dzos or yaks. Families in the richer kingdom of Nagar, on the other side of the Hunza River, may have up to ten of the bigger animals. In winter, livestock are allowed either to wander loose in the village or are kept in stables attached to the houses and fed on hay, straw and poplar and willow leaves. In May they are usually taken up to the lowest summer pastures and then, by stages, to higher pastures as the snows melt. At the end of the summer season they come down again by stages back to the village. A few animals may be kept in the village all summer for milk.

Each village has its own traditional grazing area; a rich village is one with plenty of good grazing along a large glacier, which provides a reliable supply of water. In most areas, overgrazing is a problem.

The routes up to the summer pastures are the usual trekking paths; they can be surprisingly difficult across glaciers, over scree and along narrow cliff paths. On one particularly vertiginous cliff path in Baltistan, when Ben and I were encouraging each other along and trying not to look down, our pride in our 'brave' achievement was severely deflated when we came across a fresh cow pat in the middle of our 'impossible' cliff ledge.

In the summer pastures the sheep and goats are rounded up into pens at night and milked morning and evening. If the pass out of the pastures is secure—that is, high and difficult to cross—the cattle are driven above the summer settlement in April or May and left to wander unguarded in the high pasture. They have to wander far to get enough fodder, and they give so little milk that it is not worth the effort of rounding them up at night. These untended mountain cattle climb up to the most inaccessible places far from the summer settlements. Some die in falls, under landslides and in fights among themselves. The owners come up occasionally to check on them—so you may find your porters dashing off as soon as you reach camp to check on their animals. At the end of September the owners round them up (it can take days to find them) and bring them down.

The shepherds make the milk into butter and cheese, using a variety of churning methods in different valleys. Some ethnic groups have big copper pots with a vertical paddle held firmly at the neck of the churn and in a rafter above, and rotated by means of a leather thong wound round the vertical bar. Other tribes favour a complete goatskin, the legs and neck tied closed, which they cradle in their laps and rock back and forth. Yet others churn the milk with a vertical plunger in a tall, hollow cylinder of wood virtually identical to churns we have seen in mountain museums in Switzerland and France. The cheese is usually made by boiling up the whey in huge metal pots until it is reduced to a solid. This is then made into balls and dried on the roofs or on high wooden platforms out of reach of the animals.

The butter and cheese is sold or stored. Stored butter was the traditional banking system: in Baltistan butter was kept up to 50 years wrapped in silver birch bark and buried. You still often see butter in wooden cages in the streams (ask your porters to show you some). Different areas distribute the milk products in different ways, but much of it becomes the property of the shepherds, their payment for looking after the village's animals.

Shepherds: The custom of who accompanies the animals to the summer pastures varies with the different cultures. In some secluded valleys, women go up alone, but this usually happens only if the valley has no other way in, so the men know that their women are safe. For female trekkers these are wonderful communities to visit. You can camp with the women and watch them at work all day. Once you have made friends, they usually love having their photos taken, provided that there are no men around to see and disapprove. You should always ask permission first, note names and addresses and send them copies.

In other communities only the men go up to the pastures. Many villages in these areas keep fewer herds these days, as the men have alternative sources of income, such as portering for tourists and factory work in Pakistan. Since it is the more intelligent men who get better-paying summer jobs down in the valleys, it is often the less so-phisticated—sometimes simpletons—who accompany the remaining herds. In some areas, female trekkers should consider this when thinking of wandering alone far from camp, though we have never heard of any particular nasty incident.

The shepherds carry up with them all their pots and pans and blankets, as well as cooking oil, flour and tea. These are loaded on yaks, dzos or donkeys or carried in large wicker baskets, depending on the local custom. But in all areas the shepherds' summer diet is mostly milk and milk products. On our very first trek we were served a quite palatable fondue of cheese and chapatties by the women along the Batura Glacier.

Our porters on the Batura spent most of their rest day shearing goats. Only men are allowed to shear these animals or weave their hair. 'Unclean' women are allowed to milk them, but nothing more. Goats are related to the ibex, which are believed to be the pet animals of mountain fairies; they symbolise fertility and prosperity and are therefore sacred. You find ibex carved on rocks all through the mountains, and in some areas the people still perform ritual ibex dances, in which a holy man dons an ibex headdress and drinks ibex blood (or nowadays the blood of an ordinary goat), then falls into a trance and proceeds to tell fortunes and answer questions about the future.

Few shepherds (except Gujars) keep dogs in the mountains because they are not needed to protect against predators—there are no jackals, and only the occasional fox, wolf, bear or snow leopard. Besides, dogs are expensive to feed and are considered unclean by most Muslims.

The **Gujars** are a tribe of professional migrant herders, who usually spend the winter in the plains of the Punjab and move up to the mountain valleys in summer. Originally they were nomadic pastoralists scattered over the entire northern half of the subcontinent, but in the sixteenth century they were brought into the Punjab in large numbers to populate and garrison the new towns there and to guard the then-new Shahi (Grand Trunk) Road. They gave their name to Gujranwala, Gujrat and Gujar Khan in Pakistan, and to Gujerat state in India.

Many Gujars are still migrant labourers or herders. You find them in April and May moving up the Swat and Kaghan valleys, or returning in September and October. Traditionally they camped in black homespun woollen tents, but since the Afghan war most use canvas tents originally destined for the refugees. Their striking womenfolk stride along wearing full skirts over ballooning trousers, with wicker baskets of pots and pans, crockery and chickens on their heads. The men drive herds of sheep, goats, cattle and buffalo and lead donkeys and camels laden with blankets and other household goods, calves, lambs, children and anyone unable to walk. Most speak good Urdu, and we have found them extremely hospitable to female trekkers, though Ben discovered, as he passed from teenager to manhood, that he could no longer approach their camps. Beware of their fierce dogs and make sure they are chained before you approach. Arm yourself with a couple of stones, just in case.

One August when we were crossing the Deosai Plateau, a huge expanse of rounded hills at about 4,500 metres, we stopped for lunch beside a stream. We had not seen a soul all day, until a lone man strode over a hilltop about a kilometre away carrying an enamel bowl. We joked and took bets on what he wanted. He turned out to be a Gujar herder who told us it was the feast of Eid (the biggest festival in the Muslim calendar), that he had killed a goat and, in line with tradition, was bringing a gift of meat to his nearest neighbours—us. We never saw his camp and would never have known he was there, had he not appeared with his gift. Our return offering of cigarettes seemed embarrassingly inadequate.

There are other Gujars who have settled in villages, usually at the top end of some valleys. These often act as herders for the whole valley, taking all the animals from the different villages up to the pastures in return for some of the milk products and offspring. They lock up their winter villages completely and move up as entire families to the summer pastures.

We describe in the trekking chapters covering the various valleys the different cultures of the other tribes found in each.

WILD FLORA

Once you leave the irrigated oases, you trek up through different zones of natural flora. Population pressure and the need for fuel has denuded many hillsides once clothed with scattered scrub, and indiscriminate felling of trees in some places has reduced many hillsides to a forest of stumps, leading to tragic erosion and loss of wildlife. Yet much remains to delight the trekker.

The area surrounding most mountain villages is semi-arid desert with clumps of scented artemisia, pale-blue and white globe thistles (*Echinops*), some berberis, the odd juniper or pine tree and scattered buck-thorn bushes (*Hippophae rhamnoides*) covered in orange berries in autumn. Along the river valleys you find several kinds of tamarisk (*Tamarix indica* and *Tamaricaria elegans*) with long feathery heads of pink flowers. In parts of Chitral, Swat and Indus Kohistan, the lower slopes are covered with evergreen holly-oaks (*Quercus ilex*).

As you rise the air gets cooler and less dry. From about 2,000 to 3,100 metres in some of the more remote and sheltered valleys, there are quite large coniferous forests of Himalayan blue pine (*Pinus wallichiana*), silver fir (*Abies pindrow*) and spruce (*Picea smithiana*). On the drier slopes are scattered stands of the magnificent deodar (Himalayan cedar, or *Cedrus deodara*), some specimens up to 50 metres tall with trunks ten or 11 metres in circumference, and a few chalgoza pine (*Pinus gerardiana*) with smooth, grey bark peeling in dappled flakes. These trees bear cones that contain nutritious oily seeds

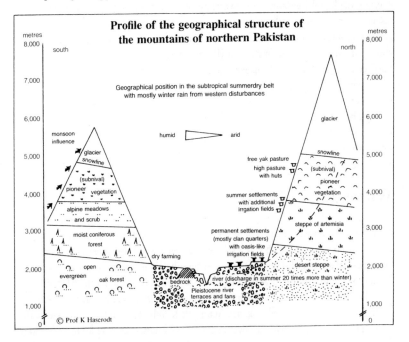

Profile of the geographical structure of the mountains of northern Pakistan

© Prof K Haserodt

that are delicious roasted.

Above this, to over 4,000 metres, dwarf or creeping juniper (*Juniperus communis*), willow and Himalayan birch (*Betula utilis*) reach tree size at the lower altitudes but crouch as bushes higher up. The birch trees are easily identified by their brown and white peeling bark, which still serves in some areas as paper and to wrap up butter for storage. Scattered throughout is the juniper, still burned for its purifying smoke. The smoke is used to induce a trance in shamans or fortune tellers in some valleys. This is probably a carryover from pre-Islamic times.

Above the tree-line, the moisture content of the air drops and you enter alpine meadows covered in a variety of flowers. In rocky places are saxifrages (*Bergenia*), pea-flowered *Astragalus*, spurges (*Euphorbia*), stonecrops (*Sedum* and *Rhodiola*), edelweiss and rock jasmines, with carpets of potentillas, primulas and gentians on the meadows. You also find taller, bright-pink and yellow louseworts (*Pedicularis*), yellow fumitory (*Corydalis*) and the pretty fringed white flowers of alpine campion (*Silene*).

On our first treks, we were surprised at the flowers, which no one had mentioned: enormous dark-pink rose bushes up to five metres high and bristling with thorns; spectacular displays of red willow herb on lateral moraines; whole slopes carpeted with purple geraniums, several species of tall blue delphiniums, the creamy-white spires of *Sorbaria* and, on the damper slopes, pink bistort (*Polygonum affine*); individual clumps of nectar-filled columbines (*Aquilegia*); mauve asters, white anemones, the drooping blue bells of campanulas (*Codonopsis*), lilies, buttercups and tall spires of poisonous monkshood (*Aconitum*).

The best book to take along is Oleg Polunin's *Flowers of the Himalaya* (Oxford University Press, 1987). It is perhaps too heavy to carry in your day pack but is worth delving into in the evenings, especially if you collect and press some leaf or flower samples found along the way.

WILD FAUNA

Northern Pakistan was once crawling with wild game—the trophy books of the 1930s in the officers' mess at Drosh give exciting (and depressing) lists of each year's bag—but times have changed. Population pressure and the abolition of the feudal kingdoms has meant the loss of the royal hunting reserves. Worst of all, the war in Afghanistan, fuelled by American and Chinese arms, has resulted in every village in northern Pakistan having access to sophisticated weapons. Automatic Kalashnikovs and accurate rifles with telescopic sights, coupled with no government control whatsoever, have led to a slaughter of almost all of the game. Army officers have even been rumoured to go on machine-gun shooting sprees from helicopters.

So, do not expect to see any big mammals: snow leopard, brown and black bear, or the various wild goats and sheep (ibex, markhor, Marco Polo, blue bharal or urial sheep). A few do still remain, in ever diminishing numbers, but they are so eagerly hunted by everyone from high officials to mountain shepherds, whatever their endangered status (the animals, not the officials), that they are now extremely timid, confining themselves to the most remote and inaccessible areas.

Brown bear are still relatively plentiful on the Deosai, and you sometimes see them on the passes between Chitral and Yasin. We even saw bear droppings on the Biafo glacier. Our guide pointed out ibex footprints along the Baltoro Glacier, and early in the morning with a good pair of binoculars you can see ibex in Khunjerab National Park. If you know what to look for, you can also find snow leopard scrapings in the Khunjerab.

Wolves still roam in the remoter valleys of Gilgit, Nagar and Hunza, especially in the far eastern parts of the Shimshal Valley, where you may also see bharal blue sheep and the occasional wild ass. Lynx, stone martens, stoats and Altai weasels still live in the northern reaches of the Kaghan Valley, as well as in Gilgit and Hunza. There are musk deer on the Deosai, in parts of the Neelum and Kaghan valleys and in the wilds of Indus Kohistan.

What you stand a good chance of actually seeing in broad daylight are Himalayan fox on the hillsides, cape hares scampering along the ablation valleys and golden marmots standing outside their burrows and emitting the piercing whistles that echo through the Khunjerab National Park and across the Deosai. In Kaghan and Azad Kashmir, you see the darker-backed long-tail marmots. Most charming of all are the little mouse hares, or Indian pikas, which are about the size of a guinea pig, with cute round ears and silky grey fur but no tail. They play in the rocks and are surprisingly tame. Where there are good populations of pikas, the rare Pallas' cat still survives.

You may also catch a glimpse of migratory hamsters in the drier Northern Areas and forest dormice, though most small rodents, such as voles and shrews, are nocturnal.

In Islamabad on the Margalla hills (a wonderful place to walk while you wait for permits, if it is not too hot—see *Hiking Around Islamabad*, by Hans van Hoeflaken) you are quite likely to encounter rhesus monkeys. Very early in the morning or late in the evening, you can sometimes hear the raucous bark of the muntjak deer or see a grey goral standing like a sentinel on some rocky outcrop. Driving at night up the Daman-e-Koh road, you may come across snuffling porcupine or pangolin, herds of wild boar and packs of jackal—you frequently hear the jackals howling in the evening. In the park beside Rawal Lake there is a tree full of fruit bats that take off in a flapping cloud if you disturb them. When we lived in Islamabad, a pair of mongoose occupied our garden.

Entertaining and informative reading on Pakistan's mountain wildlife is available in George Schaller's *Stones of Silence*, a description of his 1972–75 survey of Chitral, Hunza and Baltistan. This can also be depressing reading, as Schaller felt even then that wildlife was disappearing to the point that the mountains would become silent stones. The most complete work on the subject is T J Roberts' *The Mammals of Pakistan*, a huge tome describing 158 species with exquisite drawings.

BIRDS

T J Roberts, author of the hefty, two-volume *The Birds of Pakistan*, has kindly helped us describe the birds you are most likely to see above 2,000 metres in summer:

Pakistan is extremely rich in bird life, with about 661 species. This is a result of its favoured position straddling two major zoogeographic zones, the Palearctic and the Oriental. The Indus is one of the major bird migration paths of the world for Palearctic species, which breed in the north in the summer and fly south to the Indian Subcontinent for the winter. They are on the move spring and autumn, using the major north-south valleys as convenient freeways through the mountains. Hundreds of species, from large geese and cranes down to the tiniest warblers, fly thousands of kilometres each year.

Though you miss the main migration if you are in the mountains only in the summer, you are still likely to see circling in the main valleys Black Kite, which are easily distinguishable by their V-shaped tail. More exciting are the Bearded Vultures or Lammergeiers, with their distinctive slender wings and pointed tail, and the huge Himalayan Griffon Vulture, with a rounded tail and a wingspan of up to three metres. Long-legged Buzzards sometimes stop and breed in Pakistan's mountains instead of continuing further north, and the occasional Golden Eagle soars high over the mountain ridges (immature Golden Eagles are distinguishable by the whitish marks under their wings and tail). Watch the skies for Booted Eagles, Hobbies and wedge-tailed Jungle Crows, as well as nesting colonies of Swifts, House Martins and Rock Martins.

On remoter passes between 4,000 and 4,500 metres, you may see Himalayan Snow Cock, a large, lumbering bird the size of a domestic duck. (To our horror, our porters killed two near the top of the Thui Pass—though we were not too proud to eat them.) These birds try to escape by running away uphill; you may hear their wild whistling cries on the slopes above, together with the staccato chatter of the Rock Partridge or Chukar. Occasionally, you may spot the beautiful grey- and white-patterned Snow Pigeon flying across some alpine slope. Alpine and Red-billed Choughs wheel overhead in flocks and, together with Ravens, visit you in camp right up to 5,000 metres.

You will certainly come across lots of Hoopoe, with their distinctive black and white stripes, fawn head and fan-shaped crest. They follow you along the glacier, fluttering round camp and digging up refuse pits.

In alpine meadows, you may see the handsome white-capped Güldenstädts Redstart, with chestnut belly and tail, and Great Rose Finches (*Carpodacus rubicilla*), with their thick bills, the males boasting red heads and breasts speckled with white. There are also Black Redstarts, flocks of sooty-headed Brandt's Mountain Finches and, in drier regions, Mongolian Trumpeter Finches and the black- and white-headed Alpine Larks, the last of which run mouse-like over the ground. On grassy patches you may be lucky enough to find the Himalayan Gold-finch, flocks of Red-fronted Serins and, lower down, the common Rose Finch (or Scarlet Grosbeak).

Common visitors to mountain streams are White-capped Riverchats, with black backs, chestnut breasts and a distinctive white cap, pumping their tails and darting from rock to rock; Citrine Wagtails and Grey Wagtails (with yellow belly and grey back), wagging their tails and sitting on rocks; and Plumbeous Redstarts, the male with a reddish tail that it scissors open and closed, the female speckled grey and white with conspicuous white panels in its tail. In the higher, more northerly river valleys, you may see White-breasted Dippers walking under water and bobbing up and down while standing on rocks (hence their name). The common, all-brown Pallas' Dipper bobs on every mountain torrent in lower Gilgit, Kaghan and Chitral. You will also see Common Sandpiper and occasional Green Sandpiper. Sometimes a migratory Great Cormorant, its wingspan up to 150 centimetres, fishes along the streams, and in September you may see the large Grey Heron returning for the winter.

Blue Rock Thrushes point their bills skywards as they perch on the cliff tops in rocky gorges, and Rock Pigeons croon even in the remotest valleys. The Eurasian Cuckoo, an elusive blue-grey bird, calls in high alpine pastures in May and June. Some of them call backwards: *Koo-kuk*.

In Chitral one recent summer we saw frequent Golden Orioles, superb song-birds serenading from the trees or swooping in streaks of brilliant yellow from one tree to the next. There were also brilliant turquoise European Blue Jays (Rollers) and, in forested areas, the occasional Scaly-bellied or Himalayan Pied Woodpecker. High in the trees, you often hear the mouse-like squeak of White-cheeked Nuthatches or the loud double-tremulo whistle of the Black and Yellow Grosbeak. Flocks of Tits and Tree-creepers fly rapidly through the trees foraging for insects, buds and seeds.

The best pocket bird book to take with you is R L Fleming's *Birds of Nepal* (Kathmandu, 1976). The illustrations are poor, but it does cover most of the Himalayan birds. Salim Ali's *Indian Hill Birds* (Oxford University Press, Bombay) is even less well illustrated but gives more detailed accounts.

HISTORY

We offer here a brief overview. For a more detailed history of each area, look in the trekking chapters.

ANCIENT INVADERS, TRADERS AND PILGRIMS

Small communities of hunters and herders first visited the mountains of northern Pakistan at least six thousand years ago. Traders and pilgrims have been finding their way across the mountain passes dividing China, India and the West at least since ancient Greek and Roman times and probably earlier.

The Aryans invaded northern Pakistan from Central Asia in the eighteenth century BC, and we know from their religious text, the *Rigveda*, that they fought battles on the banks of the Suvastu River, now called the River Swat. Darius the Great of Persia took part of northern Pakistan in the seventh century BC, and Alexander the Great of Greece passed through Swat on his way to India in the fourth century BC. The rulers of Hunza and the Kalash of Chitral both tell picturesque legends in which they claim to be descended from Alexander and his troops.

Later came the heyday of the Silk Route, during which time Central Asians became rich as the middlemen in the trade between China, India and the Roman Empire. Merchants' caravans struggled through the mountains, following various trails across 4,000- to 5,500-metre passes both south and west from Kashgar. Silks, ceramics, lacquerwork, bronze, iron, furs and spices came from China, and wool, linen, ivory, gold, silver, precious and semi-precious stones, asbestos, glass, perfumes, horses and other animals and plants were traded in exchange.

The trade started during the Han Dynasty (206 BC to AD 220), which had its capital at Xi'an. The Chinese sold their merchandise to Central Asian middlemen, first the Scythians (Iranian nomads) in the second and first century BC, then the powerful Parthians (from east of the Caspian Sea) who grew rich on the trade. In 53 BC, the Parthians defeated the Romans in battle by waving silken banners that were so fine and light that the Roman soldiers fled in terror, thinking the material could only be the work of sorcerers. Next to reign in Central Asia were the Kushans, who established themselves at the centre of the lucrative silk trade, Roman demand for the gossamer fabric having by this time become insatiable.

The Kushans established the winter capital of their Gandhara Kingdom at Peshawar, and by the second century AD had reached the height of their power, with an empire that stretched from eastern Iran to the Chinese frontier and south to the Ganges River. The Kushans were Buddhist, and their most famous king, Kanishka (ruled circa 128-151), built thousands of monasteries and stupas (solid structures representing Buddha's funeral cask), while Buddhist missionaries joined traders travelling the treacherous routes through the mountains. Soon pilgrims from the east joined the traffic across the passes, heading to Gandhara in search of the holy sites, scriptures and original sources of Buddhism. Trekkers in Pakistan still find thousands of Buddhist carvings left by these pilgrims along the Indus, Gilgit, Hunza and Chitral rivers and near the tops of the passes. Most of the monasteries and stupas, however, have been destroyed.

The most famous Buddhist pilgrims to cross the mountains of Pakistan were Fa Xian in 403, Song Yun in 519, Xuan Zang in 630 and Wu Kong in 750, all of whom left impressive accounts of their journeys (see page 201).

As the Kushan Empire declined between the third and fifth centuries, the northern reaches of the empire were absorbed by the Sassanian rulers of Persia. With the rise of the Tang Dynasty (618–907) in China came the golden age of the Silk Route, as more traders, missionaries and pilgrims than ever moved through the high mountain passes. The most famous of all Buddhist missionaries, Padmasambhava, left Swat in Pakistan for Tibet during this time, in 747.

But by the end of the seventh century the Persians had discovered the secret of making silk, and by the end of the eighth century sea routes had been opened for East–West trade. The Arab expansion caused political instability in Central Asia, breaking the area up into tiny principalities and making the land routes unsafe. These developments conspired to rob the Silk Route of its value.

When the Mongols united Central Asia with their Yuan Dynasty (1279-1368) in China, the trade routes opened again for more than a century, allowing Marco Polo to pass through in about 1273 and reviving strong cultural and commercial links through the mountains.

The next strong central power was the Moghals, who stabilised India throughout the sixteenth and seventeenth centuries, allowing trade to resume through the mountains to China.

EXPLORERS AND MAPPERS

Mountain exploration began in Europe only in the eighteenth century. Until then the mountains were feared, with most cultures believing them to be the home of hungry dragons and fairies able to seduce the unwary to an untimely death. The climbing of Mont Blanc in 1786 created the kind of attitude necessary for the exploration of the greater Himalayan ranges, and this coincided with the expansionist plans of the British East India Company.

The company had started trading in India in the seventeenth century. By late in the eighteenth century, it was looking north to Central Asia for the lucrative markets in the legendary cities of Khotan, Yarkhand, Kashgar, Tashkent and Samarkand. But it was many years before the British fully appreciated the barrier between their Indian domains and their hoped-for markets: a solid block of high mountains stretching 500 kilometres from south to north, their passes high and difficult and their inhabitants divided into hostile kingdoms. Though local traders and pilgrims had been crossing the mountains for thousands of years, there were as yet no maps of the area. Most of the early information on the mountains was collected by the famous pundits, Indian surveyors specially trained by the founder of the Indian Army's Intelligence Department, Sir Charles MacGregor, the prototype for Rudyard Kipling's Lurgan Sahib in his Great Game novel *Kim*. The pundits, disguised as pilgrims or traders, explored and surveyed much of the Karakoram, the Himalaya and Tibet during the second half of the nineteenth century.

In the wake of the pundits came the European explorers and mappers, often disguised as hunters or parading in local costume, sporting huge turbans. They suffered extraordinary hardships probing the passes of the Himalaya, Karakoram and Hindu Kush, looking hopefully for possible trade routes and fearfully for lines of invasion open to the Russians.

Two Jesuit missionaries reached Leh in 1631 and 1715, but it was not until 1808 and Mountstuart Elphinstone's mission to Kabul that the first map showing the upper Indus River, the 'Kurrakooram' and the 'Hemalleh' mountains was drawn by the British.

In 1820 William Moorcroft, a British explorer and trader already aged 55, did the round from Kulu to Leh and Srinagar, in what is now India. The first qualified veterinary surgeon in England, Moorcroft had come to India to manage the British East India Company's stud farm, and his first journey, in 1812, had taken him to Tibet, disguised as a Hindu holy man, in search of the goats that produce the fine peshmina wool coveted for making shawls. Moorcroft later went to Bukhara to buy Turkoman horses. He was poisoned near Bukhara in 1824, so never returned with his horses, but his papers were collected by later travellers and published in 1841.

It was not until 1835 that the Karakoram, in what is now Pakistan, was first visited by a foreigner who lived to write about it. Godfrey Thomas Vigne (pronounced 'Vine') left Srinagar that year. Posing as nothing more than an English gentleman travelling for his health, Vigne crossed the Burzil Pass and the Deosai Plateau to Skardu. He became friends with Raja Ahmed Khan of Skardu and spent four summers exploring the area, right up to the Hispar and West (New) Mustagh passes, quietly assessing the possibility of Russian forces advancing through the Karakoram. The East (Old) and West Mustagh passes had been used for trade between Baltistan and Yarkhand, but both were blocked by advancing ice by the mid-nineteenth century. Vigne also tried to reach Gilgit via Astor but was turned back before crossing the Indus at Bunji. His name is given to a difficult pass, the south side of which he may have visited, and one of the glaciers flowing into Concordia, which he could never have seen.

The second Westerner to reach Skardu was a Scottish adventurer and doctor named John Henderson, who in October 1835 followed the Indus down from Leh and then crossed south to Srinagar. Wearing tattered native dress, he met Vigne in Srinagar.

In 1847 another Scot, Thomas Thomson, a botanist working with the Boundary Commission demarcating the boundaries of Kashmir, travelled from Ladakh down the Shyok River through Khaplu to Skardu, where he spent the winter before crossing the Zoji La Pass to Srinagar. He took many plants back to England with him and ended his days happily in Kew Gardens in London, recognised as one of the greatest botanists of his day.

The real giants of the Karakoram were not sighted until 1856, when Thomas G Montgomerie, of the Grand Trigonometrical Survey of India, standing on Haramukh Peak in the Pir Panjal, spotted two huge peaks about 220 kilometres away, which he labelled K1 and K2, the K standing for Karakoram. K1 turned out to be Masherbrum, which was measured that same year by Adolf Schlagintweit, a German now largely forgotten at least in the English-speaking world, though he was one of three brothers who undertook extraordinary journeys through the Himalaya; his measurement of 7,821 metres is still accepted today. The Schlagintweit brothers were the first to cross the Karakoram Pass, and Adolph was the first European to reach Yarkhand. He was murdered somewhere near Kashgar.

Not until 1858, two years after its sighting, was K2 measured at 8,622 metres from a vantage point on the Deosai Plateau. The mountain was measured again by Henry Haversham Godwin-Austen in 1860 at 8,611 metres and again in 1988 by Professor Ardito Desio at 8,616 metres. Godwin-Austen wrote from the Deosai: 'Peak K2 appeared of an airy blue tint surrounded by the yellower peaks K1, K3 and others all over 24,000 feet [7,315 metres] in height. Other minor peaks by hundreds thrust up their heads— some snow-capped, some rounded, some bare and angular, running up as sharp as needles.'

Godwin-Austen then ascended the Panmah Glacier and attempted the West Mustagh Pass but, like Vigne, failed. He next headed up the Baltoro Glacier as far as Urdukas and climbed above the camp to a point from which he could see K2 over the intervening mountains. This was the mountain's first close sighting, which established its position on the Central Asian watershed.

The first European to record his visit to Gilgit was Dr Gottlieb Wilhelm Leitner, who crossed the Indus at Bunji in 1866 and marched up to Gilgit, which was then in the charge of a Dogra garrison of the maharaja of Kashmir (Alexander Gardiner claimed to have passed through Gilgit in the 1830s, but his story is so incredible that few believed him). Leitner, an indefatigable ethnographer and linguist who spoke 20 languages, stayed 36 hours recording local culture and language. Though he never returned to Gilgit, he produced *The Languages and Races of Dardistan* in 1877, coining the name Dardistan (never a local name) to cover most of the area described in this guide. He published *The Hunza-Nagyr Handbook* in 1889.

The next Westerner to visit Gilgit was the celebrated George Hayward, who spent the winter of 1869 there, before moving on to Yasin for the spring. He returned again in the summer of 1870 with the intention of crossing the Darkot Pass in his search for the source of the Oxus but was murdered near Darkot (see page 279).

In 1874, John Biddulph explored the Pamirs and the north side of the Hindu Kush. He discovered how low and green the Boroghil Pass was, raising the alarm of how easy it would be for the Russians to ride in from the north. In 1876, he became the first Westerner to visit Hunza and left a vivid description of the road into the remote kingdom in his *Tribes of the Hindoo Koosh*:

> For nearly half a mile it was necessary to scramble over rocky ledges, sometimes letting oneself down nearly to the water's edge, then ascending 300 to 400 feet [100 or so metres] above the stream, holding on by corners of rock, working along rocky shelves three or four inches wide, and round projecting knobs and corners where no four-footed animal less agile than a wild goat could find a path.

Today's easy two-hour drive up the Karakoram Highway is somewhat less adventurous.

In 1877, Biddulph was made the first British political agent to Gilgit, a lone British officer in what was then the remotest outpost of the British Empire. In 1878 he visited Yasin, made the first crossing of the Shandur Pass and walked down to Chitral town to meet the ruler Aman ul-Mulk. The vulnerable Gilgit Agency was closed in 1880 after an attack by the ruler of Yasin. Biddulph would probably have been killed had not Aman ul-Mulk seen this as his chance to attack and take Yasin. The agency did not open again until 1889.

William MacNair, disguised as a Muslim doctor (*hakim*) became the first Westerner to cross the Lowari Pass to Chitral in 1883. He visited the Kalash and saw the Dorah Pass, the main trade and pilgrim route used for thousands of years between Central Asia and the Indian Subcontinent. He left via the Shandur Pass to Gilgit, going from there to Srinagar.

In 1885, Colonel William Lockhart, Charles MacGregor's friend and deputy, mounted the first British mission to Dardistan, taking along 300 mules laden with gifts (mostly beads) for the locals. His party explored the Yasin, Darkot, Boroghil and Shandur passes before descending to Chitral town. They managed to visit Drosh, the Dorah Pass and Kafiristan, recording all they saw, before returning via Gilgit to Srinagar. They compiled the first gazetteer to Chitral.

The following year Lockhart and his company struggled up to Hunza. By appeasing the *mir* (king) with promises, they secured permission to continue over the Kilik Pass into China. They came back around via the old trade route down the Wakhan Corridor and through Badakhshan, inspecting the north side of the Hindu Kush, before returning to Chitral via the easy Dorah Pass.

Francis Younghusband made the first European crossing of the high Karakoram in 1887, using the East (Old) Mustagh Pass, and then spent two years exploring all of the passes between Hunza and China (see page 260) and between Chitral and Afghanistan, thus completing the line of India's defences against Russian or Chinese attack. The British Boundary Commission followed in his wake, drawing the northern border of the Indian Empire.

The outline of the empire being complete, it remained to fill in the blanks on either side of the border—those areas still marked with the challenge 'unexplored' on early twentieth-century maps. The major valleys in the central Karakoram were mapped before Independence in 1947, and Eric Shipton and Harold William Tilman filled in the last great blank when they surveyed the north side of K2 and Snow Lake. Yet, to this day, the glaciers radiating out from Snow Lake are not fully mapped. Similarly, although most of the valleys of the Hindu Kush have been explored, modern maps are hopelessly inaccurate regarding the side valleys of the Indus in Kohistan. The Kohistanis, fanatically fundamentalist Muslims, keep all strangers out, so the necessary surveys have never been done. We have peered longingly at the valleys of Kohistan from a helicopter but consider the risks of going in to be too dangerous.

MODERN MOUNTAINEERING AND TREKKING

Hunters stalking the snow leopard, ibex, markhor and elusive Marco Polo sheep were the first to visit the mountains purely for pleasure. Officers in remote postings spent their free time in the hills. Others took leave from the Indian hill stations of Simla, Darjeeling and Murree for their hunting sprees.

One of the first real mountaineering expeditions was in 1892. Sir W Martin Conway, with the painter A D McCormick and others, took a Swiss guide from Saas, set off from Hunza, crossed the Hispar Pass and gave the name Snow Lake to the great white expanse below the Hispar Pass. They descended the Biafo Glacier to Askole, then explored the Baltoro Glacier and gave to the confluence of glaciers at its head the name Concordia, after the Place de la Concorde in Paris. They made an attempt on Baltoro Kangri, reaching the top of a spur on the north side, which they called Pioneer Peak.

In 1895, A F Mummery, the veteran of the Alps, made the first attempt on Nanga Parbat. He approached by the Rupal valley, climbed Tarashing Peak and crossed the Mazeno Pass, only to be killed on the Diamer face. Thereafter, Nanga Parbat was left to the Germans, who made five attempts on it in the 1930s, losing 30 climbers and porters and giving it the nick-name Killer Mountain (see page 175).

Fanny Bulloch Workman, the indomitable American who ostensibly travelled for her health, pioneered trekking for pleasure with her husband, William Hunter Workman, between 1898 and 1912. The Workmans made eight expeditions to the Karakoram and Kashmir and explored the Biafo, Hispar and Chogo Lungma glaciers. They wrote several books, speculating that Snow Lake, which they guessed to measure 300 square miles (777 square kilometres), might be an icecap like those in the polar regions, from which glaciers flowed out in all directions (in fact, Snow Lake is only a tenth as large and is not an icecap). Fanny held the world altitude record for women for 28 years, having in 1906 climbed to 6,932 metres on Spantik in Nagar, which the Workmans named Pinnacle Peak. Workman Peak, overlooking the Hispar Pass, which the Workman team climbed in 1899, is named after them.

Other expeditions followed: Oscar Echenstein's to K2 in 1902, A C F Ferber's to the Mustagh Pass in 1903, and the 1909 push to Concordia by the famous Prince Luigi Amedeo of Savoy, the duke of Abruzzi. Abruzzi gave his name to the southeast ridge of K2, and his expedition almost climbed Chogolisa (Bride Peak), reaching the altitude of 7,488 metres, which stood as a record for 13 years. The most lasting results of the Abruzzi expedition are perhaps Vittorio Sella's magnificent photos, still considered some of the best of the area.

Then came Tom Longstaff's exploration in 1909, during which he and Arthur Neve 'discovered' the Siachen Glacier, crossed the Saltoro Pass from Saltoro to Siachen and crossed the Ganse Pass from Kharmang to Khaplu. Filippo de Filippi explored the Rimo Glacier and the sources of the Shyok and Yarkhun rivers in 1914. In 1929, the duke of Spoleto led an Italian group that included Ardito Desio to the Baltoro Glacier. Desio crossed the Mustagh Pass, explored the Shaksgam Valley and scouted the easier Sarpo Lago Pass (later crossed by Eric Shipton and H W Tilman in 1937). Desio returned to the Baltoro in 1954, leading the Italian expedition that made the first ascent of K2, and was back again by helicopter in 1988, aged almost 90, to take another measurement of the height of K2.

The exploration of the Hunza mountains began only after World War I. In 1925, Dr Philip Christian Visser trekked the Batura and Shimshal valleys and added to the myth about Snow Lake by suggesting that the Virjerab Glacier flowed out of it. Colonel R C F Schomberg lent the myth even more credibility when he visited Shimshal in 1934 and gave the Braldu Glacier its name, thinking it flowed out of Snow Lake and was of the same drainage system as the Braldu River. Not until Shipton and Tilman's expedition in 1937 was the knot of mountains and glaciers around Snow Lake finally sorted out.

For other exploration, see the bibliography and the list of expeditions in the appendices.

TREKKING STYLES

There are four basic styles of trekking. The one you choose depends on your experience and finances. Backpacking is cheap, but for most people is not feasible for long treks. Self-organised treks can be difficult and time consuming to negotiate without a fair command of Urdu. Going through a local agent is more reliable and removes the need for some equipment without taking with it all of your flexibility, but it can be expensive. Trekking with an international adventure-travel company is very expensive, catering for those with little experience or time.

Whatever style you choose, remember George B Schaller's warning that each trekking or mountaineering party 'represents another wedge of destruction onto a fragile environment and culture'—and step lightly.

Talking of stepping lightly, a word of warning here about glaciers. Do not venture out on a glacier without a guide unless you are experienced with them. Most Karakoram glaciers are covered in gravel and boulders, and some are deeply crevassed, particularly where two glaciers meet or where a glacier is surging forward. Other glaciers may be smoother and less covered in rocks, particularly higher up, and some are like kilometre-wide motorways of ice with only small crevasses. In August, you reach patches of permanent snow starting between 4,500 and 5,000 metres; here glaciers become very dangerous, as the crevasses are hidden. Trekkers who venture this far must walk in single file, probing forcefully in front with a long pole to find the crevasses. It is best to rope up at least the first two or three in line. Mid-afternoon is the most dangerous time, when the snow is at its softest. Someone in the group should be trained in crevasse rescue.

Also a word of warning about bridges: some are washed away each season and only the locals know which are in place and safe. If you are trekking unguided, be sure to ask frequently about the condition of the path and bridges ahead.

BACKPACKING

The cheapest way to trek is to do everything yourself: find the cheapest flight to Pakistan; travel by public transport to the beginning of your chosen trek; then put your kit in a bag and set off without guides or porters. This has become very popular in Nepal, where it is possible to live off the land, sleeping and eating in the local villages and so reducing to a minimum the load in the backpack.

Backpacking does not work as well in Pakistan. Most of the trekking here is higher than the permanent villages, so there are no shops, tea houses or hotels along the trails. This means that you must carry everything with you and that, unless you are a particularly fit and experienced trekker aware of your own capabilities, your range is reduced to a few days. Backpacking does, though, provide maximum flexibility. You can go wherever you like as quickly or slowly as you wish.

We would recommend trekking in pairs or groups of three or four. If you trek completely alone there are some dangers to think about, even for the experienced explorer. Many of the trails you follow are merely goat paths, which are not marked and are often unclear, especially across glaciers. These areas are sparsely populated, and if you became lost or injured you might never be found. In Pakistan the valleys are so remote and large that it is difficult to give anyone precise details of your intended itinerary, so it is almost impossible for anyone to organise a search party if you do not return.

The added problem for women is that Pakistan is a Muslim country, where a woman out alone is a provocative figure—local women never leave their home area unescorted. Long day walks around villages and long afternoon walks away from camp can be considered in some places, but even women who speak some Urdu and know their way round reasonably well are unlikely to feel comfortable spending the night alone.

If you really must trek alone, the best precaution is to pay a local farmer or shepherd to walk with you. They are happy to do so, and the cost is comparatively low. Although very few people outside of the main towns speak English, and in the higher villages many cannot speak Urdu either, you can communicate with surprisingly few words (see the glossaries in the appendix). Not only does your farmer or shepherd provide help in an emergency, but he also knows where to find water and can tell the other shepherds who you are and smooth out any problems such as where you can or cannot camp. Chances are that he has friends and relatives higher up the valley and will invite you into the shepherds' huts for tea and bread. This is the only way that you will get to see exactly how the locals live, which is a wonderful experience, as housing, clothing, customs and language change from one valley to the next.

SELF-ORGANISED TREKS

Organising your own treks entails getting yourself to the village closest to the start of the trek and hiring porters on the spot. A smattering of Urdu is essential, as the porters speak no English. This is our usual style, unless our trek takes us onto a difficult glacier, for which we need an expert guide with mountaineering experience.

For beginners it is advisable to hire a guide as well, but finding a good one can be a problem. As there is no guides' association in Pakistan, there is no special training or exam to pass. Anyone with a little English can pose as a guide, so be sure to ask advice and see letters of recommendation. You can ask trekking agencies (see appendix) to recommend a freelance guide, or you can ask around in hotels in Skardu, Gilgit, Hunza or Chitral. If you are lucky, you may find an experienced guide who is between jobs for one of the bigger agencies. You want someone who can tell you what equipment and food to take and maybe even fill you in on the customs and folklore of the area. You may also need him to suggest an itinerary, hire porters and settle porter disputes.

Trekkers with experience and confidence can trek without a guide, as local porters usually know the routes better than any guide. When hiring porters, ask for references, though most have none to show, leaving you with nothing to go on but instinct. If your porters turn out be good, give them letters of recommendation for future use. For the rules and regulations governing the hiring of porters, see page 83.

WITH A LOCAL TREKKING AGENT

Pakistani trekking agents (see the listing in the appendix) can arrange a trek, either by mail, telex or fax before you leave home, or after you arrive in Islamabad, Rawalpindi, Skardu, Gilgit or Chitral. Again, getting a good guide is the secret to success. Even those employed by agencies vary enormously in competence. It is best to take quotes from several companies to find out exactly what they provide in the way of porters, food and equipment, how much they charge and what experience they have.

Although using a local agent is more expensive than organising a trek yourself, it still leaves you free to fix your own itinerary and change it, if necessary, as you go along. It also relieves you of the worry of finding a guide and porters, as well as of the expense of buying equipment that you may never use again.

WITH AN ADVENTURE-TRAVEL COMPANY

There are several international trekking and adventure-travel companies that arrange group treks in northern Pakistan (see the listing in the appendix). For one price they provide airfares, hotel rooms, guides, porters, food and most of the equipment you need. They offer a number of treks from which to choose, giving a description of each. This is an expensive way to trek, but, for those with deep pockets and little time, going with an adventure-travel company is the best way to ensure that you spend your holiday on the trail, not in the hotel.

For those not experienced with either trekking or travelling in Asia, international adventure-travel companies can remove the worries and many of the potential pitfalls. This is perhaps the ideal way to go on your first trip. Then, when you have seen how the system works, you can go back and organise a second trip by yourself.

That said, the drawbacks are many. Due to time limitations, organised treks must run to strict itineraries, covering the prescribed distance each day even if members are feeling ill. Also, the companies offer only the six or eight most popular routes, where you have little chance to get away from other foreigners or see local communities unblemished by tourism. Worse yet, you can find yourself stuck with strangers whose personalities or physical capabilities make them far from ideal as trekking companions.

If you decide to go with an international company, choose one that a previous customer can recommend—though, ultimately, it will be only as good as its local Pakistani ground agent and your assigned guide.

PREPARATION

The more you know about the area you are going to, the more you will enjoy your visit. Check the appendix for books on the areas you plan to visit and guidance to what is available in such publications as the *Alpine Journal* and the *Himalayan Journal*, which are available in many libraries.

MAPS

We have included sketch maps in this volume that give an idea of terrain, but if you plan to venture off the recognised trails you should rely on a local guide rather than a map to show the way.

All of the old British maps of what is now Pakistan are restricted in Pakistan. Some photocopies (which you must promise not to take into Pakistan) are available in the map room of the Royal Geographical Society in London. Also, mountaineers and trekkers with a liaison officer can borrow the restricted army maps from the Pakistani Tourism Division.

The maps available to the general public, even the most modern, are on scales between 1:200,000 and 1:500,000 and are none too accurate. They do not show the terrain in any detail, and marked bridges may have since washed away and been relocated. The best route up a valley or over a pass is not always the most obvious one. Even a small river not featured on your map can prove to be a major obstacle.

These maps are, however, useful for planning the general route for the trek and allow a rough estimate of distances and altitudes. They also give a good idea of the geography of the region and can be fun to pour over before, during and after the trek.

Good maps are not available new in Pakistan (although you may be lucky enough to pick some up second hand), so buy your maps before you leave home. As you probably have to order them, leave plenty of time.

The best map of the Karakoram is the orographical sketch map published in 1990 by the **Swiss Foundation for Alpine Research**, in Zurich. Printed to the scale 1:250,000, it comes in two sheets (four sheets in the United Kingdom). The map shows the main mountain ridges and gives contour lines for every 1,220 metres. Although these maps do not show international boundaries with India and China, nor many of the modern jeep roads, their village names, trekking routes, passes and mountain names and heights are more accurately recorded than on the U502 maps covering this region.

The best contour maps are the **American Military Service** (AMS) U502 series, which are also drawn to the scale 1:250,000. However, road detail and village names are up to 50 years out of date. Also, the cease-fire line between India and Pakistan is not marked, so if you are trekking in Kashmir or Baltistan you must find out where it is. Take careful note of the reliability diagram on each map, rating the areas as good, fair or poor.

The U502 maps for northern Pakistan are: NJ 43-13 (Mastuj) for northern Chitral; NJ 43-14 (Baltit) for Hunza; NJ 43-15 (Shimshal) for Shimshal and Hispar; NI 43-1 (Churrai) for upper Swat; NI 43-2 (Gilgit) for Gilgit and Nanga Parbat; NI 43-3 (Mundik) for Skardu; NI 43-4 (Siachen) for Concordia and K2; and NI 43-6 (Srinagar) for Azad Kashmir and the valley of Kaghan. The maps covering the border areas with Afghanistan (NJ 42-16 and NI 42-4) are restricted.

Another good set of maps is published in Japan in the book *Mountaineering Maps of the World: Karakoram, Hindu Kush, Pamir and Tien Shan* (1978), on the scale 1:200,000. The text is in Japanese, but the maps are labelled in Roman script. The maps cover most of Pakistan's mountain region (including Nanga Parbat) and are reasonably complete and accurate, though they do not show modern jeep roads. The cartographers put question marks wherever they are not sure of the terrain. The book is hard to find and is very expensive, but a good map shop may have black-and-white or colour photocopies.

There are two superb 1:50,000 German maps—one of Nanga Parbat and the other of the Minapin Glacier—made by the **Deutsche Himalaya Expedition** in 1934 and updated in 1980.

There is also an excellent Chinese map of the Batura Glacier on the scale 1:60,000. It was compiled in 1978 by the **Institute of Glaciology, Cryopedology and Desert Research, Academia Sinica**, Lanzhou.

The aeronautical maps compiled and published by the **Defense Mapping Agency Aerospace Center, St Louis Air Force Station**, Missouri, scale 1:500,000 are fairly accurate for heights of mountains, courses of rivers and names of major towns, but they show few roads and almost no villages, so are not particularly useful to the trekker.

Maps can be ordered from good map centres such as:

Stanford International Map Centre, 12-14 Long Acre, London WC2, United Kingdom; tel 01-836-1321. Maps cost about £5 each. Access and Visa cards are accepted by phone.

McCarta Ltd, 122 Kings Cross Road, London WC1X 9DS, United Kingdom.

Cordee Books, 3A De Montfort Street, Leicester LE1 7HD, United Kingdom.

Library of Congress, Geography and Map Division, Washington, DC, 20054, United States.

Geo Center GmbH, Honigwiesenstrasse 25, Postfach 80 08 30, D-7000 Stuttgart 80, Germany.

Geo Buch, Rosental 6, 8000 Munchen 2, Germany.

Travel Bookshop, Rindermarkt 20, 8001 Zurich, Switzerland.

Artou, 8 rue de Rive, 1204 Geneva, Switzerland.

Bauer SA, 1 route de Crissier, 1020 Renens, Switzerland.

Liberia Alpina, Via Coronedi-Berti 4, 40137 Bologna, Zona 3705, Italy.

PAPERWORK

INSURANCE

Accidents and theft are always possible, so be sure to take out a good holiday insurance policy. If you are planning really remote and difficult trekking, this should include coverage for rescue by army helicopter. If you plan only ordinary trekking and the crossing of relatively easy passes, you may decide that coverage for helicopter rescue is not necessary, as you would possibly get out more quickly carried by porters on a makeshift stretcher than you would if you sent someone to alert the army and then waited for the helicopter to arrive. See page 78 for details of helicopter rescue and where it is available.

VISAS

All visitors to Pakistan must have a passport valid for six months after their intended departure from Pakistan, and most nationalities need a visa. Application forms are available from Pakistan embassies and Pakistan International Airlines (PIA) offices. Rates vary depending on nationality. They are expensive for British—single entry £30, multiple entry £50 in 1989. If applying in Britain by post, allow at least two months, but you can usually get a visa in 24 hours if you go to the Pakistan Embassy in London. Provide two passport-sized photographs, proof of a return ticket and details of your intended itinerary.

TREKKING PERMITS

The official Pakistani definition of trekking is walking below 6,000 metres. Trekking areas are divided into three zones: open, restricted and closed. No permit is required for the open zone, which covers most of Pakistan. The restricted zone covers the border areas with India, China, Afghanistan and Iran and includes most of Baluchistan and some of Chitral. It also covers certain very popular treks in Baltistan, where the number of trekkers needs to be regulated.

Border areas are generally defined as being within 48 kilometres of the frontier, though there are exceptions—in Azad Kashmir, for example, the restricted zone is within 16 kilometres of the border. India and Pakistan have been fighting on the Siachen Glacier since 1984, so all of the Siachen area is now closed.

The Ministry of Tourism has approved ten treks in restricted zones, for which permits are required and a trekking fee of Rs100 per person is levied. Five of these treks are along and around the Baltoro Glacier, including the Vigne, Gondogoro and Masherbrum passes (all of which lead onto the Baltoro Glacier from the south) and the Panmah Glacier (north of the Baltoro Glacier, towards the Chinese border). The remaining five restricted treks are in Chitral: the three Kalash valleys of Birir, Bumburet and Rumbur and the Utak Pass connecting Rumbur to Garam Chashma; from Garam Chashma up the Shishgol, close to the Afghan border; the trek into Tirich Mir from Barum; the Shah Jinali Pass; and the Thui Pass. These last two have recently been reclassified from closed to restricted.

Permits are issued by the Tourism Division (College Road, F7/2, Islamabad) within 24 hours of application, which must be made in duplicate through an approved trekking-tour operator (see listing in appendix) and accompanied by two passport photos and passport details of all participants. An approved guide must accompany all treks in restricted zones, and guides and porters must be insured for the sum specified by the government. All trekkers must be briefed in Islamabad before departure and register at the checkposts along the way.

It is possible, but difficult, to get permission to trek along restricted routes other than the ten mentioned above. This takes time. Applications must be made through a recognised trekking-tour operator and accompanied by a route map, photos and passport particulars of all trekkers. If permission is given, a liaison officer will be assigned to accompany the trek.

For detailed information on all the trekking rules and regulations, apply to the Tourism Division in Islamabad. Mountaineering rules and regulations, which are different from trekking ones, are available from the same source. Specify that you require the rates for hiring porters and jeeps, as these are a special appendix and not in the trekking and mountaineering rules booklets (rates vary in the different valleys).

The regulations detail the open, restricted and closed zones and conditions for the hire of porters, guides and liaison officers. The exact duties of liaison officers, mountain guides and high- and low-altitude porters are all specified by the government—as are their equipment and food rations—making for pages of surprising reading. Groups of more than five members must have a doctor or someone qualified in first aid with them, and there are rules governing photography, foreign exchange, insurance, security and what to do in case of accident.

CLOTHING AND EQUIPMENT

The clothing and equipment that you need depends on your trekking style, the time of year you go and the length, altitude and difficulty of the trek. Thought and preparation are required, as too little or inadequate equipment is not only a discomfort but a potential danger, and too much is expensive to porter and may be difficult to shift to the start of the trek. Obviously, those carrying their own packs should take only the essentials; those using porters or pack animals, however, can afford to take a few luxuries. If you go at the very start or end of the season (June or October) you need warm and waterproof gear more than if you go in August. For a one- or two-day hike you need no more equipment than you would take on a walk of similar length at home, but for a long trek a much more comprehensive list is required. Generally the higher you go, the colder the nights are, and if you plan to walk for any length of time above the snow-line waterproofs are essential.

Second-hand shops in the Gilgit and Skardu bazaars are good sources of good, cheap equipment that has been sold by departing expeditions, but it is safer and surer to bring most of it with you. At the end of your trip, you can sell your leftover food and unwanted equipment. In Gilgit, Dad Ali Shah of Hunza Handicrafts, beside the Park Hotel, and the G M Baig bookshop, in Jamat Khana Bazaar, buy and sell second-hand equipment, food and books.

Pakistanis rarely throw anything away and consequently have become a nation of handymen. If any equipment breaks, take it to any shop. If they cannot fix it themselves, they will know someone who can.

CLOTHING AND TOILETRIES

Walking boots are worth spending considerable time and money getting right, as uncomfortable feet are a real misery on a trek. Generally, you get what you pay for, but a good salesperson should be able to tell you the real value of a boot. Boots must have plenty of ankle support and a sole rigid enough to take the sharp edges of rocks with ease. A Gortex lining, though not necessary, is very good if you can afford it, as it keeps your feet dry when walking through wet grass or shallow streams. Unless you plan to do any technical climbing, double-lined plastic boots suitable for attaching crampons are not necessary.

Use your boots as often as possible before you go, to walk them in, toughen your feet and ensure that they are not going to cause problems. Ask whether the boots need to be waterproofed. If so, make sure that this is done properly, or they can literally fall apart at the seams as the stitching rots (keep the receipt just in case). We carry a box of wax to apply every so often, impregnating the leather to prevent mildew and water rings and to keep the leather soft and the stitching sealed (beware of wax in tubes, which can split).

On the trail, the secret to healthy feet is to keep your nails very short and to give your feet as much fresh air as possible. Take your boots and socks off at lunchtime and leave them on a rock in the sun to air. If your feet get hot, dip them in a stream.

Second-hand boots are available in Pakistan but, like borrowed boots, are not recommended.

For **camp shoes**, a comfortable, light-weight pair of sneakers or tennis shoes make a pleasant change and are also useful if you have to wade rivers and do not wish to get your boots wet. Some people prefer to use these on the trail when the path is free of stones and not too steep. Rubber **thongs** are invaluable on hot afternoons in camp or when bathing in rocky streams. They are extremely light and take up very little space.

Special hiking **socks** of a nylon-wool mix are best, as they are thick at the heel and toe (where you need padding most) and dry more quickly than pure-wool socks. Sweaty socks are a major cause of blisters, so carry two pairs and wash them regularly. Some people like to wear easy-to-wash cotton liners to help keep the outer socks clean.

Trousers should be made of a strong material and have a baggy cut but must not be too heavy. We prefer colourful French sports trousers made of cotton-polyester Supplex with draw-string waists and elasticated ankles. Army combat trousers have good pockets and are cheap but are also a little hot. The local *shalwar*, worn by all Pakistanis both male and female, are comfortable and light, but they have no pockets and do not offer much protection or resilience against thorns and rocks. They do, however, make excellent pajamas that can double as spare trekking trousers. They can be bought or tailor made in any town in a few hours.

Shorts may be the obvious choice for walking in hot weather—and they may be used by trekkers elsewhere in the Himalaya—but bare flesh, especially on women, offends the Pakistani Muslim sense of propriety. Wearing shorts in Pakistan—even in high pastures—is as inappropriate as treating an English village green as a nudist beach. Also, shorts give no protection; legs get scratched and may turn sceptic.

Shirts should be loose fitting and light weight; for women, long-tailed men's cotton shirts are best. Button-down pockets are very useful, and a collar keeps the sun off the back of your neck. One loose T-shirt is useful for sleeping and as a change when you wash your trekking shirt. For men, T-shirts are acceptable, but at higher altitudes sunburn becomes a real hazard, so one long-sleeved shirt is a good idea.

A **sweater** or pullover should be warm but not bulky. A large, thin, woollen polo-neck is best.

Long **thermal underwear** is essential, not only because nights can be very cold at high altitudes, but also because, if you get caught in a storm and soaked to the skin, you need a means of getting warm. Helli Hansen or Damart are recommended; silk feels wonderful but is expensive.

Boxer shorts are preferable to Y-fronts for men, as they are less likely to cause crotch rot in the heat. Women need three pairs of easily washed **panties**. Do not be tempted to take disposable panties; they are difficult to burn and, if you bury them in Pakistan's dry soil, take years to decompose.

We recommend taking two **jackets**, one light-weight water- and windproof outer shell, preferably light-weight (but very expensive) Gortex or something cheaper (K-Way 2000) with a cotton liner to absorb the moisture. It must be large enough to fit over your second jacket, which should be warm—either fleece or a synthetic ski jacket that is comfortable but not bulky. If you plan to spend any time above 4,000 metres or travel early or late in the season, consider buying a good down jacket that is light and packs into a small space. Nothing is warmer than down, but it is expensive and needs special care to keep it dry. Your jacket stuffed into your sleeping-bag cover doubles as a pillow at night.

A **rain cape** is advisable, even though there is little rain in northern Pakistan. A plastic poncho takes up little space and can also cover your backpack. We also carry cheap plastic over-trousers, with full zips up the outside of the legs. These are easy to put on and useful in the cold and wind, as well as in rain.

Cheap cotton **gloves** are available in Pakistan and keep the hands warm when cooking at night and in the morning. They also protect them from sunburn during the day. Warm, waterproof ski gloves are necessary only if you plan to spend considerable time in the snow or are travelling early or late in the season. Gloves allow more mobility than mittens, but Gortex over-mits are a good idea at high altitude in the snow.

A broad-brimmed **sun hat** that covers the face and back of the neck is essential. A badly burned face can be a very serious problem, especially when blisters become infected, leaving scars for life. The hat should have an elastic strap or string to keep it on, as the winds can get very strong in the mountains. A warm **ski hat** that covers the ears is also needed in the evenings and early mornings. A **cotton balaclava** can be useful if caught in a storm at high altitudes, to wear under your hat to protect your face.

Light plastic **gaiters** with a strap to keep them down should be brought along to keep your feet dry in case you run into unexpected snow. If you plan a long trek up a glacier or to travel early or late in the season, good Gortex gaiters are worth the expense. Try to get ones with Velcro fastenings, as zips freeze overnight and are difficult to do up.

Many people wear **sunglasses** in the towns and on the trail. However, on snow you should wear **glacier glasses** with side flaps to keep out the glare. Snow-blindness is not only extremely painful but can be permanent. Check that the glacier glasses cut out ultra-violet rays. Take extra pairs for your porters.

Women with any boobs at all need a **bra** for modesty. One is enough if you wash and dry it in your tent overnight. You can buy tampons and sanitary napkins only in Islamabad, Lahore and Karachi, so it is best to take a full supply. Disposing of them is a problem, as they do not burn and the dry sand of the mountains harbours few bacteria to decompose them—and Hoopoes (the digger birds) like to dig them up. The best solution is to wrap them in plastic and carry them out.

Women may find it very useful to have a **sarong** of light-weight cotton two metres by one metre, like those worn in many parts of Asia and Africa. This can provide a modicum of privacy when washing and can also be used as a head shawl to avoid offending the strict Shia Muslims of some villages.

Moisturising cream or lotion in a strong, screw-top plastic bottle keeps your skin from getting too dry. After-sun lotion is also a good idea, as it does not sting. Also take a good hand cream or barrier cream (we like Neutrogena) and some good lip protector.

Such personal items as **towels, lavatory paper, washing soap, shampoo** and **shaving cream** are available in Pakistan, but are often of poor quality. We recommend doing without lavatory paper—learn to use water as the Pakistanis do (see page 81).

EQUIPMENT

You need your own **tent** if you are not trekking with a local agent or an adventure company. A good camping-goods shop should be able to advise you on what to buy, but make sure that it is double walled and able to withstand strong winds. Though expensive, domed tents are ideal, as they are light, sturdy and easy to erect.

Remember that your tent is your home for the duration of the trek. You may find that, on a long trek, a large tent is a worthwhile luxury, not only for privacy but also to provide a place for protecting gear from weather and theft. Ones that open at both ends have good ventilation and are relatively cool at low altitudes. We recommend North Face tents; Wild Country tents have a bad reputation for faulty zips and poles, which apparently are not covered by the guarantee.

A silver **groundsheet** under your tent protects the tent floor, adds insulation and reduces condensation. Buy one the exact size of your tent floor. You can also use it to sit on when eating.

Backpackers need a **rucksack** large enough to carry all their equipment and clothing, but those using porters need only a **day pack** in which to carry a camera, a water bottle, lunch and the odd item of clothing. Even day packs should have moisture-absorbing sections against the back to avoid prickly heat rash. I (Ben) prefer to carry all my own clothing and the lighter items of equipment, leaving the porters to carry the food, tents and cooking utensils. A 60-litre rucksack is sufficient for this, and an internal frame provides the most comfort. Do not spend a fortune on a large rucksack to be used by porters or loaded onto ponies. Porters have their own means of carrying equipment and often handle brand-new rucksacks with less care than their owners would like.

Porters need a **carry-all** such as a large army sausage bag or a canvas sack, one for each 25 kilogrammes of load. You can buy these in the bazaar in Pakistan. Most expeditions use large hard-plastic barrels, which are excellent, especially for keeping food from becoming crushed or wet. These are usually available in Rawalpindi.

Plastic stuff bags are useful to protect your clothing, as most rucksacks and hold-alls are not waterproof. These can be bought in camping shops, but strong, clear-plastic freezer bags with plastic twist ties (not paper and wire) are cheaper and allow you to see what is in each. Take various sizes, as they are always useful. Include a few strong 35- and 60-litre garbage bags for lining your rucksack for double protection.

Sleeping bags should be light and warm, but the crucial factor is warmth. To be safe you should have a four-season sleeping bag rated to at least -10°C, with a hood and drawstring. Buy a bag with a full-length zipper so you can open it out and throw it half over you on warm nights at lower altitudes. Down bags are the warmest, lightest and least bulky, but be careful to keep them dry and air them in the sun at every opportunity. Bags filled with Quallofil are advertised as being nearly as warm as down and still 85 percent effective when wet (we have not tried one and do not know if this is true). Quallofil is about half the price of down, but twice as heavy.

A **cotton sleeping-bag liner** not only eliminates the nightmare of trying to keep your sleeping bag clean but can also be used as a clean sheet in cheap hotels.

A **space blanket** is fantastic for providing extra insulation or driving out a deep chill. As an emergency blanket for someone who has had an accident, it can be a life saver.

A good **insulating foam mat** can make all the difference between a night of misery or of rest, especially when sleeping on snow. For those who prefer a little extra comfort, a Thermorest self-inflating air mat is well worth the investment. We prefer full-length mats, as with shorter mats your feet hang over the end and get cold.

For a **pillow**, use your jacket in your sleeping bag cover or buy an air pillow at a camping shop.

A ten-litre soft plastic **water container**, available in camping shops, is invaluable. It rolls up when not in use but needs careful packing inside something else to protect against punctures. The best container hangs up and has a tap about five centimetres above the bottom. In Pakistan your water supply is often a clouded river or irrigation channel. Fill the container as soon as you arrive in camp, and any sediment will have settled in about an hour, leaving clear water for cooking and washing hands.

A **stove** is necessary, as severe deforestation has led to a chronic shortage of wood in the Northern Areas. Trees in the valleys are all owned by the villagers and are reserved for building. Wood for fuel—also owned by the villagers—is collected off the ground. Government regulations stipulate that you must provide one stove for every eight porters. For small groups the best option is probably a good kerosene primus stove, as kerosene is available in most villages. Keep your stove clean and in good repair. Soak the cup washer on the end of the pump stick in oil to soften it before use. If it dries out, it will crack and you will not be able to pump up the pressure.

Most trekkers in Europe and America use small gas stoves, but canisters of camp gas (Gaz) are not available in Pakistan, and you are not supposed to carry them with you by air. If you are lucky, you may be able to buy some from departing expeditions, but do not count on it. In Islamabad, Expedition Pakistan may have some Gaz for sale; in Gilgit, try Dad Ali Shah's Hunza Handicrafts beside the Park Hotel.

Expedition Pakistan also sells single-burner gas cookers with a three-kilogramme container of liquid gas. For larger groups, we recommend two-burner gas stoves with large gas 'bombs' weighing 25 kilogrammes (one porter load). These are cleaner and less wasteful than kerosene—easy to use but difficult to steal. Stoves and gas are available in Rawalpindi on The Mall opposite Flashman's Hotel. You leave a refundable deposit of about US$40 for the 'bomb' and pay about US$3 for the gas; refills are available in Gilgit, Skardu and Chitral. You need an adaptor available in Rawalpindi for European stoves, or you can buy Pakistani cookers at the same place for about US$10.

Fuel containers for large expeditions, 25-litre jerry cans, are available in Skardu, Gilgit and Chitral. For small groups, tubular aluminium one-litre containers are best. Small leak-proof containers are not available in Pakistan, unless you can find some second hand in Gilgit or Skardu.

A **funnel and filter** is necessary, as kerosene in Pakistan is often contaminated with bits that can block the jets of your stove. Balls of cotton wool make a good filter. You can buy plastic funnels in any village in Pakistan.

A **pressure cooker** is invaluable, available in Islamabad and Rawalpindi for about US$15. At higher altitudes, water boils at lower temperatures (at 3,000 metres, 90°C; at 4,000 metres, 86.6°C; at 5,000 metres, 83.3°C; at 6,000 metres, 79.9°C) so you need a pressure cooker to cook even dehydrated packet foods that require water at 100°C to rehydrate them (a good pressure cooker should boil water at 100°C at 5,000 metres).

Buy a couple of cheap, light-weight **cooking pots** (called *dechi*) with lids at the bazaar. For each person, get one aluminium **plate**, **spoon**, **fork** and **mug**. Chinese enamel mugs with lids are the best if you can find them in Gilgit bazaar—a half-litre mug doubles as a bowl for cereal or porridge. In the United States, Aladdin Stanley Company sells 12-ounce thermal mugs in thick plastic with a lid for about US$5. You will also need a **tin opener**.

A **Swiss army knife** is an invaluable tool.

A small aluminium **washing bowl**, available in the bazaar, is invaluable for laundry, washing up, cleaning lentils, holding water and shovelling snow. It can also provide a private bath in your tent.

The local variety of **washing powder** is kind to neither hands nor clothes. We fill a half-litre plastic flask with good detergent from home.

Pot scourers and **washing-up sponges** make life easier when washing up. The sponges are also useful for wiping condensation off tents before folding them up in the morning.

A **drying cloth** prevents pots and plates getting dirty again while packed.

A one-litre plastic or aluminium **water bottle** per person is usually enough, but it is wise to have a spare bottle or two for the occasional days when no water at all is available and to store water in when in camp. Be sure that your water bottles are distinguishable from your fuel containers. Half-litre plastic scotch or gin bottles are ideal. Take half a dozen with you—full, if you think you can smuggle them in. Customs officers love to find scotch; they just smile and confiscate it.

For a **cooking oil bottle**, a half-litre plastic flask is good. If you are using only imported dehydrated food, you will not need oil, but frying up onions and potatoes before you add the dehydrated mix and water makes a tastier meal.

Empty **film cannisters** are good for carrying spices.

Details of a recommended **medical kit** are laid out in the health and safety section (page 76).

A **small head torch** is much easier to use than a hand-held torch when you need two hands for cooking, arranging your tent, writing your diary or even reading.

A simple **spring balance**—available in Gilgit, Skardu or Chitral—is useful for checking load weights and preventing arguments among the porters.

Thin nylon cord serves as washing line or guy ropes and for making repairs. String is always useful.

A **money pouch**, either hung around the neck or worn around the waist, reduces worries while travelling. We prefer a small waist purse, as a money belt worn inside can cause prickly heat rash in summer.

One or two telescopic **ski poles** are invaluable when crossing rivers, glaciers and screes, and to take the strain off the knees when climbing and descending.

A small **umbrella** is sometimes useful on very hot days at low altitudes.

A **fishing rod** is handy, as the mountain streams are filled with unsuspecting trout. Remember to buy your fishing permit in Gilgit, Skardu or Chitral.

Locally available Chinese **batteries** may spell doom for your trusty Walkman, but good batteries of all sizes are available in Islamabad. Most batteries contain mercury, which, if it gets into the water supply, can kill any animals or humans that drink there. Carry all of your used batteries out and dispose of them as safely as you can.

Pliers are useful for mending zippers. If your tent zipper no longer closes, gently squeeze the sides of the slider to tighten its grip on the zipper teeth.

A **sewing kit** is needed on the trail, but in the towns tailors will mend anything very cheaply and well.

Take **safety pins** to keep your washing from blowing off the line.

Waterproof matches really do work. Carry ordinary matches for most days and save the waterproof ones for emergencies.

A **compass** and **altimeter** are optional extras for budding explorers. It is fun to know how much altitude you have gained each day. Altimeters work by atmospheric pressure, though, so daily changes in pressure cause variations of hundreds of metres in the reading, meaning that you cannot measure your absolute altitude unless you can adjust your altimeter daily to a known height.

Do *not* take **crampons, ice-axes, rope, harnesses** or **karabiners** unless you know how to use them.

A **whistle** is good for attracting the attention of others when they get far ahead.

Take a **trowel** for burying faeces. (Burn or carry out your rubbish; leave your campsites as you would wish to find them—see page 79.)

A **plastic tarpaulin**, available in Pakistan, is needed to cover your supplies in camp when it rains. It also doubles as a kitchen shelter and shelter for porters.

FOOD

Cooking an imaginative meal on a primus stove at high altitudes takes practice—though, fortunately, you are usually so hungry that you will eat almost anything. You can manage perfectly well on food available in Pakistan, but if your baggage is not already too heavy it helps to take some extras and treats from home.

The main problem in the mountains is rubbish disposal, so try to restrict yourself to food in packaging that you can burn. Aluminium packets can be burned to a solid lump, then carried out. Tins should be avoided.

FOOD TO TAKE FROM HOME

Packet soups and **bouillon cubes** make warming hot drinks as well as good bases for sauces and flavouring. Packet soups sold in Pakistan are not very tasty, so we always bring a good supply with us. Allow two portions per person per trekking day.

The **dehydrated meals** available in camping shops tend to be expensive and poor value, so we prefer to scour the supermarket shelves. Our favourites are Beanfeast Mexican style (a sort of chilli con carne), mild curry and Bolognese style. Burgermix and Vegeburger are also good, not only for burgers but also as stew—just add more water. Batchelors, Vesta and Doll all make dried meals, and no doubt there are other brands. We prefer to add more water than is suggested and cook it longer. You can add spices or herbs and dried vegetables (see below) for a variety of flavours—or fry up some onions in oil as a base.

Instant mashed potato mix is lighter to carry and quicker and much easier to cook than Pakistani rice, making it an excellent starch accompaniment to dehydrated meals. Our favourite brands for high-altitude cooking are Knorr and Yoeman, but there are many others. Try them out at home first, as some are horrid.

Instant noodles are also light, quick and tasty.

Dried vegetables should be quick cooking. The best we have found are the Irish Erin brand, whose peas, beans, carrots and so on cook in five to seven minutes and do not need pre-soaking. We just add them to the dehydrated meals described above.

You can also buy dehydrated mushrooms, tomatoes, green peppers, mixed vegetables and onions. If you are in the United Kingdom and cannot find them in the supermarket, try an Indian or Pakistani corner shop. These shops may sell them only in small packs, but they usually have them in stock.

You can get cornflakes and porridge in Pakistan, but we are devoted to our **muesli** and try to take a kilogramme for each person from home. We mix it with dried fruit, nuts and boiling water for breakfast. You can make it last longer by mixing in some Pakistani cornflakes.

Dried fruits (apricots and dates) are available in Pakistan, but you do not know how clean they are or under what conditions they were dried. Besides, they need to be soaked overnight before use. (The Hunza apricots you can buy in the United Kingdom probably come from Turkey—certainly not Hunza.) We take dried mixed fruit and apples from home. You can buy packets of imported raisins and sultanas in Islamabad. Apple sauce, raisins and nuts make a delicious dessert.

You can buy fresh cheddar and tinned **cheese** in Pakistan, but you must carry out the tins. We take whole small Dutch cheeses from Europe. Protected by their red wax coating, they last better than any of the others we have tried, easily surviving two months' travel. Smoked cheese in sausage-shaped wax coating travels well, too. We also take tubes of Primula cheese spread and carry out the empty tubes.

Black-eyed beans do not need soaking but take 30–40 minutes to cook (or 10–15 minutes in the pressure cooker). They are comparatively heavy but are also nutritious, have a delicious, earthy flavour and go well with rice (especially the imported brown rice available in Islamabad).

Dried sausages and **salami** travel well and make good snack lunches if you like them. As they contain pork, do not offer them to your guide or porters.

Energy bars and **chocolate** are always welcome. Test a variety at home and take your favourite. We like the high-energy fruit and muesli bars available in health food stores and Nestlé's Fitness chocolate, which is specially packaged to withstand travel and heat.

Isostar and **Tang** are good for flavouring water.

FOOD AVAILABLE IN PAKISTAN

We have listed what you can buy in Skardu, Gilgit and Chitral separately in the trekking section. We usually do most of our shopping in one shop in either Rawalpindi or Islamabad—and then bargain for a hefty discount.

Rice, lentils and wheat flour (*chaavel*, *dhaal* and *atta*) are available most places, even in some remote village shops, but are cleaner and better quality if you buy them in Islamabad or one of the bigger towns. There are a dozen varieties of rice and lentils to choose from; these are sold from big, open jute sacks standing in rows in the grocery store. A reliable shopkeeper, your guide or a Pakistani friend can help you choose the best. Be sure that the lentils are the quick-cooking variety (*mung dhaal*)—which take about ten minutes at low altitudes—and are clean. Wheat flour is useful only if you know how to make chapattis or can get a porter to make them, and then only if you carry a wooden rolling pin and metal griddle.

Powdered milk is available in smaller towns, but is best bought in Rawalpindi or Islamabad in large, imported tins (Nestlé's or Cow & Gate). When empty, the tins are excellent for storage and make good presents at the end of your trek. The locally produced powdered milk, which is sold from open sacks, is not good. It lumps up when you try to mix it, is often stale or diluted with flour and does not taste very nice.

Buy sugar and black tea in Skardu, Gilgit or Chitral, where you find the same quality as you do down-country.

Green tea, Nescafé, Ovaltine and custard powder are best bought in Rawalpindi or Islamabad, to ensure that you find them. They are, however, usually available in the three northern towns.

Pakistanis make excellent biscuits and crackers. The best selection—and freshest product—is in Islamabad, but some sort of biscuit is available almost anywhere.

Cooking oil tends to come in large tins that, once opened, are impossible to transport. We decant it into plastic flasks. Good olive oil is available in Islamabad in small tins.

Cornflakes and porridge are always available in the capital and usually so in the mountains.

Honey, jam and tomato ketchup come in glass jars or bottles. We decant them into plastic flasks.

Spaghetti as the Pakistanis make it is not very nice, but it makes a change.

Tinned corned beef, Heinz baked beans, sardines and tomato paste are available in Islamabad. The Danish corned beef is best, but you must carry the tins out with you.

For herbs and spices, we buy curry powder, *garam masala* (mixed spices without the chilli), pepper, dried garlic and mixed herbs. These are best bought in Islamabad, where they are properly packaged and clean. You can also get the spices separately, but this is more expensive. Be sure the spices are ready ground. Film cannisters make good containers; double bag them in plastic for safety. Thyme grows fresh in the mountains.

Marmite, a savory yeast-extract spread that is indispensable in most English households, is available in Islamabad.

Fresh onions, garlic, potatoes, cabbage, cucumber, carrots, apples—or any fruit or vegetables in season that you think will travel well—are all best bought in Skardu, Gilgit and Chitral.

TRAIL RECIPES
Here are a few recipes to help you get started. Look through your recipe books for more ideas.

LENTIL SOUP
Oil, onion, carrot, garlic, celery, cabbage, tomatoes (or whatever fresh or dried vegetables you have), cleaned and washed lentils, water, stock cubes, salt and pepper. Soften the onion in the heated oil and throw in everything else in whatever proportion tastes good. Cook until ready.

LENTIL CURRY
Everything in the above recipe, plus curry powder, but less water. Fry up the onion, garlic and curry powder, then add the rest and cook.

LENTIL AND TOMATO SOUP
Oil, onion, eight ounces (230 grams) tomatoes and one cup (250 millilitres) tomato juice (or use tomato paste), four ounces (115 grams) lentils, bouillon cube, thyme, Marmite, salt and pepper. Fry chopped onion in oil, add tomato and all of the rest, cover and simmer. (From Beverly Barnett.)

SAUCES
Add about half of the recommended water to a packet of dried cream soup (leek, asparagus, mushroom, etc). You can change the flavour by adding cheese, herbs, spices or dried vegetables. Serve on rice or mashed potatoes.

CORNED BEEF AND BAKED BEANS
Oil, onion, garlic, curry powder and/or garam masala, corned beef, baked beans, dried vegetables and water. Fry up the first 4/5 of the ingredients, then add the rest and cook. Serve with mashed potatoes, rice, spaghetti, noodles or chapattis.

Wild rhubarb grows around 4,000 metres and makes a good dessert with custard, but you need to add plenty of sugar. Beware of its purgative effect.

HEALTH AND HYGIENE

The risk of dying while trekking was calculated in the 1980s to be only 14 in 100,000—mostly from falls rather than disease. By comparison, the risk of dying in a car accident in the United States was 24 in 100,000, and the risk of being murdered in New York City was 20 in 100,000. So it may be safest to spend the rest of your life trekking. That said, there are a number of precautions to take.

BEFORE YOU GO

Talk to your doctor, who should know your own particular problems and weaknesses. We recommend **immunisation** against typhoid, tetanus, diphtheria and polio—and whooping-cough, measles and mumps, if you have not had them. Cholera vaccine is only 50 percent effective and may have quite severe side-effects, so is not always recommended. Some doctors suggest a gamma globulin injection a few days before departure. This gives 80 percent protection for five months against hepatitis, which is prevalent in Pakistan.

Malaria exists year round in the whole of Pakistan below 2,000 metres. As Islamabad is in the malaria belt and it takes a few days to reach a malaria-free altitude, malarial prophylactics are recommended. Some doctors suggest that you do not take daily or weekly pills if you are in the danger zone for only a short period, recommending instead that you carry larium to be taken only if you have an attack of malaria.

Government regulations require yellow fever and cholera vaccination certificates if you are coming from an infected area.

ON THE JOURNEY

Your main medical problem on holiday is likely to be **travellers' trots**—an upset stomach. The chief risk is from water-born organisms, either cysts, bacteria or viruses. Beware of all water in Pakistan, whether served on your PIA flight, drawn from the tap in the Islamabad Holiday Inn or taken from a clear spring in the mountains. Ignore claims of purity.

Giardia lambia is a troublesome parasite now infesting many rivers in Europe and America as well as Asia. It lies dormant in cyst form, waiting to be ingested by a new host. The cysts and bacteria can be killed by boiling or with one drop of iodine per litre, or filtered out by a filter with a pore size of 0.2 microns.

Viruses can be killed by iodine or boiling. You do not need to boil the water for long, even at high altitudes, to kill all cysts, bacteria and viruses. However, as fuel is always a problem, it is easier just to treat the water with water purification tablets and then add a drop of iodine. Water purification tablets are unstable, so buy a new supply each season.

Carry your water bottle and purification tablets at all times. Use them on PIA flights and all public transport, in all hotels and even when visiting friends. Beware of ice, which is made with tap water.

Safe bottled water and soft drinks are available in all major towns and many smaller ones, but beware of the straws, which are reused. Ask for a glass and be sure it is clean, dry and uncracked—or use your own cup. Tea is usually safe if the cup is. Pakistanis boil milk, making it safe in your tea.

For a second opinion on water purification, see Dr John Shephard's comments below on page 77.

Contaminated food can be as much a problem as water. Seasoned travellers in Asia may have developed some immunity and know by experience what they can and cannot eat, but new arrivals should avoid eating anything that has not been freshly cooked, especially salads, sliced tomatoes and even sliced, raw onion. Remember the motto: 'Boil it, bake it, peel it or forget it.'

Buffet meals in first-class hotels pose a special risk, as food kept warm for long periods is likely to be contaminated.

Food from roadside stalls is usually safe, but make sure it is served from a boiling pot onto a clean, dry plate. Chapattis and dhaal are available in most stalls and make a good, cheap, high-protein meal. Fresh yogurt is usually safe; if flies have been sitting on it, dig some out from underneath. The best rule for roadside stalls is to eat where the crowds are, as the most popular stalls have the best—and freshest—food.

Fruit is particularly good in Pakistan, but, unless you have picked it yourself, peel it with a clean knife. Cut fruit, mixed fruit juices and ice cream sold in the bazaar spell danger to all but the most seasoned of Asian travellers.

Be fastidious about washing your hands. Pakistanis eat with their right hand, and you will too when you get the hang of it (or you can keep a spoon handy in your bag).

ON THE TREK

To help avoid **diarrhoea**, set up a bar of soap and a water container with a tap or long-handled spoon on the edge of camp. Be sure hand washers do not contaminate the clean washing water. If you are cooking for yourself you are unlikely to get sick, but if you have hired a cook he will need careful supervision. (He would not be alive if he had not developed immunities to the bacteria, viruses and cysts around him. He has no idea that you are not immune, too, and cannot understand why you are so fussy.)

If, despite your precautions, you still get diarrhoea, drink plenty of water to avoid becoming dehydrated. It is essential to take rehydration salts and to follow the directions exactly, or they will dehydrate you more. Imodium will help clog you up and prevent too much water loss; it provides some relief, especially for bus journeys, but is not a cure.

Altitude sickness can be fatal. Read up on it before you leave home, so you know how to recognise and treat it. It is caused by a lack of oxygen above 2,500 metres. The usual signs are a combination of any of the following: headache, nausea or vomiting, irregular breathing, dry cough, loss of appetite, lassitude and fatigue, loss of coordination and loss of judgement. Another symptom is oedema, which results in swollen face and hands, reduced urine output (you should produce at least one pint of urine a day) and, in severe cases, pneumonia and waterlogged brain. These symptoms should be taken seriously. The cure is to go to a lower altitude and rest. The best preventative is to gain altitude slowly; the height at which you sleep should not increase by more than 300 to 400 metres per day, though it is all right to climb higher and return.

Some people take Diamox 250 milligrams to reduce altitude sickness. We found it made our fingers and toes tingle, forced us to pee every hour and did nothing to help us acclimatise. Discuss it with your doctor.

Some people are more prone to **strep throat** (an infection caused by the bacteria *Streptococcus*) and **chest infections** than others. We have had strep throat in Pakistan annually for the past five years, so now we always travel prepared with a ten-day course of fenoxypen, an antibiotic. A treatment for chest infection and cough is ciprofloxacin antibiotic.

A good patent treatment for a **blister** is to prick it and cut off some of the loose skin. Add a blob of zinc oxide ointment and cover with Spenco second skin. Surround the spot with a lint ring and tape in place with surgical tape. (From Mark Schleinitz, professional athlete.)

When walking in bright sunlight on snow, put sun cream inside your nose, as reflected rays can badly burn your nostrils.

MEDICAL KIT FOR PARTIES WITHOUT A DOCTOR

We asked Dr John Shephard, MD, an expedition doctor who accompanied us to K2 Base Camp, to suggest a medical kit and offer a little professional advice. The size of your medical kit will depend on the size of your party and the length of time you plan to be trekking without access to other medical help. Talk to your own doctor, especially if you are pregnant, as some of the suggested medications should not be taken during pregnancy.

BANDAGES, PLASTERS AND PADDING

Assorted sticking plasters, Elastoplast or Band Aid
Elastic bandages in various sizes for binding sprains
Steri-strips or Butterfly sutures for taping wounds closed
Surgical tape or Micropore for taping on dressings
Blister plasters, circular type (see patent blister treatment above)
Corn plasters, Scholl type
Netolast, finger size for binding finger injuries
Alco-wipes or Sterets for wiping round wounds and grazes
Cotton-wool balls
Gauze pads
Gauze ribbon
Melolin dressings

MEDICATIONS AND SKIN PROTECTION

Aspirin (enough for locals and porters too)
Brufen 200 milligram, an anti-inflammatory (not for those with stomach ulcers)
Piriton 4 milligrams, antihistamine for allergic reactions
Antiseptic liquid and ointment such as Savlon spray and ointment
Antibiotic such as ciprofloxacin 500 milligrams or septrin for bacterial diarrhoea with
    temperature and chest infection
Metronidazole for treating amoebic dysentery and Giardia
Pivampicillin antibiotic for treating streptococcus sore throat
Imodium 2 milligram capsules, for symptomatic relief of diarrhoea
Rehydration salts (ORT) such as Dioralyte
Chloramphenicol eye drops (enough for treating the locals too)
Mebendazole 100 milligrams for treating worms

Diamox 250 milligrams for mountain sickness (ask your doctor)
Mosquito repellent
Flea powder
Total sun block and high-factor sun screen
Lip protection
Zinc oxide ointment for noses, lips, other sticky-out bits and for blister treatment

MEDICAL EQUIPMENT
Eye bath
Cotton buds
Forceps and scissors
Disposable scalpels
Space blanket
First Aid handbook
AIDS protection kit
Safety pins and paper clips
Thermometer (if you think it helps to know what your temperature is)
Disposable needles and syringes in case you need an injection at a local clinic

WATER PURIFICATION
Hydro Clonazone, Micropur or Puri-tabs
Iodine, one bottle with dropper per person
H_2O K water filter

Water-borne diseases are your greatest enemy while abroad or trekking. Their onset is sudden and their effects debilitating, sometimes even life threatening. An attack of dysentery can halt a trekking party for days, destroying schedules and ruining the holiday. Yet these diseases are easily avoided, provided scrupulous care is taken over water purification.

The routine I operated while trekking to K2 caused some amusement but ensured that we remained free of infection for the six weeks we were in Pakistan. Take your water from the purest source available and purify it in your water bottle with Hydro Clonazone, Micropur or whatever tablets you have, following the instructions. After the stipulated time for the purification tablet to work (ten minutes to one hour), add one drop of iodine to kill off any cysts, then pour the water through the H_2O K filter, back into the water bottle. This filter is extremely effective in getting rid of the taste of the tablets and iodine. Add Isostar or Tang to the finished product to improve the taste.

Some trekkers swear by their **water filter** and recommend the Katadyne filter from Water Quality Inc, PO Box 1871, Boulder, Colorado 80306 ($170; replacement filter $90, or from most pharmacies in Switzerland for about SFr250). The makers claim that the Katadyne filters out anything bigger than 0.2 microns, which includes Giardia and all bacteria.

This is an expensive piece of equipment, but it does not remove viruses and has the added problem that the water is only as clean as the container you store it in after filtering. If your bottle is contaminated, you will recontaminate the water again after filtering. I think it is better to purify at the same time both your water and the bottle with pills and iodine. A filter does, however, remove objectionable silt out of river and irrigation-ditch water, making it clean and palatable for use after further purification.

See the appendix for various diseases you may encounter.

HELICOPTER RESCUE

The army will send a rescue helicopter only if you have guaranteed full payment in advance and collected the necessary authorisation. This is worth getting only if you are trekking on or near the Baltoro Glacier, which is the line of supply for the Pakistani army in its continuing struggle with India over the Siachen area. There is a strong army presence along the glacier, with several helipads and at least five radio stations, from which you can call for help. In addition, army heli-pilots know the region well and can come quickly to your aid.

To organise rescue by army helicopter on the Baltoro, get a letter before you leave home from a bank guaranteeing to pay US$4,000 to the Ministry of Tourism in Islamabad in the event that you need a helicopter rescue. (For security, Pakistani army helicopters always fly in pairs, which partly explains the expense.) On arrival in Islamabad, show this letter to the Ministry of Tourism during your briefing session. They will give you your helicopter clearance forms. Be sure that you have at least three copies, and that they are *all* stamped and signed.

In Skardu, give the original copy to the Force Commander Northern Areas (FCNA), whose office is on the left a little beyond the PTDC K2 Motel. Have the two other copies signed by the officer in charge at FCNA. This signature is very important. Distribute these two copies to two members of your expedition and be sure that everyone knows where they are stored.

If you have an accident and need a helicopter, send someone (preferably your guide, if you have one, or your expedition leader) with your stamped and signed clearance form to one of the army camps at Dassu, Paiyu (the army camp is across the Braldu River, about two hours' hike via the Baltoro Glacier from the Paiyu trekking campsite), Goro One, Goro Two or Concordia. The camp commander will authorise his radio officer to radio to Skardu, and a helicopter will come as soon as one is free and weather permits. (When we needed one, it was delayed by a storm but still arrived within five hours. Some months later we got a little change out of our US$4,000 deposit, but not much.) Goro One to Skardu takes 80 minutes by helicopter.

If you are not in the Baltoro region, it is probably quicker to construct a makeshift stretcher and be carried out by porters. The only other radio stations are at police posts in the most important villages in each valley. Mountaineering expeditions usually carry their own radios and have a pre-arranged contact in Skardu, Gilgit or Chitral. Trekkers have no such luxury, so if you have an accident you must send out your helicopter clearance form with an expedition member or a porter on foot, which may take days. You then have to convince the unwilling policeman that your clearance is valid. If you are lucky, the police radio the army; otherwise you have to go to army headquarters. They may well radio the Ministry of Tourism in Islamabad (closed Friday and Saturday) for confirmation. Even then, a helicopter is sent only when one becomes available and only if they have a pilot who knows the area of your accident.

WASTE DISPOSAL

We are lucky enough to visit some of the most beautiful and fragile spots on earth, so surely the least we can do is show some respect for those places . . . Sensitivity for one's immediate surroundings should influence everyone who goes to the mountains . . . Leave the area as you find it. Don't leave it to the last minute, in the rush to leave there will not be time. Process all your litter right from the start. Dig latrine pits, burn paper, collect plastic, flatten tins and bag them for carry-out.

Steve Venables, *High*, June 1990

Set a good example; do not follow the bad example of others.

The most popular treks in Pakistan (Baltoro, Masherbrum, Gondoghoro, Rupal and Fairy Meadows) are already polluted to the point of being dangerous to health. Piles of human faeces and mountains of rusting cans surround most campsites. The Pakistan

Ministry of Tourism shows little interest in controlling the problem. Briefings before expeditions warn only against photographing local women, bridges and military installations, ignoring suggestions from environmental groups such as Mountain Wilderness to organise the training of guides in sanitation and the carrying out of rubbish. In Pakistan most rivers contain Giardia cysts, and typhoid, tetanus and cholera are also endemic. Care needs to be taken to protect yourself and others from infection.

Americans are most advanced in their disposal ideas; we can only hope their care will spread throughout the world. Since 1979, Grand Canyon National Park has had strict rules about disposal of human waste, and pages of instructions are distributed to all trekkers and rafters, requiring among other things that all solid human waste be packed out in watertight boxes. No group is allowed in without ample containers, proper education and a vowed commitment to pack it all out.

We do not suggest that you do the same in Pakistan, but do be aware of the health hazards from unburied faeces around camp and take a few simple precautions.

TOILET HOLES

Wherever possible, dig holes with an ice axe, spade or trowel at least 50 metres away from camp and above the high-water level of the river. This will ensure that Giardia cysts, bacteria and viruses are not carried by flying insects back to the food at camp or drain into nearby surface water or rivers. Dig one hole for the trekkers and one or more for the porters. Leave a pile of earth beside each hole, a little of which can be kicked in by each person after defecating.

Because of Muslim taboos, you may encounter resistance from your porters. Diplomacy and care are needed in introducing the idea, but the idea is not new in Baltistan, where each village has *chaksas* (pit toilets) that the villagers have used since childhood. Do not ask the porters to dig or fill in your hole, as Muslim purity laws are very strict, but make sure before you set out that the porters understand that one of their number will have to dig their toilet holes and fill them in. Determine before you start who this will be. Muslims, like Hindus, have a caste system, so you may have to hire a low-caste porter specially for the toilet holes—and pay him extra.

The expedition leader must select the toilet sites and check that they are properly dug and correctly filled in afterwards. Pack the earth down tightly and place a large stone over the top to seal the hole and prevent the Hoopoes (digger birds) from opening it again. (We have seen Hoopoes in abundance busy digging at up to 4,500 metres.)

Al Burgess suggests carrying lime to sprinkle in the pit to dampen the stench. We think this sounds a good idea but wonder if it may slow decomposition. Under the best conditions, human faeces can take more than a year to decompose. In the barren areas of Pakistan, which lack the necessary bacteria to break down the faeces, the process can take years; on glaciers or above the snow-line, where it is almost impossible to dig a hole, the freezing temperatures will preserve faeces for centuries. In these circumstances, try to find a good toilet site well away from camp and the melt pools that are the water supply for you and those who follow you.

Toilet paper and alternatives
In 1990 we walked down from Concordia against the tide of a French expedition heading up to climb. They all had the trots, and the glacier was covered in coloured toilet paper that they had made no effort to hide or collect.

We suggest that during the day all members carry plastic bags to collect any used paper, which you can bury or burn in the evening. Again, be aware of Muslim sensibilities: Muslims will not cook over a fire in which anything unclean has been burnt. Leave your burning until after dinner—do *not* leave it until morning, when you are too rushed packing up. The expedition leader must check everything personally, as guides and porters cannot be trusted to burn all paper or close the toilet holes satisfactorily.

Try to persuade your group to use water instead of toilet paper. This is the preferred method of Pakistanis. Just leave a bucket and plastic scoop beside the toilet hole (or carry your mug full of water with you from camp). Pour with the right hand and wipe with the left. The atmosphere is so hot and dry that you dry off in a moment. Alternatively, you can use a small, smooth stone, grass or leaves.

When peeing, you should get well away from the trail and camp. As there is little rain to wash urine away, the stench can become unpleasant.

If you wish to use the privacy of your tent, buy a large plastic mug in Skardu, Gilgit or Chitral. Remember when washing it out not to contaminate the river or surface water. Use a second scoop or bucket to carry water away from the river before starting to wash your dirty container. A plastic bottle or bag is a wonderful boon on cold wet nights, but remember to carry all plastic away with you. Do not try to burn or bury it.

Feminine funnels, oval funnels attached to a hose allowing women to pee into bottles, may be worth trying. In the United States you can get reusable plastic models from Sani-fem Corporation (7415 Sewart & Gray Road, Downey, CA 90241)—ask for a Freshette. In Paris, Vieux Campeur stock a device called Freelax that allows women to pee standing up. Ben refuses to hunt for feminine funnels in Britain, so please send information about what to ask for and where.

For more ideas and comfort tricks, read *How to Shit in the Woods*, by Kathleen Meyer (Ten Speed Press, PO Box 7123, Berkeley, CA 94707).

RUBBISH

Try to buy food in biodegradable or burnable packaging. Carry out the rest. Plastic emits poisonous fumes when burned, and aluminium packets just melt into a lump. Mountain Wilderness have calculated that 350 squashed cans weigh 25 kilograms, or one porter load. There is no excuse for leaving rubbish behind: as you have to pay half wages to porters going home empty, it is no great sacrifice to pay full wages to one or two porters to carry out the rubbish. You can sell the cans in Skardu, Gilgit or Chitral for Rs4 per kilo.

HIRING GUIDES AND PORTERS

If you are trekking in the open zone and hiring your own porters, the best plan is to take a jeep to the nearest point to your chosen trek and hire porters at the village where you leave the jeep. Always try to hire porters from the valley in which you will be trekking, as they know the way and the best sources of water. Also, locals have family and friends in the high pastures, so are more likely to enjoy the trip and cause fewer problems.

Expect to bargain hard, as porters naturally try for the best possible deal. Be careful not to overpay them, as this sets a precedent for future trekkers. Japanese and some trekking companies have a particularly bad reputation for pushing the prices up, making it difficult for others to compete.

Be prepared for porter strikes. Porters in Nagar and Diamer have a particularly bad reputation in this regard.

It is a good idea to have every porter sign a contract specifying exactly what is expected of him, even though these contracts have no legal force. If he cannot write, take a thumbprint. Keep a record of all the porters you have hired, and cross them off as you dismiss them. Otherwise, it is very easy to be tricked.

Tradition has divided most treks (except in Chitral) into stages, presumably a suitable day's journey when driving a herd, most of which are shorter than you may be used to walking in a day. An official stage can be as little as a flat 90-minute walk and is often only a two- to three-hour walk. Find out how many stages your chosen trek is before you start hiring. Explain exactly what you want and be sure that the porters know that you understand the pay stages and local customs.

There are recognised stopping places and it requires tact and determination to get the porters to walk further. It is perfectly possible to walk two stages in one day, but porters charge double wages. Make it clear to the porters that you will pay double if you expect them to walk two stages, but be careful not to force your porters to move on unless you are sure there is a suitable campsite ahead (we have tried to indicate most of the possible campsites along each trek).

Agree on the wages to be paid on rest days (usually about half) and forced rest due to bad weather (normally full wages), and on the porter's wage if walking back unladen (usually half or less). It is often better to agree on a set price for the whole trek, rather than a daily wage. It is acceptable to pay 50 percent of the first week's wages in advance; the rest is usually paid at the end or when the porter is dismissed.

The rules and regulations for hiring porters are clearly defined by the government. The official wage per stage differs in each valley: 1992 prices for low-altitude porters are Rs90 in Baltistan (Skardu) and Diamer (Chilas and Nanga Parbat), Rs100 in Chitral and Rs110 in Gilgit, Hunza and Nagar. High-altitude porters and porters in glaciated areas charge Rs150 in Baltistan and Diamer, Rs130 in Chitral and Rs180 in Gilgit, Hunza and Nagar.

When trekking where there are villages or shepherds' settlements, you can pay each porter the government-stipulated Rs30 daily food ration. This is usually cheaper than hiring extra porters to carry food for the porters. When you are only one or two nights away from shepherds' settlements, the porters usually prefer to be paid the Rs30 and carry their own food, but check carefully to make sure that each porter is actually carrying enough food for the trek and that he knows you will not be supplying any extra. They often think that they will be able to eat your left-overs (we never have any).

On longer treks, when you may spend ten days or so up glaciers where there are no shepherds' settlements, you have to carry the government-stipulated rations for each porter. This gets expensive, especially on the Concordia trek, where you must calculate up to 2.5 porters per expedition load of 25 kilograms. Climbing expeditions usually calculate 1.8 porters per expedition load if all of the porters are sent back with no loads on arrival at base camp.

If you have more than 25 porters, government rules state that you must hire a *sirdar* (head porter) to be in charge of them.

Government-approved daily rations for porters:

wheat flour (*atta*)	22	ounces	625 grams
meat	3.5	ounces	100 grams
lentils (*dhaal*)	3	ounces	85 grams
cooking oil	2.5	ounces	70 grams
sugar	2	ounces	56 grams
tea	0.5	ounce	14 grams
milk (fresh or tinned)	2	ounces	56 grams
salt	0.5	ounce	14 grams
dried onion	0.25	ounce	7 grams
curry powder	0.25	ounce	7 grams
tobacco	10	cigarettes	
matches	one box per week		

A quick calculation shows you need about one kilogram of food per porter per day. We usually provide more lentils and no meat. On longer treks you are expected to buy a goat (about Rs500–1,000 depending on the region) for the porters or pay them Rs25 extra each—or buy them a meal in a restaurant.

We provide only one cigarette daily.

The required **clothing allowance** for porters is one pair of rubber bootees, one pair of gloves, two pairs of woollen socks, one rain cape or plastic sheet, and one pair of sunglasses. Most porters do not demand any of these, but prefer to be paid Rs150 instead. Be sure to check that each porter's clothing is adequate. They often have no socks or gloves and sometimes no hat.

It can be extremely cold at night on a glacier above 4,000 metres, so for glacier treks you must have a tarpaulin or heavy plastic sheet measuring 4x4 metres for every eight porters. If walking on glaciers, porters also need dark glasses and a warm jacket. You must have one cooker and fuel for every eight porters.

All these items are available in the bazaars in Skardu, Gilgit and Chitral, but it is cheaper to buy them in Rawalpindi.

As leader, you are responsible for the safety of all those fingers, toes, ears and eyes. It is better to buy the gear than to treat the frostbite or snow-blindness. If travelling in a small, private group of two or three trekkers with three or four porters, it is easy to lend jackets and socks at night and collect them later. Likewise, you can lend goggles or dark glasses when walking on the snow in bright sunshine.

If you feel you need a **guide**, ask around for advice in Skardu, Gilgit or Chitral before setting out. Professional guides from the big companies cost about Rs300 per day, plus food. Locals with less experience charge Rs150–200. Be sure to get recommendations, as anyone with a little English can say he is a guide.

Government rules dictate that you must hire a cook and, if you number more than five, also a cook's assistant. We ignore this and do our own cooking. If you do hire a cook be mindful of his cleanliness. Personally supervise his hand washing, and see where he gets your water from and how he washes and prepares your food.

Guides and cooks are paid by the day, not by the pay stage.

If you are trekking without a guide, be sure that at least one porter knows the way. If there is a glacier crossing, ensure the porter has crossed it recently, as the route changes constantly. If you are alone, keep your porter with you at all times.

Finally, if you are satisfied with your porters, write them references to show to other prospective employers.

GETTING ALONG

Pakistanis usually have beautiful manners, so take time to enjoy them. Learn your porters' names and greet them every morning. Shake hands and ask polite questions about health and family—this is the Pakistani way. Remember that they are family men doing their job to support themselves and their loved ones.

It also pays to be friendly with those in authority, such as the deputy commissioner and the police. They are all-powerful and can be easily irritated; no matter how frustrated you become dealing with them, stay relaxed and cheerful to get them on your side and keep them there. Arguing gets you nowhere.

Your Pakistani assistants are Muslim and do not eat pork, so do not ask them to touch or cook pork for you. Goat and mutton are the favourite meats in northern Pakistan and are more expensive than beef.

Muslims eat with the right hand and wipe their bottoms with the left. Consequently, the left hand is rightfully considered unclean, making it rude to use it to offer or accept anything (though in Pakistan this is far less marked than in some other Muslim countries, such as Indonesia). Pakistanis are fussier than Westerners about sharing cups or eating utensils, so do not stick your spoon in the cooking pot to taste the food. The cooking fire is sacred. Never burn rubbish in your porters' fire. Make a separate fire for rubbish.

Pakistanis are very modest about their bodies. Even men keep themselves completely covered—torso, arms and legs, rolling their trouser legs up only when crossing a river. Westerners need to be sensitive about this and not show themselves shirtless or wearing shorts. Do not strip completely naked when bathing. Pakistani men squat to pee because it is considered vulgar to stand.

Women need to be particularly careful about wearing a bra and loose-fitting clothes— an extra-large T-shirt or man's shirt over baggy, draw-stringed trekking trousers is an ideal outfit. Wrap up in a sarong when bathing in the river and try to keep out of sight.

Remember that certain areas of Pakistan are still hostile to outsiders and are dangerous for Pakistanis and foreigners alike. All such areas are clearly indicated in this guide. If you go near them, inform the police of your whereabouts for your own protection and follow their advice.

Be aware of the dangers around you, human or otherwise. Many of the trails are vertiginous, unstable and steep—and are all the more dangerous for being remote. Ask those you meet about the state of the paths and bridges ahead. Every year some are washed out and relocated, and there may be different routes for different seasons depending on the height of the rivers. Make yourself known; tell villagers and shepherds where you are going, so the authorities will know where to look for you if you go missing.

Above all, trekkers in Pakistan should be flexible, ready to change their plans at a moment's notice. If your flight is cancelled due to bad weather, take a bus. If your chosen trek is closed, choose another one.

PRESENTS AND BEGGING

Do not encourage begging by handing out gifts. This is not hard hearted: begging lowers the self-esteem of the people, and giving sweets and biscuits to children is actually cruel, as there are no dentists to fill their cavities.

In most touristy areas the children have learned the Nepali mantra: 'One pen! One pen! One pen!' They use chalk and slate at school, so do not need pens, and in any case they often sing the mantra mainly to make contact with you, using the only English they know.

VISITING MOSQUES AND SHRINES

Tourists are welcome in mosques and shrines, provided that they remove their shoes, show respect and are suitably dressed. Women should cover their head and shoulders. A pair of socks (or the little bootees that airlines hand out in business class) can keep your feet off the stones, which get painfully hot in summer. Women are not allowed into the inner sanctum at some shrines but may look in through a side window. Many mosques close their doors to tourists half an hour before prayers.

During **Ramazan**, the fasting month, no food or drink is sold during the day except in the dining rooms of large hotels (poolside service is usually suspended) and in some restaurants. Travel during this month is difficult; tourists should be careful not to eat, drink or smoke in public.

WOMEN ALONE

Pakistani women never travel alone. Indeed, many never even leave the house unless accompanied by a family member, friend or servant. Foreign women tourists are therefore advised not to travel alone in Pakistan, not because it is dangerous, but because it offends good Muslim males to see women so immodest as to travel unaccompanied.

TRAVEL INFORMATION

The Pakistan Tourism Development Corporation (PTDC) is the main source of information inside Pakistan. The PTDC arranges trips, accommodation and transport and publishes a series of booklets on areas of tourist interest.

The PTDC head office is at House 2, Street 61, F 7/4, Islamabad. For PTDC hotel bookings, contact PTDC Motel Head Office, Block B-4, Markaz F-7 (Jinnah Market), Bhitai Road, Islamabad. PTDC has offices in the Metropole Hotel in Karachi, Faletti's Hotel in Lahore, Dean's Hotel in Peshawar, Club Annex in Abbottabad, PTDC hotels in Balakot and Naran in the Kaghan Valley, Swat Serena Hotel in Swat, PTDC Motel in Chitral, Chinar Inn in Gilgit, K2 Motel in Skardu. The PTDC arranges tours, accommodation and transport and publishes a series of booklets on areas of tourist interest.

The government-run Pakistan Tours Ltd (Room 30, Flashman's Hotel, The Mall, Rawalpindi; tel 565449, 563038, 581480; telex FH PK 5620) also gives information and runs tours, but it is more expensive than privately owned tour and trekking companies.

Outside of the country, Pakistan International Airlines (PIA) offices and Pakistani embassies and consulates supply information.

MONEY

The Pakistani unit of currency is the rupee, which is divided into 100 paise. Rates are about Rs25 to the US dollar, Rs45 to the pound sterling and Rs15 to the Deutschmark, but they differ depending on the town and the bank.

Any amount of foreign currency or travellers' cheques may be brought into Pakistan, but only Rs100 in Pakistani cash may be taken in or out. Also, you may change only Rs500 back from rupees to foreign currency. Save your encashment slips, as you may need to show them upon leaving. It is an offence to sell foreign currency in Pakistan except to authorised dealers (foreign banks, the National Bank of Pakistan, the Habib Bank and some big hotels and tourist shops), and the black market rates are not much better anyway. Banking hours are 9 am–1 pm.

US currency in cash or travellers' cheques is handiest, but sterling and Deutschmarks are also widely accepted. Travellers' cheques can be changed at the major cities and at some divisional headquarters and big hotels (guests only). Big hotels also accept credit cards. American Express has offices at Karachi, Lahore, Islamabad and Rawalpindi.

If you need money sent to you in Pakistan, it is quicker to have a bank draft sent registered air mail to a specific address than having it sent bank to bank.

CUSTOMS REGULATIONS

Alcohol is not admitted to Pakistan; bags are sometimes searched, and any alcohol found is impounded. A non-Muslim can buy liquor if he has a liquor licence, which is obtainable in some large hotels authorised to sell alcohol to hotel guests and from government liquor shops in the main cities, provided that he has a permit from the Excise and Taxation Department of that area.

Official import limits for other items are 200 cigarettes, 1/2 pint of perfume and one camera, tape recorder and typewriter. Officials are not strict with most tourists, but Indians and visiting Pakistanis are thoroughly searched.

Antiques may not be exported from Pakistan. Jewellery and precious stones are allowed out only if worth less than Rs10,000; carpets must be worth less than Rs25,000. You may be asked to produce foreign exchange certificates sufficient to cover the purchase price. Unaccompanied baggage needs an export permit.

Airport tax is Rs300 for international flights and Rs10 for domestic flights and must be paid at the airport by all travellers.

GETTING TO PAKISTAN
BY AIR

Over 20 international airlines fly to Pakistan from more than 40 countries. Most flights arrive at Karachi, but a few go to Islamabad, Lahore or Peshawar. Pakistan International Airlines (PIA) flies to a number of destinations in South Asia and the Gulf (and on to Nairobi) and has direct flights to some European cities, with flights continuing to New York. PIA also has a limited Far East network.

Pakistan's international airports have banks that change travellers' cheques and foreign currency in the main arrival hall, so you can change money while waiting for your bags to arrive. This is quicker and easier than at banks in town, which offer the same rates.

There are taxis and public buses from the airports to city centres. It is best to bargain with the taxi driver and agree on a fare before setting off. From Karachi airport to the downtown hotels should cost about Rs70 by taxi, Rs10 by airport coach and Rs2 by bus. From Islamabad Airport to Islamabad is about Rs80 by taxi, Rs5 by wagon and Rs3 by bus. From Islamabad Airport to Rawalpindi is about Rs60 by taxi and Rs2 by bus.

OVERLAND

From China: The Khunjerab Pass is open from May 1 to October 31 for tours and to November 30 for individual travellers. Customs, immigration and health formalities at Sost, the border post, can be completed daily until 11 am for outgoing travellers and 4 pm for incoming travellers. The travel time from Sost to Tashkurgan, the first Chinese town, is five hours, not counting formalities at the Chinese border post at Pirali.

From India: There is a daily train connection from Amritsar to Lahore. India and Pakistan have agreed to open the railway line from Jodhpur in Rajasthan to Hyderabad in Sindh, but as we go to press this has not yet happened.

From Iran: The border is open only at Taftan, from where it is a 15- to 24-hour bus ride to Quetta in Baluchistan. Quetta is the only place in Baluchistan open to foreign tourists without a special permit.

From Afghanistan: Afghanistan is still closed to foreigners. The two possible entry points from Afghanistan, from Kabul via Torkham and the Khyber Pass, and from Kandahar via Chaman and the Khojak Pass, are both closed except to local traffic. Check with other tourists for the latest information.

TRAVELLING INSIDE PAKISTAN

BY AIR

PIA operates flights to most big towns in Pakistan. Flights to Gilgit, Skardu and Chitral are extremely good value. These tickets are cheaper if bought in Pakistan, working out to about three times the bus fare. However, the flights operate only when visibility is good and so can be delayed for some days.

Journalists and groups are eligible for discounts. Apply to the public relations officer at the PIA office in Karachi, Lahore, Rawalpindi, Peshawar, Multan or Quetta.

The domestic airport tax is Rs10.

BY TRAIN

This is the best way to get around if you have enough time. The trunk lines run from Karachi via Multan, Lahore and Rawalpindi to Peshawar, and from Karachi via Sukkur and Quetta to the Iranian border. There is an extensive network of branch lines. Trains run frequently, but they are slow, unpunctual and crowded.

There are two classes of train (express and ordinary) and three classes of compartment (air-conditioned, first and second). Air-conditioned and first class have sleeper compartments, and there are special ladies' compartments recommended for women travelling alone. Air-conditioned class is almost as expensive as flying, and you usually need to book several days in advance, especially for sleepers. Most passengers bring their own bedding, but it can sometimes be hired at major stations. Buying a ticket can be time consuming and frustrating, so an agency or hotel employee willing to handle it is a great asset. If all else fails, you can pay a station porter (recognisable by his red turban and armband) to buy you a ticket and find a seat.

Foreign tourists can get a 25 percent discount (50 percent for students) on most rail fares. Apply to the divisional superintendent with your passport (and student card) at Karachi, Lahore, Rawalpindi, Peshawar, Quetta, Sukkur or Multan railway stations for the necessary concession order before buying your ticket. You may also need a tourist certificate from the local tourist officer to claim your rail discount. Indians and visiting Pakistanis are not eligible.

BY ROAD

Public buses are the cheapest but most uncomfortable and dangerous way to travel in Pakistan. They go everywhere. The bus station is usually near the railway station (if there is one) or near the bazaar in smaller places. On longer journeys, buses make scheduled stops for food, but it is wise to take food (especially fruit) and drink with you. Seats cannot always be reserved in advance.

The Northern Area Transport Company (NATCO) runs buses and jeeps up the Karakoram Highway and into some of the side valleys off the main road. They offer a discount to a limited number of Pakistani and foreign students on each vehicle.

Minibuses are faster, more comfortable and only slightly more expensive. Seats can be booked in advance. Minibuses often use different stations from the regular buses. There are several private luxury bus services plying between the major cities.

Jeeps are the public transport in northern valleys, where roads are too narrow for buses. The drivers are excellent, but the jeeps are neither cheap nor comfortable, with as many passengers as possible perched on top of the cargo (usually sacks of grain or fertiliser) and crouched on the front and back bumpers. They do not run to a timetable and, in the remoter valleys, are quite rare.

SELF DRIVE

The main roads are surfaced and generally in reasonable condition, but drivers are not conscientious about observing traffic rules, so those unused to driving in Asia (or on the left) may find it harrowing and dangerous. The main Karachi-Lahore-Rawalpindi-Peshawar highway is always very crowded with particularly reckless drivers. The minor roads are often impassable for ordinary cars, so four-wheel-drive vehicles with high clearance are recommended. In the mountains it is essential to have a small four-wheel-drive vehicle, as roads and bridges are very narrow.

Signposts are few and are often written only in Urdu, which makes finding your way difficult and frustrating, particularly in big cities. Driving at night is especially hazardous, as trucks, bicycles and bullock carts rarely have lights. It is dangerous to drive in Sindh because of the bandits. Distances are measured in kilometres.

If you still want to drive, you need only a valid driving licence.

Rental cars with drivers can be hired at the airport and big hotels. Hotel cars are fairly expensive (more so if air-conditioned), but may be worth the extra cost, as the drivers speak some English. Ensure with the hotel rental agency that the driver knows where you want to go before you set off. If you wish to visit several places, the best solution is to hire a local taxi (black with a yellow roof) in the street, which costs about Rs400 for the day. Local taxi drivers usually know only the main locations in town and will expect you to direct them to offices or private homes.

Jeeps with drivers are readily available in the mountains. The government-approved rate in 1992 in the Punjab, on the Karakoram Highway and in Gilgit District is Rs6 per mile and Rs75 overnight charge. In Chitral the rate is Rs8 per mile and Rs30 overnight charge, and in Skardu it is Rs10 per mile and Rs200 halt charge. No one keeps to these rates, so you will need to bargain.

PUBLIC TRANSPORT IN TOWNS

In big cities, buses run along set routes but not to a schedule. Datsun wagons and Suzuki vans run everywhere possible; in the towns the fare is usually Rs2. There are few designated stops, so simply wave down a passing wagon or Suzuki and ask the driver if he is going in your general direction. In some towns there are also motorised rickshaws charging about half the local taxi fare.

TIME AND ELECTRICITY

Pakistan is five hours ahead of Greenwich Mean Time. Darkness falls at about 5 pm in winter and 7.30 pm in summer.

Business hours are 7.30 am–2.30 pm in summer and 9 am–4 pm in winter. Banks are open 9 am–1 pm. Friday is the weekly holiday, when all shops and offices are closed. Most offices remain closed on Saturday.

Electricity is 220–240 volts, with brown-outs down to a few volts. In the north, the electricity supply is very erratic, and paraffin lamps or candles are usually supplied in hotels. Electric hairdryers and razors are usable only in large cities.

PHOTOGRAPHY AND FILM

Pakistan, its people and mountains are superbly photogenic. Few travellers have the time to wait for the perfect light, but beware the noon-day sun, which tends to flatten the subject and dull the colours. For best results, take photos before 10 am and after 4 pm. Underexposing midday shots by half a stop or more can help, as will a polarising filter.

Film for colour prints is widely available in Pakistan, but it is often old and heat damaged. Film for colour slides and black-and-white prints is available only in Karachi, Lahore and Islamabad. Enthusiasts are advised to bring all of the film they need with them and to store it in as cool a place as possible.

You are not allowed to photograph military installations, airports or bridges. Pakistani men generally like to be asked permission before being photographed, then they usually assume manly poses and stare straight into the camera; a telephoto lens may be useful for spontaneous shots, but remember that big lenses are big attention getters. Men should not attempt to photograph women, though female photographers usually have no problem at all, especially if there are no men around to disapprove and if a little time is first spent making friends and asking permission.

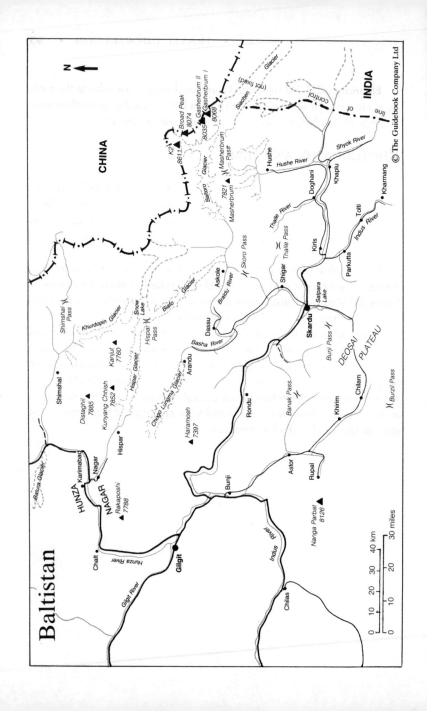

BALTISTAN

Baltistan is the northeastern district of Pakistan, sandwiched between China and Indian-held Kashmir and bisected by the Indus River. North of the Indus, the Karakoram Range rises in a serried wall 150 kilometres thick, with over 100 peaks higher than 7,000 metres. South of the Indus, the uninhabited Deosai Plateau separates Pakistan from India.

Until this century Baltistan was an unexplored dead end, with only two difficult trade routes from Tibet and Ladakh, following the Indus and Shyok rivers, and another crossing the deserted Deosai Plateau from Srinagar. Only one snow-bound pass led across the Karakorams to China, and even that was blocked by ice early in the nineteenth century. The route down the Indus, a series of dangerous gorges guarded by hostile tribes, was impassible.

BALTISTAN HISTORY

The Balti people are a mixture of Tibetan and Caucasian stock who speak Balti, an ancient form of Tibetan. Originally they probably practised animism (worship of inanimate objects and natural phenomena) and shamanism (the use of shamans or priests to influence these gods of nature). Sometime around the fourth century AD, Buddhism spread from its centre in Swat to Baltistan and Ladakh, and from there on to Tibet. By the eighth century, Baltistan was ruled by Tibet and was known as Great Bolor. By the eleventh century, the region of modern Pakistan known as the Northern Areas was a powerful independent kingdom, equal in strength to Kashmir. Sometime thereafter but before the seventeenth century, the area was converted to Shia Islam by way of Kashmir. Almost all Baltis are still Shia, the strictest sect of Islam.

Baltistan was divided into four kingdoms: Skardu, the richest and most important, in the centre; Khaplu, which controlled the trade route east along the Shyok River to Ladakh; Shigar, which held the Shigar River to the north; and Rondu, which guarded the Indus Gorge to the west. There were also four lesser principalities: Kiris, on the Shyok, and Parkutta (now called Mediabad), Tolti and Kharmang, which were on the Indus and controlled the path to Leh.

In 1840 the raja of Jammu (later to become the maharaja of Kashmir), Gulab Singh, who was a Rajput Hindu and a member of the Dogra tribe, overran Baltistan and imprisoned the reigning raja, Ahmed Shah. This ended Baltistan's independence, and the maharaja of Kashmir ruled Baltistan for the next 107 years. The British held only a minimal interest in the area, as they considered it of little strategic value. At Independence in 1947, Baltistan was assigned to India, but the Balti people, aided by a small number of freedom fighters including the Gilgit Scouts, rebelled against their Hindu Kashmiri rulers and became part of Pakistan.

There are 230 villages in Baltistan, with a combined population of 272,000, averaging eight people per household. The average farm size is half a hectare, on which is grown wheat, barley, millet, buckwheat and maize. Vegetables—peas, tomatoes, onions, potatoes, turnips, cabbage, spinach, lettuce, beans, cucumbers, radishes, chilli and carrots—were introduced about 50 years ago. Fruits and nuts are important crops, with each family owning 20 to 30 apricot trees and at least some mulberry, apple, pear, peach, plum, walnut and almond trees, as well as a few grapevines. Dried fruit and nuts are a vital part of the winter diet.

Each household owns an average of ten goats and sheep and two or three head of cattle, yaks or dzos (a cross between the two). The animals spend the summer in high pastures and the winter in stalls in the ground floor of the houses. Butter was once used as a currency; it was 'banked' underground for up to 50 years and withdrawn to buy goods and make loans. Some households own a few chickens, and in some villages you find donkeys.

About 10 percent of households send a man up to summer pastures with the animals. Some 20 percent of Balti households have a member earning a regular income either outside of the district or as shopkeepers, village craftsmen or drivers, and about 30 percent of households have a man working as a temporary day labourer, such as portering for expeditions.

SKARDU INFORMATION

Skardu, the capital of Baltistan, has a population of about 15,000 and stands at an altitude of 2,340 metres. It serves as the starting point for some of the most scenic and adventurous trekking in the world.

WHEN TO GO
Mid-June to mid-September is the best time to trek, though in June you will be camping on snow. In August, the high season, the flowers in the summer pastures are in full bloom. Ordinary tourists usually visit Baltistan in April, May, September and October, when the main Indus Valley is not too hot and the trees are covered in spring blossom

or autumn gold. About 70 percent of the annual rainfall of 202 millimetres falls between January and May. For the past 30 years the driest months have been June, September, October and November.

GETTING TO SKARDU

By air: Boeing 733 flights from Islamabad to Skardu are scheduled daily at 10 am. One-way fare is US$50 if booked overseas, Rs560 for foreigners if booked in Pakistan. On Sundays there is also a Fokker flight costing Rs483 one way. Pakistanis get a subsidised fare of Rs247 on either flight. On a fine day this is one of the most spectacular flights imaginable, with views of seemingly endless rows of peaks, dozens of which are over 7,000 metres and five of which soar above 8,000 metres. Nanga Parbat is on the right, and K2 and the Gasherbrums are straight ahead (you can ask to go into the cockpit for photos). The flight goes only in fine weather, so be prepared for delays of several days.

A weekly flight from Gilgit to Skardu departs at 1.15 pm on Thursdays. One-way fare for foreigners US$40 if paid overseas or Rs329 in Pakistan; the fare is Rs170 for Pakistanis.

PTDC reserves two priority seats on each flight for tourists, so if the flight is full apply to Flashman's Hotel in Rawalpindi, the Chinar Inn in Gilgit or the K2 Motel in Skardu. Ask for a special booking for these reserved seats and receive a note of confirmation to take back to PIA.

Skardu Airport is 14 kilometres west of town. Public Suzukis and jeeps meet the plane and charge about Rs10 for the 30-minute ride to Skardu. The Shangrila Tourist Resort lies in the opposite direction from Skardu and sends a vehicle to collect guests.

By road: Those loaded with trekking gear may find it less frustrating to go by road. From **Rawalpindi** check first at Flashman's Hotel to see if there are any mountaineering expeditions heading for Skardu, as you may be able to hitch a ride. Few public buses or wagons go directly from Rawalpindi to Skardu, a journey of 20 to 25 hours, but several leave daily for the 15-hour ride to Gilgit (see Getting to Gilgit, page 000). Take the Gilgit bus and ask in Chilas if there is a bus to Skardu. If not, continue to Gilgit and rest for a day.

NATCO (Northern Areas Transport Company) buses leave **Gilgit** for Skardu at 6 am; Masherbrum Tours buses leave at 7 am. The fare for the 207-kilometre run to Skardu is Rs40. Several wagons leave throughout the day for Rs60. The journey takes six to eight hours if there are no landslides.

Jeep: You can hire a private jeep for the official government rate of Rs6 per mile plus an overnight charge of Rs75. Rawalpindi to Skardu is about 735 kilometres. Well-known travel agents are the most reliable, but jeeps can also be hired in the bazaars. Check the tyres, keep an eye on what the driver smokes, and allow him frequent tea and food stops.

The route follows the Karakoram Highway for 565 kilometres to the junction of the Indus and Gilgit rivers, 37 kilometres south of Gilgit. It then turns east and follows a metalled road along the north bank of the Indus for the last 170 kilometres through the Rondu Gorge to Skardu.

SKARDU TOWN

The **Tourist Information Centre** is in the K2 Motel. Your best source of information is other trekkers and mountaineers, and the best place to meet them is the K2 Motel.

Habib Bank and **National Bank of Pakistan** are in the bazaar. They are open 9 am–1 pm from Monday to Thursday and 9 am–12 pm Saturday and Sunday. Sterling and US dollar travellers' cheques are accepted with good identification.

The **Post Office**, near the football ground, is open 8 am–2 pm. The nearby **telephone and telegraph office** is open 24 hours a day, seven days a week. The direct dialing code for Skardu is 0575. You can make international calls and send cables.

The **hospital** is at the east end of town. There is a doctor on duty for emergencies, but do not expect much. It is best to try to find a foreign expedition doctor and beg help. You can buy drugs in pharmacies without a prescription, but be sure you know what you are doing.

All basic supplies are available in Skardu's Naya (New) and Purana (Old) **bazaars**: flour, rice, lentils (*dhaal*), sugar, powdered milk, salt, tea, biscuits, curry powder, dried tomato, dried onion and garlic. When buying dhaal, get the fast-cooking kind—and beware of shopkeepers who will tell you that everything is fast cooking. In season you can find potatoes, onions, cabbage and apples. The Purana Bazaar has local rope, plastic string, all shapes and sizes of aluminium cooking pots, local kerosene cookers, metal plates, mugs and cutlery. Tarpaulins and canvas bags are rare, but you will find old sugar and flour bags and large rolls of thick plastic sheeting. Also available (albeit more expensively and in a smaller selection than in the Raja Bazaar in Rawalpindi) is all of the gear you need for your porters: rubber boots, socks, gloves, woolly hats and sunglasses.

You will also need aspirin, antibiotics and bandages for your porters.

The bazaar offers surprisingly little expedition equipment, such as climbing rope, ice axes, boots, crampons, tents and sleeping bags. Ask around, but do not count on finding anything. Try the shop at Satpara Lake, to the right of the entrance to the PTDC Rest House (we found gaiters there). Your best bet for equipment and camping food is to buy from departing expeditions.

TREKKING AGENCIES

Himalayan Trekking, PO Box 621; tel (0575) 280; Cable BAT SKARDU. Muhammad Ali Chengezi, the owner, is a Skardu man—knowledgeable, reliable and a skilled guide. His Rawalpindi address is 112 Rahim Plaza, Murree Road; or PO Box 1769; tel 63014; cable HIMALAYA.

Karakoram Treks and Tours, Karakoram Yurt and Yak Serai, Link Road, Satellite Town; tel (0575) 856; cable YURT SKARDU. Raja Alamdar, from the Khaplu royal family, knows the area intimately and is reliable and extremely helpful. The head office is in Islamabad (see page 000).

Pakistan Tourist Development Corporation (PTDC), K2 Motel; tel (0575) 946.

Baltistan Tours, Link Road, Satellite Town; PO Box 604; tel (0575) 626. Muhammad Iqbal organises the Karakoram Experience tours—pricy but knows his stuff.

Siachen Tours, Link Road, Satellite Town; PO Box 613; tel (0575) 844 or 951; cable SIACHEN.

Ask at your hotel for ideas and guides.

HIRING GUIDES AND PORTERS

Read the section on hiring (page 83).

If you are preparing for the Concordia trek, you will have your obligatory guide, who will do all the shopping and hiring for you. We recommend that you accompany him so you can check all your supplies and speak to your porters, using him as an interpreter as you explain your plans. Make a list of your porters' names and write each one's load beside his name. Every few days you pay off porters and send them back. Do this yourself, thanking them personally and checking them off your list.

On the Concordia trek, it is usual to pay the porters an extra Rs30 a day so they can provide their own rations as far as Paiyu, beyond which you must carry the government-approved rations—about one kilogram of food per day per porter.

If organising your own trek in an open zone without a guide, start by asking around to find out the latest Skardu rules and what to expect regarding porter equipment, pay stages and local customs. Try to find someone who has done your proposed trek so you can learn about the latest conditions and how many stages the porters expect you to

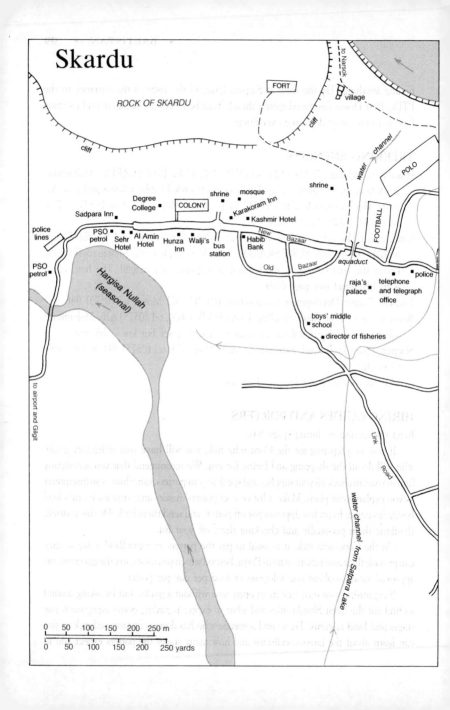

Skardu

ROCK OF SKARDU

to Narsok

FORT

village

cliff

cliff

cliff

water channel

POLO

shrine

mosque

shrine

FOOTBALL

Degree College

COLONY

shrine

Karakoram Inn

Sadpara Inn

Kashmir Hotel

police lines

PSO petrol

Sehr Hotel

Al Amin Hotel

Hunza Inn

Walji's

New Bazaar

bus station

Habib Bank

aquaduct

PSO petrol

Old Bazaar

police

Hargisa Nullah (seasonal)

raja's palace

telephone and telegraph office

boys' middle school

director of fisheries

to airport and Gilgit

Link Road

water channel from Sadpara Lake

0   50   100 150 200 250 m

0   50   100 150 200   250 yards

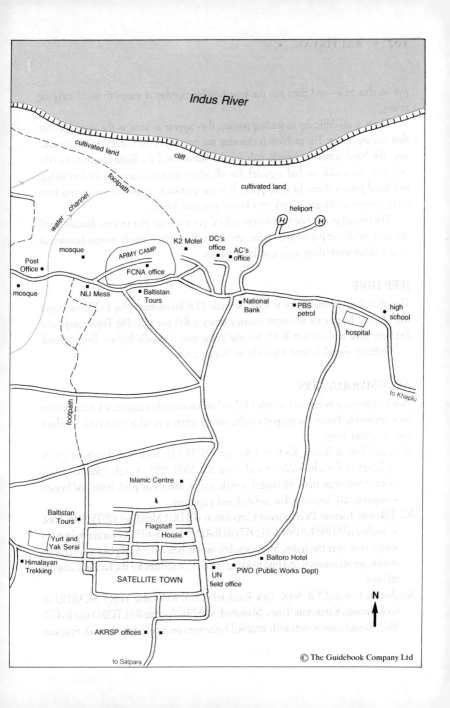

pay on that trek—and then pay the least possible number of stages to avoid inflating prices.

There is no difficulty in finding porters; they appear as soon as the word goes out that you are hiring. The problem is choosing the best out of the hordes crowding round you. We hired porters in Skardu only for the Baltoro and the Biafo-Hispar treks (the only treks for which we had a guide). For all others we took a jeep to the last village and hired porters there. In some places it is the custom to employ a few porters from each of several villages. Check this before you start hiring.

The official porter rate in Baltistan is Rs90 per pay stage plus rations. Bargain hard, stay firm and do not pay more than the agreed rate. Portering is hugely overpaid compared to any other work these men can hope to get.

JEEP HIRE

The official government rate is Rs10 per mile (1.6 kilometres) plus Rs200 overnight halt charge; the rate for an empty return journey is Rs5 per mile. Big Toyota jeeps cost Rs12 per mile and tractors Rs15, but the going rate is usually higher. Bargain hard.

Ordinary **petrol** is available only in Skardu town.

ACCOMMODATION

Hotel prices given below are for early 1992 and are meant to be a guideline for comparison between hotels. Prices rise proportionally, except when a hotel is renovated, in which case its prices jump.

Shangrila Tourist Resort, Kachura Lake; tel (0575) 235; book Rawalpindi tel 73006 or 72948 or Karachi 520261/5 (s/d about Rs1,100/1,500). Lovely lakeside setting planted with fruit trees. 96 bungalow-style rooms, swimming pool, boats and horses. Comparatively luxurious but isolated and expensive.

K2, Pakistan Tourism Development Corporation (PTDC) Motel; tel (0575) 946; book Islamabad tel 819384, 815653, 812957 (s/d Rs425–525/525–625). Great central garden with a view over the Indus. Most expeditions stay here, so a good place to exchange stories, get information and find trekking mates. Convenient for the bazaar. Camping allowed.

Karakoram Yurt and Yak Serai, Link Road; tel (0575) 856; cable YURT SKARDU or book through Karakoram Tours, Islamabad; tel 829120; cable BALTORO (s/d Rs450/ 550). Round canvas yurts with attached bathrooms on a peaceful side road. Spacious with good food, but new, so rather empty and isolated. Storage facilities for expeditions. Camping allowed.

Sehr, College Road; tel (0575) 771 (s/d Rs350/500). Attempts to be upmarket but has small rooms (only two of which with a view) and no garden.

Al Amin, College Road; tel (0575) 576 (d Rs300–450, camping Rs20). Two rooms have lovely views south across the nullah to the mountains, but other rooms are claustrophobic. Helpful management.

Sadpara Inn, College Road; tel (0575) 951 (s/d Rs250/300). New, small, airless rooms but trying hard.

Hunza Inn, College Road; tel (0575) 570 (Rs120–200). Best value. Older place with rooms set round a small garden. Popular with backpackers. A good meeting place with a good, cheap restaurant.

Karakoram Inn, Yadhar Chowk; tel (0575) 449 and 452 (s/d/t Rs150/200/250). Multi-storey, noisy and sleazy. The food tastes okay, but we were poisoned.

Baltoro, Satelite Town (d Rs100). New and a bit isolated but good value.

Northern Areas Public Works Department (NAPWD) rest house (also at Shigar, Khaplu and Machlu). Book through NAPWD headquarters; ask at Tourist Information, PTDC, for details.

Camping is allowed; ask at Tourist Information for details.

SHORT WALKS IN AND AROUND SKARDU

Skardu Fort, perched halfway up the enormous Rock of Skardu, is an easy half-hour walk up a sloping ramp from the bazaar. Variously known as Karpochu, Askandria or Mindoq Fort, the present structure was built on the site of an earlier fort by the Kashmiri Dogra troops when they captured Baltistan in 1846. You can explore the many ruined rooms and walls or just go for the view.

Intrepid rock climbers can keep in form by shinning to the top of the rock, which is 350 metres high. This is best attempted from the western end, behind the Degree College, and is only for the experienced.

> Follow a path that diverges from the airport road . . . paralleling the talus slopes at the base of the rock. Continue past the first slopes to a farther, larger slope that is lighter in hue, with a visible stock trail ascending it. You must keep going up the talus and figure out the difficult route to the

left as you approach the top. Several zigzags along exposed ledges require the use of both hands.

Hugh Swift, *Trekking in Pakistan and India*

On the rolling, grassy top are the ruins of another fortress built in the 1930s. A sublime panorama of valleys, cliffs, terraces and mountains rewards the climber. On the south you look straight down to Skardu, with the hills leading to the Deosai Plateau behind. The Shigar Valley, broad and fertile, runs down from the north to join the Indus, which sweeps around the foot of the rock. The Shigar and Indus valleys were both filled with glaciers in the last ice age.

Narsok, a tiny village huddled in a small oasis by the Indus on the northeastern side of Skardu rock, is another possibility for a short walk from the bazaar. Follow the path from the polo ground or the K2 Motel through cultivated land to a village at the eastern end of the rock, and continue on a cliff path above the Indus round toward the northern side.

Satpara Lake, eight kilometres south of Skardu, is a 20-minute drive or a steep walk away. Follow the irrigation channel from the aqueduct in the centre of town to the jeep road, and continue south. There is a stunning view north and south from the top of the ridge before the lake. You can row out to a small islet in the boat moored by the PTDC rest house (Rs350 per double, bookable at the PTDC in the K2 Motel or in Islamabad). It is a good place to camp and rest, and the lake is well stocked with fish. A fishing licence and tackle are available from the PTDC rest house.

The **Satpara Buddha**, on a large rock facing the road halfway between Skardu and Satpara, is clearly visible from the edge of the ravine a few metres to the right of the road. It is an easy 15-minute detour across the Satpara River and up the slope on the other side. The meditating Buddha, which was carved in about the seventh century, is surrounded by dozens of small bodhisattvas.

SOUTH OF SKARDU

THE DEOSAI PLATEAU

Warnings: Be sure you know the position of the ceasefire line with India, and stay at least 16 kilometres away from it. You need a permit from the Ministry of Tourism to cross the Deosai, but you can explore the northern edge without one. Buy all your food supplies in Skardu, as there is nothing available along the way.

The Deosai features rolling pastureland of rounded hills, knee deep in summer grass and flowers, inhabited by whistling marmots and boasting views of giant mountains in the distance. It offers gentler walking than the Karakoram, with its jagged towers of granite and narrow valleys. Billed as the highest plateau in the world, the Deosai stretches south for about 65 kilometres, blocking the way from Skardu via the Burzil Pass to Srinagar. A treeless wilderness at 4,000 metres—uninhabited and inhospitable in winter, snow-covered for eight months of the year and well-known for its ferocious wind storms—the plateau is nonetheless enchanted on clear August days. Our only problem was the cloud of enormous, vicious mosquitoes, which make effective insect repellent and mosquito-proof tents essential.

ROAD TO CHILAM AND ASTOR
Map: U502 NI 43-3 (Mundik) and NI 43-2 (Gilgit), reliability poor.
Restricted zone; easy in good weather (dangerous in a storm); three days; maximum height 4,266 metres; August.

The jeep road across the centre of the Deosai from Skardu to Chilam is often blocked by landslides, snow or broken bridges but is an easy three-day walk or horse ride. Horses are available in Skardu for Rs300 per day from Karakoram Tours, at Karakoram Yurt and Yak Serai (Raja Alamdar there can organise your trip anywhere in Baltistan). We did the trip in the opposite direction, as in August horses are easy to find in Chilam, costing about Rs200 per day (the owner walks with it); we paid an extra Rs200 per horse for their return. We describe the trip below from Skardu to Chilam.

Stage 1: Satpara Lake to the edge of Deosai Plateau, about 25 kilometres up the steep, narrow Satpara Gorge. Even descending, we were glad to be riding, as it would have been a long trudge on foot. There are many possible campsites before you enter the gorge proper (if starting in Skardu, just go as far as you can). At the top of the

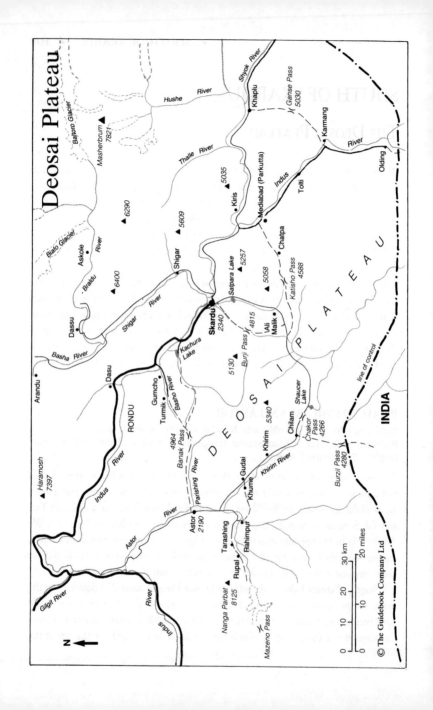

gorge is an adequate campsite at about 3,800 metres, on a bed of edelweiss beside the Satpara River. The view to the north reaches down the gorge and on to the endless serried peaks of the Karakoram Range; the view to the south extends over rolling plains to gently rounded hills.

Stage 2: Across to the *dak* bungalow, six hours and 25 kilometres or so. You climb gently up to **Ali Malik** (4,084 metres), where a track branches due north to the **Burji Pass** (see below). A kilometre further on, another path cuts east to the **Katisho Pass**, a three-day hike to the Indus Valley at **Mediabad** (old name Parkutta; see below). The jeep road to Chilam continues southwest over rolling plateau, crossing five good-sized rivers (water up to our thighs) that flow south into India before joining the Indus.

The scenery changes little as you move across an enormous marshy bowl, green and flower covered, with birds, marmots and a fair chance of seeing one of the last remaining Himalayan brown bears. You are unlikely to see another human, though, because the Gujar herders who come up to the plains in August with their herds (they winter down in the Punjab) keep to the western edge of the Deosai. The clear air deceives, so that distances are greater than they seem. The view on all sides is of low, rounded hills rising to about 5,000 metres; only the snow patches and your shortness of breath betray the altitude. Camp by the river near a ruined *dak* bungalow, a relay post that is a remnant from British days. Leave no food out that may attract bears.

Stage 3: On to Chilam, about 30 kilometres. This is the most euphoric part of the trip. You climb gently past the deep blue **Shaucer Lake** to the top of the **Chakor Pass** (4,266 metres), then down past three villages and herds of horses, mules, yaks and goats to Chilam, an army post at the top of the Khirim Valley with a clinic, primary school and shop. Jeeps from Astor arrive almost daily. If you are heading for the Rupal Valley (see page 176), try bargaining a special rate direct to Tarashing. Failing that, ask to be dropped at the *chai-khana* on the Astor-to-Tarashing road near the junction to Chilam. Pray for a passing jeep, or start walking to Tarashing, 17 kilometres away.

For a more adventurous route to Tarashing, leave the jeep road halfway down the Khirim Valley at **Gudai**, cross the river on a footbridge to the left bank, and climb steeply up from **Khume** to summer pastures with some shepherds' huts. Continue west to the top of the ridge for stunning views west to Nanga Parbat, about 25 kilometres away, rising from the green Rupal Valley. Camp by the first water for terrific morning views. The trail comes out at **Rahimpur** (Rampur on the U502 map), about seven kilometres downriver from Tarashing.

BURJI PASS
Map: U502 NI 43-3 (Mundik), reliability poor.
Open zone; strenuous; three to four days; maximum height 4,815 metres; August.

The Burji Pass (4,815 metres) is best approached from the Deosai Plateau, as the trail up from Skardu is a very steep two-day climb. We suggest going up to the Deosai via Satpara and down via the Burji Pass. We have not been there, but Hugh Swift makes it sound enticing:

> The view from [the Burji Pass] looking northward is one of the most magnificent in the whole of the Himalayas. Personal observation confirms that the great peaks along and at the head of the Baltoro Glacier are visible on a clear day from the pass. They are astounding even 50 to 80 miles [80 to 130 kilometres] away . . .
>
> The location of the pass may be difficult to determine on the northern side . . . and the uppermost reaches of the trail are virtually nonexistent from infrequent use. Look for the true low point above a permanent snowbank toward the Satpara (eastern) side of the bowl at the head of the valley.

Swift describes the approach from the south as being near two lapis-blue lakes. The trail passes the smaller of the two lakes and cuts back and forth up the pale-yellow slope. Way off in the distant south, you can see the Pangri Range, identified geographically as within the Himalaya. (This description is vague enough for us to suggest taking a porter with food and warm clothing from Satpara to show the way.) Swift continues:

> Those who don't mind melting snow for water may succumb to the great temptation to camp at the pass in order to seek an elevated viewing spot on the ridge to the east. Gypsy Davy, who did just that in 1924, said: 'It was such an expanse of immensity as I have hardly imagined . . . It seems you cannot talk in a matter-of-fact way in a place like that . . . [T]he eastern down-sweeping horizon brought K2 into the sun's rays several minutes before Nanga Parbat to the west got any light. I thought the Sierras were large, but here, where we could see three or four score miles [100 to 130 kilometres] north, south, east and west, and see only mountains, and most of them

above twenty thousand feet [6,000 metres], the Sierras seem like sand dunes . . .'

Hugh Swift, *The Trekkers Guide to the Himalaya and Karakoram* (1982)

K2 is not mentioned in the 1990 edition of Swift (*Trekking in Pakistan and India*), so perhaps it cannot be seen from the ridge above the pass.

Kachura Lake and the Shangrila Hotel is another starting point from which to reach the Deosai Plateau. We have not been that way, so ask instructions at the Shangrila Hotel.

BASHO RIVER TO BANAK PASS

Map: U502 NI 43-3 (Mundik), reliability poor.
Open zone; strenuous; three to four days; maximum height 4,964 metres.

The Basho River (not to be confused with the Basha River further north) flows into the Indus about 11 kilometres downriver from Kachura. A jeep bridge across the Indus connects this valley with the main Skardu-to-Gilgit road. The jeep road climbs steeply up through villages and wheat fields to **Gumcho**, a village surrounded by apple, apricot and peach trees festooned with grapevines. Another couple of hours on the jeep road takes you to **Turmik**, which has a forestry rest house set in a pine forest. The jeep track ends about one kilometre past the rest house. We have not been there, but apparently the footpath follows the river up through pine forest for at least three or four hours and would eventually come to **Banak Pass** (4,964 metres), from where a path leads down the **Parishing Valley** to **Astor**. (Information from Philip Astley.)

MEDIABAD, TOLTI AND KHARMANG

Map: U502 NI 43-3 (Mundik), reliability poor.

Following the Indus upriver from Skardu, you come after about 35 kilometres to the confluence of the Indus and Shyok rivers. Jeep roads follow each river, one east along the Shyok to the old kingdom of Khaplu, and the other south along the Indus through the old principalities of Parkutta (now called Mediabad), Tolti and Kharmang, before continuing on to India (foreigners are not allowed along the Shyok River within 16 kilometres of the cease fire line). The sign at the junction reads: 'Tolti 36 kilometres,

Hamzigond 75 kilometres, Olding 91 kilometres.' India, not marked, is 95 kilometres.

At **Mediabad** (Parkutta on the U502 map), about 11 kilometres south along the Indus, the green Katisho Valley runs down from the Deosai Plateau. From the old Balti fort at Mediabad, it is 27 kilometres to the top of the **Katisho Pass** (4,588 metres). A jeep road follows the river as far as **Chatpa** (Chaltha on the U502 map), which is set in terraced fields at the tree-line. It is a two- or three-day hike to **Ali Malik** on the Deosai Plateau, and then two days down to Skardu (see above). This looks worth exploring; as we have seen it only from a helicopter, please send more information. Tolti and Kharmang, further south along the Indus, also look enticing, but do not get too near the Indian border, which is about 30 kilometres beyond Kharmang.

EAST OF SKARDU

Map: Swiss Karakoram map, reliability good; U502 NI 43-3 (Mundik) and NI 43-4 (Siachen), reliability poor.

KHAPLU

Khaplu, 103 kilometres east of Skardu, was the second-largest kingdom in old Baltistan and guarded the trade route to Ladakh along the Shyok River. At an altitude of 2,560 metres, it is slightly cooler than Skardu, with enough of interest to keep you occupied for a couple of days.

Public and cargo **jeeps** ply regularly between Skardu and Khaplu, charging Rs20-30 one way (ask around in Skardu bazaar). Another option is to rent a private jeep in the bazaar or from one of the hotels or tour agents. There is a **Post Office** and **telephone exchange** in the village and a missionary **dispensary** on the jeep road near the river.

For **accommodation**, camping by the river is best. The NAPWD rest house is bookable in Skardu (ask at the PTDC office in the K2 Hotel). The friendly Khaplu Inn is on the village main street.

Khaplu stretches in a wide fan from the base of a semi-circular wall of mountain, dropping some 300 metres to river level. The scattered hamlets set amid terraced fields are connected by paths and irrigation channels. The people here belong to the Nurbashi sect of Islam and are slightly more liberal and tolerant than Shias. The women are unveiled, like the Ismailis in Hunza, and a lone female tourist is more easily accepted here than in Skardu.

A rough jeep road winds up through the hamlets of Khaplu to the ex-raja's **palace**, built 150 years ago in Tibetan style. Its carved wooden balcony has a commanding view over the kingdom, as well as north across the Shyok and up the Hushe Valley to the white pyramid of Masherbrum Mountain, at 7,821 metres the 24th-highest peak in the world.

Further up the valley behind the palace you pass **Chak-Chang**, a carved wooden mosque. Supposedly the oldest mosque in Baltistan, it shows Buddhist influence and is reminiscent of Tibetan architecture. Somewhere there is the ruin of the **old fort**, but we did not find it. Another couple of hours along the old road takes you up to a plateau about ten kilometres long, with superb views north up the Hushe Valley, edged by sword-shaped peaks. About five minutes up from the Khaplu Inn is a steep short-cut to the plateau; it is difficult to find but saves about an hour compared to following the old road. The road crosses the plateau and winds down again to **Surmo**. Return to Khaplu by the new jeep road, which is cut into the cliff and follows the river.

Another possibility is to trek due south from Khaplu across the steep **Ganse Pass** (pronounced 'Gansay'), about 5,030 metres high, with superb views back to Masherbrum. It is about 27 kilometres to Kharmang and takes three or four tough days.

Zak raft across the Shyok: In summer, when the river is in spate, an inflated cowhide raft crosses the Shyok from Khaplu to Saling—an exciting ride not to be missed. In winter the river is low enough to cross on tempory wooden bridges spanning the several channels. Alternatively, you can reach the Hushe Valley via the jeep bridges upstream at Surmo or downstream at Yugu.

SALTORO, KONDUS AND SIACHEN

The whole area east of Khaplu—the Saltoro and Kondus rivers and the entire Siachen area—is closed because of the conflict with India. The ceasefire line between India and Pakistan was never fixed east of the Shyok River to the Chinese border, but for some years it was vaguely thought to run roughly from Siari on the Shyok to the Karakoram Pass. Pakistan's main claim to the area is that access to the mountains in the Siachen area has traditionally been through Pakistan. Trouble started in 1978 when the two sides began moving into the area. Full-scale war developed in 1984, and the Indians captured the whole of Siachen Glacier. The Pakistani army is now camped on Conway Saddle (6,300 metres), at the head of Abruzzi Glacier, to prevent the Indians penetrating to Concordia.

HUSHE VALLEY

The Hushe Valley (pronounced 'Hoosh-ay') runs from Masherbrum Mountain (at 7,821 metres, the 24th highest in the world, first climbed by the Americans in 1960) south to the Shyok River, opposite Khaplu. Hushe, the last village up the valley, is about 140 kilometres east of Skardu and is the starting point for treks to various summer pastures up five glaciers. The American Nick Clinch astonished the people of Hushe by making the first crossing of the Masherbrum Pass from the Baltoro in 1974. Until then the villagers had thought their valley was impenetratable from the north (see Nick Clinch, *A Walk in the Sky*).

The Swiss Karakoram map is best for this valley. The U502 series NI 43-3 (Mundik) is fairly reliable, but many of the jeep roads, footpaths and shepherds' summer settlements are not marked.

Transport: A private jeep from Skardu to Hushe takes about six hours and costs Rs1,200–1,500, returning empty. Cargo jeeps go occasionally but not to a set schedule.

A private jeep from Khaplu to Hushe takes about two hours, following the east bank of the Hushe River—price negotiable. At **Hulde** (pronounced 'Hulday'), a branch road follows the **Saltoro River** east to **Kondus** and the **Siachen** area (closed zone, see above).

Alternatively, you can take a public jeep to Khaplu, cross the Shyok River on the *zak* raft to **Saling** and walk, in two days, to Hushe along the jeep road up the west side of the river (or hope to flag a rare passing jeep). The hike along the jeep road is hot but rewarding, with magnificent views of Masherbrum surrounded by lesser peaks that soar straight up from the valley floor. Granite cliffs hundreds of metres high are surmounted by impossible jagged spires, looking like illustrations in a fairy story. Most tourists jeep in, so walkers are greeted with surprised friendliness by the villagers along the way.

From **Kande** (pronounced 'Kanday'), about 20 kilometres from the junction of the Hushe and Shyok rivers, you can cross the Hushe River on a footbridge and head east up the **Nangmah Valley**, a narrow gorge of savage beauty, with enormous 1,000-metre cliffs that overhang the valley floor and seem almost to meet overhead. **Nangmah** summer settlement is surrounded by gigantic rock towers of reddish-brown granite. The **Nangmah Glacier** leads to the south side of K6 (7,281 metres), which was first climbed in 1970 by the Austrians.

Hushe village, at the end of the jeep road, was very poor before the advent of trekking. As it is too high for fruit trees or double cropping, the villagers survive on sparse crops of wheat, barley, potatoes, peas and turnips—as well as their herds of animals.

Hushe is being spoiled by too many tourists; children beg and are a nuisance around the camp. Despite the money gained from portering, the inhabitants are the dirtiest we have seen in northern Pakistan. That said, they are wonderfully hospitable and friendly.

Flour, rice, sugar, biscuits and kerosene are usually available in the village shop called Masherbrum, which sometimes has a surprising supply of climbing gear, but it is better to bring all food supplies from Skardu. Aslam Khan, the shop owner, and his famous brother, Rosi Ali, the high-altitude guide, are the best sources of information and are helpful in finding good porters. (Beware—Rosi Ali is a common name.) Horses and donkeys are not available, but there are usually plenty of porters, unless your presence coincides with the harvest in August or a big group trek (Karakoram Experience and Sherpa organise treks to this valley).

The usual campsite is five minutes' walk beyond Hushe village, beside a stream and

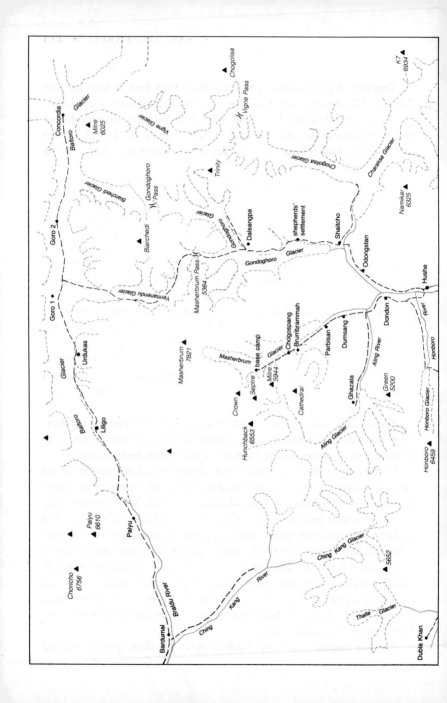

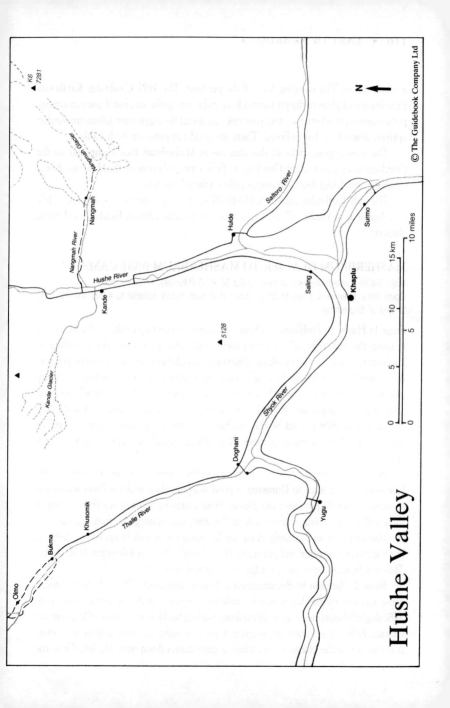

© The Guidebook Company Ltd

N

▲ K6 7281

Nangmah Glacier

Nangmah River

Nangmah

Saltoro River

Hushe River

Hulde

Kande

Kande Glacier

▲

Saling

Khaplu

Surmo

▲ 5128

Shyok River

Doghani

Thalle River

Olmo

Bukma

Khusomik

Yugu

Hushe Valley

0   5   10   15 km

0   5   10 miles

a saline spring. The camping fee is Rs10 per tent. The 1991 Cambridge Karakoram Expedition had plans to dig pit latrines here and clean up the site, but if you can arrange porters quickly it is better to start your trek and spend the night a few kilometres further upriver, where it is less polluted. There are good campsites on both banks.

The most popular treks in this area are to Masherbrum Base Camp and up the Gondoghoro Glacier to climb Gondoghoro Peak. Optional extras are the Honboro, Aling, Charaksa and Chogolisa (sometimes called Trinity) glaciers.

The only **footbridge** across the Hushe River when the river is in spate during July and August is at Hushe village. Cross here for the Masherbrum, Honboro and Aling glaciers.

MASHERBRUM GLACIER TO MASHERBRUM BASE CAMP

Map: Swiss Karakoram map is best; U502 NI 43-3 (Mundik), reliability poor.
Open zone; strenuous; three to seven days; maximum height optional to 4,200 metres; June to end of September.

Stage 1: Hushe to Parbisan, two hours. A scenic, flat and easy hike to the best place to camp the first night, if you set off early in the afternoon. Cross the footbridge in Hushe to the west bank and walk for 20 minutes through fields of barley, peas and potatoes (in August) to a footbridge by a mill across the Honboro River—an optional side trip (see below). The marshy area beyond the fields leads to scrubland covered with wild roses, willows, juniper and thorn bushes, followed by a large settlement of stone huts with a mosque that is used by the shepherds as soon as the snows melt in April or May. By early July, the higher pastures are usually clear, and the shepherds move further up.

Beyond the settlement, a footbridge crosses the Aling River—an optional side trip (see below)—and leads to **Dumsang**, a good stopping place under willows and beside a stream, about 90 minutes from Hushe. From Dumsang you can see the meeting of three valleys: the Aling coming in from the west, the Gondoghoro from the east and the Masherbrum from the north. A further 30 minutes' easy walk brings you to Parbisan, the traditional first camp and pay stage, which is only about six kilometres from Hushe. This is a beautiful spot on the edge of a tamarisk wood.

Stage 2: Parbisan to Brumbrammah, three to four hours. The trek starts through dense tamarisk jungle that is marshy underfoot, beyond which the terrain changes to difficult glacial moraine—a gravelly expanse of sliding boulders at the snout of Masherbrum Glacier. Follow the stream up, keeping it on your right, to about 200 metres before it comes out of the glacier snout, where a gully comes down from the left. Cross the snowdrift at the bottom of the gully, and follow the almost vertical, ill-defined path up the right (north) side of the gully, which goes straight to the top of the western lateral moraine of the Masherbrum Glacier—a one-hour climb. You may need a guide to point out the way, and there may be a gentler path up the moraine from the end of the tamarisk wood. In August the top of the moraine is a sea of purple vetch, with clumps of columbine, potentila, rockroses and willow bushes. The walk along the top of the moraine, still climbing, is the prettiest of the whole trek. You wade through flowers with superb views on your right over the Masherbrum Glacier, south to craggy spires and sheer cliff faces, and north to Masherbrum Peak.

Brumbrammah (meaning 'between mountain and willow bush') campsite is down to the left of the lateral moraine below the mountain wall, on a wide, flat, sandy area surrounded by willow bushes, edelweiss and many other flowers. This is a lake in July, but the water supply dries up in mid-August. If you are fit, it is only a five- or six-hour walk from Hushe, but the porters charge two stages. Joining the main valley here is **Bruni Brama**, a side valley leading up to Cathedral, Mitre, Sceptre and Crown peaks.

Stage 3: Brumbrammah to Masherbrum Base Camp, two to four hours. Two paths lead north, one along the base of the mountain in the ablation valley, and the other along the crest of the moraine, to **Chogospang** (meaning 'big grassy place'), 30 minutes away. Here in square, flat-roofed stone huts about five women spend the summer looking after about 1,000 sheep and goats and an equal number of yaks and cows (including the various crosses between the two: yakmo, dzomo and dzo). The mountainside above the settlement is green and criss-crossed with animal paths—a friendly place to camp if you are not in a hurry. The porters expect you to buy a sheep or goat (about Rs500) for a feast and singsong in the evening.

The path climbs from the settlement up the lateral moraine, then follows the top for a few minutes before dropping onto the edge of the glacier and losing itself amid the boulders. You need a guide to show the way for one hour to Masherbrum Base Camp, at about 4,200 metres, a small grassy patch below the cliff face, looking across the glacier at the fluted ice gullies and steep rock ridges of Masherbrum. This is the top of the valley, a dead end in a wide bowl completely filled with the glacier. Ice faces soar out of deep crevasses, sheer rock walls enclose the bowl, and a curtain of 7,000-metre peaks prevents access to the Baltoro Glacier beyond.

In July there is a clear, icy lake just above the base camp. A two-hour walk on the lateral moraine towards Masherbrum leads to another campsite strewn with flowers. Climbers can make an attempt on the ridge above the base camp for excellent views across to Masherbrum.

Stages 4 and 5: return to Hushe, by the same route. This can easily be done in one day.

HONBORO GLACIER

Map: The Swiss Karakoram map is best; U502 NI 43-3 (Mundik), reliability poor.
Open zone; easy; four to six hours; maximum height optional; June to October.

This is a return day hike from Hushe. Follow the west bank for 20 minutes to the Honboro tributary and follow it up, keeping the tributary on your left, for about two hours and 600 vertical metres, to the summer settlement of a dozen huts and a mosque. From here it is an hour's walk up the wide stream bed to the glacier snout. On the left a bridge leads to a path up the Dara and Baoujul peaks—a steady one-hour ascent to the ridge is rewarded with bird's-eye views of Hushe Valley and village. (Information from Philip Parnell and Beverly Barnett.)

ALING GLACIER

Map: The Swiss Karakoram map is best; U502 NI 43-3 (Mundik), reliability poor.
Open zone; easy to strenuous, depending on what you choose to do.

The Aling River joins the Hushe River from the west about 90-minutes' walk from Hushe. A two-day hike following the north bank of the Aling River takes you up through Aling Base Camp to **Ghazala,** a summer settlement where about five women tend the herds from July to September. We have not been there, and reports are conflicting, but it seems that there is a good campsite about 16 kilometres from the Hushe River junction, by an icefall at about 3,650 metres, where a few rosebushes grow. From there you can climb **Green Mountain** (about 5,200 metres) for good views. Green Mountain stands by itself in the middle of a cirque of higher peaks rising to 6,700 metres; its flanks are covered in flowers, and the summit just touches the July snow-line.

From Aling Glacier two difficult technical treks (demanding mountaineering experience) lead north to Bardumal on the Braldu River (permit required) and west to the Thalle River, each taking about six days.

GONDOGHORO, CHARAKSA AND CHOGOLISA GLACIERS

Map: Swiss Karakoram map is best; U502 NI 43-3 (Mundik), reliability poor. Note that Gondoghoro is spelled Chundugaro on the U502.
Open zone; strenuous; minimum six days; maximum height 4,000 metres, optional to 5,650 metres; June to September.

Stage 1: Hushe to Shaitcho, three to four hours. Follow the east bank of the Hushe River along on a flat, easy path through fields of barley and peas, then turn east to follow the Charaksa River through scrubland and sparse willow woods to **Odongstan**, which is two hours from Hushe. This is a shepherds' summer camp, used in the second half of April and all of May, in the woods beside a stream. A further hour takes you past the junction of the Gondoghoro and Charaksa rivers, across a good wooden bridge to Shaitcho (Chospah on the Swiss map), a large shepherds' settlement with its own mosque, used in May and June. This is the traditional first camp, set in a forest of juniper, cedar and willow trees, with giant bushes of wild roses and a good water supply. About 100 metres upriver from the bridge on the south bank there is a fresh spring that is good for washing, as it is cleaner than the river and not as cold.

At Shaitcho, the Charaksa Valley joins the Gondoghoro. The path to the **Chogolisa and Charaksa glaciers** follows the north side of the Charaksa River, leading to the base camp of K6, K7, Dripikar and Namikar mountains. From this side, K6 is a vertical wall about 2,000 metres high, much more imposing than from the other side. It takes about 45 minutes to walk to the top of the terminal moraine of the Charaksa Glacier, or two hours to the junction of the Chogolisa and Charaksa glaciers, following the northern lateral moraine or the ablation valley most of the way. There are no shepherds' summer settlements up these valleys, as it is more barren than the Gondoghoro, but the climbing possibilities are inviting.

Stage 2: Shaitcho to Gondoghoro summer settlement, two to four hours. The path follows the highest ridge of the lateral moraine through roses, gooseberries, cedar and tamarisk bushes, with views left leading down across the glacier and back to sheer rock walls and jagged crags. Masherbrum stands guard ahead. The track is dusty and stony— a steady, but not too steep, climb to the main summer settlement occupied by about ten women and children in July and August. Stages 1 and 2 add up to only five hours' walk from Hushe and can easily be covered in one day by those who are fit.

The campsite is in a wide, sandy bowl with a shallow stream and willow bushes. The women in the settlement are friendly and happy to pose for photographs in return for supplies. Organised treks are expected to buy a goat here and have a singsong with their porters.

Stage 3: Summer settlement to Dalsangpa, two to four hours. The path continues north, outside of the lateral moraine, crossing several side streams. The willow bushes by the last stream mark the tree-line. About 200 metres later the path forks to circumvent a spur of rock that juts down to the glacier. The more attractive path, following the top of the moraine, soon peters out. The trekking path turns steeply down the lateral moraine to the edge of the glacier, 300 to 400 metres beyond the last stream. The next hour is an unpleasant scramble along the stony, sliding glacier edge, with huge boulders poised above, ready to fall. The ordeal ends with a steep climb up a gully in the lateral moraine, into a grassy field filled with flowers and wild rhubarb. The next half-hour up to Dalsangpa is the prettiest part of the trek.

Dalsangpa, meaning 'field of flowers', lives up to its name. It is a beautiful campsite at about 4,150 metres, set between two lakes, with Masherbrum Mountain and the white glacier cascading down from Masherbrum Pass reflected in the still water. A climb to the top of the lateral moraine gives an even more spectacular view of glaciers and jagged spires. Below the campsite are two shepherds' huts, occupied in July and August, where the women make butter in a big copper pot.

Masherbrum Pass, leading to the Baltoro Glacier and Concordia, is in a restricted zone (permit required). It is an extremely difficult technical climb requiring the scaling of several ice faces with ropes and pitons (see page 136).

Stage 4: Dalsangpa to Gondoghoro Base Camp, four to six hours. The path follows the ridge of the lateral moraine for a short while before dropping down onto the glacier. You pick your way across moving boulders and ice, finally crossing the glacier to reach Gondoghoro Base Camp, a grassy field at about 4,600 metres, below the north face of Trinity Peak (6,700 metres) and offering views of the peaks of Leila (6,400 metres), Basso, Jinaji and Gondoghoro (5,650 metres). A stone circle provides some shelter for porters.

Gondoghoro Peak is a comparatively easy climb of six to eight hours up and three hours down. No permit is needed, but it is recommended only for those with some climbing experience, as crampons and ice axes are essential. Set off at 1 am in order to be back before 10 am, when the snow gets too soft. From the top are views of Masherbrum, Gasherbrum I (or Hidden Peak), Chogolisa, part of Broad Peak, Mitre Peak and Gasherbrum IV. (Gondoghoro Peak information from Beverly Barnett.)

Gondoghoro Pass and Vigne Pass, leading to Concordia, are in the restricted zone and require technical mountaineering skills (see page 137).

Stages 5 and 6: Return by the same route.

THALLE VALLEY

Thalle (pronounced 'Thallay') is the next valley west of Hushe, which it parallels. Access is by cargo jeep from Skardu to **Doghani**, at the junction of the Thalle and Shyok rivers.

Get off at the *chai-khana* (local restaurant) on the west side of the Thalle River, from where, with luck and about Rs200, you may be able to find a jeep to take you about 20 kilmometres up the Thalle River to **Khusomik**. This is a large village at about 3,400 metres, with narrow streets and a carved mosque, where you can arrange porters and guide. The jeep road ends at **Bukma**, about an hour's hike above Khusomik. Horses, donkeys and porters are easily available, and you can take a horse across the pass. A private jeep all of the way from Skardu costs about Rs1,000.

THALLE VALLEY OVER THALLE PASS TO SHIGAR

Map: Swiss Karakoram map is best; U502 NI 43-3 (Mundik), reliability poor.
Open zone; strenuous; three to five days; maximum height 4,572 metres; July to early October.

Stage 1: Khusomik to Dubla Khan, four to five hours. Follow the jeep track for one hour to Bukma, then a path across cultivated fields for another hour to **Olmo**, the last permanently inhabited village, after which the valley narrows and the track is squeezed between steep cliffs and the swift river. Above the gorge there are no more trees, and

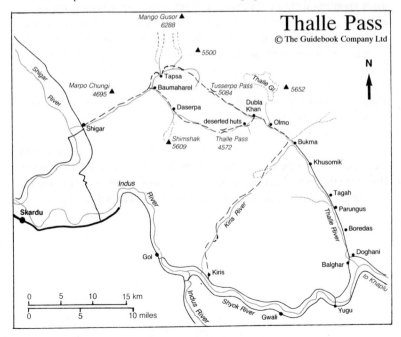

a short, steep climb brings you after a third hour to the first shepherds' summer settlement, with huts set amid rolling pastures. An hour later you arrive at Dubla Khan, the last shepherds' settlement, where rather unfriendly men and boys look after a large herd of dzos and live all summer in primitive hovels.

Stage 2: Dubla Khan across the Thalle Pass to Daserpa, seven to eight hours (four hours up, three hours down). At Dubla Khan the valley divides; the northern branch leads to the Tusserpo Pass (5,084 metres), the western branch to the Thalle Pass.

The well-made path to the Thalle Pass follows the south bank for one hour to some abandoned shepherds' huts, a good possible campsite near where a tributary enters from the south. Cross here to the north bank and follow the main (right-hand) valley on a clear, zigzagging donkey path for two hours to the top for views of the western Masherbrum Range and Mango Gusor (6,288 metres). The descent is steep at first, then you follow a grassy ridge down for an hour to a roofless stone shelter. Continue down across a few side streams to the first bushes—from where there are views south to a chain of snowy mountains dominated by Shimshak (5,609 metres)—past herds of dzos, sheep and goats, to the summer settlement of Daserpa, where men and boys live in about eight stone huts. This is an ideal campsite. Many trekkers take two days for this stage.

Stage 3: Daserpa to Shigar, five to six hours. The path is excellent, maintained by the woodcutters who come up from Shigar for fuel. One hour from Daserpa, at the junction of the two rivers at **Baumaharel,** the path from the Tusserpo Pass rejoins the Thalle route. Below this junction the valley is barren, the way passing through several gorges with high cliffs. The usual lunch stop is under a lone cedar tree three hours further on. Just before Shigar there is a rock formation making an impressive gateway to the village. Just beyond this gateway on the right is a small, pagoda-shaped mosque, with delicate carving, and the raja's old palace, from the days that Shigar was a kingdom. Descend to the bridge, beside which stands the K2 Hotel, where, with luck, you may get a lift to Skardu on a passing jeep. (Information from Elisabeth Gardner.)

NORTH OF SKARDU

SHIGAR AND BRALDU VALLEYS

The broad, fertile Shigar Valley runs down from the north to join the Indus opposite Skardu. The road into the valley bridges the Indus upriver from the confluence and then crosses rolling sand dunes, before climbing over a ridge for an expansive view reaching 50 kilometres up to the head of the valley, where the Braldu and Basha rivers join to form the Shigar.

The **Braldu River** flows from the Baltoro Glacier and leads to the famous treks into Concordia and K2 and to the strenuous trek north along the Biafo and Hispar glaciers to Hunza. The **Basha River** (misspelled as Basna on the U502 map) empties from the Chogo Lungma Glacier and leads to hikes around Haramosh.

Public cargo jeeps travel every few days up the valley to the road heads at Askole on the Braldu River and to Doko on the Basha River (this road is being extended to Bisil). You can hire a private jeep to either road head—bargain hard.

Shigar town, the first stop up the main Shigar Valley, was once the capital of the relatively prosperous, independent kingdom of Shigar. It boasts some of the most finely carved wooden houses and mosques in Baltistan, including one mosque with a pyramidal, three-tiered roof, which was built several hundred years ago by Kashmiri carpenters. Guarding the town is the abandoned four-storey ex-raja's palace.

For the trek from Shigar across the **Thalle Pass** to the Shyok River, see page 121.

The trek from **Skoro**, six kilometres northwest of Shigar, across the **Skoro Pass** (5,073 metres) to **Askole**, 30 kilometres away, can be done relatively easily in three or four days. Crampons are recommended for about 50 metres of steep glacier on the Askole side of the pass. This is the route taken by the Skardu Marathon, a gruelling six-day race from Skardu to Askole and back that is held in July most years and organised by Sylvain Saudan of Chamonix. Both these passes are in the open zone, requiring no permit.

BRALDU VALLEY TO BALTORO GLACIER, CONCORDIA AND K2

Map: Swiss Karakoram map, reliability excellent; U502 NI 43-3 (Mundik) and NI 43-4 (Siachen), reliability poor, with insufficient mountain detail.
Restricted zone; very strenuous; 18 to 24 days; maximum height optional but normally about 5,000 metres; June to September.

It is an open zone to Askole (pronounced 'Askolay') and up the Biafo Glacier but restricted beyond Askole and up the Baltoro Glacier. Permits are obtainable only from the Ministry of Tourism in Islamabad and only through a recognised travel company. You must be briefed in Islamabad before you start (see page 59).

The **Baltoro Glacier** is the most popular trekking and mountaineering area in Pakistan—with good reason, as clustered around the end of the glacier are eight of the world's 30 highest mountains. Rows of needle spires, granite towers, shining, glaciated mountains and snowy domes line the glacier, providing perhaps the greatest mountain scenery in the world.

The glacier was closed to foreigners from 1961 to 1974. Since its reopening, this area has been the focus of attention for many climbers. In 1990, 52 mountaineering expeditions and numerous trekking tours followed the main trail up the glacier, each group serviced by between 15 and 200 porters, with some unfortunate results. Many campsites are crowded, littered and polluted, and most villages in the area have lost their charm. There is hardly any wildlife left; in 1975 George Schaller estimated that only 100 ibex survived here. On top of it all, porters are spoiled for choice, making wages high and attitudes sometimes surly. To compensate for this, the scenery is truly magnificent. Like the Taj Mahal, these mountains never disappoint.

Expenses: The Concordia trek is by far the most expensive we have done. Organising it ourselves, with an official guide recommended by Ashraf Aman of Adventure Tours Pakistan, it cost us over US$1,000 each (for six people), but we were moving slowly, taking 12 days to reach Concordia, as our oldest member, André Roch, was 84 years old (still the grand old man of Swiss mountaineering, Roch was filming, painting and telling stories all the way).

Concordia was not in the style of our usual treks—which are do-it-yourself budget jobs without guide or cook—but we felt it was worth it. If you are fit and well organised, you can reach Concordia in six to eight days, meaning that you carry much less food and need fewer porters to do so. However, according to government rules, you must take a guide and cook—expensive extras—and you need to buy insurance for them all.

Plan to pay a camping fee of about Rs100 for each tent at Askole. Also, allow for Rs10 per person and Rs5 per load crossing the Dumordo River on the wire pulley (*jola*).

Headaches: This is definitely the most strenuous trek we have done, with dangerous, vertiginous cliff walks and six days of stumbling over rocks on the glacier itself. Joe Tasker called it 'as hard as anything I have come across which is not actually climbing'. For **helicopter rescue**, see page 78.

There is much less human interest than on any other trek we have done, as the villagers in Askole see too many foreigners, there are no summer pastures along the way (so you never camp with shepherds) and there is less flora and fauna to enjoy. Besides all this, it is crowded: in 23 days we met 18 mountaineering expeditions and seven trekking groups. We were lucky with the weather, though, and Concordia justifies all superlatives: for sheer mountain grandeur there is nothing like it anywhere else in the world. We are glad to have been there but would not do it again.

Porters: Be prepared for porter strikes. On the Baltoro trek, where there are usually new expeditions setting out every day, some porters prefer to return to the start after a few days and sign on afresh with a new group so they work only the easier lower stages. Show your porters the tarpaulins (one for every eight porters) and sheets of plastic to protect against rain (one for every porter)—it will make them happier.

Expeditions doing the one-way trip to K2 or Gasherbrum base camps usually calculate 1.8 porters for every porter load of 25 kg. Trekkers going up and back (and therefore carrying more porter food) need to calculate about 2.2 porters per load.

Custom dictates that you pay 20 pay stages (more if the jeep road is blocked before Askole) plus three rest days to Concordia and back, no matter how quickly you trek, plus half pay for however many days you stay at Concordia. Make sure your porters know that you understand this. The more quickly you trek, the less food you will need, and the porters like to move quickly, as they can take their full wages and sign on with another expedition.

See pages 83 and 99 on hiring porters.

Only the very experienced—with mountaineering skills and fully equipped—should wander unguided in the open zone up the Biafo Glacier to Snow Lake (see page 137).

Stage 1: Skardu to the end of the jeep road at Askole. The mountain is so unstable between Apaligon and Hoto that there will always be landslide problems in this area. If the road is blocked, there is a good chance there will be jeeps trapped the other side of the landslide, so you can carry your loads across and hire new jeeps beyond.

Shigar is a traditional stopping place, where more porters are usually hired. You will be expected to stop for breakfast or lunch (*chai* and *chapattis*) here. Everyone will move slowly, as they want to make the trip last the whole day. Be patient and cheerful; keep your porters happy while still keeping them moving.

The jeep road crosses the Braldu three times to pass the villages of **Dassu, Apaligon, Pekora** and **Hoto**. If the new road is open all of the way and you are flying by in a jeep, ask to stop at **Dungo Zamba** (meaning 'narrow bridge'), a few kilometres beyond

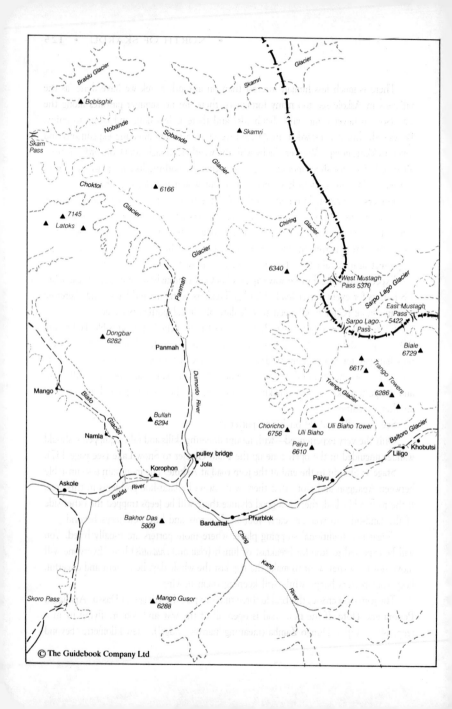

© The Guidebook Company Ltd

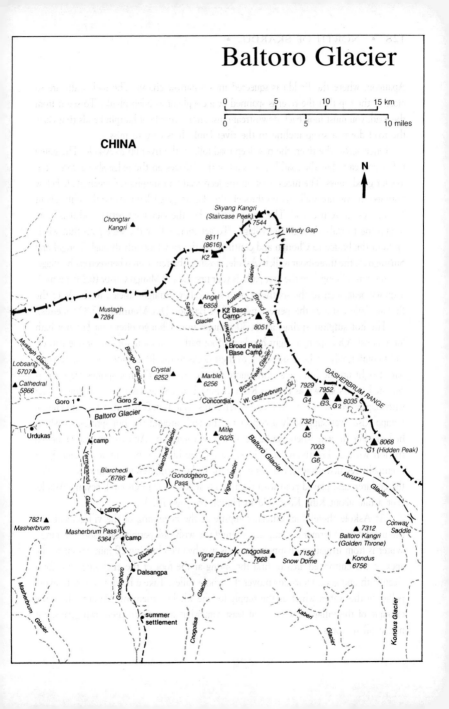

Apaligon, where the Braldu is squeezed into a narrow chasm. The rock walls are so close at the top that the river is spanned by a couple of wooden planks. To see it from the road, you must look back downstream just after a couple of hairpin bends that carry the road down a steep incline to the river bank. It is easy to miss.

Once across the river, the new jeep road follows the river up to Askole. The going is fast and easy, but the road bypasses all of the villages on the ledge above and is too low for good views. The nicest spot on the jeep road for camping is a green glade below Surungo. If you are walking, go through the flat, irrigated land above the cliff, about 100 metres above the road. The way is longer, but the views are better, and it is more interesting to walk through the villages. To get there follow the wide path that winds up from the bridge to **Chongo** and continue on the easy footpath through **Tongol** and **Surungo** for the three-hour walk to Askole, crossing a barren stretch between each village.

Just past Chongo, on the foot path, is your first view of **Mango Gusor** (6,288 metres), a snowy peak seen to the southeast up a side valley. Straight ahead, in the V of the Braldu Valley, stands the perfect pyramid of **Bakhor Das Mountain** (5,809 metres).

The **hot sulphur springs** about 30 minutes from Chongo offer your last hot bath for a month. One spring is right beside the foot path, with room for four or five bathers to sit comfortably on large stones up to their necks in the 40°C water. Two more pools out of sight up the hill are slightly more private. Around the hot springs are copper-coloured stones known as **Lompo Kiser** (Kiser's Fort). King Kiser was a mythical ruler with magical powers—dozens of legends tell of his exploits in Baltistan, Nagar and Hunza. Lompo Kiser was supposedly a copper fort he built around the hot springs, in which he locked up his wife whenever he went away on campaigns. An evil *jinn* (giant) melted the fort with his breath and stole Kiser's wife, vanishing up the Baltoro Glacier. Kiser eventually rescued his wife, but not before she had two children by the jinn. Kiser killed the children and played polo with their heads at Kiser's Polo Ground, beyond Askole. (For a tale about King Kiser told in Hunza, see page 242.)

At **Askole** there is an official campsite at the beginning of the village, but you can usually pay a farmer to camp elsewhere if you wish (ask permission before camping). Water is from irrigation channels, but it is worthwhile climbing 20 minutes up to the apex of the cultivated area to find the spring at the foot of the enclosing cliff, for a clean bath and good views down over the whole valley. Take a bowl with you to avoid polluting the water, which is the supply for the whole settlement. Do not follow the example of the villagers, who are at least somewhat immune to their own germs, but not at all to yours.

Askole was founded about 500 years ago, according to local legend, by a prince from Nagar, who, fearing he would be killed by his brother the king, fled across the Hispar Pass and discovered the flat, watered land of the Askole Valley. He married a Balti girl from Shigar and settled in the secluded valley. Until the middle of the eighteenth century, Askole was on a trade route to China across the two Mustagh Passes, but when glacier movement made the passes impassable for ponies, the trade stopped. Francis Younghusband surprised the villagers in 1887 by appearing from China. He remarked in *Heart of a Continent*: 'That was a dirty little village! . . . The houses and the inhabitants were repulsively dirty.'

Askole now consists of 40 houses in a tight cluster in the centre of a large, terraced alluvial fan about 3,000 metres above sea-level. Narrow alleys wind between flat-roofed stone houses, each with a wicker cage on the roof, in which the family sleeps in summer. At ground level is the summer living room with a fireplace in the centre. Near the fireplace, a hole in the floor lets down to a warm underground winter room beneath. Each house has a toilet similar to those in Ladakh and Tibet, a wooden platform with holes in it, high over a dusty pit. The dust smothers all foul smells.

About 35 of the village boys attend the village primary school, but most of the villagers are illiterate. The people speak Balti and are all strict Shia Muslims, so tourists should be careful not to offend them with their dress or behaviour.

The women's costume in the Braldu Valley is unlike anything elsewhere in Baltistan. They wear baggy cotton trousers under a long black or beige homespun shirt, usually decorated with red trim on cuff and hem and tied tightly round the hips with a cord. The head is covered with a cap faintly reminiscent of Tibetan style, decorated with buttons, medals, coins, zippers, metal watchstraps—anything silvery.

The valley used to be self-sufficient for the most part, but this is changing since 1974, with the present wave of tourism bringing jobs as porters. The people here grow their own cereals, vegetables and fruit, and they own large herds of sheep, goats, yaks and dzos, which spend the summer up in the summer pastures along the glaciers and the winter in the villages or at Paiyu.

There is one small shop in Askole, and the village headman, Haji Mehdi, sometimes has flour, kerosene and some climbing equipment for sale.

Below the village a traditional **birch-twig bridge** (the last in the valley) crosses the Braldu River, giving access to the villages on the other side and to the **Skoro Pass**, which leads to Shigar (see above). It is in very poor repair and no longer safe. Use the new pulley bridge further upstream.

Stage 2: Askole to Korophon, four to six hours. There is good drinking water about 40 minutes beyond Askole, where a slender waterfall sprays down a cliff. Askole to the Biafo Glacier is an easy two to three hours across waste land, with a rest stop beside a stream just before the green grass of Kiser's Polo Ground (marked by a red star on the U502 map). Across the river to the south, **Testa** (spelled Ste Ste on the U502 map), the last village of the valley, guards the entrance to the gorge leading to the Skoro Pass.

The **Biafo Glacier** (*biafo* meaning 'rooster' in Balti), a tortured ocean of moving boulders and crevasses two kilometres wide, takes about 90 minutes to cross. (For the open zone, 13-day trek up Biafo Glacier, across the Hispar Pass and down to Nagar and Hunza on the Karakoram Highway, see page 137.) Once off the glacier, it is about ten minutes to Korophon, a green campsite with sandy river water beside willow trees and thorn bushes at about 3,100 metres. The big stone that gives its name to Korophon (*koro* meaning 'cup' in Balti) is about 20 minutes further on. Shepherds have built a shelter against the stone, but there is little shade or water.

Trekking companies often do a double stage here and continue to Jola.

Stage 3: Korophon to Jola, three to four hours. From mid-June to the end of August the Dumordo River, draining from the Panmah Glacier, is too swollen to wade, so you must trek about a kilometre upriver to Jola Bridge, a pulley with a toll of Rs10 per person and Rs5 per bag. The route is a vertiginous 'path' across the cliff face with a death drop into the swirling river below. At the bridge you may have to queue, as the crossing is slow. Jola is a rather dusty camp surrounded by a few bushes about 20 minutes beyond the bridge, with a silted side stream for water.

Many of the sheep, goat, cattle and yak herds of the Braldu Valley spend the summer in pastures along the Panmah Glacier. There are several treks up this glacier, some peeling off west to loop back to Snow Lake, the Biafo Glacier and the Hispar Pass, and others turning east to the New Mustagh Pass (5,370 metres), once a trading route to Xinjiang. Eric Shipton was first to explore and map this area in 1937, though Henry Haversham Godwin-Austen had been there before him in 1861 and 1887 (see Shipton, *Blank on the Map*). This is a restricted zone, requiring permits.

Stage 4: Jola to Bardumal, three to four hours. The trail here is comparatively easy, with occasional exposed scrambles across the rock. The first good water is a thin waterfall after about two hours. There are several campsites called Bardumal along a two-kilometre stretch of sandy river beach scattered with thorn bushes and tamarisk. The altitude is about 3,200 metres. Mouse-hares or pika (Latin name *Ochotona*), charming little rabbits with mouse ears, scamper in the rocks. Just beyond Bardumal at **Phurblok**

is the grave of a young porter who died in 1987, where the porters stop to pray. Nearby is a large cave, providing good shelter for porters in bad weather. Water is fetched from side streams.

Opposite Bardumal, the Ching Kang River offers a possible route to the Aling Glacier and Hushe, but we have met no one who has done it. This route is for fully equipped mountaineers only. To cross the Braldu River, use the Baltoro Glacier above Paiyu. Most trekking companies do a double stage from Jola to Paiyu.

Stage 5: Bardumal to Paiyu, two to four hours. This is an undulating walk, difficult at times, with the first views of dramatic mountains ahead. There is a rest stop by some tamarisk trees beside the stream flowing down from **Paiyu Peak**, where we saw ibex tracks and fox spore. The trail climbs to a vantage point from which you see the snout of Baltoro Glacier and, in the far distance, a magnificent panorama of the Cathedral Towers and, left of them, the unmistakable triangle of K2. The last hour involves an exposed cliff walk followed by a paddle along the river's edge.

Paiyu (meaning 'salt' in Balti and misspelled Paiju on the U502 map), at about 3,600 metres, was disgustingly polluted in 1990, but many expeditions still chose this camp for their rest day. Empty cans are scattered everywhere, and piles of excrement greet you in every direction. A spring gives rise to a now-polluted stream that runs steeply down through a grove of mature willow and poplar trees. Tent platforms are cut beneath the trees beside the stream. The site is always crowded, theft is a problem, and the place is a real health hazard. Probably the best bet is to camp higher up, away from shade and water, on a flat shoulder with panoramic views up and down the valley. There are a couple of shepherds' huts at Paiyu; some of the Askole herds winter here, as it is sheltered and there is less snow here than in the village.

The porters use their rest day here to kill a goat, driven from Askole, and sing and dance through most of the night.

Stage 6: Paiyu to Liligo or Khobutsi, five to eight hours. After 90 minutes, the path divides at the snout of the Baltoro Glacier. The left branch goes to the base camp of Trango Towers and the Sarpo Lago Pass, which was discovered by Ardito Desio in 1929 and crossed by Eric Shipton and Harold Tilman in 1937. The right branch drops down past some tamarisk trees before climbing up onto the glacier, where the Braldu River roars out of a black hole as from a sluice gate. The glacier stretches up the valley as far as the eye can see—a vast turbulent sea of rocks and gravel two kilometres wide and 62 kilometres long. The porters stop and chant a hymn before crossing the glacier: 'Oh God, peace be upon the holy Prophet and all his family'—repeated over and over.

You walk across the boulder-strewn ice, up and down great grey slag heaps, climbing steadily for two to three hours on a long diagonal to the other side. Then you follow the southern edge of the glacier across sand and rock for 60 minutes to Liligo or Liliwa (both names are in use), the traditional campsite and pay stage. From the glacier are spectacular views across to the white, vertically striated pyramid of **Paiyu Peak** (6,600 metres) and north up the glimmering Trango Glacier to the jagged granite needles and blocks of **Trango Towers**, one of which, **Nameless Tower**, soars to 6,239 metres. The usual campsite has been wiped out by a landslide, and people now camp 15 minutes further along, on a flat, sandy area of the lateral moraine, beside a roaring, silted glacial melt river. Clearer water is ten minutes back along the track towards Liligo. If camping here, pitch your tent near the water, out of danger of the sliding cliff.

It may be better to continue for another 90 minutes to Khobutsi, a lovely walk on a yak track built by the yak handlers to carry goods up to supply the army camps at Goro One and Concordia. Khobutsi campsite is the other side of the river flowing from the Liligo Glacier. The river is usually too deep to wade, and the easiest way across is to detour out onto the Baltoro Glacier. Do not camp immediately, but continue for another 300 to 400 metres to a higher, nicer campsite at about 4,000 metres, with shade under rocks, a small, clean stream and delicious waterfalls.

Stage 7: Khobutsi to Urdukas, two to three hours. This is a lovely walk mostly along the crest of the lateral moraine, but with one river and a side glacier to cross. There are stunning views across the Baltoro to the serried teeth of Paiyu, Choricho, Uli Biaho, Trango Towers, Cathedral and Biale. Urdukas, one of the most magnificent campsites of the trek, is set at 4,200 metres, about 100 metres above the lateral moraine. The tent platforms here were cut in 1909 by the duke of Abruzzi, and there are natural rock shelters for the porters (*urdwaa-kas* means 'a stone with cracks'). Covered in grass and flowers, it faces the panorama of the Baltoro Glacier flowing in front of a continuous wall of granite needles and towers that rise sheer to over 6,500 metres.

Like Paiyu, this site is over-used and horribly polluted, with cans and excrement everywhere. The main health hazard here is the swarm of flies that live and breed on the excrement and crawl in a thick layer over everything. An Australian cork hat would be appreciated. We devised a sort of bee-keeper's outfit, placing gauze veils over our hats and tucking them into our shirts. Check to see where your cook is getting water, as the supply is poor. There is a dirty well to the east of the camp and a tiny, cleaner trickle of a stream a ten-minute climb up the mountain to the west. At the east end of the campsite, to the left of the path, is an inconspicuous porters' graveyard.

Urdukas was the highest point reached by Colonel Godwin-Austen in 1861. He climbed 600 metres above the camp and saw the gigantic silhouette of K2. The peak was first sighted in 1856 by T G Montgomerie, who noted a cluster of high peaks from a survey point 219 kilometres away and named them K1, K2, K3, K4 and so on, with K standing for Karakoram. He recognised K2 as the highest and measured it to be 8,619 metres, only three metres more than its new (1988) official height of 8,616 metres, as measured by Professor Ardito Desio of Italy (though most sources still say 8,611 metres). The British usually used local names for mountains: K1 is Masherbrum, and K3, K4, K5 are the Gasherbrum Peaks. K2's local name is Chogori (meaning 'big peak'), and it is often known as Mount Godwin Austen (a name never recognised by the Survey of India), yet it is still commonly called K2.

In 1887, Francis Younghusband visited this part of the Baltoro Glacier, arriving from China across the Old (East) Mustagh Pass (5,422 metres), which was a trade route until it was blocked by ice in the middle of the nineteenth century. He walked down to Askole in three days wearing sheepskin slippers. He had no previous mountaineering experience; in fact, this was the first time he had seen a glacier (see Younghusband, *Heart of a Continent*).

Stage 8: Urdukas to Goro Two, six to eight hours. From Urdukas on you walk on the glacier all the way and may need to wear gaiters early or late in the season. The first hour is across difficult side crevasses; once out in the centre, the way is smoother and the going easier, but you walk on stones all the way, with only a rare glimpse of white ice. Two to three hours from camp, you are opposite the Yermanendu Glacier, which flows down from the Masherbrum Pass (5,364 metres). (For the difficult, technical hike out over this pass see below.) This point is known as Goro One (old name Biango), a pay stage and the traditional lunch stop. Few people camp here, but if you have plenty of time and can persuade your porters, it is worthwhile spending the night here for the clear morning views of **Masherbrum**, the snowy triangle to the south. At 7,821 metres, it is the 24th-highest peak in the world, first climbed by the Americans in 1960.

For the next three to four hours to Goro Two, you walk east up the Baltoro Glacier, following the telephone wire from the army headquarters at Goro One straight towards **Gasherbrum IV** (the name derived from *gashay*, meaning 'beautiful'). At 7,929 metres, this is the 17th-highest peak in the world, a sheer-sided pyramid with a flattened top. Over its right shoulder peeps the soaring point of **Gasherbrum II** (8,035 metres), ranked number 14. Goro Two Camp, at about 4,500 metres, is pitched on the rough stones and ice in the centre of the glacier, with water from glacial melt. It is impossible to dig a toilet pit here, and it is all too easy to contaminate your drinking supply. The leader should designate a toilet area west of camp and make sure the porters use it, too.

Stage 9: Goro Two to Concordia, four to six hours. Excitement mounts on the last day. The walking is slightly easier, and soon after Goro Two you get the famous view north to **Mustagh Tower** (7,284 metres), seen from here as a gigantic stone axe—apparently sheer sided and unclimbable—at the head of Biango Glacier. It was first climbed from the west by the British in 1956, who made it to the top only five days ahead of the French, who were approaching from the east. Ahead up the Baltoro, you still see Gasherbrum IV, but Gasherbrum II has disappeared. On the southern side, overshadowing Concordia, is the cleft top of Mitre Peak (6,010 metres).

A domed army hut signals your arrival at Concordia, at about 4,700 metres. About ten minutes further on, **K2** finally appears on the left, 12 kilometres away. Your porters will want to camp here, where there are stone circles built on the glacier. But, if you can coax them to continue another 20 minutes, you come to a less-polluted site with a better view of K2, which is seen as a near-perfect cone with granite precipices jutting through the glaciers and snow. It stands isolated from its neighbours, rising 3,600 metres straight from Godwin Austen Glacier. K2 was first climbed in 1954 by the Italians.

Concordia, the joining of five glaciers so named in 1892 by Martin Conway after the Place de la Concorde in Paris, is an immense sea of ice covered in stones. Glacial fingers reach up to clasp at the surrounding giants. In every direction the views are stunning. To the right of K2, the notched dome of **Broad Peak** (local name Falcon Congri) crests at 8,060 metres (old measurement 8,051 metres)—a first for Herman Buhl with Kurt Diemberger in 1957. Next is **Gasherbrum IV**, decorated with a vertical vein of rose-coloured marble, conquered in 1958 by the Italians Walter Bonatti and Carlo Mauri. In the southeast, the shining, glaciated **Baltoro Kangri**, or Golden Throne, is a giant armchair soaring to 7,312 metres at the end of Abruzzi Glacier. The Swiss André Roch and Jimmy Belaieff made the first ascent of the southeast peak of Baltoro Kangri in 1934 and then skied down from about 7,000 metres, creating a world altitude record on skis (see André Roch, *Karakoram-Himalaya, Sommets de 7000 metres*).

To the right of Baltoro Kangri, the smooth white slopes of Kondus are topped by a perfect nipple. Nearer to camp, in the southwest, one of the slender twin peaks of the **Mitre** (6,025 metres) towers over head. Due west is the view down the Baltoro Glacier to Paiyu Peak. On the north side of the Baltoro Glacier at Concordia is the sharp ice point of **Crystal Peak** (6,252 metres) glinting like cut glass beside **Marble Peak**, which occupies the Godwin Austen-Baltoro corner. Coming full circle you see the smooth white wedge of **Angel Peak** thrusting above the left shoulder of K2. Hidden from view are the 8,068-metre **Hidden Peak** (Gasherbrum I), which was first climbed by the Americans Andy Kauffman and Pete Schoening in 1958, the 8,035-metre Gasherbrum

II, which was taken in 1956 by the Austrians, and the 7,952-metre Gasherbrum III, which was conquered by the Polish women's team led by Wanda Rutkeiwicz in 1975. Within a radius of 15 kilometres are 41 peaks higher than 6,500 metres, many of them unnamed.

Martin Conway was, in 1892, the first person to explore Concordia. He made an attempt on Baltoro Kangri, reaching the top of a spur on the north side, which he called Pioneer Peak.

Stage 10: Concordia to K2 Base Camp, five to six hours. The first few kilometres from Concordia is across difficult crevasses and glacial rivers. You will save hours by hiring a porter who knows the way to lead you across the snow bridges. Follow a medial moraine north up the Godwin Austen Glacier, with magnificent views back to **Chogolisa** or Bride Peak (7,668 metres). This is the snowy tomb of Herman Buhl, who fell through a cornice in 1957; the peak was finally conquered in 1975 by the Austrians. The duke of Abruzzi had come to within 150 metres of the summit in 1909.

As you approach K2, you look back to Concordia and see the zebra-striped glaciers sweeping round the corner and disappearing down the Baltoro. The striped effect is from the lateral moraines of side glaciers that, as they join the main iceflow, are squeezed into long, parallel ridges of ice bordered by lines of rock and gravel. The lateral moraines having become medial moraines, they sweep dramatically round at Concordia, accentuating the flow of the ice. The easiest walking is on the ice. Stop for lunch at Broad Peak Base Camp. Camp at about 5,000 metres.

The **memorials** to those killed on K2 are about 20 minutes north of K2 Base Camp, on the rock face above the junction of the Savoia and Godwin Austen glaciers. Walk to the foot of the rock, then scramble up about 30 vertical metres on a rocky path to the memorials, a collection of saucepan lids with the climbers' names and dates hammered onto them. Return by scrambling down the other side of the ridge to the Savoia Glacier.

By 1990, 55 people had climbed K2, and 25 had died on the mountain. The worst year was 1986, when five separate expeditions were on K2 in early August. Sixteen climbers reached the summit, but 13 died (two British, two American, two French, three Polish, two Austrian, an Italian and a Pakistani), most caught in a storm above 8,000 metres. The first memorial, placed in 1953, was for the American Art Gilkey. Suffering from flebitis in his leg, Gilkey was being dragged down the mountain by Pete Schoening and others, who left him anchored to an ice axe on a steep slope while they prepared the route ahead. When Schoening went back to fetch Gilkey, he was gone, carried off by an avalanche.

Stages 11 and 12. Tours usually allow several nights at Concordia, a veritable tent city, to give people time to explore. It is well worth hiking southeast up the Abruzzi Glacier for views of the hidden Gasherbrum peaks I, II and III. Another option is to climb a little way up the dividing ridge between the Baltoro and Godwin Austen glaciers for magnificent panoramic photos of the joining glaciers.

It is possible to trek back to Askole in four or five days if you are fit, but tour groups allow six days. (Additional information from Ashraf Aman, Muhammad Ali Chengezi, Kent Obee, Larry True and André Roch.)

CONCORDIA OVER MASHERBRUM PASS TO HUSHE

Map: Swiss Karakoram map, reliability excellent; U502 NI 43-3 (Mundik) and NI 43-4 (Siachen), reliability poor, with insufficient mountain detail.
Restricted zone to open zone; technical; five days; maximum height 5,364 metres; August to mid-September.

An alternative to returning from Concordia down the Baltoro Glacier is to exit via the Masherbrum Pass (5,364 metres). This technical trek requires crampons, ice axe, climbing harness, rope, gaiters and perhaps short ice-climbing axes and ice screws. You also need a good guide and fully equipped high-altitude porters. Do not attempt this pass unless you have ice-climbing experience.

This pass was first crossed in 1974 by the American Nick Clinch, much to the surprise of the villagers of Hushe, who thought their valley impregnable from the north. They remembered Clinch from 1960, however, when he led the successful ascent of Masherbrum Peak from Hushe, and gave him a warm welcome.

Stage 1: Concordia to Yermanendu Glacier. Descend to Goro Two and continue a further couple of hours to the junction of the trail south to the Yermanendu Glacier, which is marked with a small stone cairn. After a short and gradual descent, mount the end of the Yermanendu Glacier and continue for two hours, heading towards the closest ridge that runs down to the east side of the glacier. A 30-metre climb over the lateral moraine brings you to the campsite, which consists of four small tent platforms cut into the grassy hillside.

Stage 2: To Masherbrum Pass Base Camp. Descend to the glacier and rope up, as crevasses, especially in the flatter portions, are often hidden. Crampons are not necessary. Thread your way up the glacier, alternating between the glacier proper and both edges. Where the glacier steepens and you have to climb along the eastern lateral moraine, finding the route is a little tricky. Head for the north face of the long eastern ridge of Masherbrum, which arises from the Masherbrum Pass, then gradually turn eastwards with the glacier until you can see the pass ahead. Camp on a flat snow-rock area near the north side. Melt snow for water.

Stage 3: Across the Masherbrum Pass. Prepare for a long day, rope up and, keeping to the north side of the glacier, head toward the lowest point of the pass, which is to your left. Finding the route through the crevasses on this side of the pass is challenging but not as laborious as on the south side. From the top of the icefall, the final ascent to the pass is a gradual slog up a flattish snowfield about two kilometres long—hot and exhausting at this altitude. Descend fairly easily for two hours, dropping about 200 vertical metres to the top of the icefall. Camp on the glacier at about 5,200 metres. Melt snow for water.

Stage 4: Down the icefall. A laborious and tedious day. Finding the route down the icefall is difficult; it entails climbing and abseiling. Head first to the east (left) side of the glacier, then, using crampons, climb generally down the centre of the icefall. Camp on uncomfortable rocks at the base of a ridge, near the bottom of the icefall, on the right side. Melt snow for water.

Stage 5: To Dalsangpa Lake. Zigzag down the icefall and cross to the left lateral moraine below the junction with Gondoghoro Glacier. Just outside the lateral moraine is a lone shepherds' hut that is occupied from July to September. At a slightly higher level, Dalsangpa Lake reflects stunning views of the Masherbrum Pass and Masherbrum Mountain. It is an idyllic campsite. From here it is one or two days down to Hushe (see Gondoghoro trek, page 118). (Information from Larry True, Linda Brown, Kent Obee and Cynthia Brown.)

CONCORDIA OVER VIGNE OR GONDOGHORO PASS TO HUSHE

You can also exit from Concordia up the Vigne Glacier and over the Vigne Pass to the Chogolisa Glacier, or up the Biarchedi Glacier and over the Gondoghoro Pass to the Gondoghoro Glacier. Both routes lead down to Hushe. David Hamilton leads tours over the Gondoghoro Pass each summer, and one Japanese expedition made it to Hushe this way in 24 hours. The French company Allibert also leads treks over the Gondoghoro Pass.

BIAFO GLACIER OVER HISPAR PASS TO NAGAR AND HUNZA

Map: Swiss Karakoram map is best; U502 NI 43-3 (Mundik), NJ 43-15 (Shimshal) and NJ 43-14 (Baltit), reliability poor but better than nothing.
Open zone; very strenuous; 12 to 14 days; maximum height 5,150 metres; July to September (on skis in February or March).

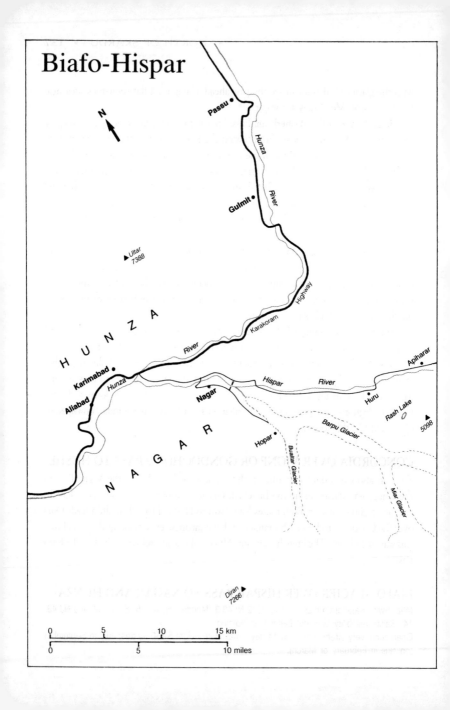

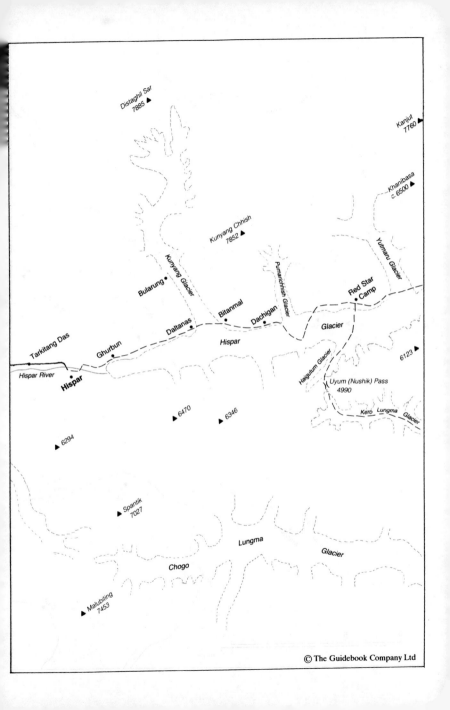

Distaghil Sar
7885 ▲

Kanjut
7760 ▲

Khanibasa
c. 6500 ▲

Kunyang Chhish
7852 ▲

Yutmaru Glacier

Kunyang Glacier

Bularung •

Punarichhish Glacier

Red Star
Camp

Bitanmal •

Dachigan •

Glacier

Daltanas •

Hispar

Ghurbun •

6123 ▲

Tarkitang Das

Haigutum Glacier

Uyum (Nushik) Pass
4990

Hispar River

Hispar •

Kero   Lungma   Glacier

6470 •

▲ 6346

▲ 6294

Spantik
7027 ▲

Lungma

Glacier

Chogo

Malubiting
7453 ▲

© The Guidebook Company Ltd

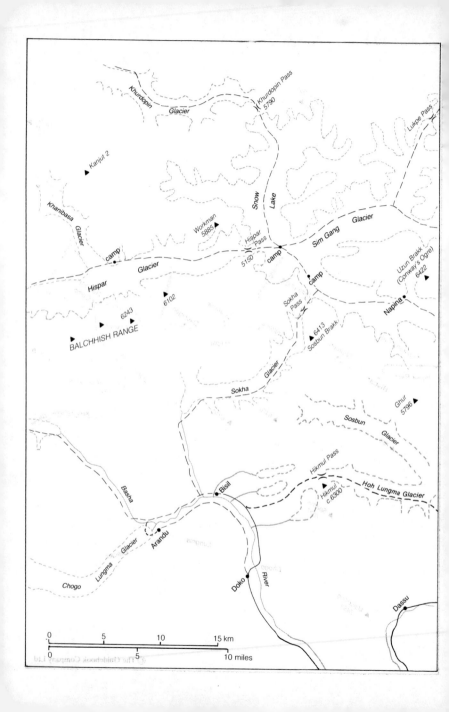

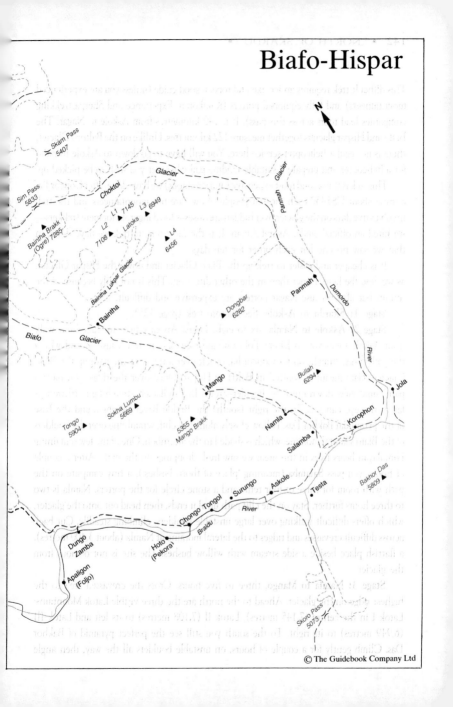

Biafo-Hispar

N

Skam Pass
5407

Sim Pass
5833

Choktoi
Glacier

Panmah Glacier

Baintha Brakk
(Ogre) 7285

L2
7108

L1 7145
Latoks

L3 6949

L4
6456

Baintha Lukpar Glacier

Baintha

Dongbar
6282

Panmah

Dumordo

Biafo
Glacier

Bullah
6294

River

Mango

Jola

Tongo
5904

Sokha Lumbu
5669

5365
Mango Brakk

Namla

Korophon

Salamba

Testa

Bakhor Das
5809

Chongo Tongol
Braldu

Surungo

Askole

River

Dungo
Zamba

Hoto
(Pekora)

Skoro Pass
5073

Apaligon
(Folio)

This difficult trek requires an ice axe and rope, a good guide (unless you are experienced mountaineers) and fully equipped porters (Karakoram Experience and Sherpa trekking companies lead tours across this pass). It is 140 kilometres from Askole to Nagar. The Biafo and Hispar glaciers together measure 122 kilometres. Unlike on the Baltoro Glacier, there is no regular helicopter service here. You will have to go down to Askole to radio for a helicopter and prepare a suitable landing pad wherever you wish to be picked up.

This trek is the second most expensive (and strenuous) we have done, after Concordia, costing about US$450 each for four people. As we are not mountaineers and the trek involves five days on the glacier over hidden crevasses—too dangerous for mere trekkers—we hired an official guide, Ashraf Aman. It is the most remote trek we have done, in that we saw no one but each other for ten days.

It is cheaper and easier to trek up the Biafo Glacier and down the Hispar Glacier, as we describe here, rather than in the other direction. This is not only because of the terrain but also because Nagar porters are expensive and difficult.

Stage 1: Skardu to Askole. See Baltoro trek (page 125).

Stage 2: Askole to Namla, six to eight hours. An easy two- to three-hour walk from Askole takes you to Kiser's Polo Ground (see Baltoro trek), just beyond which the path forks, straight on for Concordia, or left over a ridge for the path up the Biafo Glacier (biafo meaning 'rooster' in Balti) to Hispar. Once over the ridge, you have a panoramic view down onto the boulder-strewn Biafo Glacier, stretching northwest as far as the eye can see. To the right (south) the Braldu River sweeps round the base of the pyramidal Bakhor Das. Follow closely along the cliff, scrambling over the boulders of the Biafo's lateral moraine, which is shaded in the afternoon. One of the few remaining Himalayan bears lives in this area; we saw fresh droppings on the path. After a couple of hours, you pass **Salamba** (meaning 'place of thorn bushes'), a tiny campsite on the path with room for three or four tents and a stone circle for the porters. Namla is two to three hours further. Stay on the cliff path until it ends, then head out onto the glacier, which offers difficult walking over large unstable boulders, climbing steadily. Cut back across difficult crevasses and ridges to the lateral moraine at Namla (about 3,400 metres), a flattish place beside a side stream with willow bushes. The site is not obvious from the glacier.

Stage 3: Namla to Mango, three to five hours. Cross the crevassed area to the highest ridge on the glacier. Ahead to the north are the three visible Latok Mountains: Latok I in the centre (7,145 metres), Latok II (7,108 metres) to its left and Latok III (6,949 metres) to its right. To the south you still see the perfect pyramid of Bakhor Das. Climb gently for a couple of hours, on unstable boulders all the way, then angle in across the crevasses to Mango, an ablation valley with grass and willow bushes by a side stream flowing from the striated snow ridge and glacier of the 5,355-metre Mango Brakk (*brakk* meaning 'mountain' in Balti). The view back across the glacier runs to the granite northern wall, flecked with snow and rising to over 6,000 metres. The campsite, at about 3,650 metres, has stone circles for the porters and ample tent space. Herds of yaks, dzos and cattle are unattended by shepherds, who are up the Panmah Glacier with the milk herds. Hoopoes and Rock Buntings hop among gentians and geraniums.

Stage 4: Mango to Baintha, four to six hours. This is a lovely, easy day starting with a short walk along the ablation valley past a small lake, then heading out across the lateral crevasses to the smooth, white centre of the Biafo Glacier. Ahead is your first view of the Hispar Pass. The mountain walls on either side rise to 6,000 metres, the southeastern wall being covered with snow and ice, the northwestern wall a line of serrated rock. You cross two medial moraines and climb the lateral moraine to find a green ablation valley and follow it up to Baintha, a grassy area with a clear stream flowing through dense willow shrubs surrounded by flowers—the last greenery and flowing water you will see for five days.

Baintha is also known as Conway's Camp, as Sir W Martin Conway camped here in 1892. There are rock shelters for porters. An hour's walk beyond camp, the Baintha Lukpar Glacier flows down from the Latok Group, offering interesting side treks to explore those peaks. Viewed across the Biafo Glacier, Tongo (5,904 metres) and Sokha Lumbu form a jagged wall of ice and granite. Camp at about 4,020 metres.

Stage 5: Baintha to Glacier Camp or Napina, four to six hours. Start with 45 minutes of easy walking up the ablation valley past several small lakes surrounded by flowers and willow bushes (we saw bear droppings and ravens), followed by 30 minutes of crossing difficult crevasses out to the easy white ice. Do not get too close to the Baintha Lukpar Glacier, as the ice is churned up where the two glaciers meet. The next few hours is an easy stroll up smooth ice, stepping over frequent small crevasses. If the glacier is snow covered, you must rope up and walk in single file all the way across the pass. The Biafo is hemmed in by gleaming glaciers on the south and jagged granite on the north.

Napina is a green campsite in the northern ablation valley, with fresh water but no bushes. If you do not wish to detour into Napina, you can camp out on the ice in the middle of the Biafo at about 4,400 metres and collect water from glacier melt. On the southern side of the Biafo, the **Sokha Pass** (guarded by Sosbun Brakk, 6,413 metres, first climbed by the Japanese from the south in 1981) leads to the Sokha Glacier and the Basha Valley. The Sokha Pass, first crossed by H W Tilman in 1937, is a steep snow slope on both sides and should be attempted only by those with mountaineering experience and equipment.

Tilman reports that he twice saw 'yeti footprints' on Snow Lake and followed them for about a mile. His Nepali Sherpas assured him that they were made by the smaller, man-eating yeti (as opposed to the larger, yak-eating sort). Tilman adds: 'My remark that no one had been here for nearly thirty years and that he must be devilish hungry did not amuse the Sherpas as much as I expected!'

Stage 6: Napina or Glacier Camp to Hispar Pass Base Camp, four to five hours. This is a steady plod on snow-covered ice (rope essential, gaiters recommended), zigzagging to cross the crevasses but keeping slightly right of centre. Wag Tails and Ravens follow you up. Snowy peaks adrip with glaciers wall you in on the south, as do granite towers on the north. At the intersection with the Sim Gang Glacier and Snow Lake (or Lukpe Lawo), the route to the Hispar Pass leads off to the west. The ice here is about 1.5 kilometres thick and flowing at about 300 metres a year. Camp at about 4,780 metres in a flat bowl of ice several kilometres wide and surrounded by jagged black and white mountains. From here treks lead north across Snow Lake and the Khurdopin Pass (5,790 metres) to the Shimshal Valley, and east up the Sim Gang Glacier across the Sim Pass to the Panmah Glacier (only for those with mountaineering experience and equipment).

The name Snow Lake was given in 1892 by W Martin Conway, the first foreign visitor (see *Climbing and Exploration in the Karakoram–Himalaya*). In 1899, the husband-wife team of William Hunter Workman and Fanny Bullock Workman came and speculated that Snow Lake might be an ice-cap like those in the polar regions, from which glaciers flowed out in all directions, and estimated its size at 300 square miles (777 square kilometres). It was not until Eric Shipton and H W Tilman explored the area in 1937 and 1939 that the true geography was known; the estimated size of Snow Lake shrank by a power of ten to 30 square miles, or 77 square kilometres (see Shipton, *Blank on the Map*).

Stage 7: To the top of Hispar Pass, two to three hours. Rope, gaiters and waterproof boots are essential. It is an easy, steady climb to the top of the pass (5,151 metres) but quite strenuous at this altitude. The route wends gently up the centre, with giant crevasses and striped, greenish-blue seracs on either side.

Looking back across Snow Lake gives a feeling of vast snowy space, without a hint of vegetation. Coiling out from Snow Lake, smooth glaciers writhe between nameless unclimbed peaks. The highest peak, due east up the Sim Gang Glacier, is the Ogre (local name Baintha Brakk, 7,285 metres), which was first climbed in 1977 by Chris Bonington and Doug Scott, who broke both of his legs just below the summit and had to crawl down (see *American Alpine Journal*, 1978).

Camp on the wide, flat top of the pass, which is hemmed in by crevasses and 6,000-metre peaks. Just north of the pass, Workman Peak (5,885 metres) forms a white pyramid; to the south, avalanches dislodged by the afternoon sun crash at the base of the great ice wall. In the west, the Hispar Glacier, rough and snow-covered, stretches down as far as the eye can see, separating the Hispar Mustagh Range on the right (north) from the Rakaposhi and Balchhish ranges (*chhish*, appearing as *kish* on some maps, means 'mountain' in Burushaski).

Stage 8: Hispar Pass to Khanibasa, three to five hours, depending on snow conditions. Even in the early morning, the snow can be so soft that you sink up to your calves. Undulate for one hour across the top of the pass, then plod sharply down the centre on smooth snow, jumping small crevasses for another hour or so. Beware of hidden crevasses, rope up, and walk in single file. Large crevasses and seracs border the glacier on both sides. The base camp for those crossing in the opposite direction is at the bottom of the steep part (we saw fox tracks there).

A further hour takes you across deep snow and hidden crevasses to the northern lateral moraine and the usual lunch stop by a trickle of fresh water. Two more hours of boulder hopping on scree and moraine leads to a small green campsite just before the junction with the Khanibasa Glacier, with room for four or five tents at 4,580 metres. Carry water up from glacial pools below. You look across the Hispar Glacier to the sheer white wall of the Balchhish Range, which rises to over 6,000 metres; Wedge Peak and the Sugar Loaf are at the western end. Edelweiss, gentians and asters surround the camp.

Stage 9: Khanibasa to Yutmaru, four to six hours. It takes about 90 minutes to cross the Khanibasa Glacier. It is relatively easy going, with a fine view north (right) to the smooth white dome of **Kanjut Sar**, at 7,760 metres the 29th-highest peak in the world. There are six possible campsites between the Khanibasa and Yutmaru glaciers, two of which have stone circles used by hunters in winter. Much of the way is along a clear path high on the lateral moraine about 30 metres above the glacier, with magnificent views across to the hanging glaciers and frequent avalanches on the southern ice wall. Camp about an hour before the Yutmaru Glacier in a flat, sheltered field in the ablation valley, which offers room for many tents. There is running water until mid-August; thereafter, it is a short walk to a silted river. A few small willow bushes and flowers surround the site, which is at about 4,330 metres.

Stage 10: Yutmaru to Red Star Camp, five to seven hours. The Yutmaru Glacier takes at least two hours to cross, with high ice walls and deep crevasses to negotiate. Fill your water bottles before leaving the glacier, especially late in the season. On the other side, climb steeply up under the cliff to a good possible campsite with a panoramic view back to the Hispar Pass (but no water in September). Follow a high path 50 or 100 metres above the Hispar Glacier. You will have to cross a few screes, and there is a shortage of water, but flowers and fine views make this otherwise idyllic. There are at least five possible campsites along the way. The lower path, following the edge of the glacier, is more difficult and not as scenic.

Red Star Camp (marked by a red star on the U502 map) is a large field at 4,150 metres with stone shelters and circles and silty river water. Opposite, to the south across the Hispar Glacier, the Haigutum Glacier leads to the difficult **Uyum Pass**, which crosses to the Chogo Lungma Glacier and Haramosh—a technical climb up an ice wall (see below). The Uyum Pass is the lowest point in the 6,000-metre wall of the Balchhish Range.

Stage 11: Red Star Camp to Dachigan, four to six hours. The Pumarichhish Glacier flows south off Kunyang Chhish, at 7,852 metres the 22nd-highest peak in the world, and blocks your way. Since 1988 the Pumarichhish Glacier has been racing forward, pushing three-quarters of the way across the Hispar Glacier and creating a violently contorted mess of towers and pinnacles of ice that is impossible to cross. You must head out across the Hispar Glacier to get round it—a tiresome day of boulder hopping, with your last view of the top of the Hispar Pass from the middle of the Hispar Glacier. From here you can follow either side of the Hispar Glacier down to Hispar. We chose the northern side. Just past the Pumarichhish, the ablation valley widens into a sheltered, grassy pasture at Dachigan, an ideal spot for a rest day, with interesting walks exploring up the Pumarichhish Glacier. Another good campsite is about 30 minutes further down from the Pumarichhish Glacier, in summer pastures with a good water supply, stone circles for the porters, a grove of stunted willows and herds of yaks and cattle. Camp at about 4,050 metres.

Stage 12: Dachigan to Hispar village, five to seven hours. This is an easy day of walking through pastures in the ablation valley past willow and cedar shrubs. In one hour you reach the deserted shepherds' summer settlement of **Bitanmal** (meaning 'shaman's field'—*bitan* is Burushaski for 'shaman' or 'witch doctor'). Bitanmal is another good spot for a rest day, on the edge of the Kunyang Glacier, which you can explore. It is possible to climb a ridge for views of the giant mountains to the north: Kunyang Chhish and, in the distance, the serried peaks of Distaghil Sar (7,885 metres).

The easy crossing of the Kunyang Glacier takes about an hour, followed by a gentle four-hour walk to Hispar village down the ablation valley and past herds of goats, cattle and donkeys. There are a couple of shepherds' settlements, which are deserted or occupied only by men. You may be able to buy yogurt and watch the men make butter in tall wooden churns. For the last hour, you see on the south bank Hispar, a wide alluvial fan rippling in terraces down to a cliff above the Hispar River. Cross the river on a pulley (Rs10 per passenger) and climb up the mud ramparts to fields of wheat, buckwheat, peas, beans, turnips, poppies and marijuana, with a few scattered apricot trees, willows and poplars.

Hispar village, with a population of nearly 1,000 strict Shia Muslims, is a tight knot of narrow streets tying together 120 houses, a boys' primary school, an empty clinic and a small wooden mosque rising above it all. You can pay the *chowkidar* to camp in the grounds of the empty guesthouse above the village at about 3,250 metres. The guesthouse has no cooking, washing or toilet facilities.

Hispar people are notoriously difficult. Fanny Bullock Workman was complaining about them in 1906, and Steve Venables calls them 'the most expensive and bloody-minded porters in the Himalaya' (*Alpine Journal*, 1983). They may try to insist that you hire Hispar men for the walk out to the Karakoram Highway. This is an expensive proposition at three days out and one-and-a-half days back, at Rs110 a day plus rations, besides having to pay your Skardu porters for walking out empty. It takes skill and diplomacy to talk your way out of it.

In any case, by the time we go to press, the jeep road will probably be open all the way to Hispar.

Stage 13: Hispar to Huru, five to six hours. Start out on the south bank for about an hour of walking through irrigated wheat fields to the footbridge. Cross to the north bank and continue down through the hot Hispar Gorge. In 45 minutes you will reach **Tarkitang Das,** which consists of a few willow trees beside a spring, with two houses, trees and fields above on the cliff top—the last greenery until Huru. **Apiharar,** an hour downstream, has two huts beside a spring but no shade. You join the jeep road a few minutes later, but in 1989 landslides and side streams made it impassable for vehicles for the first six kilometres.

Huru, three hours' barren walk from Apiharar, is a lone shepherds' hut perched on a shelf about 150 metres above the river and surrounded by walnut, apricot, mulberry and willow trees and fields of wheat and potatoes. Huru means 'water shoot', and the place is so named for the trickle of water that shoots down the smooth, barren hillside to a small holding pond beside the hut. Camp at about 2,800 metres. We paid the camping fee with surplus flour and biscuits. **Rash Phari** (meaning 'sparkling lake') sits high on the steep ridge above Huru. Reputedly, you can see K2 from the ridge about 300 metres above Rash Lake (see page 228).

Stage 14: Huru to Nagar and Hunza. Unless you have arranged to be met, there is no chance of finding a jeep or tractor at Huru. Your porters may insist on going to Nagar village, three hours on foot from Huru, but it is shorter and more convenient to walk straight to the Karakoram Highway (KKH), a five-hour waterless walk to Ganesh Bridge. Either way, you walk two and a half hours from Huru to the jeep bridge across the Hispar River and another 30 minutes to the footbridge that leads back to the Nagar side. This is where you have to decide to either turn to Nagar or continue straight to Hunza and the KKH. If you turn, it is a 30-minute climb up to Nagar, which boasts three shops and a few scattered houses but no guarantee of transport. If you continue toward the KKH, it is one hour to the jeep bridge connecting Nagar to the KKH, where you may be lucky enough to find some sort of transport for the remaining three kilometres to the KKH (we got a tractor and trailer).

If you have the time and energy, though, it is worthwhile spending a day exploring Nagar, a small kingdom once ruled by a *mir* (king), the last of whom still lives in his palace above the village. A visit to Hopar is also recommended (see page 225).

There are always plenty of vehicles passing on the KKH, and private jeeps park at Ganesh Monument to take tourists up to Karimabad. Private wagons are usually available in Aliabad. A public bus from Ganesh to Gilgit costs Rs30 per person.

BASHA AND HARAMOSH VALLEYS

The Basha River basin divides the Haramosh Range from the Rakaposhi Range. Fed by the Chogo Lungma and Kero Lungma glaciers (*lungma* meaning 'valley' in Balti), the Basha flows down a fertile valley with villages connected by footpaths along either side. The river is crossed by one of the last remaining birch-twig bridges in Pakistan.

A jeep road leads part of the way up the valley. When completed, it will end at **Bisil**, about two hours' walk below **Arandu**, the last permanent village. It is a two-day walk to Arandu from **Tisar**, which is 65 kilometres north of Skardu, where the Braldu and Basha rivers join to form the Shigar River.

A recommended tour is to take a jeep to **Doko**, where the new jeep road crosses from the west to east side of the Basha River. Then walk upriver along the west bank, spend a week or so exploring the lower Chogo Lungma and Kero Lungma glaciers, and return via the east bank (see below). A guide is necessary if you wish to cross the Haramosh Pass (about 4,800 metres) at the head of the Chogo Lungma Glacier or the Uyum (Nushik) Pass (4,990 metres) at the top to the Kero Lungma Glacier.

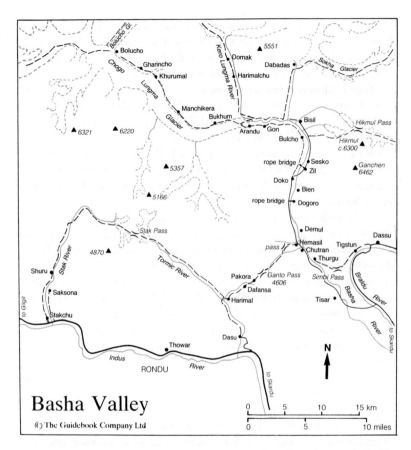

Basha Valley

(C) The Guidebook Company Ltd

    Two treks from the lower Basha Valley lead west to the Indus and east to the Braldu
River, offering interesting routes by which to leave the valley. Most confusingly, they
each end up at phonetically identical villages—one spelled Dassu, the other Dasu. We
describe these before proceeding up the Basha.

CHUTRAN OVER GANTO PASS TO DASU ON THE INDUS

Map: Swiss Karakoram map is best; U502 NI 43-3 (Mundik), NI 43-2 (Gilgit) and NJ 43-15
(Shimshal), reliability poor.
Open zone; strenuous; two to four days; maximum height 4,606 metres; June to October.

Chutran, a prosperous village on the west bank of the Basha River about 72 kilometres from Skardu, has a hot spring, bath house and government rest house. The little-used, roughly 18-kilometre trek from here to Dasu on the Indus crosses two steep passes and is recommended only for the experienced and confident.

Stage 1: Chutran to summer settlement, five to six hours. Two gullies come down near Chutran; the one further north, at **Hemasil** village, leads to the pass. Follow a shaded path through giant walnut trees and climb for three hours up a steep logging path to the top of the ridge. Beware of tree trunks hurtling down the logging shoot, as the loggers shout a warning only if they see you. The top of the ridge is extremely narrow and jagged, with no room to pitch a tent. The descent down the other side is a vertiginous cliff path with a drop of several hundred metres into the other gully, which descends to Chutran.

A shepherds' summer settlement, used in June and July, nestles into the base of the cliff, where the path descends to the river. You can camp here, but it is better to climb for another hour up a steep path to the higher summer settlement, the last in the valley, used in August and September. Here the water is cleaner, flowing out from under perpetual snow. In this area, only the men go to summer pastures with the animals.

Stage 2: Across the Ganto (Holtoro) Pass to Pakora, six hours. A steep three-hour climb takes you to the top of the Ganto Pass, at the end of the valley on the right. The top is a grassy saddle with a giant slab of rock thrust vertically up on one side. Magnificent views lead east across the Basha River to serried peaks and, to the west, down to Pakora summer settlement in a green valley. The descent is across a steep, rolling hillside through knee-deep grass and flowers—gentians, edelweiss, anemones, buttercups and geraniums.

The people of Pakora have a markedly different culture from those in the Basha Valley. The entire family comes up to the pastures for the summer, locking up their winter houses in the village below. The women's headdresses are decorated with coins, silver beads and a brown felt tail hanging down behind. The people are Shia and speak Balti (see the Rupal Valley section of the Nanga Parbat trek for other members of the same tribe).

Stage 3: Pakora to Dasu on the Indus, four to five hours. An easy two-hour descent—first down a narrow gorge, then following an irrigation channel through plantations of poplars and willows and past the deserted winter village of **Dafansa**—brings you to the village of **Harimal** on the **Tormic River**. You can follow the Tormic Valley up for 19 kilometres to the **Stak Pass**, then follow the Stak River down for another 19 kilometres to join the Indus at **Stakchu**. Alternatively, you can head down the Tormic River from

Harimal through continuous green and shaded villages, arriving after about 90 minutes at Dasu and the end of the jeep track. The last three kilometres from Dasu down to the Indus is totally barren—a remarkable contrast to the lush Tormic Valley hidden upriver.

Once on the Gilgit-to-Skardu highway, you can easily hitchhike or flag down a bus going to either Gilgit or Skardu.

DOKO OVER SIMBI PASS TO DASSU ON BRALDU RIVER

Map: Swiss Karakoram map is best; U502 NI 43-3 (Mundik), NI 43-2 (Gilgit) and NJ 43-15 (Shimshal), reliability poor.
Open zone; easy; two days; maximum height about 3,500 metres; cool weather only.

Start at the jeep bridge across the Basha River at Doko, a friendly village shaded by huge walnut trees about 85 kilometres from Skardu. Sugar, rice and biscuits are available in the village shop, but it is better to bring all your supplies from Skardu. Horses and donkeys are not available, but there are plenty of porters, who appear as soon as you arrive.

Walk downriver on the east bank through the fertile village oases of **Bien**, **Dogoro** (where there is an old birch-twig footbridge across the Basha) and **Demul** to **Thurgu**, where you can camp high above the Basha Valley. As these villages are seldom visited by tourists, they are unspoiled. From Thurgu, a two-hour steep walk along a clear path across the barren hillside takes you to the top of the **Simbi Pass**; your reward is an impressive view down the wide Shigar Valley and other views up the Basha and Braldu rivers. For the next two hours descend on a good path to **Tigstun** on the Braldu River. Thirty minutes' walk along the jeep road brings you to Dassu, where you can wait for a jeep to take you back to Skardu. Another option is to hike on for three days to **Askole** (see the Concordia trek, page 123). (Information from Elisabeth Gardner.)

LOWER BASHA RIVER: DOKO TO ARANDU AND BACK

Map: Swiss Karakoram map is best; U502 NI 43-3 (Mundik), NI 43-2 (Gilgit) and NJ 43-15 (Shimshal), reliability poor.
Open zone; easy; two to three days; maximum height about 3,000 metres; April to November.

Ascending the ten kilometres from Doko to Arandu takes four to five hours. The jeep road crosses a new bridge to the east bank and is complete for a few more kilometres, but take the footpath up the west bank, starting from behind the shop in the centre of Doko. The path sets off through walnut groves and across fields of hay, with views across the river to cultivated land and villages. It is an easy stroll along a once-jeepable road that undulates across the hillside with little altitude gain. Though reasonably green with thorn, willow, gooseberry and rose bushes, it is hot in summer. The path crosses a couple of side streams but, on the whole, is too high above the river for easy access to water.

Opposite **Zil**, at four shepherds' huts, a birch-bark bridge gives access to Zil and Sesko, on the east bank. Beyond this the path becomes stony, and several landslides falling sheer into the river are slippery to cross. There is a good possible campsite at **Bulcho**—three shepherds' huts with fresh water—after which the valley opens out. You cross some waste land to **Gon** village, a lush, green oasis surrounded by poplar trees. From Gon to Arandu takes another hour across more scrubland. Camp above the village at about 2,950 metres.

A recommended day walk from Arandu is to climb steeply up the moraine beside the snout of the Chogo Lungma Glacier, a black tunnel out of which gushes the Basha River. Follow the southern lateral moraine, with patches of grass and flowers, for panoramic views up the glacier and down the Basha River.

There is no bridge at Arandu. To return down the east bank you must continue up to the glacier and cross on the ice—a 90-minute detour. A good bridge crosses the Kero Lungma River, from where it takes two hours, on a well-made path across the barren mountainside and then along the river, to the first terraces of **Bisil**, an attractive, fertile village with a hot spring in the centre.

A little south of Bisil, a trail climbs east over the Hikmul Pass to the Hoh Lungma Glacier, which was explored by W H Tilman in 1937 (see Eric Shipton, *Blank on the Map*), and on to join the Braldu River at Chakpo.

Continue from Bisil down the Basha River through the fertile village of **Sesko** to the jeep bridge at **Doko**. We recommend that you continue on foot to Dassu on the Braldu (see above).

KERO LUNGMA GLACIER OVER UYUM PASS TO HISPAR

Map: Swiss Karakoram map is best; U502 NI 43-3 (Mundik), NI 43-2 (Gilgit) and NJ 43-15 (Shimshal), reliability poor.

Open zone; technical; about seven days; maximum height 4,977 metres; August and September.

This strenuous technical trek requires mountaineering skills (we have not done it). Do not attempt it unless you are experienced and fully equipped and have a guide. The path heads north from Arandu up the Kero Lungma River, past **Harimalchu** settlement to the first camp at the shepherds' summer settlement of **Domak**, eight kilometres away. From here it is 13 kilometres to the head of the Kero Lungma Glacier, which leads to two passes: the **Bolucho Pass** (5,462 metres) leading west and then south, down the Bolucho Glacier and back to the Chogo Lungma Glacier; and the Uyum (Nushik) Pass (4,977 metres), which leads north, down a sheer ice cliff to the Haigutum Glacier, which joins the Hispar Glacier about halfway down (a two-day hike above Hispar village; see page 146).

CHOGO LUNGMA GLACIER OVER HARAMOSH PASS TO THE INDUS

Map: Swiss Karakoram map is best; U502 NI 43-3 (Mundik), NI 43-2 (Gilgit) and NJ 43-15 (Shimshal), reliability poor.
Open zone; very strenuous; seven to ten days; maximum height 4,800 metres; August and September.

This very strenuous trek should be attempted only by those who are experienced and fully equipped with rope, harness, ice axe and so on—and only with a guide. Muhammad Ali Chengezi of Himalayan Trekking is the best guide for this pass. Karakoram Experience also leads tours here.

Stage 1: Arandu to Bukhum, five to eight hours. Follow the Basha River up to the snout of the Chogo Lungma Glacier. It takes one hour to cross the glacier to the northern lateral moraine—a difficult route to find. Follow the moraine along a good path west for three to five hours to the summer settlement of Bukhum, used by shepherds for a couple of weeks at the end of June on their way to higher pastures. Camp.

Stage 2: Bukhum to Khurumal, five to eight hours. Continue with views of the perfect pyramid of Spantik (7,027 metres), which guards the head of the valley, to **Manchikera**, another summer settlement (and a good campsite) where the shepherds cultivate a small vegetable plot and field. Follow the ablation valley between the lateral moraine and the mountain to the summer settlement of Khurumal. Camp.

Stage 3: Khurumal to Bolucho, four to five hours. You pass the summer settlement of **Gharincho** and a small lake (both possible campsites) and continue with magnificent views of Spantik and Laila peaks to Bolucho, at the base of the Bolucho Glacier, which leads to the Bolucho Pass (see above). There is no shepherds' hut here; the shepherds are on the other side of the glacier. You camp at about 3,900 metres on a green pasture beside a good water supply.

Stage 4: Bolucho to Laila Base Camp, five to eight hours. Cross the Chogo Lungma Glacier. The first 20 minutes is on nasty rocks, until you reach the smooth, white central part. Turn southwest up the Haramosh Glacier to Laila Base Camp. Karakoram Experience tours take a couple of rest days here for acclimatisation and to climb a lesser peak for panoramic mountain views.

Stage 5: Laila Base Camp to Haramosh Base Camp, four to six hours. Walk up the Haramosh Glacier, with views of the pass ahead. The last hour is across big rocks and crevasses, requiring that you rope up. Camp on the glacier on a bed of rocks.

Stage 6: Haramosh Base Camp to the top of Haramosh Pass, eight to ten hours. Walk on the glacier, keeping a little towards the south side and crossing many crevasses. After about two hours, you are threatened by avalanches coming down from the left, so move across the glacier towards the north side and continue up. At one point you will need to use about 20 metres of fixed rope. Beware of avalanches from the right

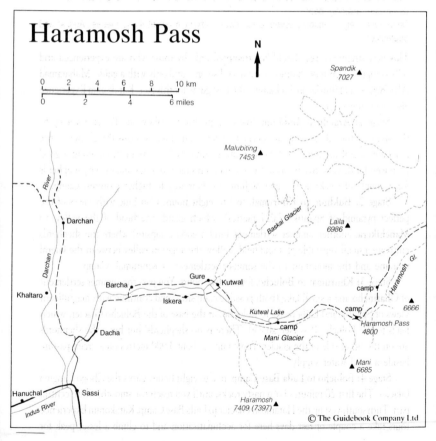

Haramosh Pass

about 40 metres below the top. At the top of the pass is a stone circle, where you can camp. You will find good views of Haramosh (7,409 metres, first climbed in 1958 by the Austrians), Laila and, after a short climb up to the right (north), Rakaposhi. Below, you see Kutwal Lake and trees.

Stage 7: Top of Haramosh Pass to Kutwal Lake, seven to eight hours. You need a rope to get down the first 40 metres or so across the snow. Then you descend (unroped) across loose sliding rocks. After four to six difficult hours, you reach grass and trees, from where it is an easy walk along the Mani Glacier for at least another hour, down to the shepherds' huts at Kutwal Lake, where you camp at about 2,500 metres in green

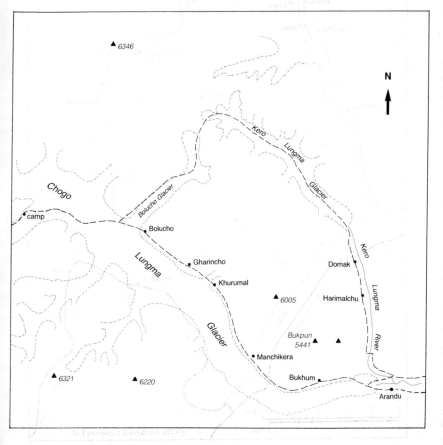

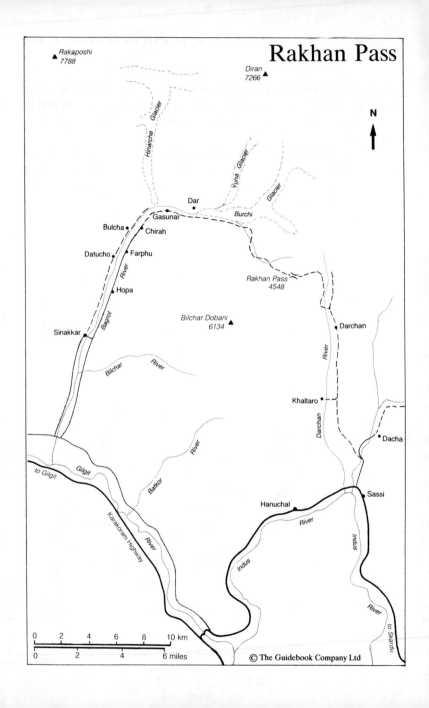

pastures. This is the ideal spot for a rest day. (If you need it, there is a campsite less than half way down, but exposure to rockfalls makes it rather dangerous.)

You are now in the top end of the area known as Haramosh, where the people are Shia Muslims, speak Shina (pronounced 'She-naa'), as in Gilgit, and are on the whole conservative and poor. The area is of interest to anthropologists because of the traces of pre-Islamic culture still found here.

Stage 8: Kutwal Lake to Dacha, nine hours. Walk down from the lake through green pastures for one hour, to where the path forks. The direct route down is half an hour across the Mani Glacier (sometimes, like the glacier on the other side of the pass, called the Haramosh Glacier) and then down to **Iskera** summer village, at about 2,000 metres, which is occupied from May to November.

Alternatively, you can continue down the right side of the Mani Glacier and cross the Baskai Stream to the shepherds' summer settlement of **Gure**, where Dr Karl Jettmar, the German anthropologist, describes finding a stone altar where the women worshipped the goddess Murkum (see Jettmar, *Bolar and Dardistan*). They still leave juniper branches as a good luck offering on the old altar stones. Murkum, the protectress of mothers and children, was believed to live on Haramosh.

A path down the right bank connects Gure to **Barcha**, below which is a bridge across to the left bank, connecting with the path down from Iskere. Follow the water channel down through trees and fields to Dacha (often pronounced Dassu—not to be confused with the two others in Baltistan, never mind the one in Kohistan) and camp for the night. This is supposed to be the end of the jeep road, but it is sometimes blocked. Even when it is open, there are few jeeps.

Stage 9: Dacha to Sassi on the Indus, two to three hours walking down the jeep road. A couple of kilometres downriver from Dacha, a path leads northwest up the Darchan River to the Rakhan Pass (see below). Once on the main Skardu-to-Gilgit road, it is easy to hitchhike the two hours to Gilgit. If you are desperate, there is a good *chai-khana* at the bus stop at Sassi, where you can stay the night. (Information from Muhammad Ali Chengezi and Karakoram Experience.)

HARAMOSH VALLEY OVER RAKHAN PASS
TO BAGROT VALLEY

Maps: Swiss Karakoram map is best; U502 NI 43-3 (Mundik), NI 43-2 (Gilgit) and NJ 43-15 (Shimshal), reliability poor.
Open zone; strenuous; maximum height 4,550 metres; June to September.

We have not done this trek, but it looks worth exploring (please send information). Rakhan Pass (4,550 metres) crosses the ridge that joins Miar and Dobani peaks. It is approached up the Darchan River, which joins the Indus at the latter's most northern point, where it makes a right angle turn south between Sassi (marked Sasli on most maps) and Hanuchal.

The path—said to be forested—follows the north bank of the Darchan River through the villages of **Khaltaro** and **Darchan,** then crosses the pass and comes down to the Burchi Glacier, with views ahead, up the Yuna Glacier, of Diran (Minapin) Peak. Follow the Burchi Glacier east to the first shepherds' summer settlement of **Dar**, at the top of the Bagrot River (pronounced 'Bag-roat'). Bagrot Valley is also Shia, Shina speaking and conservative. The track follows the river through **Gasunar** summer settlement, then turns due south to the end of the jeep road at the first permanent village of **Chirah**.

From here it is a four-hour drive to Gilgit, but jeeps are rare, so be prepared to walk down through **Farphu**, with its wide street that was probably once a polo ground, and **Datucho**, to the main village of **Sinakkar**, which is two hours by jeep from Gilgit. You may find yourself riding with blocks of ice, cut from the Hinarche Glacier and jeeped down to Gilgit bazaar to cool soft drinks and make ice syrups.

GILGIT

Gilgit, the capital of the Northern Areas of Pakistan, is a thriving frontier town that has expanded rapidly to about 30,000 inhabitants since the Karakoram Highway opened in 1978, connecting Gilgit with the rest of Pakistan and with China. The bazaar is full of traders from all over Central Asia: Punjabis, Pathans, Chitralis, Tajiks and Uyghurs speak a babble of languages, as Chinese silk and porcelain, Punjabi cotton and steel and mountain fruits and vegetables change hands.

Hot in July and freezing in February, Gilgit huddles in a wide, irrigated bowl 1,500 metres above sea-level at the eastern end of the Gilgit Valley. The snow-covered pinnacle of Dobani (also called Domani, 6,143 metres) stands guard at the eastern end of town, and a semi-circle of barren peaks about 4,500 metres high encloses the valley on the other three sides. Gilgit is a desert, with only about 130 millimetres of rainfall annually, so all agricultural land must be irrigated with water from the melting snows of higher altitudes. Every available square metre of suitable land has been terraced; the tiny fields and fruit gardens stacked up the lower slopes of the mountains contrast vividly with the surrounding grey.

GILGIT HISTORY

Gilgit has been inhabited for thousands of years. The various waves of invaders that passed through Pakistan also reached Gilgit, and their various beliefs and customs were layered one on top of the other. The animism of the early inhabitants was overlaid by fire worship brought in from Iran, which was modified in turn by Hinduism following the Aryan invasion of about 1700 BC.

From the first century BC, Gilgit, like Kashgar, was an important staging post on the Silk Route from China, and the Chinese wielded considerable influence in the area. Inscriptions and pictures carved on rocks throughout the region give snatches of its history, as does the collection of the sixth- to eleventh-century Buddhist manuscripts discovered in Kargah, ten kilometres west of Gilgit, in 1931.

From the fourth to the eleventh century, Gilgit was mostly Buddhist. Gilgit and Yasin together were called Little Bolor (Xiao Po-lu) according to the Chinese Tang Annals, with its capital in Yasin. Early in the eighth century, three great powers—China, Arabia and Tibet—jostled for control here. A rock in Dainyor lists the Tibetan kings

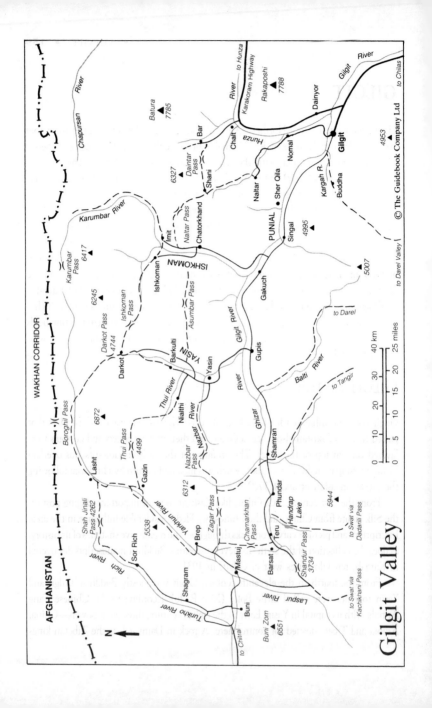

Gilgit Valley

© The Guidebook Company Ltd

who ruled in the seventh and eighth centuries. In 725, according to the Dainyor rock, the kingdoms of Great and Little Bolor merged under Tibetan suzerainty. There was a short Chinese interlude from 747 to 751, when the Chinese invaded successfully across the Boroghil and Darkot passes and captured Yasin, before being driven back by the Arabs from the west (see page 279).

Less than a hundred years after the prophet Muhammad's death in 632, Arab Muslim forces invaded Pakistan from the south by sea, simultaneously reaching Xinjiang in the north. Muhammad bin Qasim was successful in the south, but the northern invasion was repulsed.

The tenth century brought the invasion of the Shins, a Europoid people who spoke Shina (pronounced 'She-naa'), still the language of the main Gilgit Valley, and drove the native Burushaski speakers up into Hunza, Nagar and Yasin. The Shins may have been Hindu, as were the Hindu Shahi kings, who then ruled upper Pakistan from their capital at Hund on the Indus, just below the modern Tarbela Dam.

It was not until early in the eleventh century that Mahmud of Ghazni invaded from Afghanistan, overthrowing the Hindus at Hund and finally winning the plains of Pakistan for Islam. At the time, Gilgit was part of the powerful independent mountain stronghold of Dardistan. Gradually, though, central power waned, and each isolated valley became a small kingdom, speaking its own language and following its own customs. There were seven different kingdoms along the Gilgit and Hunza rivers alone (Gilgit, Punial, Ishkoman, Ghizar, Yasin, Hunza and Nagar), speaking at least three distinct languages (Shina, Khowar and Burushaski). Each tiny kingdom was autonomous and usually at war with the next. Indeed, Marco Polo, who passed through Badakhshan (northeastern Afghanistan) in the thirteenth century, called the area 'noisy with kingdoms'. The better situated of these grew rich by taxing the traffic to and from China.

Sometime after the fifteenth century, the whole area gradually converted to Islam. Pathan Sunnis came up the Indus from Swat in about the sixteenth century, and Shia Muslims spread into Baltistan from Kashmir before the seventeenth century. Finally, early in the nineteenth century, the *mir* (king) of Hunza, Silum Khan III, who had been in temporary exile in Badakhshan, was converted to the Ismaili creed by a *pir* (religious leader) there. Most of his subjects in Hunza and Gojal (upper Hunza) followed suit. Ishkoman, Yasin and the top end of Chitral are now mostly Ismaili, followers of the Aga Khan. Though northern Pakistan is virtually 100 percent Muslim, the people still hold a strong belief in fairies, witches and *jinns* (wizards), and there survive vestiges of pre-Islamic planting and harvesting ceremonies.

In 1846, the British sold Kashmir, Ladakh, Baltistan and Gilgit to the raja of Jammu,

Gulab Singh, and appointed him the first maharaja of Kashmir. But the maharaja's Hindu soldiers could do little to subdue the Muslim tribesmen, despite repeated campaigns in the 1850s and '60s.

After the first Anglo-Sikh war in 1845-46, the British began to worry about a possible Russian invasion through the mountains to Kashmir, inducing them to take a more active interest in the northern frontier. In 1877 they sent a political agent to Gilgit (see pages 49–50), the most isolated outpost of the British Empire, to prevent the Russians destabilising the remote mountain kingdoms with influence gained through gifts and promises. This was the world of Rudyard Kipling's *Kim* and the Great Game, aptly described by John Keay in *The Gilgit Game* as 'a shadowy see-and-run contest between Britain and Russia in the highest mountains'. There was also the fear that, in the event of a Russian invasion of India, which was expected via the Bolan and Khyber passes, secondary light-weight Russian thrusts might penetrate the Karakoram and Hindu Kush passes.

Totally cut off by snow for eight months of the year, the first British agency failed. It was too small and isolated to make its presence felt, and it ended abruptly in 1881, when it was nearly overrun by Yasin.

The second agency, established in 1889, fared better. By then the route from Srinagar via Astor had been improved; there was a telegraph link, and the agency included a full compliment of British soldiers. There followed a series of campaigns to subdue the surrounding kingdoms: in 1891 the British, led by Colonel Algernon Durand, overran Hunza; in 1893 they strengthened the fort at Chilas to defend the new road over the Babusar Pass against the Kohistani tribes. The year 1895 saw the dramatic rescue of the garrison at Chitral Fort by 500 troops from Gilgit, who marched across the Shandur Pass through the April snows (see page 291).

In 1935, the British leased the agency back from the maharaja of Kashmir, built an airfield at Gilgit and formed the Gilgit Scouts, a force of 600 men raised to guard against invasion and to maintain peace. The Scouts were mostly the sons of royalty from the seven kingdoms, commanded by a subadar major, usually a brother of one of the kings, under the direction of the political agent. The Scouts' bagpipe band wore the Black Watch tartan and, even today, practises in the Chinar Bagh, near the river.

At Independence in 1947, British India was divided into Hindu-majority India and Muslim-majority Pakistan. One of the many vexing problems brought about by the split was what to do with the hundreds of princely states, which theoretically had the right to remain independent. The vast majority were Hindu and were easily persuaded to join India, and the Muslim states in Pakistan were absorbed by Pakistan. The rub was Kashmir, a Muslim-majority state ruled by a Hindu maharaja.

Maharaja Hari Singh let the Independence Day accession deadline pass without joining either Pakistan or India—an apparent bid for independence or at least a favourable autonomy arrangement. Two weeks before the August 14 Independence Day, the political agent of Gilgit handed over power to a new Kashmiri Hindu governor, Ghansara Singh. The Gilgit Scouts were left in the charge of Major William Brown, a British officer who had volunteered to see them through Independence. In Punjab, grisly bloodshed marked Independence, as ten million Hindu, Sikh and Muslim refugees fled in opposite directions across the new border. Gilgit waited in suspense while the maharaja dithered.

On October 26, Pathan tribesmen from the North-West Frontier Province invaded Kashmir, declaring a *jihad* (holy war). Hari Singh fled to Delhi and begged for help, agreeing to accede to India, subject to a general referendum. In Gilgit, Major Brown sent Subadar Major Babar Khan, brother of the mir of Nagar and commander of the Scouts, to arrest Governor Ghansara Singh on October 31. The next day Gilgit was declared 'the independent Republic of Gilgit', which later acceded to Pakistan. The Gilgit Scouts and Muslim soldiers of the Kashmiri army then joined the war against India, winning Baltistan for Pakistan. There is a memorial to Babar Khan in the Chinar Bagh.

A charming but unfounded legend tells of the Indian air force attempting to bomb Gilgit while all the Scouts were away fighting. The story goes that the Indians were mocked by the Scouts' pipe band, whose members stood on the airfield throughout the raid, playing as loudly as they could.

The first war for Kashmir ended in January 1949, with a United Nations-sponsored ceasefire. Pakistan retained the Northern Areas (Gilgit, Hunza, Diamer and Baltistan) and Azad (Free) Kashmir, while India held the Kashmir Valley and Ladakh. The Kashmir question remains the core issue behind most of the disputes between India and Pakistan since Independence. The two countries declared war in 1965 and 1971, and in 1985 fighting flared again on the Siachen Glacier.

Until 1974 the seven feudal kingdoms along the Gilgit and Hunza rivers remained more or less autonomous, with the mirs or rajas in control of the administration, police and justice. Between 1972 and 1974, the Pakistani government relieved the kings of most of their powers, and the kingdoms became incorporated into Pakistan. The Northern Areas are now divided into five administrative districts: Diamer (administered from Chilas), Baltistan (Skardu), Ghanche (Khaplu), Ghizar (Gakuch) and Gilgit (Gilgit town, which is also the headquarters of the chief administrator of the Northern Areas). Hunza is part of Gilgit District, which has a population of 277,000—a threefold increase since Independence.

The referendum promised in 1947 was never held. Pakistan is loath to make the Northern Areas a province of Pakistan, as this could be construed as permanent acceptance of the ceasefire line. Officially, the region is called a 'federally administered area' and is looked after by a special ministry in Islamabad. Because of its sensitive position bordering China and Afghanistan—and a stone's throw across the Wakhan Corridor from the former Soviet Union—Pakistan has made a concerted effort to develop the area, improving the irrigation and road networks, building schools, hospital and medical centres, and developing training and marketing programmes. But signs painted on walls and rocks saying 'We want the vote' illustrate the underlying frustration of people barred, not only from voting, but also from appealing to the Pakistan Supreme Court. The people of the Northern Areas fought to join Pakistan, and now they feel excluded and exploited.

There is also smoldering religious tension. In May 1988, the Sunnis of Chilas attacked the Shias of Gilgit, ostensibly because the Shias finished the Ramazan month of fasting one day ahead of the Sunnis. Hundreds were killed. In November 1989, Sunnis again attacked Shias, leaving several dead.

GILGIT INFORMATION
WHEN TO GO
The wettest months are March, April and May; the driest June, October and November. That said, the average rainfall of about 130 millimetres per year is variable, and every month of the year has been without rainfall in at least one of the past 20 years. Passes over 5,000 metres are best attempted between mid-August and mid-September; lower treks are usually open from mid-June to mid-October. Walks in the main valley can be done all year round, though it is very hot in July.

GETTING TO GILGIT
By air: Three flights are scheduled most mornings from Islamabad to Gilgit at 7, 7.15 and 11.45. A one-way ticket for foreigners is US$40 if bought overseas and Rs461 if bought in Pakistan. Pakistanis fly for the subsidised price of Rs236. The flights go only in clear weather, so no firm bookings are made. You must reconfirm your flight the morning before at the PIA office in Rawalpindi (tel 67011, 66231). Be prepared for cancellations. The 70-minute flight is spectacular, with the 8,125-metre Nanga Parbat visible out the right side, towering above the twin-engine Fokker Friendship, which can fly no higher than 6,000 metres.

There is a flight from Skardu to Gilgit once a week at 12.40 pm on Sundays. Tickets cost US$40 if bought overseas or Rs329 if bought in Pakistan (or Rs170 for Pakistanis). The flight offers another spectacular fly-past of Nanga Parbat, this time out the left side.

PTDC reserves two priority seats on each flight for tourists, so if the flight is full apply to PTDC in Rawalpindi at Flashman's Hotel (tel 581480/4), in Skardu at the K2 Motel or in Gilgit at the Chinar Inn. Ask for a special booking for these reserved seats and get a note of confirmation to take back to PIA.

By road: It is often less frustrating just to get on a bus and go by road, especially if you are loaded down with trekking gear.

The journey from **Rawalpindi** to Gilgit is 603 kilometres, taking 15 hours.

NATCO (Northern Areas Transport Company, Rawalpindi tel 860283) runs buses to Gilgit at about 4 and 9 am and 1, 5 and 11 pm in summer (timings flexible); the fare is Rs90. The 4 am bus travels in daylight, making it marginally safer and allowing you to see the scenery. The 9 am bus is deluxe, with softer seats and a fare of Rs120. You can book your seats in advance; the best are numbers 1 and 2 for single travellers; for couples, 3 and 4, or 5 and 6.

Masherbrum Tours (Rawalpindi tel 863595) runs buses from Pir Wadhai Bus Station to Gilgit for Rs90 at about 2 and 4.30 pm. They also have two Toyota wagons, which are quicker and more comfortable and cost Rs120. These do not even pretend to run to a schedule—they leave when full. Buy your tickets from a man sitting on a chair at the east end of the station.

Sargin Travel Service and Prince Tours are reputed to run wagons to Gilgit from Saddar and Raja bazaars in Rawalpindi. Saeed buses leave from Raja Bazaar and are considered to be safer than NATCO.

Buses and wagons leave **Skardu** daily for the six- to eight-hour, 207-kilometre journey to Gilgit.

GILGIT TOWN

The **Tourist Information Centre** is in the Chinar Inn, PTDC hotel. **Habib Bank** and **Allied Bank** are in Saddar Bazaar by the Post Office, and **National Bank of Pakistan** is near the deputy commissioner's house off Bank Road. Banks are open 9 am–1 pm from Monday to Thursday and 9 am–12 pm on Saturday and Sunday. Closed on Friday. Sterling and US dollar travellers' cheques are accepted with identification.

The **Post Office** (GPO), in Saddar Bazaar, is open 8 am–2 pm from Saturday to Thursday. The **telephone and telegraph office** is in Upper Hospital Road, past the hospital on the right. It is open 24 hours, seven days a week. You can make international calls and send telegrams. The Gilgit telephone code is 0572.

District Hospital and **Ladies Hospital** occupy opposite sides of Hospital Road. Do not expect much. There are several private doctors. I can recommend Dr Ejaz Tahseen beside the Park Hotel, but if you know what you want, you do not need a prescription to buy drugs at any of the pharmacies. Know your medicines and read the labels—I was offered penicillamine in place of penicillin.

Gilgit is the only market town for hundreds of kilometres in every direction, and the **bazaar** is packed with traders every day except Friday. Good buys include Chinese silk and porcelain, irregularly shaped seed pearls, cashmere sweaters, garnets and rubies.

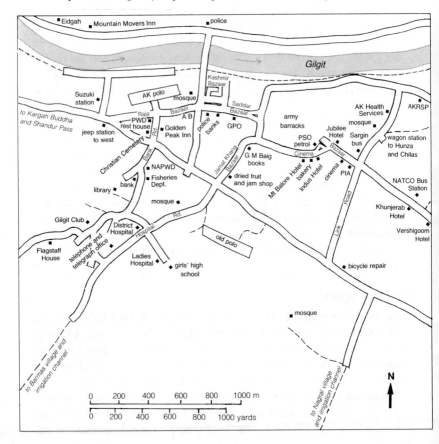

Trekkers will find all basic supplies in the grocery shops along Airport Road and in the fruit and vegetable market beside the big mosque: flour (*ata*), rice, lentils (*dhaal*— be sure to buy the quick-cooking kind—*mung dhaal*), sugar, powdered milk, Nestlé tinned cream, salt, tea, instant coffee, Ovaltine, Glucodin (disgusting), biscuits in good variety, curry powder, dried tomato, dried onion, garlic, ketchup, cooking oil, cornflakes, porridge oats, tinned peas, tinned sweet corn, tinned fruit, very strong tinned curry, packet soup (not recommended), spaghetti, potatoes, onions, cabbage, apples and lavatory paper. The best jam, honey and dried apricots are from Anwar Ali's Hunza Jam Shop in Jamat Khana Bazaar; Anwar Ali makes them himself using the best available ingredients.

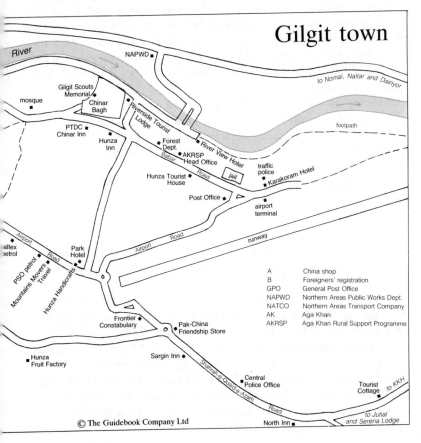

Gilgit town

River

NAPWD

to Nomal, Naltar and Dainyor

mosque

Gilgit Scouts Memorial

Chinar Bagh

Riverside Tourist Lodge

footpath

PTDC Chinar Inn

Hunza Inn

Forest Dept.

River View Hotel

AKRSP Head Office

Babar Road

jail

traffic police

Hunza Tourist House

Karakoram Hotel

Post Office

airport terminal

Airport Road

Road

runway

altex petrol
PSO petrol

Airport Road

Mountains Movers Travel

Park Hotel

Hunza Handicrafts

A	China shop
B	Foreigners' registration
GPO	General Post Office
NAPWD	Northern Areas Public Works Dept.
NATCO	Northern Areas Transport Company
AK	Aga Khan
AKRSP	Aga Khan Rural Support Programme

Frontier Constabulary

Pak-China Friendship Store

Hunza Fruit Factory

Sargin Inn

Shahrah-e-Quaid-e-Azam

Central Police Office

Tourist Cottage

to KKH

© The Guidebook Company Ltd

Road

North Inn

to Jutial and Serena Lodge

Dad Ali Shah's Hunza Handicrafts, beside the Park Hotel, often has dried camping food packs, but these are of uncertain date and may have instructions in such languages as Japanese. You can sometimes find climbing rope, harnesses, crampons, gaiters, boots, glacier glasses, sleeping bags, tents and primus stoves—all extremely cheap. He usually has a supply of camping gas, which is not cheap.

Small gas stoves and 25-kilogram gas 'bombs' are sometimes available by the Aga Khan Polo Ground. Try also opposite the mosque or near the dental clinic on the continuation of Pul Road.

All shapes and sizes of aluminium cooking pots, local kerosene cookers, metal plates, mugs, cutlery, plastic string and local rope (which is *not* suitable for climbing) are available in the hardware shops. You can sometimes find pressure cookers, but it is better to buy these in Islamabad or Rawalpindi (see page 67). Tarpaulins of all sizes, metal boxes, heavy sheet plastic and canvas stuff bags are sold in Kashmir Bazaar, where you can also find such porters' gear as rubber boots (about Rs20), socks, gloves, woolly hats, jackets and sunglasses.

You will also need aspirins and bandages for your porters.

Books and some maps relevant to the Northern Areas are usually available from Dad Ali Shah, of Hunza Handicrafts beside the Park Hotel, and from G M Beg bookstall in Jamat Khana Bazaar. G M Beg was killed in the Gilgit plane crash of August 1989, but his son has kept the shop going.

Renting equipment: Trekking agencies rent tents and equipment if they have any spare, so ask around.

TREKKING AGENCIES

Mountain Movers, Airport Road opposite Park Hotel; tel (0572) 2967. Musarat Wali Khan, the owner, is a Gilgit man, treks himself and is knowledgeable, charming and reliable.

Walji's Adventure Pakistan, Babar Road near the airport; tel (0572) 2663; also at Serena Lodge. Reputable, reliable and well organised, with good guides—but more expensive.

Adventure Center (Pvt) Ltd, PO Box 516, Gilgit; tel (0572) 2409; fax (92 572) 2409. Owner Ikram Beg runs the best bookshop in Gilgit (G M Beg bookstall) and is an experienced guide. A small company specialising in the Gilgit–Hunza area.

Himalaya Nature Tours, Gujal House, Riaz Road, Khomer Gilgit, or Silk Route Lodge, Gulmit; tel (0572) 2617; fax (92 51) 824245. Owned by Mirzada Shah Khan, an interesting prince from upper Hunza and well-known guide of the 1950s.

Pamir Tours, JSR Plaza; tel (0572) 3939.

Ashraf Aman, who runs Adventure Tours Pakistan, and Nazir Sabir, of Nazir Sabir Expeditions, are both Hunza men who know the area well. They have both climbed K2 and are extremely reliable but much in demand for big expeditions. Contact them in Islamabad. Karakoram Tours and Sitara have local offices in Gilgit on Airport Road but are best contacted in Islamabad and Rawalpindi.

Asif Khan, the PTDC tourist information officer at the Chinar Inn, knows his way round and can find guides. Dad Ali Shah, of Hunza Handicrafts in Airport Road beside the Park Hotel, knows some excellent, reliable guides and is a good source of information. Finally, ask in your hotel for suggestions.

HIRING JEEPS, GUIDES AND PORTERS

The official government rate for jeep hire in Gilgit on surfaced roads is Rs6 per mile plus a Rs150 overnight charge. The only surfaced road is the Karakoram Highway, so you need to compare prices and bargain for remote destinations. Jeeps are available from NATCO, PTDC, Mountain Movers, Adventure Pakistan, Park Hotel, Hunza Inn and several other hotels and in the bazaar. Ask around.

Ordinary **petrol** is available in Gilgit, Jaglot, Chitral, Chalt, Aliabad and Sost.

The government rate for porters in Gilgit and Hunza is Rs110 per stage plus Rs30 daily for food rations. See page 83 for hiring porters.

ACCOMMODATION

Hotel prices given below are for early 1992 and are meant to be a guideline for comparison between hotels. Prices rise proportionally, except when a hotel is renovated, in which case its prices jump.

MODERATE

Serena Lodge, Jutial, Gilgit; tel (0572) 2330/1 (s/d Rs850/1,100). Outside town with view of Dobani (Domani) Peak. Comparatively luxurious with videos and the best food in town, including an all-you-can-eat buffet for Rs65. Free shuttle Suzuki to town.

Chinar Inn, PTDC, Chinar Bagh; tel (0572) 2562 (s/d Rs450/550 plus tax). Central location, popular with tour groups, but overpriced.

Hunza Tourist House, Babar Road opposite jail; tel (0572) 2338 (s/d Rs300/450). New with excellent management, nice central garden, great food and bicycles for rent. Good meeting place.

Hunza Inn, Chinar Bagh; tel (0572) 2814, 3814 (d Rs120–450, dorm Rs50). Has peaceful central garden, maps, trekking information and good food. Popular with independent travellers and a great place to meet people.

Park, Airport Road; tel (0572) 2379, 2679 (d Rs300–400). Central, modern and noisy with no garden and nowhere to meet people. Good food but slow service.

Gilgit Alpine Motel, on main road near Serena Lodge; tel (0572) 3434 (s/d Rs250/350). New, too far out of town.

River View, on riverside near bridge; tel (0572) 3568, 3508 (d Rs350). Good site but bare, isolated and, with no transport, inconvenient for town. Camping allowed.

Riverside Tourist Lodge, Chinar Bagh (d Rs300). Calm, relaxed and friendly, with nice garden (cool in summer) beside the river. Good food, but isolated.

JSR, JSR Plaza, Airport Road; tel (0572) 3954, 3971 (s/d Rs250/350). Centre of town near PIA office but noisy and overpriced.

Mount Balore, Airport Road; tel (0572) 2709 (s/d 150/250). Convenient in centre of town, with large, quiet garden and helpful management. Guides and jeeps available. Camping allowed.

Sargin Inn, Shahrah-e-Quaid-e-Azam; tel 3538 (d Rs200). New, on main road into town and convenient for public transport.

Mountain Movers Inn, tel (0572) 2967. Other side of the river, west end of town. Belongs to Mountain Movers travel agent. Jeeps, guides and camping equipment available. Camping allowed.

Cheaper

Golden Peak Inn, Bank Road, Raja Bazaar; tel (0572) 3911 (d/t Rs80–120/120, dorm Rs35, tent Rs20). In the town house of the mir of Nagar, with shady walled garden where you can pitch your tent. Central, with relaxed management. Popular with backpackers and good meeting place.

Vershigoom Inn, Airport Road; tel (0572) 2991 (s/d Rs50–80/55–120). Central, with large courtyard and good food. Drab, but popular with backpackers.

Tourist Cottage, Jutial; tel (0572) 2376 (d Rs100, dorm Rs35). Scruffy and none too clean. Popular with down-and-outers.

Masherbrum Inn, Airport Road; tel (0572) 2711 (d Rp80–100). Seedy.

Jubilee, Airport Road; tel (0572) 2843 (s/d Rs80–120/100–200). Noisy and filthy.

Karakoram, opposite airport terminal (s/d/t Rs50/100/130). Convenient for the airport, but bottom of the list.

The NAPWD (Northern Areas Public Works Department) runs rest houses for government officials in Gilgit, Singal, Gakuch, Chatorkhand, Gupis, Yasin, Phundar, Teru, Nomal, Naltar, Chalt, Minapin, Karimabad and Nagar. If they are not full, tourists can use them for about Rs60 per double room. Book all rest houses through the Administrative Officer, NAPWD, Bank Road; tel (0572) 2515. He will give you a chit for the rest house *chowkidar* (guardian). Take your own food and bedding. You can usually camp in the gardens. Some of the remoter rest houses are just two rooms with a roof but not a stick of furniture, nor any cooking or toilet facilities. The best, like Phundar, are comparatively luxurious.

SHORT WALKS IN AND AROUND GILGIT

The **Kargah Buddha**, a rock carving beside the Kargah Nullah (stream) six kilometres west of Gilgit along the old road to Punial, is the most popular short outing from Gilgit. Take a public Suzuki (Rs2) west for 15 minutes from Gilgit, get out just before **Baseen** village, and walk up the old jeep track for about a kilometre (ten minutes) to a bridge across the Kargah Nullah. From here you can see the Buddha halfway up the cliff face on your left. The figure is about three metres tall and looks down protectively over Gilgit. To reach it, walk up the east (Gilgit) side of the stream for ten minutes on a rough path, then follow the irrigation channel round to the base of the cliff.

The Buddha was carved in the seventh century. A monastery and three stupas (solid domes, similar to chortens in Ladakh and Tibet) about 400 metres upriver from the Buddha, were excavated in 1938–39, following the discovery of the so-called Gilgit manuscripts in 1931. Written in Sanskrit, the manuscripts comprise Buddhist texts and documents that reveal the names and dates of some of the local rulers and various important pilgrims. More manuscripts were found in 1939 and 1956; all are now housed in museums in London, Delhi, Srinagar, Rome and Karachi.

The local legend about the Buddha tells of a man-devouring ogress called Yakhshini who lived at Kargah. The villagers asked a passing saint to help them get rid of her. The saint succeeded in pinning the ogress to the rock and told the villagers that she would be unable to escape during his lifetime or even following his death, if the villagers buried him at the foot of the rock. The people immediately killed the saint and buried him as instructed.

You can follow the irrigation channel to its source in the Kargah Valley and continue on a track along the Kargah Nullah for 17 kilometres to **Jut**. The U502 map NI 43-2 (Gilgit), which is unreliable in this corner, shows trails continuing for another 50 kilometres across the **Kali Pass** (over 4,000 metres) to the top end of the **Darel**

Valley and a further 30 kilometres down to the Indus at **Shatial**. The German archaeologist Karl Jettmar describes this as 'a very easy path', the main pilgrim route from Gilgit to Swat (see Jettmar, *Bolar and Dardistan*). The map shows the mountains in this area rising to about 5,000 metres and crisscrossed with trails.

Be warned, though, that the area is dangerous. The Kohistani tribesmen of Darel and Tangir have a ferocious reputation, and the police, who have no control over them, advise all outsiders—both Pakistani and foreign—to stay away. It is foolhardy to disregard the police warning, especially as there are more interesting hikes elsewhere. But, if you must trek here, go in a group of at least four, get advice, take a guide, and inform someone in Gilgit of your itinerary.

For your short walk from the Kargah Buddha, return to Gilgit along the irrigation channel, an easy two-hour stroll on a flat path through villages and farmland, with magnificent views down over Gilgit and the valley. The irrigation channel ends near the Serena Lodge, from where you can catch a Suzuki back to Gilgit for Rs2.

Jutial Nullah is behind the Serena Lodge. Like most valleys in the Northern Areas, Jutial has a very narrow mouth, but a six-kilometre walk along the stream, through the steep-sided gorge, takes you to coniferous forests and pastureland. Follow the irrigation channel behind the hotel to the cleft in the cliff face, then take the goat path into the gorge, keeping to the right of the stream. There are good campsites beside the stream.

The trail continues over the **Khomar Pass** (4,500 metres) to the **Pahot and Sai valleys**—eventually, after about 50 kilometres, meeting the Karakoram Highway at Jaglot. Several of the web of trails shown on the U502 map appear to cut straight south to Chilas. Remember, though, that this is a remote area and the dangers cited above are real.

The **Gilgit River** itself provides a pleasant walk. Follow the right (Gilgit) bank of the river for kilometres in either direction.

For the **Bagrot Valley**, entered from about 15 kilometres downriver of Gilgit town, see the Haramosh Valley (page 157). You can get from Gilgit to **Sinakkar**, the main village in the Bagrot Valley, in two hours by public bus from the bus stand, or by jeep from the Ghari Bagh jeep stand opposite the GPO.

SOUTH OF GILGIT

The Gilgit River flows into the Indus about 40 kilometres south of Gilgit. Here the Skardu road branches east to Baltistan following the upper Indus River, the dividing line between the Himalaya and Karakoram ranges. The river was there before the mountains, which have grown up on either side during the past 55 million years. From the junction of the Indus and Gilgit rivers (at about 1,300 metres, the lowest point of the Karakoram) you look south to magnificent views of the Nanga Parbat Massif, the western end of the Himalayan Range.

NANGA PARBAT—SOUTH SIDE

ASTOR VALLEY

The Astor Valley is the starting point for several treks east to the Deosai Plateau and south and west to Nanga Parbat. The annual rainfall here has averaged 501 millimetres over the past 25 years, about four times that of Gilgit. More than half the rain falls in March, April and May. June, July, September, November and December are the driest months.

NATCO runs daily **public jeeps** from Gilgit to Astor town, 112 kilometres away. The fare is Rs70, and the trip takes about six hours. Or you can hire a private jeep for about Rs1,200 returning empty. (We recommend that you bargain for the jeep to take you on to Rama.)

The Astor road leaves the Karakoram Highway at Jaglot, the last reliable source of diesel and petrol, 57 kilometres south of Gilgit. It crosses the Indus, giving superb views of Nanga Parbat, then winds up past the regimental headquarters of the Northern Light Infantry, goes through **Bunji** and follows the left bank of the Indus for ten kilometres, finally turning southeast to go up the Astor River.

The **Astor Gorge** is 30 kilometres long, with sheer sides. The new road was cut in the 1980s along a shelf in the cliff face far above the river. This was the nightmare section of the first route to Gilgit, a difficult trail from Srinagar over the Burzil Pass (4,200 metres), which was open only four months of the year. The British improved the route in the 1890s, building a mule trail through the gorge. They later bypassed the problem altogether by opening a new track from Rawalpindi over the Babusar Pass, making Gilgit more accessible.

Above the Astor Gorge the valley is wider, with tiny villages perched on either side of the river for the next 20 kilometres to Astor.

Nanga Parbat

Astor town is set above the road, to the right as you approach, at about 2,150 metres. This is a military post where foreigners must show passports and register. Consider the trekking options, clockwise from the east.

The **Parishing Valley** leads east from Astor across the **Banak Pass** (4,964 metres) to the **Deosai Plateau** (see page 109). A jeep road leads part of the way up the valley. We have not been there, but it looks interesting. More information is welcome.

At **Gurikot**, about ten kilometres south of Astor, a jeep road follows the fertile, wooded **Khirim Valley** for 40 kilometres to the army post at **Chilam** and continues across the **Deosai Plateau** to Skardu (see page 105).

The best-known treks from Astor lead west and southwest, to the east and south sides of **Nanga Parbat**. This huge mountain is not a single peak but a series of ridges culminating in an ice crest 8,125 metres high—ranked ninth highest in the world and second in Pakistan after K2. The name Nanga Parbat is Kashmiri for 'naked mountain', so called because some of its slopes are so steep that they are bare of snow or vegetation.

Early disasters on Nanga Parbat gave it the nick-name Killer Mountain or *mangeur d'homme*. Twelve climbers and 18 sherpas had died there by 1937. The monster was finally conquered in 1953 (one month after the ascent of Everest) by a joint Austrian-German expedition; Hermann Buhl made the final ascent in a gruelling 41-hour solo ordeal without oxygen. Today's death score is 47—far fewer than have lost their lives on Everest.

You can trek all the way round Nanga Parbat at about 3,500 metres, with passes rising to 5,300 metres. The three most famous treks are to Rama on the east side, the Rupal Valley on the south, and Fairy Meadows on the north. Adventure Pakistan (Walji's) claims to have guides who know the routes for the complete tour of the mountain, but we have not met anyone who has done it.

ASTOR TO RAMA

Map: Deutsche Himalaya Expedition map of Nanga Parbat, reliability excellent; U502 NI 43-2 (Gilgit), reliability good.
Open zone; easy; about three days; maximum height optional to about 3,800 metres; June to September.

Six kilometres up a steep jeep track west of Astor is Rama, a beautiful site at 3,150 metres that is good for at least two nights and should not be missed. There is no public jeep up, so your options are to hire a private jeep in Astor or walk.

The road to Rama runs up from Astor's main bazaar and winds west across green, rolling fields, which in July are knee deep in flowers—purple clover, geraniums, mint and thyme, blue cornflowers and several varieties of orchid. The slopes above are thickly forested with huge pine, fir, cedar and juniper trees. Rama Rest House, bookable through the Forestry Department in Rawalpindi or Gilgit, stands on the edge of a wide field that is covered in edelweiss, with a stream flowing through, a helipad in the centre and forest all around—the perfect campsite.

The steep jeep track continues for about another four kilometres, if not blocked by landslides, stopping a few kilometres short of **Rama (Sango) Lake**, at 3,482 metres. From here you can trek up the Sachen Glacier on the east face of Chongra Mountain (part of the Nanga Parbat Massif) for magnificent views in all directions. The shepherds are welcoming, and you can buy from them butter, yogurt and cheese.

RUPAL VALLEY: UP AND BACK OR
OVER MAZENO PASS TO DIAMER

Map: Deutsche Himalaya Expedition map of Nanga Parbat, reliability excellent; U502 NI 43-2 (Gilgit), reliability good.
Open zone; easy to strenuous; four to fourteen days; maximum height optional from about 4,000 to 5,377 metres; June to September (August is best for Mazeno Pass).

This is a popular trek offered by international trekking companies. It can be an easy week, recommended for beginners, with two days at Rama followed by a four-day round-trip hike up the Rupal Valley to about 4,000 metres and back, with no guide needed. Or you can continue across the Mazeno Pass (5,377 metres), a strenuous trek requiring rope, crampons and a fully equipped professional guide.

From Astor, the jeep road continues south for 28 kilometres up the Astor River to Tarashing, the beginning of the Rupal Valley trek. There is no regular public jeep service, but if you have time to wait you will probably find something heading that way. Otherwise, you can book a private jeep for Rs300–500 from Astor. A private jeep from Gilgit to Tarashing costs about Rs 1,500, returning empty.

Guides, porters, donkeys and horses are readily available at Tarashing, with no need to book in advance.

From Tarashing you can either continue directly west up the Rupal Valley or take an extra day to do another recommended side trip, north up the **Chungphar Valley**, for a four-hour hike to the shepherds' summer settlements on the south flank of Chongra Mountain and back.

Stage 1: Tarashing to Bazhin, four hours. The trail climbs steeply from Tarashing (2,911 metres) up the lateral moraine of the Tarashing Glacier, then crosses the glacier in 30 minutes along a clear path. **Rupal**, on the other side, is a large settlement with a lower and an upper village, each surrounded by fields of wheat, barley, beans, peas and potatoes. The people of **Lower Rupal** originated from Baltistan and still speak a form of Balti mixed with Shina. The women wear Balti headdresses—decorated with silver beads and buttons and a brown felt tail hanging down the back—reminiscent of headdresses in Ladakh.

Upper Rupal has two compact villages, the houses so close together that a laden donkey cannot pass between them. Here the people are Gujars, and the women wear round pill-box hats covered with veils. The two settlements of Upper Rupal are completely closed up in summer, when the inhabitants all move further up the valley with the herds to summer pastures. The houses are half underground, with round, excavated food stores nearby. In winter the snow is more than a metre deep, so everyone stays indoors for three months.

The first good campsite, until after the harvest, is beyond Upper Rupal, two hours from Tarashing. If necessary, you could camp in the school yard in Lower Rupal.

From Rupal, the path climbs steadily up a narrow green valley, through groves of willow, poplar and juniper. The mountainside is covered in forget-me-nots, lavender and edelweiss. After about two hours you pass a small lake and round a corner to Bazhin Camp (about 3,650), a flat, green meadow between the lateral moraine of the **Bazhin Glacier** and the mountain. Ahead towers the solid ice wall of the east face of Nanga Parbat. This is a perfect campsite—sheltered and with clear spring water, a wood full of birds and a moraine covered in primulas, thyme and other flowers.

Stage 2: Bazhin Camp to Shaigiri, five hours. Crossing the Bazhin Glacier takes about 90 minutes along a fairly obvious donkey path. The local shepherds come and go frequently, so you can follow one of them across. From the top of the lateral moraine on the western side, you look down on a huge grassy field known as **Tup** (about 3,550 metres), which must once have been the bed of a lake. Herds of horses, dzos, sheep and goats graze in the centre, and five or six summer villages are spaced round the edge. The Rupal River flows down the far side through willow and juniper woods, and a gentle stream meanders along the near side.

The summer villagers are friendly to female trekkers. Most of them are Sunni Muslims from Chorit and are not at all camera shy. They wear round pill-box hats, churn their butter in goatskins and spin sheep wool while they sit and chat, offering bread and buttermilk (*lassi*) to visitors.

The clear trail continues up the Rupal River, offering a flat walk through sparse woods. It takes about an hour to skirt round the end of a terminal moraine to a smaller flat field called **First Base Camp**. The spot is also called Herligkoffer Base Camp, after the German mountaineering organiser who has led eight expeditions to Nanga Parbat, including the first ascent by Herman Buhl in 1953. A further hour takes you round the end of a second moraine, with a lake on top, to another broad field, Latboi (meaning 'stony place'), also called **Second Base Camp**, with a summer settlement on one side. From here the path climbs gently over some moraine, then follows the north bank of the river through the woods to Shaigiri (meaning 'white stone') 30 minutes away. This is a good campsite at about 3,660 metres, with fresh water, firewood and superb views of the south face of Nanga Parbat, an awesome jagged precipice 4,500 metres high. The summer settlement at Shaigiri belongs to Tarashing people of Balti descent, strict Shia Muslims who are reasonably friendly to female trekkers but very wary of cameras. Organised treks are usually expected to buy a goat at Shaigiri and have a feast and singsong with their porters.

Stage 3: Rest day to explore or climb. **Rupal Peak** (5,584 metres), to the south of Shaigiri, is a difficult climb for trekkers but comparatively easy for mountaineers. It offers magnificent views north across the valley to Nanga Parbat. Doug Scott climbed it from the west and describes three bivouacs and some grade-3 ice climbing.

Stage 4: Shaigiri to Mazeno Pass Base Camp, three to five hours. The path follows the northern lateral moraine of the **Toshain (Rupal) Glacier** with views back to Leila and Rupal peaks on one side and Nanga Parbat on the other. The camp, in a green meadow at about 4,200 metres, with a bubbling stream and dried juniper bushes, looks down on Toshain Glacier, a 20-kilometre-long, two-kilometre-wide snake that fills the whole head of the valley.

Stage 5: Mazeno Pass Base Camp to Mazeno High Camp, four to six hours. The track turns north and climbs steadily up to the lateral moraine of the **Mazeno Glacier**, which descends gently from the clear V of the Mazeno Pass. The surrounding mountains are capped with gleaming fields of snow. Camp at about 4,700 metres on a flat, stony site with a stream about five kilometres before the pass.

Stage 6: Mazeno High Camp across Mazeno Pass to Upper Loiba, six to nine hours. The climb up is not difficult, except that the altitude is 5,377 metres. The other side is a steep drop of about 300 metres (requiring rope and crampons) down the difficult **Loiba Glacier**, which is white for a short way, then covered in gravel and rocks. Camp at Upper Loiba at about 4,200 metres.

Stage 7: Upper Loiba to Loiba Meadows, two to four hours. This is a lovely easy descent to birch woods and lush green meadows, with shepherds' settlements and herds of dzos, sheep and goats. From here you can look south up the Airi Glacier. Camp at about 4,000 metres.

Stage 8: First option, down to Zangot, about four hours.

Second option, take a two-day side trek up to the **Diamer face** (west face) of Nanga Parbat.

Third option, continue on a tour of Nanga Parbat by crossing the Kachal and Juliper passes to **Fairy Meadows** (see Fairy Meadows trek, page 180). Adventure Pakistan has a guide who knows this route.

Our choice here is the Diamer face.

First day: Loiba Meadows to Kachal, three to five hours. A lovely trek down through willow, pine and birch woods with good views of Nanga Parbat, then across the Airi River and east up through pastureland and some fields of potatoes and barley to Kachal, an isolated settlement at the foot of the **Kachal Pass**, where you camp below 3,000 metres. The Kachal Pass, about 4,400 metres, crosses to **Zangal**, from where you can either go down to the Karakoram Highway or continue over the Juliper Pass.

Second day: up to Diamer Base Camp, four to six hours. This is a steady climb along a stream up through birch woods, past towering rock faces to the fertile shepherds' settlement at **Kutgali**. From here it is another two to three hours to Diamer Base Camp. A F Mummery disappeared on the Diamer Glacier in 1895 on his first Himalayan expedition. Reinhold Messner lost his brother Gunther here after their successful ascent in 1970. Gunther was killed on the way down by an ice avalanche. Camp at 4,100 metres.

Stage 9: Zangot to Halala or Dimroi, four hours. This is a hot, steep, barren walk down the Diamer River to its junction with the Bunar River, where you join the jeep track. If there is no jeep available, it is a further four-hour walk down the Bunar River to the Karakoram Highway, from where you can hitchhike west to Chilas or east to Gilgit. (Stages 4–9 were contributed by Ashraf Aman and Haroon Pirzada. The descriptions and timings are not reliable, so please send more information.)

Chilas to Diamer Base Camp and back makes an excellent six- to eight-day trek.

NANGA PARBAT—NORTH SIDE

Access to the Nanga Parbat circuit trek from the Karakoram Highway is from three points: Raikot Bridge, the Patro Valley and the Buner Valley. Be warned that these treks are in Diamer (pronounced 'Dee-ah-mer') District, where the Kohistani people have a foul reputation for murder, theft and general surliness. Register with the police in Chilas before setting out, and tell them your plans. We recommend that you take a good professional guide with you, having made sure he really has been there. Ask for advice in Gilgit at Mountain Movers and Adventure Pakistan.

The trek from Raikot Bridge to Tato and Fairy Meadows is the most popular, but to continue the tour of Nanga Parbat in clockwise direction, we describe the points of access from west to east.

From the **Bunar Valley**, there are several trekking possibilities. The trail due south up the Bunar and Barai rivers leads in about 40 kilometres to **Barai**, thence another 40 kilometres over the **Barai Pass** (about 4,250 metres) and down to the **Neelam Valley** at **Kel**. This is close to the Indian frontier, where a permit is needed. Another alternative is a trail west from Dimroi across the **Shatuche Pass** (3,800 metres) to **Niat**.

To get to the start of the trek, take a public bus or Suzuki from Gilgit to Bunar, about 110 kilometres away, and enquire about public jeeps up the Bunar Valley. You may have to hire a private jeep in Chilas. A jeep road runs from Bunar at least ten kilometres up the Bunar Valley to **Dimroi** and **Halala**, where the Diamer River joins the Bunar. For Halala to Zangot, Kachal and the trail round Nanga Parbat, see the Mazeno Pass trek above.

PATRO VALLEY OVER JULIPER PASS TO FAIRY MEADOWS

Map: U502 NI 43-2 (Gilgit), reliability fair; from the top of the Patro Valley on (beginning with Stage 4), you can use the better Deutsche Himalayan Expedition map of Nanga Parbat. Open zone; strenuous; about ten days; maximum height 4,837 metres; August to mid-September.

Stage 1: Gilgit to Patro Valley. Take a public bus or Suzuki from Gilgit to **Gunar**, a check post with a police fort about 100 kilometres south of Gilgit along the Karakoram Highway (KKH), or 20 kilometres downriver from Raikot Bridge. Arrange porters at Gunar and, if possible, hire a private jeep to take you to the shepherds' huts high above the Patro valley. This poor jeep road leaves the KKH five kilometres upriver of Gunar, beyond the bridge across the Patro River. It would take you several hours to get there on foot, and the Indus Gorge is a burning, shadeless furnace in June, July and August. The huts have no water nearby in August, and it is an hour's walk down to the river and back—not the ideal campsite.

Stage 2: Pasture to Zangal, five to six hours. Start early to climb the steep ridge immediately behind the shepherds' huts while it is still in the shade. The path zigzags for two hours to the ridge, for your first view of the snowy shoulder of Nanga Parbat. A clear track follows the ridge up for another 90 minutes to the top of a barren, bleak hill, with the Patro River deep in a gorge below on the right. Follow a flat trail along the west side of Patro Valley, through barren landscape (some green fields are visible far ahead upriver). A further 90 minutes takes you to the first wooded area, around the village of Zangal. You will see a small spring just below the path before the first houses—the first water since you left the Indus. Camp near Zangal.

Stage 3: Zangal to Lower Khusto, five to six hours. Follow the Patro Valley, crossing several side streams and walking through pine forest and past villages with fields of barley, maize and vegetables. After three to four hours, you come out of the forest into summer pastures with magnificent views of Ganalo Peak straight ahead. Pass another shepherds' settlement, and climb another steep slope to arrive at Lower Khusto, a high pasture with streams and an ideal campsite at about 3,500 metres. A rest day to acclimatise is recommended here. You can take a magnificent two- to three-hour walk carpeted with flowers up to the terminal moraine of the Patro Glacier. Switch here to the Deutsche Himalaya Expedition map.

Stage 4: Lower Khusto to Juliper Pass Base Camp, six hours. An impressive waterfall tumbles down behind the camp. Climb steeply up the ridge beside the waterfall to above the tree-line, keeping the waterfall on your right. There are fantastic flowers in early August. Pass two settlements of shepherds' huts in which everyone is cheerful and friendly. After about three hours come to a small lake with another waterfall—a good spot for a picnic and swim at over 4,000 metres. Continue up a small stream for two more hours to a high bowl surrounded by snow-covered peaks with no obvious exit. Camp at about 4,400 metres, where it is cold at night, even in August. Catch the magnificent view of **Ganalo Peak** (6,608 metres) and, on either side of the pass, North (5,245 metres) and South (5,206) **Juliper peaks**. If you are a mountaineer and have crampons, an ice axe and a guide, you can climb South Juliper Peak from here, up and back in eight to ten hours.

Stage 5: Across Juliper Pass (4,837 metres), five to six hours. Juliper Pass is not obvious between North and South Juliper peaks, so you need a guide to point out the right place to head for. The first one or two hours is a steep and dangerous climb over huge boulders, then up more steeply over smaller, loose rocks to a big snowfield on the pass. You can avoid the snow by keeping on the rocks to the left. From the top there is a superb view of the whole Nanga Parbat group. The descent is steep and slippery on moving rocks for one hour, continuing to grassy pastures and a stream, which leads you down past willow shrubs and birch woods to the bottom of the Raikot Valley (misspelled Rakhiot on most maps). It is a very steep three to four hours from the top of the pass to **Beel Camp** (which some porters call Old Fairy Meadows) at about 3,500. It is only 90 minutes from here down to Fairy Meadows, but Beel is less crowded. From the campsite, it is a ten-minute walk up on the opposite side from Juliper Pass, through a birch wood to the top of a cliff, which offers a fantastic view down onto the Raikot Glacier. The glacier flows down from Nanga Parbat, which is framed in a V. Go carefully, as you come through the trees very suddenly to the edge of the cliff.

Stage 6: Up to Nanga Parbat Base Camp, three hours. This is a very enjoyable walk up the tree-covered Raikot Valley along a clear path, some of it through pastures, with views of Raikot Peak. Slide steeply down the lateral moraine to the glacier on an obvious path and cross a small glacier coming from the right. A clear track goes up a steep slope to a flat meadow, full of marmots and flowers and surrounding an enormous rock, to **Old Base Camp**. Climb another half hour to Drexel's Monument, built at 3,967 metres in honour of the many German climbers killed on Nanga Parbat. In 1934, four Germans (including Willi Merkl, Karl Herligkoffer's step-brother) and six porters died in a storm, and in 1937, seven climbers and nine porters were buried alive by an avalanche that covered their camp. Just behind the monument is an edelweiss-filled meadow, also called Base Camp, with fresh water springing from under a huge rock and a magnificent view of the three Chongra peaks, Raikot Peak (7,074 metres), Diamer Gap (also known as Silver Saddle), and Ganalo Peak (6,608 metres). Many old hands say it is the best mountain view they have ever seen, and it is certainly a good place to stay and explore for two or three days.

Day walk to the Great Moraine, four to six hours. To the right of camp is a steep, narrow ridge with a path along the top leading up to Camp 1. Superb views all along the walk make you feel you can touch Nanga Parbat. Continue past Camp 1, up and over a ridge, accompanied by the thundering of avalanches and falling seracs all the while. It was above Camp 1 (4,468 metres) that the avalanche of 1937 killed the seven climbers and nine porters. Descend to Base Camp on the opposite side from the ascent.

Those with climbing experience and equipment can climb Buldar Peak (5,602 metres) in two days.

Stage 7: Down to Fairy Meadows. Backtrack down to Beel Camp and continue down along a clear path to Fairy Meadows, with superb views behind you all the way.

Fairy Meadows is a big clearing that used to be surrounded by thick forest. It was perhaps the most magical and scenic of all of Pakistan's beauty spots, but is fast being spoiled. Brigadier Muhammad Aslam, owner of the Shangrila chain of hotels, has built a road up to Fairy Meadows. The villagers have sold him the forests for a pittance, and he will soon have stripped the area. There are no serious plans for reforestation.

Below the meadow and hidden in the woods is a lake good for swimming. From here, Nanga Parbat looks even bigger than from Base Camp. Camp anywhere on the meadow at about 3,200 metres.

Stage 8: Fairy Meadows to Tato. The jeep road begins at Fairy Meadows, but you can walk down all the way through lovely scenery reminiscent of Nepal, past the settlement of Fairy Meadows, which is surrounded by fields, irrigation channels and mills, then down a steep, zigzag path from the ridge, with Raikot Glacier ending on your right. Join a side valley coming down from the left—a possible campsite. The valley narrows before Tato, which is still a two- to three-hours walk. If you are walking all of the way, you can camp in front of the school at 2,585 metres (guard your gear from theft). There are hot springs in a small, attractive village 30 minutes down the old path on Buldar Ridge, and this makes a good afternoon walk.

Stage 9: Tato to Raikot Bridge, four hours if you walk all the way down the jeep road. (Information from Elisabeth Gardner.)

SOUTH OF GILGIT • **183**

RAIKOT BRIDGE TO FAIRY MEADOWS AND BACK

Map: Deutche Himalayan Expedition map of Nanga Parbat, reliability excellent; U502 NI 43-2 (Gilgit), reliability fair.

Open zone; easy; minimum four days; maximum height optional between 4,000 and 5,200 metres; June to September (August to September for higher altitudes).

Stage 1: Gilgit to Raikot Bridge and on to Tato. Take any vehicle from Gilgit down the KKH for about 90 kilometres to Raikot Bridge. Just beyond the bridge is a Shangrila Hotel (s/d Rs500/650, book in Rawalpindi; tel 73006 or 72948). From here the hotel owner, Brigadier Muhammad Aslam, has built a private jeep road to Fairy Meadows. It is worthwhile renting a private jeep to either Tato or the end of the jeep road, as the walk up is steep and extremely hot. There are no porters, guides or jeeps available at Raikot Bridge, but you can hire men at the nearest village, five kilometres away towards Chilas, near the hot springs and the truck stop. If you are walking, camp at Tato at 2,585 metres (see above).

Stage 2: Tato to Fairy Meadows, three to five hours. Two to three hours from Tato is the first Fairy Meadows village, a green meadow with trees, shepherds' huts, running water and a view of Nanga Parbat. It takes one or two more hours from here to Fairy Meadows. For the many trekking possibilities from Fairy Meadows, see above.

FAIRY MEADOWS TO ASTOR

Map: Deutche Himalayan Expedition map of Nanga Parbat, reliability excellent; U502 NI 43-2 (Gilgit), reliability fair.

Open zone; strenuous; maximum height 4,965 metres; August to September.

It is possible to complete the circuit of Nanga Parbat by trekking east to the village of **Muthat** on the **Buldar River**, then following the river up to the Buldar Glacier and crossing the **Muthat Pass** (4,965 metres). Descend to the **Lotang Glacier** and follow it down to a point where you can get across the **Rama Ridge** to **Rama** and Astor. Adventure Pakistan has a guide who knows the route, or perhaps you can find a shepherd in Muthat to show the way.

A second path from Muthat leads over to **Doian** on the Gilgit-to-Astor road. This was the route taken by the 1932 German expedition from Srinagar, which crossed the Burzil Pass to Astor before crossing from Doian to Fairy Meadows.

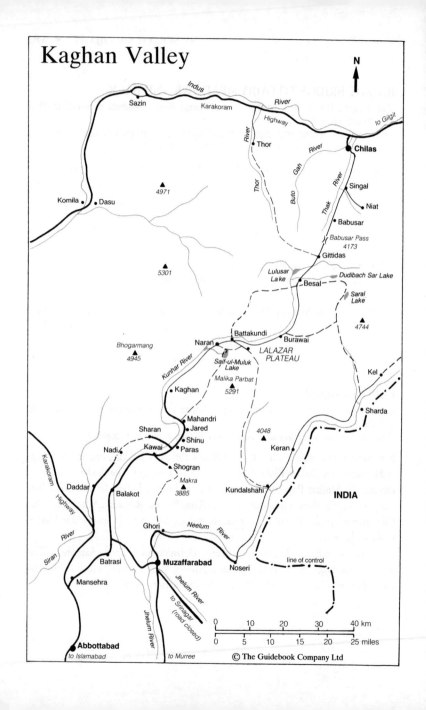

CHILAS, KAGHAN AND AZAD KASHMIR

Chilas, the capital of Diamer District (pronounced 'Dee-ah-mer'), is three kilometres south of the Karakoram Highway (KKH), out of sight of the road. A jeep track leads over the Babusar Pass (4,173 metres) to the Kaghan Valley, making Chilas the starting point for many highly recommended treks around the Kaghan Valley and across the various passes connecting Kaghan and Azad Kashmir.

Most confusingly, there is no Kaghan River. The Kunhar River drains the Kaghan Valley, and it is the insignificant village of Kaghan, 60 kilometres from Balakot (not even marked on the U502 map), that gives its name to the whole valley.

Trekking in the 160-kilometre-long Kaghan Valley is for those who love flowers, who like to walk through green mountain pastures at 4,000 metres and camp by turquoise lakes undiscovered by other tourists. Sandwiched between the Indus Valley and Kashmir, the Kaghan Valley falls just inside the monsoon belt, so it is green and forested, in vivid contrast to the barren Indus Valley. Expect rain most afternoons in August, but trekking here is cooler than in the dry valleys further north.

The mountains surrounding Kaghan range in height from 4,500 to 5,000 metres; the passes between the mountains are all around 4,000 metres. The only people you encounter are Gujar herders and their families living in summer settlements—curiously marked as ruins on the U502 map, perhaps because, in winter, the stone huts are deserted. Herds of horses, donkeys, sheep and goats—as well as the occasional camel—graze in knee-deep grass amid blue delphiniums.

Most of the treks we recommend are to the east of the Kaghan Valley, threading back and forth across the many passes connecting the Kaghan and Neelum valleys. A guide or some knowledge of Urdu is recommended, so you can ask directions and avoid wandering down to the Neelum Valley in the closed zone near the ceasefire line with India. For treks to the west, see Kohistan (page 197).

Warning: We have not trekked northeast from the Babusar Pass to either Niat or Bunar. As the Kohistani herders who wander in this area from July to October have a reputation for violence, you are advised not to walk there. If you must, inform the local police and take reliable porters with you.

CHILAS TOWN

Chilas was an important junction on the ancient trade route. Because of the fierce independence and violent fanaticism of the Chilas people, the British left them alone until the 1890s, when they built the new, shorter track across the Babusar Pass, directly connecting Gilgit and British India. Before this the only route to Gilgit had been the difficult track from Srinagar via the Burzil Pass and Astor Gorge. In 1893, the hostile Chilas tribes rose against the small garrison of Kashmiri soldiers and British officers stationed in Chilas, and a savage battle ensued. The British only just managed to quell the uprising. The Babusar road was the main route to Gilgit from the 1930s until 1978, when the KKH was opened.

Transport: There are several wagons daily from Gilgit to Chilas town for a fare of about Rs30. Otherwise take any vehicle down the KKH. Get off at the police checkpost at the turning up to the town, and hitchhike the three kilometres up to the bazaar. Register with the police as soon as you arrive.

Accommodation: Chilas town is a barren, dirty furnace in summer. If possible avoid spending the night unless you can get into the new NAPWD rest house (d Rs60), which is situated on a small road out the west side of town and has large rooms and a fine view. Book ahead in Gilgit (see page 170), as it is often full. Otherwise there are six hotels in the main bazaar, all charging about Rs80 per double. The Khunjerab has the best food and helpful management. Its small, airless rooms are ranged round a narrow courtyard. Men can sleep on *charpoys* (rope beds) on the roof for Rs10, but women must sleep indoors. Down on the KKH are four overpriced hotels: the Shangrila Midway House, tel Chilas 69 (s/d Rs500/650), the Chilas Inn (d Rs400), the New Shimla (d Rs180) and Al Kashmir (d Rs180).

The best sights in Chilas are the hundreds of **rock carvings** along the Indus below the town—a fair sampling of the 20,000 petroglyphs that are concentrated at ten major sites between Hunza and Shatial.

These are best seen early in the morning or late in the afternoon to avoid the heat. One of the more interesting groups is down a jeep track near the check post, just west of the Shangrila Midway House, and another is down the jeep track leading to the bridge to Thalpan, just east of the petrol station. The best carvings face the river.

The carvings were left by various invaders, traders and pilgrims who passed along the trade route, as well as by locals. The earliest date back to between 5000 and 1000 BC, showing single animals, triangular men and hunting scenes in which the animals are larger than the hunters. These carvings were pecked into the rock with stone tools and are covered with a thick patina that proves their age.

Later carvings, from about 500 BC, show the lifelike leopards and antelopes of the Scythians or Sakas, Iranian nomads of the first millennium BC. The best carvings of this period are on the north bank, across the Thalpan bridge, on so-called Altar Rock. A warrior with a huge knife slaughters a goat; his dress and pose are typical of the Persians of the Achaemenid Empire, who ruled this area from 516 BC. On the same rock another figure seems to be dancing, and a third strides ahead with a lowered lance. Nearby a delicately drawn horse with a tassled mane bends one knee in a typical pose for the period. Though there has never been deer in this area, a stag is depicted pursued by a predator with a small head and two hooked tails. On the Chilas side of the river, there is a realistic carving of an ibex being chased by a snow leopard.

The Parthians (first century AD) drew warriors on horseback. In Kushan times (second to fifth centuries) Buddhism was brought by missionaries on their way north to China, and, in the centuries that followed, Chinese pilgrims came to Pakistan to visit the Buddhist shrines. There are thousands of drawings of Buddhas and Buddhist stupas (solid domes) dating mostly from the sixth century and accompanied by inscriptions in various languages—Sogdian, Tibetan, Kharoshthi and Brahmi—reflecting the anxiety with which pious pilgrims approached their difficult journeys along the Indus. Many inscriptions give the date, destination and purpose of the journey.

The archaeologist Karl Jettmar has pieced together the history of the area from the various inscriptions and recorded his findings in *Rockcarvings and Inscriptions in the Northern Areas of Pakistan* and the newly released *Between Gandhara and the Silk Roads—Rock Carvings Along the Karakoram Highway*.

BABUSAR OVER BABUSAR PASS TO BESAL

Map: U502 NI 43-2 (Gilgit) and NI 43-6 (Srinagar), reliability good in Kaghan and Azad Kashmir, reliability very poor in Indus Kohistan.
Open zone; easy; one day (four days from Babusar to Naran); maximum height 4,173 metres; June to October (July to October by jeep).

The jeep road from Chilas to the Babusar Pass is safe, but beware of the side valleys. Once across the Babusar Pass and into Kaghan, in the North-West Frontier Province, you will be with Kaghani people and Gujar nomads (see page 37), who are safe and reliable.

Public jeeps and NATCO trucks run several trips daily from Chilas to Babusar (2,800 metres), the last permanent village, 13 kilometres before the Babusar Pass. The 37-kilometre journey costs about Rs20. You can hire a private jeep from

Chilas to Babusar for about Rs600. You may want to consider renting one for about Rs1,200 to Lulusar Lake or Besal (3,355 metres), about 15 kilometres beyond the pass.

Just a few kilometres above Chilas, you enter the edge of the monsoon belt, which experiences rain from the end of July to beginning of September. The valley is wide, fertile, green and wooded—though, as elsewhere, trees are being cut at an alarming rate with no apparent effort to replant.

Public jeeps across the pass are rare, but in one long day you can walk across to **Besal**, about 25 kilometres from Babusar, and pick up a public jeep from there to Naran for about Rs50.

It takes four long days to walk all the way from Babusar to Naran, following the jeep road most of the way (there are much more interesting things to do in Kaghan). The traditional stopping places are Besal, Burawai (about 20 kilometres from Besal) and Battakundi (about 13 kilometres from Burawai and 16 kilometres from Naran). You do not need camping equipment, as you can rent a *charpoy* for about Rs10 in the *chai-khanas* in each village. Battakundi also has a good youth hostel, and there are PWD rest houses at Battakundi and Burawai, which charge Rs50 a night.

If you hire porters in Babusar, it is probably best to send them back from Besal and hire Kaghan men from there, as Babusar men are not welcome in Kaghan, do not speak the language (Hindko) and are unlikely to know their way up the side valleys. If you need a guide, your best bet is to go on to Naran by jeep and hire one there.

The footpath across the Babusar Pass is open from about June, though there will still be snow most of the way, making it wise to hire a villager to show the way. The winter path keeps to the left of the valley, while the jeep road and summer footpath are more to the right. It is seven kilometres to the top by the footpath. Dervla Murphy, the intrepid Irish travel writer, carried her bicycle across in April 1964 and almost came to grief (see Murphy, *Full Tilt*). An English student was killed in June 1987 when he lost his balance and fell over a cliff from the jeep road, which was then thick with snow.

The walk is relatively easy, taking you up through what is left of the pine forest and across pastures to the flat, stony top of the pass. Views are of rolling hills covered in yellow ragwort (*Senecio*), pink bistort, blue delphiniums, edelweiss and countless other flowers reaching to distant white peaks. To see Nanga Parbat, you must hike for a couple of kilometres east along the ridge from the top of the pass. The police in Babusar asked us (two women—Ben was in China) not to camp there. If you are a larger group with men it is safer, but there is no water on the ridge.

The summer settlement of **Gittidas**, about seven kilometres south of the top of the pass and occupied from July to September, has a bad reputation. The police advised us not to camp before **Lulusar Lake** (3,355 metres), about 11 kilometres south of Gittidas. The lake is three kilometres long, with miniature icebergs floating in its brilliant turquoise waters. The banks, covered in delphiniums, slope too steeply for camping until the southern end, where a flattish shoulder is the only possible site. There is no habitation nearby. About two kilometres further down is **Besal**, a cluster of stone houses at 3,266 metres, still above the tree-line and abandoned in mid-winter. Besal has a shop and *chai-khana* where you can spend a smoky night for about Rs10.

NARAN

The tourist capital of Kaghan, Naran (about 2,500 metres) is easily accessible from Islamabad and Rawalpindi. Because of the difficulty of finding guides elsewhere in Kaghan, we describe all travel and trekking from here.

The best guide in Naran is Muhammad Bashir, son of Muhammad Zaman. He stayed with us for ten days and is a joy—efficient, honest, tactful, charming and knowledgable about all the treks described here. His is a common name, though, so check his references to be sure that you have the right one.

Transport: Several buses leave Pir Wadhai Bus Station in Rawalpindi daily for Mansehra, a four-hour journey costing about Rs15. The Flying Coach leaving from Murree Road, and the wagons leaving from The Mall, take about three hours and cost Rs20. Change at Mansehra and head for Balakot (the administrative capital of the Kaghan), a one-hour journey costing about Rs6 by bus or Rs10 by wagon. Plying daily between Balakot and Naran (82 kilometres) are several buses (fare Rs16), Datsun wagons (Rs30) and jeeps (Rs40). There are plenty of private jeeps for hire in Balakot and Naran. Daily public jeeps in summer continue up the valley to Besal, about 18 kilometres south of the Babusar Pass. A public jeep from Naran to Besal costs about Rs50, a private jeep about Rs600. A private jeep from Naran to the Babusar Pass costs about Rs1,000, to Babusar village Rs1,200.

Accommodation: The Kaghan Valley is popular in summer and therefore crowded. Balakot is the pits, so we recommend that you head straight for Naran, or at least try to get as far as Mahandri, the end point of the trek briefly described below, where you will find a rest house and some small hotels. If you absolutely must stay in Balakot, there are several small hotels. Or try the Park (s/d 300/400) or the PTDC Motel (s/ d 400/500). The youth hostel near the PTDC Motel costs Rs10 per bed.

In Naran we recommend camping on the riverbank above the town or trying one of the small local hotels offering *charpoys* for Rs15–20. The best, with good food for

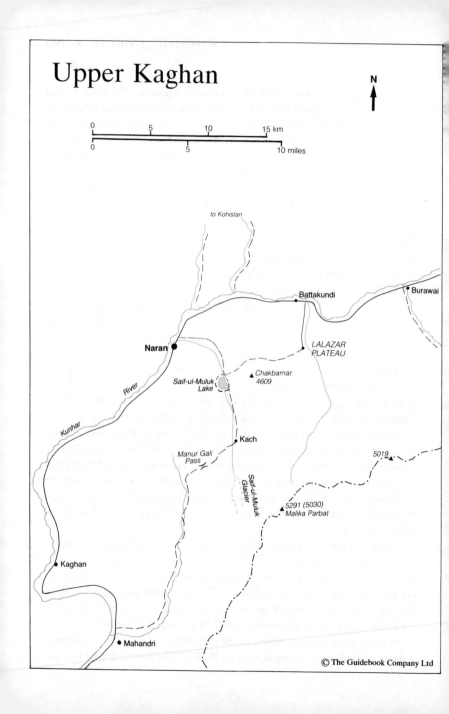

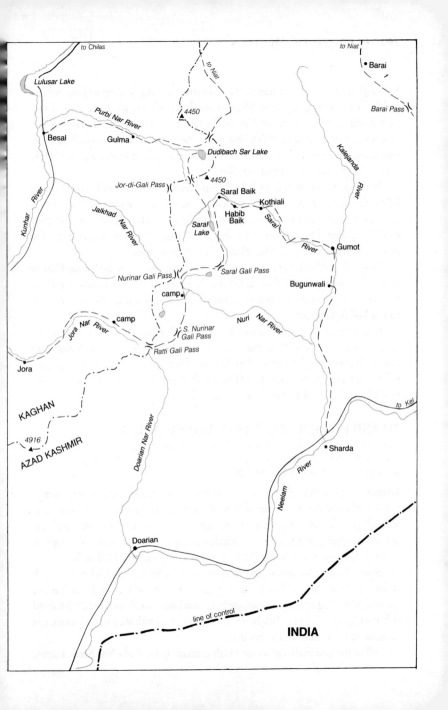

Rs10 a plateful, is on the corner of the main street and the road up to Lake Saif-ul-Muluk. The Park, Lalazar, Naran, Shalimar and Zumzum hotels all charge about Rs400 for a double, more for deluxe, and are usually fully booked in summer. Prices drop out of season, so try bargaining. PTDC has by far the best site, in the woods beside the river above the town (s/d Rs500/600–1,500 plus tax); book in Islamabad, tel 819384, 815653, 812957, or Abbottabad, tel 2446.

From Naran you can walk to **Lake Saif-ul-Muluk** in two to three hours. The path follows the jeep road up through coniferous forest, cutting all the corners; though steep, it is straightforward and easy. You can also hire horses for about Rs200 one way. Saif-ul-Muluk is spoiled by a clutter of tea and souvenir stalls, but you can get away from them by walking round the lake, which takes about an hour.

From Saif-ul-Muluk you can trek east for five hours, across to the **Lalazar Plateau** (not to be confused with Lulusar Lake), which perches above Battakundi—a guide is recommended. You can also trek south from Saif-ul-Muluk and up the stream to the **Saif-ul-Muluk Glacier.**

For a longer trek of several days, turn west (right) about two kilometres before the glacier at **Kach**, a shepherds' summer camp, and trek over the 4,237-metre **Manur Gali Pass** to shepherds' settlements on the other side. There are several more ridges to cross before you rejoin the main valley at **Mahandri** (not marked on the U502 map), so you would be well advised to hire a local as a guide.

TO AND FROM DUDIBACH SAR AND SARAL LAKES
Map: U502 NI 43-2 (Gilgit) and NI 43-6 (Srinagar), reliability good.
Open zone, with closed-zone options; easy; any number of days; maximum height optional to about 5,000 metres; August to September.

Warning: The ceasefire line with India is not marked on the Srinagar map. It is essential to know where it lies, as the area within 16 kilometres of the border is a closed zone and well patrolled. As a foreigner you are very conspicuous; word will get round, and you risk being arrested if found near the Indian frontier. The river marked Kishanganga on the U502 map is just inside Pakistan and is now called the Neelum River.

Besal (about 3,260 metres), 48 kilometres north of Naran and 18 kilometres south of the top of the Babusar Pass, is the starting point for the trek to Dudibach Sar (we recommend starting with a night camping by Lulusar Lake—see above). Besal is inhabited only from June to October. Pack horses or donkeys, along with their Gujar owners, can be hired here for about Rs150 per day.

Follow the goat path east along a high contour up the Purbi Nar River, keeping the river far below you on your left. This route is easier and more scenic than the donkey path, which follows the riverbank. You cross several small snowfields, even in mid-August, and pass several Gujar summer settlements. The hillsides are green, gentle and smooth, covered in carpets of pink bistort, blue delphiniums and purple geraniums. Three hours of steady climbing on a clear path brings you to **Gulma**, where the valley opens out to wide, flat pastureland. Gulma makes a good campsite at about 3,550 metres.

Dudibach Sar is about three and a half hours' gentle walking further up the valley through wide pastureland with Gujar summer settlements every kilometre or so. Herds of water buffalo, cattle, horses and goats graze the flower-covered slopes. The deep blue Dudibach Sar, at 3,800 metres, is surrounded by green hills at about 4,800 metres, with snow patches in the shady hollows. Uncontrolled blasting has diminished the lake's once plentiful supply of trout. You can camp anywhere round the lake.

TWO POSSIBILITIES FROM DUDIBACH SAR

One option is to climb to the top of the pass to the northeast of Dudibach Sar, which gives a view of snowy peaks. To view Nanga Parbat, however, you must make the two-hour climb from the pass to the top of the green hill. From the pass, the intrepid can trek north to Niat and Bunar (see the warning above) and continue either southeast or northeast round Nanga Parbat (see page 179).

Aurel Stein crossed from Kel to Niat across the Barai Pass in 1913. He decided this was probably the ancient supply route from Kashmir used by the Chinese in the eighth century (see Stein, *Innermost Asia*).

The other option—for a few days' gentle, safe trekking—is to turn south from Dudibach Sar and follow a high contour up the first side valley on a clear zigzag path, just passable for a laden horse, to the top of an unnamed pass at about 4,000 metres. Looking west from the top of this pass, you see **Jor-di-Gali Pass** (4,488 metres), a flat, easy route leading to the Jalkhad Nar Valley and an easy walk back to the Kaghan Valley, coming out about five kilometres south of Besal. Looking south from the top of the unnamed pass, you see a wide, green bowl covered in patches of flowers, with the sapphire-blue **Saral Lake** at the bottom. There are several Gujar summer settlements in the area, but Saral Lake, at about 3,500 metres, makes a perfect campsite.

TWO POSSIBILITIES FROM SARAL LAKE

If you have a permit for Azad Kashmir, you can follow the Saral River down to the Neelum Valley at **Sharda** in three days. Follow the right bank of the Saral River through **Saral Baik** to **Habib Baik**, then climb up to **Kothiali** to avoid the gorge, keeping the river on your left. Camp in the birch woods on the first flat spot since Saral Baik. At Kothiali, cross to the left bank of the Saral River on a snow bridge, and turn south along a trail that runs about 200 metres up the hillside above the river for two or three hours to a Gujar settlement. Ask the Gujars where to cross the river—there are usually several snow bridges, and it is easier to follow the right bank through tall grass for part of the way. Return to the left bank and trek down through juniper bushes and fir trees to **Gumot**, where the Saral and Kalejanda rivers join. There is a good campsite just northwest of the junction. A mule trail follows the east bank of the Kalejanda down to Sharda, but there is no bridge at Gumot. Follow the right bank down for one and a half hours through long grass to the nearest bridge at **Bagunwali**. Daily jeeps connect Sharda with Muzaffarabad. (Information supplied by Vaqar Zakaria.)

Those without permits for Azad Kashmir must turn to the southwest from Saral Lake and follow the Azad Kashmir–Kaghan frontier. The paths on the U502 maps are all accurately marked, and there are several possibilities, but be sure not to wander southeast into the ceasefire zone in Azad Kashmir.

From Saral Lake walk south for one hour, then turn west (right) for a long easy approach on snow for about two hours up to the **Saral Gali Pass** (about 4,000 metres). Fork right again just before the top and climb steeply up to the grassy ridge. The view down the other side is of a gentle green bowl with a small lake. Two hours' walking across thick grass takes you down past a lone Gujar hut to the **Nuri Nar River**, where you can camp knee deep in flowers at about 3,350 metres.

A mule trail (or jeep road under construction) leads from Sharda up the Nuri Nar River, over the **Nurinar Gali Pass** (about 4,000 metres) to the Jalkhad Valley, which leads in turn to the Kaghan Valley. If you wish to cut your trek short, it is a day's walk from your camp to the jeep road in the Kaghan Valley by this route.

There are two Nurinar Gali passes marked on the map, the more southerly one (also about 4,000 metres) leads over to the **Doarian Nar River**. It is an easy climb following a clear, well-made donkey path. From the top is a view east into India and snow-covered 6,000-metre peaks. The top end of the Doarian Valley is stony with snow patches and a small lake. Unless you have a permit, do not follow the river; it leads down into Azad Kashmir and comes out at **Doarian**, on the Neelum River. Instead, take a high contour to the right (north), and, without losing more than 100 metres in altitude, follow the hillside round for about an hour to the **Ratti Gali Pass** (about 4,000 metres), which leads to the **Jora Nar River.** The clear path across the pass skirts a large snowfield on the Jora side before zigzagging steeply down to the valley floor.

There is a good campsite beside the river, near a Gujar shepherds' summer settlement.

It is about six hours' walk down to Burawai and the jeep road. For the first couple of hours, the Jora Valley is wide and green, with many Gujar camps and herds of cattle, sheep, goats, buffalo, horses and donkeys—and the occasional camel. Paths lead up every side valley. Above Jora, a Gujar summer settlement of stone huts, the valley narrows to a gorge. Walking from Jora down to the Kaghan Valley takes two hours, as you pass sparse juniper bushes on the hillsides and bright patches of green elder bushes on the lower slopes and valley floor. Burawai, at about 2,800 metres, is inhabited from mid-May to mid-October and sports four shops, two local hotels and a PWD rest house. Jeeps pass daily; private hire to Naran costs about Rs500.

OTHER TREKS IN KAGHAN

There are dozens of good treks in the Kaghan Valley. The U502 map is accurate, so you can follow any of the trails.

One recommendation is **Shogran to Ghori**, which takes you from Kaghan into the Neelam Valley. You reach Shogran from **Kawai**, which is 24 kilometres north of Balakot. The logging track winds up through dense pine forest. Take the right fork where it divides. Shogran, at 2,400 metres, stands well above the valley—a lovely place to spend a few days. You can camp in the meadow or even stay in one of the Forestry Department rest houses (book through the Conservator of Forests, Hazara, tel Abbottabad 2728, or the Divisional Forest Officer, Kaghan Division, tel Balakot 17). The Park Hotel in Balakot runs two rest houses at Shogran that are adequate but have no view (s/d about 300/400); book at the Park Hotel in Balakot. From the meadow are magnificent views up the Kaghan Valley to the flat-topped mountain Musa-ka-Musalla (meaning 'prayer mat of Moses') and Malika Parbat, which, at 5,291 metres, is the highest of all the peaks enclosing the valley.

A two-hour walk along the logging track leads up to summer pastures at about 2,700 metres, where there is another Forestry Department rest house and a suitable camping ground. From here you trek for two to three days over the hill, past Makra Peak (3,885 metres) and down to **Ghori**, in an open-zone portion of the Neelum Valley. Flag down a passing vehicle to Muzaffarabad and change there for Rawalpindi.

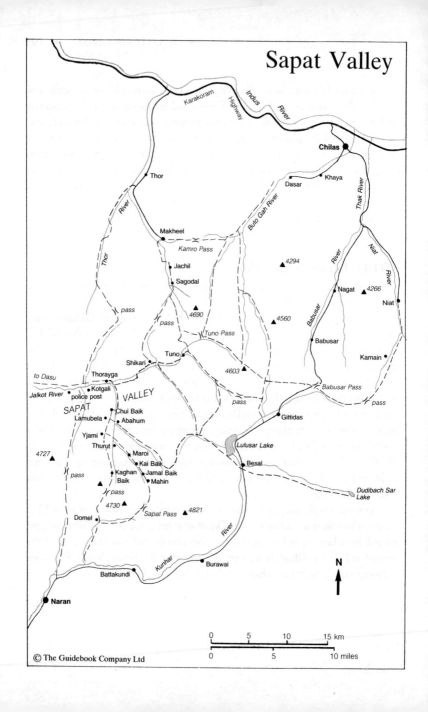

Sapat Valley

Indus River

Karakoram Highway

Chilas

Thak River

Thor

Dasar

Khaya

Thor River

Makheel

Buto Gah River

Kamro Pass

Jachil

▲ 4294

Sagodal

Niat River

Babusar River

Nagat

▲ 4266

Niat

▲ 4690

▲ 4560

pass

pass

Tuno Pass

Tuno

Babusar

Shikari

▲ 4603

Karnain

to Dasu

Thorayga

Babusar Pass

Jalkot River

police post

Kotgali

pass

SAPAT VALLEY

pass

Chui Baik

Lamubela

Abahum

Gittidas

Yjami

Thurut

Maroi

Lulusar Lake

▲ 4727

Kai Baik

Besal

pass

Kaghan

Baik

Jamal Baik

Mahin

Dudibach Sar Lake

▲

pass

▲ 4730

Sapat Pass

▲ 4821

Domel

Kunhar River

Burawai

Battakundi

N

Naran

| 0 | 5 | 10 | 15 km |

| 0 | 5 | 10 miles |

© The Guidebook Company Ltd

INDUS KOHISTAN

Indus Kohistan extends on either side of the Indus from Chilas down to Besham. The side valleys off the Indus are typically narrow and barren at their mouths but, further up, green and fertile, with thick forests of cedar, fir and spruce. Until the advent of the Karakoram Highway, Kohistan was perhaps the most remote and backward region of Pakistan. It was known as Yaghistan, meaning 'land of the ungovernable' or 'land of the savages'. It is still probably one of the wildest and most inhospitable areas of Pakistan, consisting almost entirely of rugged mountains, many of which are over 4,500 metres high, with alpine valleys sandwiched in between.

Warning: The entire Indus Kohistan area is dangerous; the British avoided it, so the reliability of maps is poor. Do not go trekking here without informing the local police and taking a local dignitary with you. The people of this area continue to be lawless, fanatical and violent. We describe a few of the larger side valleys but suggest that you ask the advice of the police and deputy commissioner in Chilas or Dasu before attempting to visit them. Note that the scenery is very similar to what you can see in Kaghan much more safely.

THOR VALLEY TO NARAN IN KAGHAN

Map: U502 NI 43-2 (Gilgit) and NI 43-6 (Srinagar), reliability good along the main Kaghan and Swat valleys, reliability very poor in Indus Kohistan.
Dangerous open zone; strenuous; about five days; maximum height about 4,300 metres; August to mid-September.

The Thor River flows into the Indus 27 kilometres downriver of Chilas. A jeep road goes 24 kilometres up the valley to **Makheel** (spelled Makheli on the U502 map). You can either take a jeep from Chilas—public jeeps go every few days part of the way up the valley—or walk to Makheel directly from Chilas up the **Buto Gah**, a green valley with many villages, across the **Kamro Pass** (about 3,650 metres) and steeply down to Makheel, which by this route is 33 kilometres from Chilas. A jeep road goes about ten kilometres up the Buto Gah.

In Makheel, contact either Sikandar Malik or his cousin Sarwar Malik, two influential men of the area. Ask advice and arrange porters through them.

The following times are accurate for a fit, young Pakistani.

A one-hour climb from Makheel takes you to **Jachil**, from where it is two hours on a steep grassy slope to **Sagodal** (Singodal on the U502 map). Camp.

It takes about four hours from Sagodal up a fairly steep gradient—on grass, neither difficult nor dangerous—to the **Tuno Pass** (pronounced 'Tunoo'), also known as **Shikari Top**, the crest of the ridge at about 4,300 metres. A track reaches this same point directly from the Buto Valley. If you find reliable men in Chilas or at the end of the jeep road in the Buto Valley, there is no need to detour round to Makheel to see Sikandar Malik.

There are routes all through the green, rounded hills from here: east to **Babusar Pass**, south to **Lulusar Lake** or west through the summer grazing grounds of the area known as **Sapat**, along the upper Jalkot River, which flows down to Dasu on the Karakoram Highway. There are several tracks from the Jalkot Valley across the ridge to the Kaghan Valley. We have sketched them in on the map but have no reliable information about them.

Heading west for Sapat and the Jalkot River, it is 90 minutes steeply down through juniper scrub to the river and a further hour to the log cabins of **Tuno**, the highest shepherds' summer settlement at the junction of two valleys. Ask for the *subadar* (headman) and spend the night under his protection.

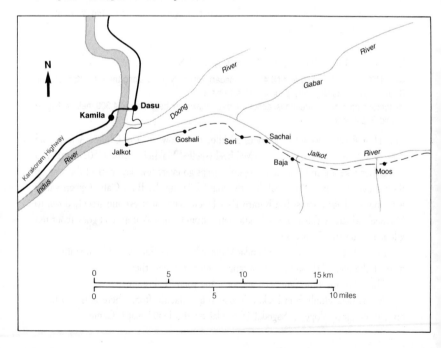

Walk down through rolling green pastures, past sparse juniper and fir trees and through the summer settlements of **Shikari** (one hour) and several other settlements to **Thorayga** (four hours), a large summer settlement on the edge of a grassy plain. Here you can camp under the protection of Malik Sakhi, the influential man of the area, described as a rifle-toting baron with a bushy red beard. The high point of the summer here is the annual horse race.

From Thorayga there is a choice of two routes: one continuing down the Jalkot River to Dasu on the Karakoram Highway (see below) and the other south through sparse woods and green pastures to the Kaghan Valley, coming out a little north of Naran.

The path to Kaghan climbs gently for four hours up the wide, grassy valley and through the settlements of **Chui Baik**, **Zhububela**, **Lamubela** (the Abahum Valley—marked Sapat on the U502 map—branches east here to Lulusar Lake) and **Shamis** to **Yjami**, where the valley divides. You can spend the night here under the protection of Mr Behrai or continue for a couple of hours up either the eastern or western branch valley, both of which lead over to the Kaghan Valley.

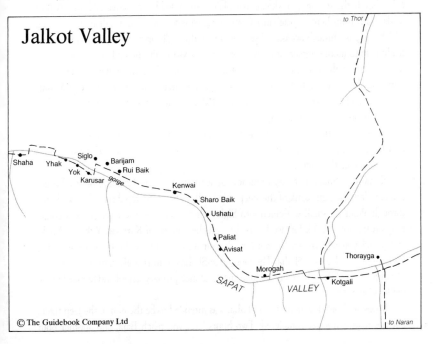

Jalkot Valley

We have no accurate information but believe the two paths join up again the other side and come out somewhere near Naran. Up the eastern branch are four shepherds' settlements before the pass, **Maroi**, **Kai Baik**, **Jamal Baik** and **Mahin**, where you can spend the night under the protection of Mr Samandar, the councillor. Up the western branch, there is at least one shepherds' settlement, **Kaghan Baik**, before the pass. Both passes rise to about 4,300 metres and are green and smooth all the way. We do not know how long it takes from the passes down to the Kunhar River, but according to the U502 map there are shepherds' settlements along the way.

THORAYGA DOWN JALKOT RIVER TO DASU ON THE INDUS
Map: U502 NI 43-2 (Gilgit) and NI 43-1 (Churrai), reliability very poor; we have little faith in the accuracy of our sketch map on pages 198-9.
Dangerous open zone; strenuous; four days; maximum height about 3,000 metres; August to mid-September.

Kotgali, 90 minutes down the Jalkot River from Thorayga, boasts a police post—a log cabin beside the stream in a wide, grassy plain surrounded by tree-covered hills. (A trail leads south from here to Kaghan.) Continuing west for two and a half hours—during which you pass through occasional settlements in the wide, green valley with side valleys leading up to more summer pastures—you come to **Morogah**, the end of the wide Sapat Valley. This is also the end of the smooth, easy walking. The valley narrows and turns northwest, and you climb along fir-covered slopes for three hours above a gorge to **Avisat**, which is shaded by about 300 walnut trees. **Paliat**, 30 minutes later, marks the end of the Sapat area. It is low enough here to grow one crop of maize a year. Camp.

Below Paliat the way is stony and tiring, and the route crosses several snow patches that have avalanched down the side streams. It is about three hours to **Kenwai**, a good place to spend the night.

Kenwai to **Shaha** is a day's journey, at least six hot and fatiguing hours. To get there, follow the right bank of the steep-sided valley above the rapid river for four hours through about six small settlements to **Siglo**, where you cross the river above a gorge. Stay on the south bank for two hours through the villages of **Karusar**, **Yok** and **Yhak**, after which you must cross to the north bank again for a difficult two hours before returning to the south bank above **Shaha**. The mosque in Shaha has intricately carved pillar heads. Other features of the settlement include an abandoned primary school and terraced maize fields. Camp.

Moos, an hour downriver from Shaha, was intended to be the end of the jeep track, but the road is not yet completed. Two hours later you reach **Baja**, and another hour takes you through **Sachai** to **Seri**, the approach to which involves a very steep climb of 300 metres up the side of the valley. From high above the river, you view the confluence of the Gabar and Jalkot rivers before descending again to river level for the final hour's hike to the end of the jeep road at **Goshali**. The road crosses the Jalkot and Doong rivers and comes out at Dasu on the Indus.

DAREL AND TANGIR VALLEYS

The people of Darel and Tangir have a bad reputation for brigandry. In addition to the advice of the deputy commissioner and police in Chilas, trekkers should have the support of Amir Jan, ex-councillor from Barijat, in Sateel, and one of the most influential men in Tangir Valley. We can offer no safe contact for the Darel Valley.

From about the fourth to fifteenth century, the Tangir and Darel valleys were on the main Buddhist pilgrim route from China to Swat. Fa Xian came this way in 403 and wrote a precise description in his diary. It took him a month to reach Darel from Kashgar, travelling via Tashkurgan and Sarhad on the Oxus, then over the Boroghil and Darkot passes to Yasin and due south to Darel. The most famous of all Buddhist monks, Xuan Zang, came to Darel from Swat in 630.

Both pilgrims travelled along the Indus and vividly describe its horrors. Fa Xian writes of a difficult and rugged path across dizzying precipices above the swirling Indus, with nowhere to put his feet: 'In former times men had chiselled paths along the rocks, and distributed ladders on the face of them, to the number altogether of 700, at the bottom of which there was a suspension bridge of ropes, by which the river was crossed, its banks being there 80 paces apart.'

Xuan Zang's journey in the opposite direction was equally terrifying, taking him 'over hills and across gulleys ascending the Indus by hazardous paths through gloomy gorges, crossing bridges of ropes or iron chains, across bridges spanning precipices or climbing by means of pegs for steps'.

Despite these difficulties, the main trade route followed the left bank of the Indus, crossing to the right bank at Dubair, and then either followed the Dubair Valley to Swat (see below) or continued down the right bank to Besham and crossed the Shangla Pass to Swat (now a paved road).

The most important of all Buddhist shrines was in Darel at **Poguch**, which boasted a wooden statue of the Maitreya Bodhisattva 30 metres high, seen by both Fa Xian and Xuan Zang. The shrine was so powerful that the whole of Swat was controlled from here. Darel was sufficiently fertile to support a large community of monks, and it was from here that Buddhism spread east to Tibet and China.

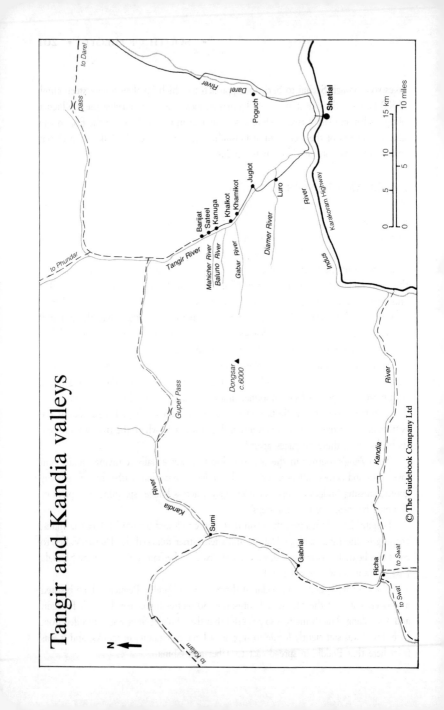

Tangir and Kandia valleys

© The Guidebook Company Ltd

Poguch is now the site of the important Muslim **Shrine of Shaha-Khel Baba**, a Chishti saint who came from Swat to convert the 'heathens' in about the sixteenth century. In the course of his pious wanderings, Shaha-Khel Baba was killed at Poguch by *kafirs* (infidels), who cut off his head and threw it in the Indus. The head miraculously flew back through the air to join the martyr's corpse—a holy sign that converted Darel to Islam.

Aurel Stein became the first Westerner to visit these valleys in 1913 (see Stein, *Innermost Asia*).

Today, Darel and Tangir still support many holy men—fanatical Sunni Muslims, violent and xenophobic, who preach against letting strangers into the valleys and periodically stir up murderous religious trouble between Sunnis and Shias. The carving on the mosques and around the tombs in Darel and Tangir still shows Buddhist influence in the choice of motifs, such as a four-leaved flower in a rectangular or round frame, entwined vine leaves and scrolls of half-opened lotus buds.

The jeep road to the Darel and Tangir valleys leaves the Karakoram Highway on a bridge across the Indus at **Shatial**. Some of the best Buddhist **rock carvings** are along this stretch of the river, on either side of the bridge (see page 186). This is about 60 kilometres downriver from Chilas, from where public jeeps go up the valleys most days. Once across the bridge, turn east for Darel or west for Tangir. Both valleys used to be filled with magnificent cedar forests, but these are fast being cut, with no plans to replant.

If visiting Tangir follow the river up for three hours (51 kilometres) to **Sateel**, the end of the road. The valley is wide and green, with fields of wheat and barley. At **Kanuga**, shortly before Sateel, are magnificent views west up the Mahichar River to Mount Dongsar (about 6,000 metres).

There are several long treks from Sateel, but we do not recommend them unless you are escorted.

TANGIR VALLEY TO SWAT OR KANDIA VALLEY
Map: U502 NI 43-1 (Churrai), reliability very poor.
Dangerous open zone; strenuous; five to seven days; maximum height 4,000 metres; August to mid-September.

We have not been here, but according to the U502 map, you can trek west from Sateel across the **Guper Pass** to the Kandia Valley, then follow it down to **Sumi**, which is about 50 kilometres from Sateel. From Sumi you can loop north then west to join the top of the Swat Valley at either **Lake Mahodand** or **Matiltan**, going from there down the jeep road to Kalam, for a total journey of about 100 kilometres.

If, instead, you continue down the Kandia River from Sumi, you come back to the Karakoram Highway after about 65 kilometres, arriving at a point about halfway between Shatial and Dasu—30 kilometres from each. There are at least two other routes through to Swat from the Kandia Valley.

TANGIR VALLEY TO PHUNDAR IN GILGIT VALLEY

Map: U502 NI 43-1 (Churrai), reliability very poor, and NJ 43-13 (Mastuj), reliability good. Dangerous open zone; strenuous; three days; maximum height about 4,000 metres; August to mid-September.

This route runs about 75 kilometres. The police and Northern Areas administration have no control here. In the past few years Kohistani tribesmen have crossed this way several times to kidnap people and disappear back into the hills.

DUBAIR VALLEY TO SWAT

Map: U502 NI 43-1 (Churrai), reliability very poor. Dangerous open zone; strenuous; three to four days; maximum height 4,250 metres, optional to 4,850 metres; August to mid-September.

Trekkers should not wander up this valley without first visiting the assistant commissioner in Patan and, through him, contacting Malik Said Ahmad, the grey-bearded patriarch who exercises complete command of the area. Malik Said Ahmad winters in Nerai and retreats to Gaydar in the hills for the summer.

The Dubair Valley joins the Indus about 50 kilometres south of Dasu, 15 kilometres north of Besham. A jeep road runs for about 16 kilometres up to **Dhar Dubair** (marked Duber Qala on the U502 map). We have not been up this valley; our timings are those of a fit young Pakistani.

It is a two-hour walk across terraced fields through **Gaya** to **Nerai**, at the junction of two cascading rivers. This is the winter home of Malik Said Ahmad and a safe place for the night.

Follow the western river along its northern bank for about two and a half hours, then cross on a log bridge to the south bank. The mountains here are steep and partly forested. Continue for 90 minutes beside the rapids to the junction of the Gaydar River, which flows in from the west, and climb up to **Gaydar**, the summer home of Malik Said Ahmad. Camp under his protection.

You can make a day trip from here to climb **Mount Chansar** (about 4,500 metres), but do not camp away from the protection of Gaydar.

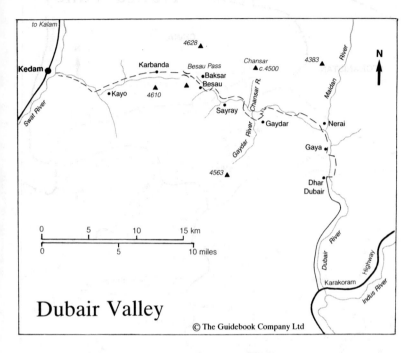

Dubair Valley

© The Guidebook Company Ltd

Gaydar to **Sayray** takes two hours, and in a further 90 minutes you reach **Besau**, where you can spend the night at a lone log cabin without a door, surrounded by grey stony slopes above the tree-line. Start very early and climb steeply up for two hours on dangerous ice to **Baksar** before the top layer of snow softens. This is the most difficult part of the trek, but you are rewarded by the view from the top of the **Besau Pass** (about 4,250 metres) of row upon row of stony hills.

Walk across the flat top of the pass for about 30 minutes, then descend down steep ice for about two hours. Cross sharp stones and boulders for another 30 minutes to **Karbanda** and the forest.

Kayo, at the junction of two streams, is about 90 minutes down a good logging track from Karbanda. Cross on a wooden bridge and follow the river down for another 90 minutes to **Kedam**, on the River Swat about eight kilometres above Bahrain.

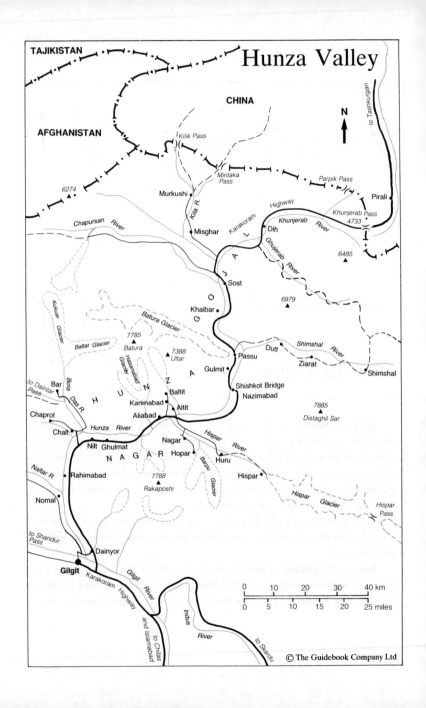

NORTH OF GILGIT

The **Hunza** is the only river to slice through the western Karakoram Range. It was there before the mountains and has maintained its flow through a cluster of 7,000-metre peaks to empty into the Gilgit River just below Gilgit town. The Karakoram Highway (KKH) hugs its banks all the way to China, giving easy access to some of the best trekking in the whole Karakoram. In several places, glaciers come right down to the road, so you can step straight off a public bus and start trekking up to summer pastures. The paths up the ablation valleys are usually safe, but you should never venture onto the glaciers without a local porter to guide you. Even if you are experienced with Karakoram glaciers, you should trek in pairs or groups.

Bordering the Hunza River are the kingdoms of Hunza and Nagar, long eulogised for their magnificent scenery—'the ultimate manifestation of mountain grandeur,' according to Eric Shipton, 'rich, fecund and of an ethereal beauty'.

A dozen main side valleys flow down to join the Hunza, each waiting to be explored. There are day walks, circular treks and up-and-back hikes along the glaciers; you can even cut across the whole Karakoram Range to Skardu. We work from south to north along the river, describing them all.

NALTAR VALLEY

Hidden in the mountains—up a dramatic, barren gorge 19 kilometres long—is the surprisingly green and lush valley of Naltar. Some climatic quirk gives Naltar about 410 millimetres of rainfall per year, more than three times that of Gilgit, and the valley is heavily wooded with pine, spruce, birch, rowan and juniper. The valley is the most highly recommended day outing from Gilgit.

Naltar village, at 2,880 metres, has an army ski-training base (not open to the public) and good walkabouts for the energetic tourist. It is also the starting point for two longer treks: one across the Naltar Pass (about 4,600 metres) to Ishkoman, and the other across the Daintar Pass (4,636 metres) to Chalt. The path across the Daintar Pass is not easy to find—and is even less obvious from the Chalt side—so a guide is recommended.

Transport: Naltar is a two-hour, 42-kilometre drive from Gilgit via the west bank of the Hunza River to Nomal, and from there northwest up the Naltar Nullah to the green meadows of Naltar.

The public jeep to Naltar leaves Gilgit every two or three days. The fare is about

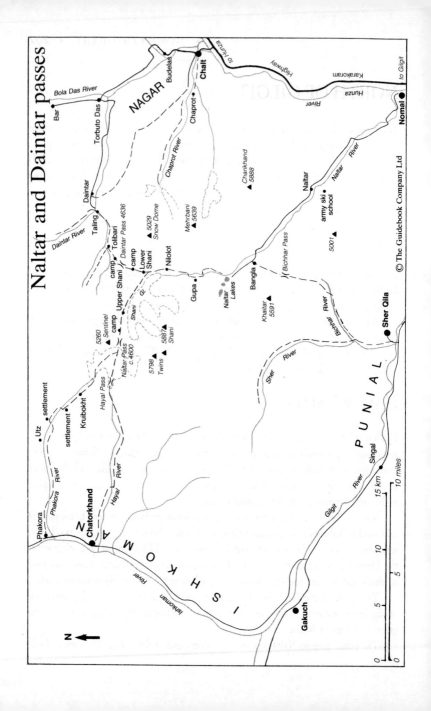

Naltar and Daintar passes

© The Guidebook Company Ltd

Rs20, or you can hire a private jeep for Rs700. Alternatively, take the daily public bus to Nomal and hike up the gorge in about six hours—but this is a hot, miserable way to start your trek, especially if you are not yet fit. The Prince Hotel, a basic doss house in Naltar, has a helpful manager who allows camping in the garden and can find porters, guides, donkeys and horses (you can use animals to just below both passes). A nicer campsite is across the river beyond the NAPWD rest house. The two tiny shops in Naltar sell cigarettes and sugar, but you should bring all your supplies from Gilgit. The people in lower Naltar are Shia Muslims; those in upper Naltar are Sunni.

NALTAR OVER NALTAR PASS TO ISHKOMAN

Map: Swiss Karakoram map, reliability good; U502 NJ 43-14 (Baltit), reliability very poor. Open zone; strenuous; five days; maximum height about 4,600 metres (4,340 metres according to another source); mid-July to September.

Stage 1: Naltar to Naltar (Kuti) Lake, about 12 kilometres. This takes four hours if you walk all the way, or one hour by jeep (Rs500). We recommend walking through the thick pine forest. Nine kilometres from Naltar (three hours on foot) the track crosses the Naltar River on a new jeep bridge. Across the bridge is **Bangla**, a summer settlement of Gujar nomads who winter in a permanent settlement at Naltar village and are paid by other villagers to take the herds up to the valley in the summer. As there is plenty of wood here, the Gujar's houses are built of birch poles covered with mud and juniper branches; some are round like a teepee, others oblong with a ridge pole. The whole family comes here for the summer, bringing their dogs and chickens (you can buy eggs for about Rs2 each). The villagers also collect birch bark, which is used as wrapping paper and sold for Rs8 per kilo. Butter is wrapped in the bark and stored in holes in the ground.

An alternative two-day trek from Bangla follows a path to **Sher Qila** in Punial across the **Bichhar Pass** (about 4,000 metres).

From Bangla to **Naltar Lake**, you pass through more forest and see more Gujar settlements. The first lake is a startlingly green pond about 200 metres in diameter, surrounded by birch, ash and pine trees. The water is still and clear, its colour rising from bright green algae on the bottom. The best campsite is beside this lake; a plank bridge leads out to a tiny island, from which the fishing is said to be excellent (get your licence in Gilgit). There are two more lakes—one a brilliant cobalt blue and the other turquoise—at a higher level about ten minutes to the west. It is very stony round the edge of these lakes, with no obvious campsite. A fourth, larger lake is still higher, about 40 minutes away to the west.

Stage 2: Naltar Lake to Lower Shani, four to five hours. Fifteen minutes north of Naltar Lake, cross the river on a log bridge and follow the east bank. From the top of the next rise, you can look back and see one of the higher lakes. Descend to a large, swampy field with herds of cattle and horses. Keep to the east of the river, crossing pastures then a stony area rimmed by a few birch trees. On the west bank about 75 minutes from Naltar Lake is the Gujar settlement of **Gupa**, surrounded by sparse pine trees.

For both the Naltar and Daintar passes, you would be well advised to hire a shepherd to show the way. If you do not have a guide and are heading for the Daintar Pass, ask the shepherds at Gupa to point it out, as it is not obvious. The pass is one of the low points in the wall of mountains, with a large field of snow below it, to the left of **Snow Dome**, a rounded mountain 5,029 metres high. Continue up to **Nilolot** (meaning 'green top'), a green hillside with birch trees and herds of cattle and donkeys, and from there to the snout of the Shani (Naltar) Glacier. Follow the east side of the glacier for several kilometres across patches of snow and stones along a clear path; you will be looking ahead to **Sentinel Peak**, the 5,260-metre (or 5,461-metre, according to Stephen Venables) cone that guards the head of the valley.

Camp at **Lower Shani**, a shepherds' summer camp comprising three stone huts used only in August. This is on the green flank of the mountain, about 300 metres above the glacier, across which are outstanding views to **Shani Peak** (5,887 metres), a dramatic triple-headed giant, with **The Twins** (5,798 metres and 5,700 metres) visible further north. Lower Shani (3,800 metres) is quite lush, fed by a small stream edged with flowers: pink bistort, purple geraniums, blue gentians, white edelweiss and many more. Herds of horses and cattle roam the hillside.

Stage 3: Lower Shani to Upper Shani and Naltar Base Camp, four to five hours. Continue west on a good path along the edge of the Shani Glacier for another three hours to **Upper Shani**, a vast area of steep pastures with a few deserted shepherds' huts. Cross a side stream and climb straight ahead on a zigzag path through knee-deep flowers and up a wide, grassy shoulder. The donkey path is further right but less attractive. You come out on a big plateau featuring herds of grazing yaks and horses and plenty of good campsites, with small clear streams and great views of huge overhanging seracs. Camp in the top left-hand corner of the high plateau, at about 4,100 metres.

Stage 4: Across Naltar Pass to Kruibokht, six hours. About two hours' climb up stones and snow takes you to the flat top of the pass, from where you can see Shishpar Peak in the distance to the northeast. Keep to the left as you approach the summit. Just beyond the summit, the route (there is no path) divides, right for Phakora, and left over the Hayal Pass to Chatorkhand (see below).

Continuing along the Phakora route, the first hour on the other side of the Naltar Pass is across crevassed snowfields to the moraine of a side glacier, which takes 30 minutes to cross. Next comes a tiring two to three hours of difficult walking along the crest of the lateral moraine of the Phakora Glacier to the first trees of Kruibokht (meaning 'red stone' in Khowar). Camp beyond a small side stream in a green pasture surrounded by birch, pine and willow trees.

Stage 5: Kruibokht to Phakora, six hours. The path is high above the river, first through pastureland then through thick forest, leading in one hour to the first summer settlement of wooden huts, below which you cross the river on a good bridge (the way is not obvious). Continue through pine and birch woods, past another settlement of solid stone huts and across another good bridge back to the left bank. Thirty minutes later you pass **Utz** (meaning 'spring' in Khowar), a village surrounded by green fields on the other side of the river. This is a pay stage. Pay another day, and you can continue down to Phakora along a well-maintained donkey path through a long, narrow gorge. The path is cut into the cliff face high above the stream and crosses three cascading side streams, the first of which is the best for bathing. It is a hot three to four hours before the gorge opens up and you reach the first trees and fields of Phakora.

Phakora is small, with a couple of shops but no hotel. The people are friendly and you can camp—ask permission first. There are several jeeps in the village, and one usually leaves at sunrise for Chatorkhand and/or Gilgit. (Information from Elisabeth Gardner.)

Chatorkhand alternative in stage 4: From the top of Naltar Pass. (We have not been this way and do not know how accurate our information is, so send information please.) Bear left after crossing the Naltar Pass and walk for an hour on rock and snow to the **Hayal Pass**. You need a guide, as it is impossible to see which point on the ridge is the pass. Walk down for 90 minutes on moraine to a pasture with a clear stream, where you can camp amid willow bushes.

Stage 5: Pasture to Chatorkhand, eight hours. Descend the Hayal Valley through a scenic, steep canyon, walking high above the left bank of the river on stones for six hours and crossing several screes, one of which is frightening. Water is available from several side streams. Descend to cross the Hayal River, then continue down for two hours past a few birch trees to the cultivated area above Chatorkhand, the capital of Ishkoman.

The people of Ishkoman are Ismaili and Sunni and speak Khowar (the language of Chitral), Shina and Wakhi. The valley belonged to Chitral and was ruled by the Kushwaqts, who appointed governors to rule Ishkoman. The raja living in Chatorkhand is descended from these. See page 270 for other treks in the area. A large new rest house is under construction in Chatorkhand.

Public jeeps leave Chatorkhand for Gilgit every morning, or you can hire a private jeep for Rs800–1,000.

NALTAR OVER DAINTAR PASS TO CHALT

Map: Swiss Karakoram map, reliability good; U502 NJ 43-14 (Baltit), reliability very poor. Open zone; strenuous; at least six days with further options; maximum height 4,636 metres; late July to September.

Stages 1 and 2. Same as the Naltar Pass route as far as Lower Shani (see above). Do not rush across the Daintar Pass, as the Naltar Valley is more beautiful and tranquil than the other side. Take a day or two to acclimatise and explore the top of the Naltar Valley. Climb to the Naltar Pass and explore Sentinel Peak, returning to Daintar Base Camp along an easy, flower-lined contour path that runs a few hundred metres above the glacier.

Stage 3: Lower Shani to Daintar Base Camp, one hour. Daintar Base Camp is an easy climb along a clear cow path, which leads back (east) diagonally up the green slope to the ridge. Follow the ridge north up to a flattish shoulder beside a stream, with panoramic views back down the valley to a ring of jagged snowy peaks, with the Daintar Pass above to the north. The hillside is crisscrossed with so many paths that it is a good idea to have someone to show the way. Camp at about 4,000 metres.

Stage 4: Across Daintar Pass (4,636 metres), six to eight hours. It is about two and a half hours to the top of the pass. Follow the crest of the shoulder all the way— the first hour on grass and flowers, followed by half an hour of steep, slippery scrambling up an unstable, fractured rock slope (roping up is recommended for the inexperienced). The last hour is less steep but still quite difficult. From the top, you look north across snowy peaks to the Batura and Passu ranges, and to the east you can just see Dobani (Domani) Peak but not the main peak of Rakaposhi. Watch for *ram chakkor* (Snow Cock), Snow Pigeon (a piebald high-altitude pigeon) and Himalayan Griffin Vulture, the biggest bird in the Himalaya.

A thick cornice of snow prevents your going straight over the pass, so turn right and follow the crest (which is very sharp and vertiginous, making ropes recommended) up to the cairn at the highest point. Continue east for another 200 metres or so, then head down an exceedingly steep shale gully, sliding at every step to a large snowfield. We could not find a path. Below the snowfield, about an hour from the top, is a large, green pasture known as **Daintar** (meaning 'green place'; about 4,000 metres), where a small stream trickles through purple and yellow flowers. In good weather, this is a lovely spot to camp, but most people continue steeply down for another two hours through dwarf juniper then birch woods to **Tolibari**, a shepherds' settlement at about 3,400 metres, where half a dozen men tend herds of sheep, goats, donkeys, horses and cattle. If you have time, you can detour upriver from here to explore the valley head.

Stage 5: Tolibari to Torbuto Das, five or six hours. Ask the shepherds for the best path. If there are snow bridges crossing the river, it is quicker to cross the river at Tolibari and follow the north (left) bank down for the first hour on a precipitous goat path about 20 metres above the river, then cross back on another snow bridge. The path following the south (right) bank all the way passes through woods, crosses pastures and fords two side streams. For the second hour, follow the well-constructed animal path on the south bank through a narrow gorge to **Taling**, a summer village at the junction of the Daintar River. Wide fields of wheat and lucerne border the river, and the polo ground above the village is used for a celebratory match at harvest time.

You are now in the kingdom of Nagar where the people are Shia. We found them unfriendly—perhaps two unescorted women (Ben was in China) upset the Shia sense of propriety. Camping is allowed only by the bridge. Again, if you have time, you can detour up the Daintar River to explore to the top of the valley.

Taling is the end of the jeep road, but even if the road is open you are unlikely to find a jeep here. It is a two- to three-hour walk along the road down to **Torbuto Das**. The jeep road passes through the irrigated fields of **Daintar** (from where a footpath cuts across the ridge to Chaprot village), then winds through the barren Daintar Gorge on a shelf cut along the cliff face above the river. It finally arrives at Torbuto Das, which is at the junction with the Garamsai (pronounced 'Gar-am-say') Valley, through which flows the Budelas River, which is marked on most maps (including ours) as the Bola Das River.

If you have time, you can detour from Torbuto Das up to the head of the Bola Das River, the upper reaches of which become the Tutu Uns River on some maps. The jeep road ends at **Bar**, which has hot springs (see the Chalt Valley below).

People in Torbuto Das are not very friendly (perhaps the surfeit of river and valley names gives them headaches). They expect a tent fee of Rs10 or more from all campers.

Stage 6: Torbuto Das to Chalt and Gilgit, three hours by jeep. Public jeeps leave Torbuto Das early each morning for Gilgit. Make arrangements with the driver the night before. The rate is about Rs20 per person and Rs15 per bag. Be prepared for a hassle, as you may have difficulty persuading the driver to take you as a public passenger. The private booking fee is Rs800. Alternatively, you can walk (see below).

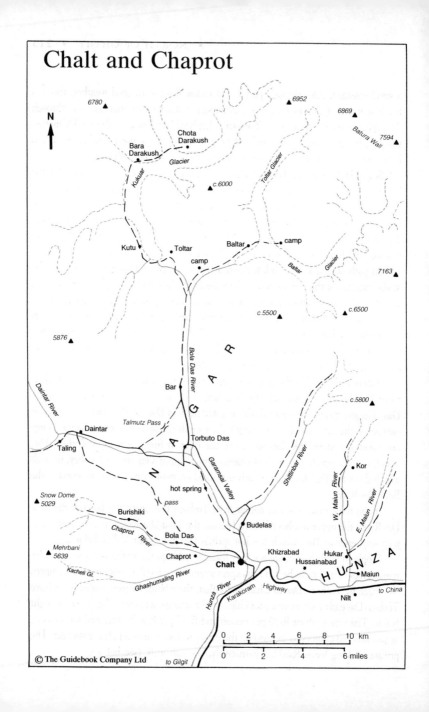

Chalt and Chaprot

N

6780

Chota
Darakush

Bara
Darakush

Glacier

Kukuar

c.6000

6952

6869

Batura Wall

7594

Toltar Glacier

Kutu

Toltar

Baltar

camp

camp

Baltar Glacier

7163

5876

c.5500

c.6500

Bola Das River

N A G A R

Daintar River

Bar

c.5800

Talmutz Pass

Daintar

Torbuto Das

Taling

Garamsai Valley

Shitinbar River

Kor

hot spring

W. Maiun River

E. Maiun River

Snow Dome
5029

pass

Burishiki

Bola Das

Budelas

Mehrbani
5639

Chaprot River

Chaprot

Chalt

Khizrabad

Hukar

Hussainabad

H U N Z A

Kacheli Gl.

Ghashumaling River

Hunza River

Karakoram   Highway

Maiun

Nilt

to China

0   2   4   6   8   10 km

0   2   4   6 miles

© The Guidebook Company Ltd

to Gilgit

AROUND CHALT

About 60 kilometres north of Gilgit, Chalt is the southernmost settlement of the old Nagar kingdom. The British arrived in 1891 with a force of 1,000 men, strengthened **Chalt Fort** and used it as their base to overthrow Hunza and Nagar in a fierce battle at Nilt, nine kilometres upriver (see page 233).

The area is Shia, like the rest of Nagar, and the people speak Burushaski and Shina. The KKH was originally planned to follow the west bank of the Hunza from Gilgit through Nomal and Chalt, but the conservative Chalt elders refused, so the road was built up the east bank instead. We found the people greedy and unhelpful, possibly because we were two unescorted women. The dour temperament cannot be explained by hardship, as Chalt is one of the richest oases along the KKH—a wide, fertile bowl fed by the waters of the Chaprot and Bola Das rivers.

Chalt lies on the line of collision between two geological plates. The Indian subcontinent is still pushing northwards into the Asian land mass, and a small island plate is being crushed between them. The deepest, oldest layers of this island plate are at Patan, further south on the KKH, and the top layer appears at Chalt. A sign on the cliff beside the KKH before Chalt reads: 'Here continents collided.'

Public jeeps leave Gilgit daily for Chalt from Bank Road and from opposite the Aga Khan Polo Ground; the fare is about Rs15. Or you can take any vehicle up the KKH and get off at the Chalt turning, from where it is a hot, barren three kilometres across the Hunza and Chaprot rivers to Chalt. You can stay at the NAPWD rest house (bookable in Gilgit, see page 170) or in a local hotel in the bazaar. The assistant commissioner of Nagar lives in Chalt. A member of the Nagar royal family, he stays in one of his family homes beside the fort.

CHALT UP CHAPROT VALLEY

Map: Swiss Karakoram map, reliability good; U502 NJ 43-14 (Baltit), reliability very poor. Open zone; easy; two days; maximum height 3,500 metres (optional); April to November (July to September if going higher).

Chaprot is thickly forested. R C F Schomberg, who travelled all over the area before World War II, enthused in his *Between Oxus and Indus*: 'The Chaprot Valley is lovely, more beautiful than any other valley in the Gilgit Agency.' You can cover the three kilometres from Chalt to Chaprot village by jeep along the north side of the Chaprot River or follow the footpath along the south bank. Just before Chaprot, the **Ghashumaling River** flows in from the southwest, offering easy walking along irrigation channels through orchards of fruit and nut trees, coming after about ten kilometres to pastures, pine forest and the **Kacheli Glacier**.

Above Chaprot village, the main donkey trail follows the north side of the Chaprot River up through **Bola Das** (note that Bola Das is not on the Bola Das River and is easily confused with Budelas, which is). The trail continues through Burishki, among other summer villages, and on to the pastures and woods at the top of the valley. A footpath cuts north from Chaprot village, over the ridge to Daintar, joining the route to the Daintar Pass and Naltar.

CHALT UP BOLA DAS (GARAMSAI OR BUDELAS) VALLEY

Map: Swiss Karakoram map, reliability good; U502 NJ 43-14 (Baltit), reliability very poor. Open zone; easy to strenuous; four to eight days; maximum height optional; roughly June to October, depending on altitude.

The jeep road to Bar, about 20 kilometres upriver from Chalt, passes through the large, fertile **Budelas** oasis, which is on the east bank at the junction of the Shittinbar River (a possible side trip). It then traverses a barren stretch before crossing back to **Torbuto Das**, at the junction of the Daintar River. The footpath stays on the west bank all the way, passing a hot spring, one of many in the Northern Areas, whose sulphurous waters are supposedly good for rheumatism and skin diseases. You can also reach the hot spring from the jeep road via a foot bridge.

At Torbuto Das, a branch jeep road follows the Daintar River up through Daintar to Taling, the beginning of the trek via the **Daintar Pass** to Naltar. Daintar Pass is more difficult from this side because of a huge snowfield below the pass and the heavy snow cornice on top of the ridge. It would be wise to take a shepherd to show the way. We describe the trek in the opposite direction (see page 212).

Bar, the road head five kilometres above Torbuto Das, is famous for its hot spring. About six kilometres further upriver, the valley divides, east to the Baltar and Toltar glaciers, and west to the Kukuar Glacier. Bar to **Baltar**, a large summer pasture between the moraines of the Baltar and Toltar glaciers, is a relatively easy two-day walk. You can continue up a difficult moraine to more summer settlements. The top ends of these glaciers are blocked by the Batura Wall, the steep, icy flanks of which soar 3,000 metres to the summit of **Batura Mountain** (7,785 metres).

If you have mountaineering experience or a professional guide, you can follow the western valley up to the Kukuar Glacier. According to the Swiss Karakoram map, there are paths up either side of the glacier that bring you after about two days to **Bara** (meaning 'big') **Darakush** (about 3,350 metres), from where it is another day's walk to **Chota** ('little') **Darakush** (about 4,250 metres). H W Tilman came this way in 1947, looking for a route over to the Batura Glacier (see Tilman, *Two Mountains and a River*).

MAIUN VALLEY
Map: Swiss Karakoram map, reliability good; U502 NJ 43-14 (Baltit), reliability poor.

The first valley in the old kingdom of Hunza, Maiun descends from the north to join the Hunza River about ten kilometres upriver of Chalt, opposite Nilt and the KKH. The Swiss Karakoram map shows footpaths up to summer pastures along both the west and east branches of the Maiun River (spelled Mayon on the Swiss map). There are several small settlements and pastures up the valley. We have not been there, but it looks interesting (please send information).

RAKAPOSHI BASE CAMPS

The KKH turns east at Chalt and hugs the Hunza River round the north side of Rakaposhi, at 7,788 metres, the 27th-highest mountain in the world. There are three possible short treks up to various Rakaposhi base camps.

OPTIONS FROM JAGLOT AND GHULMAT
Map: Swiss Karakoram map, reliability good; U502 NJ 43-14 (Baltit), reliability poor.
Open zone; easy; two to five days; maximum height optional; roughly April to November, depending on altitude.

The first starts at **Jaglot**, about 15 kilometres downriver from Chalt (not to be confused with the other Jaglot further south on the Indus, beside the turning to Astor). Jaglot is out of sight of the KKH and connected to it by a jeep track. From Jaglot village, you can trek up the north side of the Jaglot River through pine woods and wild roses to **Barit**, where you cross the stream and follow the south bank to **Dobar**, returning thence to the north side of the river. Continue through the summer settlement of **Darakush** past more pine woods, then along the ablation valley on the north side of the **Biro Glacier** to a flat pasture surrounded by birch trees, at 3,750 metres, the base camp for the northwest ridge and **Secord Peak** (first climbed by Campbell Secord and J M K Vyvyan in 1938). Alternatively, you can cross to the south bank of the Jalkot River at Darakush and find your way to the north side of the **Kunti Glacier** and the base

Rakaposhi base camps

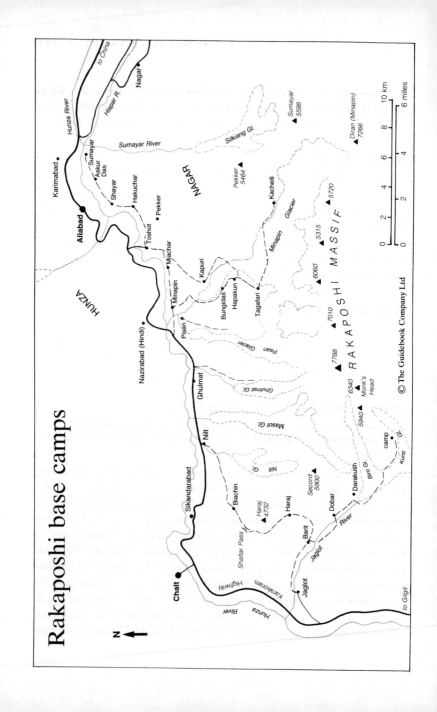

© The Guidebook Company Ltd

camp for the southwest spur and the **Monk's Head**. This is the route by which Rakaposhi was first climbed, in 1956, by Mike Banks and Tom Patey of the British Royal Navy. (Information from Alfred Tissières.)

Instead of returning to Jaglot, you can take the steep trail up from Barit to the summer settlement of **Haraj**, on the Haraj Ridge, and down through **Biachun** to **Nilt**, on the KKH.

Nilt was the site of the battle between the British and the combined forces of Nagar and Hunza in 1891; it took the British three weeks to rout the locals. It is now the home of the Pakistan Mountaineering Institute, which very occasionally runs training courses for Pakistani mountaineers (see page 233).

At **Ghulmat**, a few kilometres beyond Nilt, there is a superb view of Rakaposhi. A sign in English reads: 'Visitors please Rakaposhi on your right.' The view runs straight up the gleaming white Ghulmat Glacier—which is surrounded by white ridges and peaks and great expanses of smooth snow—to the top, 5,838 metres above you and 11 kilometres away. This is the highest unbroken slope on earth. (The famous north face of Nanga Parbat rises from 1,150 metres at the Indus to 8,125 metres at the summit of the mountain, but the subsidiary peak of Ganalo, at 6,606 metres, breaks the slope—which, in any case, is not as steep as the Ghulmat.)

The Ghulmat roadside drink stall and Rakaposhi View Hotel (Rs10 per bed in a tent) are the starting point for a trek up to the Japanese 1979 base camp on the Ghulmat Glacier. It is a hot, steep, waterless climb up the ridge between the Ghulmat and Pisan glaciers. The route offers great views of Rakaposhi but has little else to recommend it.

Beware that Ghulmat is easily confused with Gulmit, which is further up the KKH, near Passu. Some wagon drivers think it is funny to drop tourists at the wrong one.

The most scenic base camp of all is reached from **Minapin**, about 10 kilometres up the KKH.

MINAPIN UP MINAPIN GLACIER TO KACHEILI

Map: Deutsche Himalaya Expedition map of Minapin, reliability excellent; Swiss Karakoram map, reliability good; U502 NJ 43-14 (Baltit), reliability fair.
Open zone; easy; two to five days; maximum height about 4,000 metres (2,400 metres at glacier snout); April to October.

Tumbling down from the flanks of Rakaposhi and visible from the KKH, the Minapin Glacier is a wide, crevassed sheet of gleaming ice. Up the southern side, thick forests of pine, spruce, juniper, willow and silver birch surround summer pastures, grazed by herds of goats and cattle, and potato fields cultivated by the villagers of Minapin. In one or two days, depending on your strength, you can trek up this green valley to Tagafari, one of the base camps of Rakaposhi. It makes a short, safe, easy and extremely scenic hike, recommended to beginners as a first trek. Its greatest advantage is that it is accessible directly from the KKH and can, at a pinch, be completed in two days.

Transport: Take any vehicle from Gilgit toward Hunza and get off at the Pisan and Minapin turn, a kilometre before the KKH crosses the Hunza River, or about an hour's drive north of Gilgit. Pisan and Minapin are rival villages facing each other across the Minapin River. You can hire porters at the Diran Peak Hotel (very basic), which is just above the KKH to the right, at the beginning of the jeep road leading four kilometres to Minapin village. The jeep road ends at the Minapin NAPWD rest house (d Rs60; book in Gilgit, see page 170), where more porters and donkeys are available.

Porters here are expensive. The official government rate is Rs110 per day, plus Rs30 for food, but these porters charge Rs200 per day and demand six days' pay to Tagafari and back. They calculate two pay stages up, plus half rate to return empty, as they insist that you hire new porters for the return trip. They were taken to court in 1986 by Nazir Sabir, lost the case and were told (according to Doug Scott in *Alpine Journal*, vol 91, page 47): 'Minapin to Base Camp at Minapin Glacier, being an eight hour carry, counts as one day only.' They still try to charge exorbitant prices, so bargain hard. Come to an agreement before you start trekking and make your porters sign a written statement. Be firm and do not hesitate to take them to the police if there is trouble. If you were to arrive with your own porters from elsewhere, there would be a riot.

We have not trekked up the **Pisan Glacier**, but there are summer pastures also up there. The Pisan Glacier's other point of interest is the ice harvest. In the early morning, almost daily during the summer months, groups of villagers go up and cut ice blocks weighing 30 to 70 kilogrammes, carry them down and truck them to Gilgit for sale. Drinks merchants use the ice to cool bottled drinks and to make sorbets by sprinkling chips of ice with fruit syrups. Minapin and Miachar villagers also harvest ice but less frequently.

Stage 1: Minapin to Hapakun, three to four hours. It takes an hour on foot to cover the four kilometres along the jeep road from the KKH through irrigated farmland to Minapin. Continue on through the crooked alleyways of Minapin village, where you can fill your water bottles, using the wooden dippers that float in the wells. Twisted grapevines festoon the huge mulberry and walnut trees shading the alleys, from where you catch glimpses into cobbled courtyards and walled orchards through open wooden doors.

From the village, follow the irrigation channel up to a bridge that leads back across the Minapin River, then follow a well-made donkey path, keeping the river on your left (the river's exit from the snout of the Minapin Glacier is out of sight of the path). A steep climb of about an hour takes you to the forest and **Bungidas**, the first summer settlement comprising about ten shepherds' huts surrounded by juniper, willow, thorn and rose bushes, with a few fields of barley and potatoes. From March to November, the male shepherds of Minapin sleep up here, but the women come up to work only during the daytime, returning to Minapin for the night. Hapakun, another hour's walk higher, is a summer settlement of three houses surrounded by fields of hay and potatoes. At the top end of the settlement, a fresh spring beside a rock at the end of the small stream provides the best place to camp.

Stage 2: Hapakun to Tagafari, two to three hours. Follow a good path up through forest, zigzagging easily through steep pastures to the top of what looks like a pass. When you arrive there, you see that it is really the lateral moraine of the glacier, which until this moment has been hidden from view. Your reward is a panoramic view dominated by the sharp cone of Diran (Minapin) Peak (7,266 metres) and the gleaming serrated ridge connecting Diran to Rakaposhi. The entire bowl between you and the mountain ridge is filled with the swirling lines of the crevassed Minapin Glacier. The next section of the walk is difficult for those carrying a heavy pack and impossible for donkeys. You follow a narrow path across the side of the lateral moraine for about 200 metres, with a steep scree slope dropping about 30 metres down to the glacier. Vertigo sufferers will find this trying, but the path is no problem at all for those who are used to heights.

The final half hour is an easy descent to Tagafari, a long, narrow, banana-shaped field (which must once have been a lake) between the lateral moraine and the foot of Rakaposhi. A stream fed by melting snow flows through the meadow in June, July and August. Early and late in the season, when the snows are not melting, the only source of water at Tagafari is a tiny spring under a rock on the right, about 100 metres from the top end of the field. A lone shepherds' hut with two rooms and a leaky roof is occupied from May to September by about five men from Minapin, who tend about 500 goats and 100 head of cattle. You can watch them milk and make butter, *ghee*, *lassi* and cheese (*buruss* in Burushaski).

Plan to spend at least 24 hours here. From the top of the lateral moraine, you look across the Minapin Glacier to Diran (Minapin) Peak, first climbed in 1968 by the Austrians. On the other side of the field, a long ridge covered in silver birch and mountain ash runs down from Rakaposhi, protecting the meadow. A 20-minute climb to the top of this ridge gives views north to Batura, Passu, Shishpar and Ultar peaks and south to Rakaposhi and Diran peaks and the Minapin Glacier. To the northeast lies the Hunza Valley, within which you can clearly see the KKH and Nazirabad (originally called Hini and marked as Hindi on the Swiss Karakoram map). You can walk the length of this ridge and climb a little way up Rakaposhi. There are rumoured to be bears (*ridge* in Urdu) on this ridge, but in fact the last bear was shot years ago.

Stage 3: Tagafari to Kacheili, three to five hours. A guide is recommended, as you must cross the glacier from the top end of the meadow at Tagafari, where the lateral moraine meets Rakaposhi. Kacheili is another grassy meadow with flowers, which is at its best in June and July, offering superb views of Rakaposhi.

Stage 4: Return to Hapakun, three to four hours. It is safest to return by the same route. We have not tried the route along the north side of the Minapin Glacier, as it is said to be difficult and dangerous.

Stage 5: Hapakun to Minapin, two hours. Or **Hapakun to Toshot**, four hours. The second option involves crossing the Minapin Glacier on a diagonal route from a point on the southern lateral moraine behind the shepherds' hut at the top corner of the highest field in Hapakun. From the top of the moraine (a one-minute climb from the hut), looking northwest across the glacier, you can see a dip in the northern lateral moraine, marking the point where the path climbs up off the glacier. It takes about one hour to cross, but you should not attempt this without a guide, unless you are experienced with Karakoram glaciers.

Once on the other side, follow the top of the northern lateral moraine down for half an hour to the summer settlement of **Kapuri**—a lone hut surrounded by fields (and a possible campsite with water)—then scramble along the irrigation channels going north round the side of the mountain. You follow two different channels; when, after about 20 minutes the first one heads off down the mountain, leave it and cut across to a second channel further north. Follow the second channel for about half an hour to a point where you can scramble down the hillside to a wide donkey track that rides across the cliff face high above the south bank of the Hunza River. The track connects Minapin village with **Miachar** and **Dadimal** and finally comes down to the banks of the Hunza River at **Toshot**, where there is a jeep bridge.

Along the higher stretches of the path, through Miachar, you can see over the top of the **Pekker Ridge** to central Hunza. Baltit Fort and the gorge leading to the Ultar Glacier are clearly visible. On the banks of the Hunza on the Toshot side of the river is a gold panners' settlement, where you can watch the panners using their flat wooden boards to sieve the gold from the river. Cross the jeep bridge to regain the KKH, from where you can hitchhike, or take a bus or wagon, back to Gilgit or on to Hunza and China.

PEKKER RIDGE AND SUMAYAR VALLEY

Map: Swiss Karakoram map, reliability good; U502 NJ 43-14 (Baltit), reliability fair.
Open zone; easy; number of days optional; maximum height optional; April to October.

Start at the jeep bridge across the Hunza River at Toshot. Climb above Toshot to the top of the Pekker Ridge and camp for the best morning and evening photos of Hunza against the backdrop of Ultar Mountain (7,388 metres).

Follow the old contour track round the base of the ridge from Toshot to central Nagar. The trail passes through **Shayar** and **Askur Das** to **Sumayar**, at the mouth of the Sumayar River. You can trek up the Sumayar River through the gorge to summer pastures in about three hours. Follow the water channel up from the hydro-electric powerhouse. From the pastures you can continue to the **Silkiang Glacier**, flowing off Sumayar Peak, for superb views back north to Baltit, with Ultar Mountain behind, and south to Diran Peak.

In winter, when the water is low, a temporary footbridge crosses from Sumayar to the Nagar road, which leads to the KKH, but in summer the shortest way back to Hunza is via the jeep bridge below Nagar village.

CENTRAL NAGAR

According to an unlikely local legend, Nagar was first settled in about the fourteenth century by people from Baltistan, who came over the Hispar Pass and down the Hispar Glacier. Interestingly, the people of Askole in Baltistan (see page 129) believe their ancestors came from Nagar at about the same time.

In any case, Hispar, hidden 25 kilometres up a difficult gorge, is believed to be one of the earliest villages in Nagar; Sumayar, on the banks of the Hunza, is another early village of Balti descent. Meanwhile the Burushaski speakers of Gilgit, who had been driven up into the mountains by the Shins, settled in Hunza and crossed the river to Nagar in about the fourteenth century. A man called Borosh from Hunza supposedly founded the first village of Boroshal and married a Balti girl he found there. The legend says the girl and her grandmother were the sole survivors of a landslide that killed all of the early Balti settlers.

Uyum Nagar (now Nagar village and the 28 hamlets surrounding it) was settled late in the fifteenth century by Burushaski speakers from Gor, near Chilas, who built the big fortified village of Nagar, the home of the rulers of Nagar (a list of kings runs from about 1500). Early in the twentieth century, erosion underminded the village, which

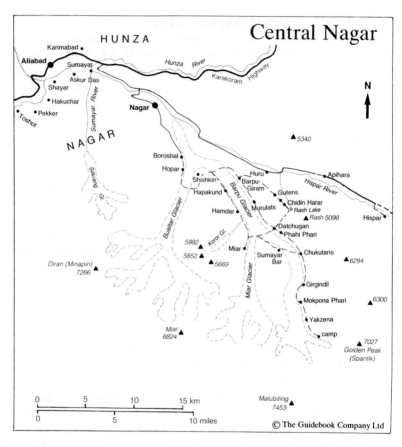

fell into the river; now only the ex-ruler's palace remains on top of the hill.

Nagar and Hunza were converted from animism to Shia Islam in the sixteenth or seventeenth century. From about 1700 on, the two kingdoms were at war with each other, continually attacking each other and stealing women and children to sell as slaves. Everyone lived in fortified villages until the nineteenth century, when new immigrants arrived, first founding Askur Das and Shayar and then, as population pressure increased, building new, unfortified hamlets.

As Nagar has always had the better water supply, it is bigger than Hunza. The present population of the bowl of Nagar is about 36,000, compared to 20,000 people in the bowl of Hunza. (The population of the whole of Nagar, from Chalt to Hispar, is 47,000; that of the whole of Hunza, from the Maiun Valley to Khunjerab, is 36,000.) The continuing conflict between the two kingdoms is exacerbated by religion, as the Hunzakuts are now Ismailis, followers of the Aga Khan, and the people of Nagar remain Shia. There is also a personality divide, which popular legend puts down to the sun: the slopes of central Hunza face south to the warming sun, while Nagar slopes north, shivering in the shadow of Rakaposhi. Consequently, the legend suggests, the Hunzakuts have a warm, open nature, while their neighbours across the river are known for their dour temperament.

Whatever the reason, trekking in Nagar can be difficult, especially for women. Porters can be extremely expensive, sometimes charging a day's wage for hikes as short as 90 minutes. The scenery is magnificent, though, equalling or bettering anything in Hunza.

Above Central Nagar, the **Bualtar Glacier**, known locally as the Hopar Glacier, drops 5,000 metres from its source on Diran (Minapin) Peak and ends at 2,270 metres above sea-level, apparently making it the world's lowest glacier between the latitudes of 40°N and 35°S. Its snout is certainly the lowest in the Karakoram-Himalaya region, with the Minapin and Pisan glaciers being close seconds, at 2,400 metres (see C Charles' doctoral thesis, *La Vallée de Hunza Karakorum*, 1985). In 1990, the Bualtar was surging along at a reckless 20 metres per day, creaking and groaning as it ground forward, churning itself into huge ice pinnacles and yawning crevasses. The Bualtar wins no speed record, however; there is a glacier in Greenland that has been clocked at 300 metres per day.

NAGAR INFORMATION

Public wagons and **jeeps** leave every morning from Bank Road in Gilgit (the Nagar enclave round the Golden Peak Inn) for Nagar village, the capital of the old Nagar kingdom. The fare is about Rs25. Some jeeps go on to the road head at Hopar, the start of the best treks. Hopar is an area comprising five hamlets, and the road ends just beyond Holshal, which is marked on both the Swiss Karakoram and U502 maps. From Aliabad in Hunza, public jeeps leave most days for Nagar and occasionally continue to Hopar. Alternatively, you can hire a jeep in Aliabad from the PTDC Hotel, the Prince Hotel or the jeep stand at Ganesh Monument to drive you in 90 minutes to Hopar (about Rs600).

The **Post Office** is in Nagar village beside the road in the bazaar. The **telephone exchange** is at the top of the hill outside the gate to the mir's palace.

For **accommodation** in Nagar village there is only the seedy NAPWD rest house (d Rs60; book in Gilgit, see page 170). In Hopar, the Hopar Hilton's tents (Rs 30 per bed) are ideally sited on the edge of the Bualtar (Hopar) Glacier. There is a stark new government rest house nearby, bookable in Gilgit.

Guides and **porters** are available at the Hopar Hilton (see the note on Minapin porters, page 220). Ghulam Nabi and Shafi Ahmad are recommended guides, but you may find that the village council has organised the rotation of local porters and you have to take the men allotted you.

Because of the troubles presented by Nagar porters, the famous trek along the Biafo and Hispar glaciers (121 kilometres of continuous ice) is best done from the other end (see Baltistan, page 137).

BUALTAR (HOPAR) AND BARPU GLACIERS

Map: Swiss Karakoram map, reliability good; U502 NJ 43-14 (Baltit), reliability fair.
Open zone; easy to strenuous; four to ten days; maximum height about 4,000 metres, optional to 5,098 metres; April to October (August to September above 4,500 metres).

Except for the first day, this is a green and relatively easy trek, recommended for first-time trekkers, following the northeastern flank of the Barpu Glacier along a flat, fertile ablation valley, where large herds of goats and cattle graze among tamarisk and willow woods in summertime. Golden (Spantik) Peak and Malubiting Mountain, two snow-covered sentinels, stand guard at the end of the glacier. Alternatively, you can make it a more challenging trek by climbing up to Rash Lake and/or continuing to Golden Peak Base Camp. Rash Lake is at 4,700 metres; if you are not already acclimatised, take some extra days on the way up.

A five- or ten-litre water container is essential on this trek, as most campsites are waterless from July on, and water has to be carried from glacier pools up to 30 minutes away.

When negotiating with porters it helps to know the recognised pay stages: Hopar–Shishkin–Barpu Giram–Gutens–Rash Lake (Rash Phari)–Phahi Phari (or Chukutans)–Girgindil–Sumayar Bar–Hamdar–Shishkin–Hopar. These ten stages make a comfortable seven- or eight-day trek. It would take five extra days to go up to Golden Peak Base Camp. Providing you agree to pay Rs140 (Rs110 plus Rs30 for food) for each stage, you should avoid porter strikes.

Stage 1: Hopar to Shishkin, three to four hours. This is a hot, dry day, so fill your water bottles. As the Bualtar (Hopar) Glacier moves quickly, the crossing is difficult and the route changes daily. Attempt the crossing only with a local escort or porter who has crossed recently.

Start behind the Hopar Hilton. Follow the new tractor road down to the glacier, then continue on the footpath east along the lateral moraine for about an hour to the crossing place (that is, the 1990 crossing place). A difficult hour on moving boulders and slippery ice slopes takes you to the other side, where a path zigzags up a steep slope to a high plateau, from where you have an extensive view back across the glacier to Hopar and the surrounding highly cultivated area. A hot, dry path leads down to the abandoned and waterless huts of Shishkin, between the Bualtar and Barpu glaciers. This may be a nice campsite in the spring with a small stream, but in July it takes an hour to fetch water from the glacier. Most trekkers continue to Barpu Giram on the first day.

Stage 2: Across the Barpu Glacier to Barpu Giram, two to three hours. Climb for half an hour on a hot, barren track up a stony gully to the Barpu Glacier, which comes in at a higher level from the southeast to join the Bualtar. Here near its snout, the Barpu Glacier is a black sea of soft mud and slippery ice, which makes for an unpleasant crossing that takes at least an hour, ending with a short, steep climb up the lateral moraine to the pastures beyond. There are no trees or water here, so continue for 45 minutes up to Barpu Giram, a cluster of shepherds' huts and goat pens occupied by Hopar men from April to mid-July, after which they move higher up the glacier. The men milk the goats into gourds, make butter in tall wooden churns and boil up the whey to make a sort of cheese. As there is a good supply of wood further up the glacier, they also spend some of their time making *charpoys* and chairs.

The stream at Barpu Giram is fed by melting snow from May to mid-July, after which water must be carried from pools on the glacier, a short hike over the lateral moraine. All the trees have been cut here, and only a few scrubby thorn bushes remain. To avoid fleas and lice, camp above the settlement at about 3,000 metres.

You will find there a view of Golden Peak (7,027 metres) framed in the V of the valley. Two yellow streaks of marble rising 1,000 metres up its north flank give the mountain its popular name. It was first climbed in 1955 by the Germans. Dr William Hunter Workman and his wife Fanny Bullock Workman had got to within 330 metres of the top in 1903 and named it Pinnacle Peak. In 1987 two British climbers, Michael Fowler and Victor Saunders, made the fifth ascent of the mountain, climbing up the marble pillar (see Saunders, *Elusive Summits*).

From Barpu Giram, you have a choice of routes. Either take the highly recommended two- or three-day detour up to Rash Lake (Rash Phari in Burushaski or Rash Jheel in Urdu), or continue directly along the edge of the Barpu Glacier (see Stage 3 alternative below).

Stage 3: Barpu Giram to Gutens, four to six hours. Start early so you will climb in shade. A good zigzag path starts just above the huts and leads steeply up to the crest of the ridge, approximately 800 metres above you, in about two hours. Here you have impressive views north across the barren Hispar Gorge to the high mountains Lupghur, Momhil, Trivor and Bularung (all over 7,000 metres). The path continues for a further two hours along the ridge and then climbs to the first shepherds' huts at Gutens, which is abandoned and waterless in August. Thirty minutes longer takes you to another cluster of stone huts on the very edge of the ridge, where shepherds tend large herds of sheep and goats. This is a good campsite, at about 4,000 metres, but it takes 45 minutes to fetch water—so pay a shepherd boy to go for you.

A steep path leads down from here to Huru, in the Hispar Valley (see page 147).

Stage 4: Gutens to Rash Lake, three to four hours. Look forward to a day of tremendous views on all sides. Follow the grassy ridge up for one or two hours to the few abandoned huts at **Chidin Harar**, and continue up a wide valley for another hour to a small pass, beyond which you cross a plateau for 30 minutes, passing the first running streams since Hopar, to Rash Lake. Camp beside the lake at 4,760 metres.

Rash Peak, at 5,098 metres on the ridge behind the lake, is a good late-afternoon or early-morning walk for superb views down into the Hispar Gorge and a 360-degree panorama of Golden Peak, Malubiting, Miar, all of Hunza with Ultar and Passu peaks, all of Nagar and the mountains to the north of the Hispar. One trekker reports seeing the distinctive triangle of K2, 170 kilometres to the east, but this seems unlikely. A few tent platforms are cut into the hill just below the summit, making this a fantastic campsite if the weather is good and you carry up your water.

Stage 5: Rash Lake to Chukutans, four to six hours. Phahi Phari is about 1,500 metres below Rash Lake, on the edge of the Barpu Glacier. It is down a very steep path with no water and is extremely hot later in the day, but the route down offers magnificent views of the Miar Glacier and the Rakaposhi Range.

Phahi Phari is a single shepherds' hut in the ablation valley beside the Barpu Glacier. In June and July, there is a small lake filled with melt water. Willow and juniper trees surround the site, and lavender and vetch cover the moraine. From the top of the moraine are marvellous views of Golden Peak and the Barpu Glacier, but Malubiting and Miar are hidden.

A gentle, steady climb through juniper and ash woods brings you in one hour to Chukutans, a summer settlement of several huts and goat pens where the men of Hopar stay from mid-July to the end of August. It makes an excellent campsite, with green grass and clear water from May through August. The camp is set a little way up the side of the hill, with extensive views up and down the Barpu Glacier and across to

Sumayar Bar summer camp—a pasture at the base of a sparsely wooded hill. Looking south up Barpu Glacier, you can just see the west shoulder of Golden Peak over a rocky projection that juts out, forcing the Barpu Glacier to sweep round it.

Stage 3 alternative: Barpu Giram straight to Chukutans, four hours. Follow the grassy ablation meadow, with clear views back to Ultar Peak in Hunza and forward to Golden Peak. From June to August, it is hot, as the altitude is only about 3,000 metres, but the flowers are at their best in June and July. You pass through a virtual forest of wild roses and tamarisk besides plentiful juniper, willow, ash and thorn trees. Dozens of black-tailed hares scamper through the rocks.

Murulats, about 90 minutes from Barpu Giram, is a lone hut occasionally occupied by shepherds. Here, as at Barpu Giram, the stream has water only when the snow melts in June and July. Phahi Phari is a steady 90-minute climb from Murulats, getting more wooded and flower-filled the further you go, as purple vetch and lavender carpet the moraine. About 30 minutes before Phahi Phari, the valley narrows at a slight rise, forming a natural gateway known as Datchugan. A rock on the left at this point is covered in ibex drawings. As this marks the beginning of one of the crossing places of the glacier, these ibex drawings are probably good-luck symbols designed to ensure a safe crossing, but they could also be fertility symbols (for the importance of the ibex in folklore, see page 37). From the top of the lateral moraine here, there is a magnificent view of the junction of the Miar and Barpu glaciers and of Miar Peak (6,824 metres) at the head of the Miar Glacier. It takes about two hours to cross the glacier here to Miar—a lone shepherds' hut with an erratic water supply.

Continue from Phahi Phari to Chukutans (see above). Alternatively, you can cross the Barpu Glacier from Chukutans to Sumayar Bar in one hour.

Stage 6 (or 4): Chukutans to Girgindil, two to three hours. Follow the lateral moraine for a short while, then drop down to the edge of the glacier to circumvent a rocky projection. Girgindil, which is easily visible from Chukutans, consists of one shepherds' hut (abandoned in August) and a herd of the fattest bullocks we have seen in the Karakorams, all enjoying this little-grazed pasture with an abundance of flowers. The side river beyond the camp is suitable for washing, but drinking water has to be fetched from the stream you cross 20 minutes before arriving at the camp. There is no shade.

A 90-minute walk leads high above the camp to the northeast, arriving at a steep ridge with three tall cairns. To get there, follow the side valley towards Golden Peak through deep flowers and past the last juniper bushes, for magnificent views of Golden Peak and the Chogo Lungma group and down the Barpu Glacier to Hunza and the high mountains beyond.

A recommended option from Girgindil is a five- or six-day trek up to **Golden Peak Base Camp**, described here.

First day: Girgindil to Mokpona Phari. Drop down to the glacier and follow a runnel of steep slurry at its edge, dodging occasional falling debris. At times, move further out on the glacier. This is a messy, awkward section, better before the sun hits it at about 8 am. Continue more easily on the edge of the glacier to arrive in two to three hours at Mokpona Phari, a small pasture with one shepherds' hut that is no longer used, as there are fewer herds since the KKH was built and more jobs became available. This makes a good campsite amid lush vegetation and breathtaking flowers, with water and a view of Golden Peak, Malubiting and the Barpu Glacier.

Second day: Mokpona Phari to Yakzena, four to five hours. Gird for a rough day up and down and across steep earth slides featuring vertiginous drops to the glacier below. Make your way as best you can along the side of the glacier—and at times up to 300 metres above it—to by-pass steep, eroded gulches. Yakzena is a collection of house-sized boulders offering shelter for porters. You are surrounded by high mountains with icy veils spreading out on both sides. There is good water nearby and stunning flowers.

Third day: Yakzena to Golden Peak Base Camp. Cross steep, hazardous earth and rock slides, then climb easy slopes carpeted in flowers all the way to the base camp, which has two stone shelters beside a running stream, with plenty of space to pitch tents. It is an easy walk up to the base of the north face of Golden Peak, right in the heart of the mountains. (Information from Joe Brennan and Steve Harvatt.)

Another report says it is only one hour from Mokpona Phari to Golden Peak Base Camp (please send more information). You can also reach Malubiting Base Camp from Mokpona Phari in two hours by crossing the glacier, which is comparatively easy.

Stage 7 (or 5) Girgindil to Sumayar Bar, about three hours. You can cross the Barpu Glacier just below Girgindil in about one hour if your guide knows the route. On the other (west) side of the glacier, the lateral moraine is less steep and greener, with occasional grazing animals. It takes about two more hours to Sumayar Bar, where you can camp beside fresh water (or continue to Hamdar).

Stage 8 (or 6) Sumayar Bar to Hamdar: three to four hours. An easy walk down the wooded lateral moraine takes you in 90 minutes to the Miar Glacier. Cross the clean, white ice, which is slippery in the early morning but easier than the last part, which is stony. On the other side, you join the path leading down the lateral moraine from **Miar**. Follow the path down. Further along it is well built, high above the junction of the Miar and Barpu glaciers and cut into sheer rock. You cross a side stream (no bridge) coming down from the **Koroi Glacier**, above which there is said to be good climbing on each of the three peaks. After another 30 minutes, reach the first terraced fields of Hamdar, which comprises six shepherds' huts surrounded by wheat and potato fields. The water channel above is filled only in the evening, so drinking water must be lifted from an underground reservoir. Shepherds stay at Hamdar for four months, from June to September.

Stage 9 (or 7): Hamdar to Hopar, four to five hours. Hamdar to Hapakund takes one hour, with views of Golden, Chukutans, Rash peaks and Barpu Glacier. **Hapakund** has seven huts surrounded by wheat, potato and hay fields and is occupied for five months from the end of April—if the water supply lasts. In one more hour you reach **Shishkin** on a path across the hillside, where you close the loop of this varied trek. Backtrack for two or three hours down to the road head at Hopar. (Additional information from Elisabeth Gardner.)

CENTRAL HUNZA

Dominated by Baltit Fort, the famous irrigated terraces of central Hunza, ranged as neatly as fish scales, ripple down the lower slopes of Ultar Mountain. Across the valley, the gleaming snows of Rakaposhi thrust a vertical five kilometres skywards. The isolation of this famous beauty spot ended with the opening of the Karakoram Highway (KKH) in 1978, and now tourism is quickly encroaching on Hunza. Yet, despite the concrete hotels that increasingly scar the hillside, the grandeur of the setting is so powerful that Hunza retains its appeal.

At an altitude of about 2,400 metres, Hunza has an average annual rainfall of about 145 millimetres. The wettest months are April, May, July and August, which together account for 65 percent of the total, leaving the valley fairly dry from October to March.

HUNZA HISTORY

The origin of the Hunza people is unclear. They look European (specifically Celtic), many with brown or russet hair and green or blue eyes. The Hunzakuts themselves tell a legend of three soldiers from the army of Alexander the Great, which passed through Pakistan in 325 BC, settling in the valley with their Persian wives and founding the first villages of Altit, Baltit and Ganesh—a pretty story, but unfounded. The old *mir* (king) of Hunza had an even better tale, reported by E F Knight in *Where Three Empires Meet*. He claimed to be descended from the union of Alexander the Great and a fairy of the Hindu Kush, giving himself, as Knight says, 'certainly a very respectable pedigree'.

What is certain is that Altit, Baltit and Ganesh were the first three villages in Hunza and were probably settled in the eleventh century. Indeed, they were the only villages until the end of the eighteenth century, when improved irrigation techniques enabled the colony to expand.

Western researchers such as Karl Jettmar and Hermann Kreutzmann think the Hunzakuts are probably descended from the original mountain inhabitants. They speak Burushaski, an autochthonous language with no apparent link to any existing language family. Burushaski speakers probably once inhabited the entire Gilgit area, as many of the place names there are of Burushaski origin. Certainly the Tibetans in the seventh century refer to the whole area as Bruza and to the people as Burushos. As noted by Jettmar in *Bolar and Dardistan*, the Tibetans record that, in 740, a king of Bruza married a Tibetan princess. In the eleventh century, the invading Shins, speaking Shina, drove the Burushaski-speakers into the Hunza and Yasin valleys (see page 161).

Hunza has been ruled by the same family since the eleventh century, which, from 1761 to 1937, paid nominal tribute to Xinjiang, but in all essentials was independent. For centuries the Hunzakuts earned their livelihood by taxing the caravans along this branch of the Silk Route between Gilgit and Kashgar—and by well-organised brigandage. They were the terror of the people between Afghanistan and Yarkhand, and made frequent raids across the Hindu Kush and Karakoram, even robbing the trade caravans as far away as Shahidula, on the route from Leh across the Karakoram Pass to Yarkhand. On one memorable occasion they captured a caravan of 50 laden camels and 500 laden ponies. Slave dealing was equally lucrative. All men, women and children taken in these raids were driven across the mountains and sold in Chinese Turkestan or to Kirghiz tribesmen.

For centuries the tiny state was impregnable. When Kashmir sent a force to attack it in 1848, the Hunzakuts captured 200 of the Kashmiris and sold them as slaves.

Hunza was considered critical to the expansionist plans of tsarist Russia and British India, as it controlled the most important mountain passes linking Russia, India and China. John Biddulph became the first Westerner to penetrate Hunza's southern defences in 1876, but he was not allowed to explore beyond the capital at Baltit. In 1888, the Russians negotiated with the mir of Hunza, offering arms and training in return for a Russian post at Baltit. The British countered by sending Francis Younghusband to explore the mountain passes and by reopening their British Agency in Gilgit in 1889. They also negotiated with the mir of Hunza, offering a subsidy in return for safe passage for trade caravans between Gilgit and Kashgar, safe passage on the Leh–Yarkhand route and the breaking of relations with Russia. It did not take the mir long to calculate that the Russian deal was better, so he returned the English representative to Gilgit.

The British decided to invade Hunza, and in December 1891 a force led by Colonel Algernon Durand advanced to Nilt. In a fierce battle lasting three weeks, the British, aided by a Nagar prince, defeated the combined forces of Nagar and Hunza, but not before Durand was wounded by a bullet made of a garnet encased in lead. The mir fled to Xinjiang, and Baltit Fort was ransacked in search of treasure. The British found little except for some beautifully decorated copies of the Koran and a secret armoury containing gunpowder, garnet bullets and a few Russian riffles.

The British installed the mir's brother, Muhammad Nazim Khan (died 1938), as the new mir and ally, ensuring free passage to Kashgar. In 1895, the Russians and British met in the Pamirs and agreed that a strip of Afghanistan, the Wakhan Corridor, should separate the two empires. There were many skirmishes along the Hunza–Chinese frontier until 1963, when Pakistan and China agreed on the present boundary, about 40 kilometres west of that marked on the U502 map, with the result that Hunza lost to China its eastern grazing lands beyond Shimshal.

From 1897 to 1947, the British kept an assistant political agent in Hunza, but the mir remained in charge of his own government and administration. Following Pakistani independence, little changed until 1974, when the building of the KKH began to open up the area and Islamabad took over Hunza's political, legal and fiscal administration. The mir's son was elected to the Northern Areas Council and is still respected by most of his ex-subjects for his lineage and wealth.

The Hunzakuts were animist until the sixteenth or seventeenth century, when they became Shia Muslims. In the 1820s, the mir was converted to the Ismaili creed, bringing most of his subjects with him to the new faith. The openness and friendliness of the Hunzakuts is in part the result of this, as Ismailis are freer in their outlook than other Muslims—as far back as 1904, for example, the reigning Aga Khan decreed that women should come out of seclusion and be educated.

The modern, green-roofed *jamat khanas* (community centres, not open to tourists) that dominate every village are the new Ismaili places of worship, introduced in 1922, and the old carved mosques are falling into ruin or have already disappeared in most villages. Notices everywhere announce the development projects of the Aga Khan, who takes a deep interest in Pakistan (see page 33).

The great myth of Hunza's tranquility, contentment and purity is perhaps the result of James Hilton's 1933 novel *Lost Horizon*, which depicted a life of bliss in Shangrila. The miracle of the Hunzakuts' longevity, supposedly resulting from their mostly vegetarian diet of cereals and fruit, was the invention of the Swiss dietitian Ralph Bircher, who in 1942 published *Hunza, das Volk, das Kline Krankbert Keunt* (*Hunza—a People Untouched*

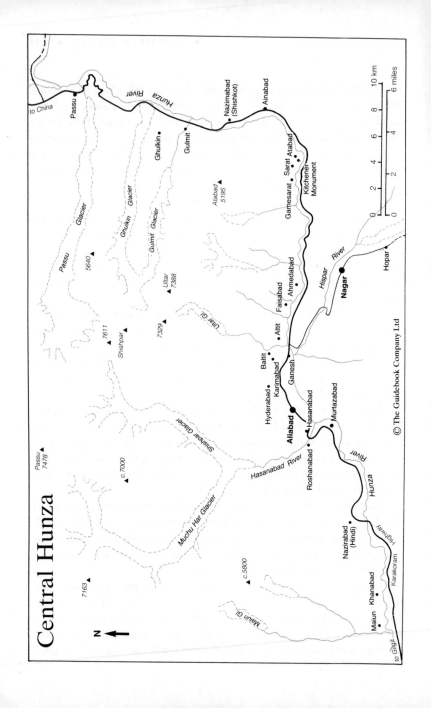

by *Illness*) without ever visiting the area. The myth got further play in articles in *Life* magazine (The Happy Land of Just Enough) and *National Geographic* in 1971 (Every Day Is a Gift When You Are Over 100).

In fact, until the 1980s, life in Hunza was as hard as anywhere else in the Northern Areas, especially in springtime, when food stocks ran low. People looked older than their years, infant mortality was as high as 25 percent, about 7 percent of those who survived suffered from cretinism and—a final gloomy note—questions of succession were generally solved by murder.

This much is true. Fruits and cereals have long been the staple diet. For centuries wheat, barley, buckwheat, millet, peas, beans and spinach have grown in Hunza. From late March to May, the valley is covered in the blossoms of apricot, apple, peach, pear and plum trees; grapevines festoon the trees and terrace walls. This century has seen the arrival of maize, potatoes, cabbage, carrots, courgettes and tomatoes. Until the 1970s, the people ate only what they could produce, but now many men find paid jobs outside of Hunza, causing agricultural production to drop but providing the means to import nearly 60 percent of the Hunzakuts' dietary needs.

The present population of the bowl of central Hunza is about 20,000; about 36,000 live in the whole of Hunza, between the Maiun Valley and Khunjerab.

HUNZA INFORMATION

Several **public wagons** and **jeeps** leave the Jamat Khana Bazaar in Gilgit daily for Karimabad, the best place to go in Hunza. The fare is Rs20. Be sure to ask for Karimabad, rather than just Hunza. The vehicles make a second stop in Gilgit, at the general wagon station, but it is better to catch them at their source, where you can wait in the shade. NATCO buses heading for the Pakistan frontier post at Sost will drop passengers at Aliabad or Ganesh for Rs15, but this is not very satisfactory, as most tourists still need to get up to Karimabad. It is a steep, hot two-kilometre hike up from Ganesh or a Rs50 ride in a private jeep, whose drivers wait for the gullible at Ganesh Monument. Local Suzukis ply up and down the KKH, charging Rs2 per ride to anywhere from Ganesh to Hasanabad. Pay as you get in to avoid a rip-off attempt at the other end.

There is a **bank** on the KKH in Aliabad (no travellers' cheques changed), and the Mountain View Hotel will change dollars. There is a **Post Office** on the KKH in Aliabad and another below the Park Hotel in Karimabad. There are **telephone exchanges** on the KKH in Aliabad and near the Mountain View Hotel in Karimabad.

Accommodation: The best place to stay is **Karimabad**, which, at about 2,450 metres, offers stunning views over the whole valley, with Rakaposhi as the backdrop. The hotels are all in a row; just walk along and choose one, as there is usually no need to book, unless you are a group.

Hotel prices given below are for early 1992 and are meant to be a guideline for comparison between hotels. Prices rise proportionally, except when a hotel is renovated, in which case its prices jump.

In the **moderate** range (about s/d Rs300/400) are:

Mountain View, tel 17. New and large, with a good view but no garden.

Hilltop, tel 10. Convenient and popular with tour groups, with hot water, good food, nice garden, great view and helpful management.

Tourist Park, tel 45. Popular with tour groups, with good food and nice garden but little view. Also offers a local house that sleeps six for Rs500.

Rakaposhi View, tel 12. Wide veranda, but most rooms have no view; the four best rooms are on lower level with garden. Owned by the mir.

Silver Jubilee, tel 62 (dorm Rs50). Magnificent view but no garden.

Hunza Lodge, tel 61. Sunny, with great view but no garden.

Garden. Overpriced.

In the **inexpensive** range (most about Rs100–250, try bargaining) are:

New Hunza Tourist (s/d/t Rs30–50/60–80/90). Recommended and a good meeting place. Quiet and well-positioned on canal near Post Office.

Hunza Inn (dorm Rs25). Bare but with sunny porch and good view.

Rainbow, tel 49. Gloomy and basic.

Village, tel 26. Furthest from the centre.

Karim. Sunny porch with a view.

Karimabad (d Rs80, dorm Rs25). Good view.

Friends (charpoy for Rs20).

Diran (tents Rs25 per bed; camping allowed at Rs15 per tent). Great view.

NAPWD rest house (d Rs60; book in Gilgit, see page 170).

In **Aliabad** and **Garelt**, down on the KKH, there are two new hotels, especially welcome if you have just come in from China, but a long haul from scenic Karimabad unless you have your own transport.

PTDC Hotel, Garelt; tel 69 (s/d 450/550). No garden, meeting place or view from rooms.

Rakaposhi Inn, Aliabad; tel 113 (d Rs375–500). Overpriced with no garden.

PTDC camping ground, Aliabad (double tent Rs80, camping fee Rs15). Hot showers.

Domani View, tel 111 (s/d Rs250/350). Scruffy but friendly.

The cheapos along the KKH in Aliabad are the Prince, Jubilee and Delux (all with dorm beds Rs50–80, camping fee Rs15 per tent). In **Ganesh**, near Ganesh Monument on the KKH, there are two really grotty cheapos, the Yadgar (Rs25 per bed) and the Ruby (Rs 20 per bed).

SHORT WALKS AROUND KARIMABAD

Baltit Fort, the old palace of the mirs of Hunza, stands guard over the whole valley. Faintly Tibetan in style, it was reputedly built about 700 years ago, when a princess of Baltistan married the reigning mir and brought with her some Balti masons to build Baltit as part of her dowry.

For the best photography of the valley from Baltit Fort, go at sunrise; to shoot the fort itself, evening light is best. The route up is obvious. Take the road uphill from the Rainbow Hotel, turn right again before the polo ground, and follow your nose. If you wish to go inside, first get the key (*chabi*) from the gatekeeper at the mir's new residence, above the Park Hotel; entry is Rs10 per person. The fort is a maze of small rooms on three floors, with a bird's-eye view over the whole valley and, to the rear, a sheer drop into Ultar Ravine. It was abandoned in the 1950s, when the mir moved down the hill to his new palace, and is now empty and in dangerous condition. There are plans to renovate the building and turn it into a museum.

Hunza exists only because of its **irrigation system**. Some of the water feeding the wide bowl of central Hunza comes from the Hyderabad (Bululo) River, but most comes from the Ultar Glacier in nine channels, five on the right bank, four on the left. The earliest channels (the Hamachi, Altit and Balti-il) were built between 500 and 900 years ago and fed the first three villages of Ganesh, Altit and Baltit. The Dala and Barber channels, both of which are over ten kilometres long, and the two Murku channels were completed by the mid-nineteenth century.

Regulation of water is central to Hunza life. The rules are precisely laid out, so that water is distributed according to a complicated code of so many hours or days of water per area. Supervisors (*yatkuin*) are appointed to maintain each channel and see that water is shared equally, and each village elects representatives to control distribution. Individual farmers guard their plots day and night when it is their turn to receive water. Most court cases in Hunza are water disputes. The fields are not irrigated in winter; when irrigation resumes in February there is a ceremony including prayers for a good harvest.

The channels also supply water for household use, so be sure not to wash your hands in them or otherwise pollute the water.

Barber Channel from Baltit to Hyderabad: Join the water channel, which was built in 1847, just below Baltit Fort. First follow it upstream a short way for views of the

Baltit Fort

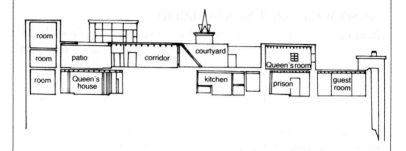

room
room
room

patio
corridor
courtyard

Queen's house

kitchen

Queen's room

prison

guest room

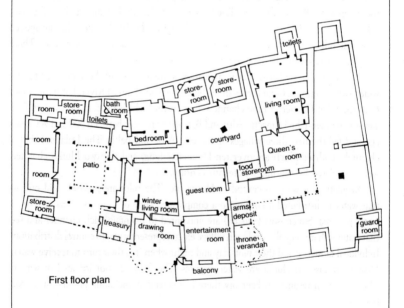

toilets

room
store-room
bath room
toilets
store-room
store-room
living room

room
bedroom
courtyard

patio
Queen's room
food storeroom

room
guest room

store-room
winter living room
arms deposit
guard room

treasury
drawing room
entertainment room
throne verandah

balcony

First floor plan

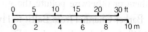

0   5   10   15   20   30 ft

0   2   4   6   8   10 m

Hughes — Lefort — Vaichere
First published in MIMAR No. 20
by Concept Media Singapore

back of Baltit Fort, then retrace your steps and follow it downstream, a flat easy walk of several kilometres with views of daily life in Hunza and the magnificent panorama of rippling terraces and Rakaposhi. Where it bridges the Hyderabad stream, drop down to the paved link road and head back. After a short while, drop down again on a rough path between houses to the **Dala (Samarkand) Channel**, which brings you back to the New Hunza Tourist Hotel and the Post Office. The Dala made possible the expansion of Hunza. It was built in about 1820, after the mir, Silum Khan III (reigned 1790 to 1824), returned from Afghanistan, where he had learned about irrigation and become an Ismaili. You can continue round the mir's new palace, past **Mominabad**, the musicians' village, to the headworks of this channel, which overlook Altit. The musicians are a separate ethnic group who speak Dumaki, which may be related to the Romany language of the Gypsies.

Baltit to Victoria Monument: Follow the Barber Channel downstream from Baltit Fort for about five minutes, then cross the channel on a log bridge just before the old watch tower, and start climbing. Once above the village, head for a small cleft in the rock face, and continue to the base of the cliff, then cross over to the monument. Locally known as the Malikamu Shikari ('Queen's Monument' in Burushaski), it was erected by the present mir's grandfather, Nazim Khan, soon after he was installed as mir by the British following their invasion in 1891.

WALKS FURTHER AFIELD OF KARIMABAD

Map: Swiss Karakoram map, reliability fair; U502 NJ 43-14 (Baltit), reliability poor.
Open zone; easy to strenuous; maximum height optional; best time depending on altitude, with something available year round.

Baltit across Ultar Ravine to Rahimabad and Duiker, then down to Altit: This can be a long day trip, but we recommend camping overnight. Follow the irrigation channel upstream behind Baltit Fort towards Ultar Gorge. Just before the gorge, a path forks right, crosses the Ultar River on a small bridge and climbs steeply up the hill on a diagonal to Rahimabad. It continues up to summer pastures at **Duiker**, from where there are fantastic views back over Hunza and Nagar to Rakaposhi. The highest summer pastures are a couple of hours above Duiker. Take water with you. Return on the jeep track from Rahimabad to Altit.

Karimabad to Altit: Either follow the Dala (Samarkand) Channel or take the jeep road from above the Hilltop Hotel, pass under the aqueduct and walk a couple of kilometres to Altit, arriving at its polo field and pond. The *chowkidar* (guardian) appears with the key and charges a Rs10 entry fee for Altit Fort, which is more interesting than Baltit Fort, as it has more intricate wood-carving and better-preserved rooms. From the roof, you peer down a 300-metre sheer drop to the Hunza River; turning the other way, you look out over the rooftops of Altit village and on up to the Ultar Glacier and Baltit.

The fort is best photographed from the hill to the east, immediately upriver. You walk through the village to get there.

Altit to Sarat: Recommended for cooler weather, this long, strenuous walk starts at Altit village and follows the old trail up the Hunza River, on the opposite side from

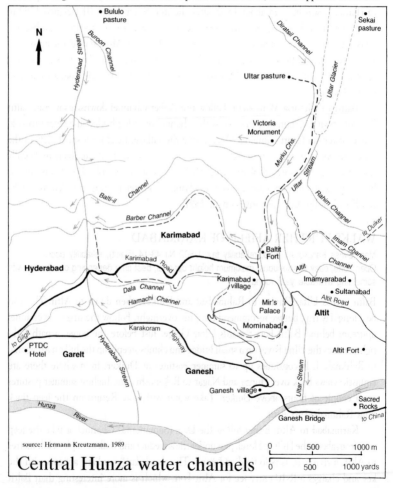

source: Hermann Kreutzmann, 1989

Central Hunza water channels

the KKH, through **Faisabad** to **Ahmedabad**, where written in white stones across the alluvial fan above the village are the words 'WELCOME AKRSP', referring to the Aga Khan Rural Support Programme. Two AKRSP irrigation channels feed some vertical fields on the alluvial fan—an impressive example of village engineering. The trail continues to **Gamesarat** and **Sarat**, about ten kilometres from Altit. Just past Sarat is the **Kitchener Monument**, which commemorates Horatio Kitchener's visit in August 1903, when he toured the frontier as newly appointed commander-in-chief of the Indian Army. From Sarat, cross the Hunza River on a jeep bridge to the KKH and hitchhike back to Ganesh. Check before setting out that the path is open and the bridge is still there.

Ganesh and the Sacred Rocks: Ganesh is a Shia village folded in an S-bend on the KKH as it snakes down to cross the Hunza River on Ganesh Bridge. The village, guarded by an old watch tower and fort, has preserved its original Shia mosques, with their intricately carved pillars. The pool in front of the tower is where local boys once learned to swim. Until this century, all boys had to swim across the Hunza to prove that they could escape or attack across the river when necessary.

In cool weather, you can walk on across the road bridge to the so-called Sacred Rocks, about 400 metres beyond the bridge, between the KKH and the Hunza River, below Altit Fort. Called 'the guest book of the Silk Route' by Professor A H Dani, Pakistan's most famous archaeologist, the rocks record 2,000 years of travels along the road to and from China. The inscriptions are in Kharoshthi, Brahmi, Gupta, Sogdian and Tibetan.

Just beyond the rocks, the old jeep road to Nagar branches right (south), from where there is a hot climb for good views across the river to Hunza. It is a dry, dusty two-hour walk to Nagar village (see central Nagar above), so take water. Or you can drop straight back down to Ganesh Bridge via the footpath.

Baltit to summer pastures by Ultar Glacier: Landslides make the way dangerous after rain, so ask first if it is safe. You can do this as a steep one-day climb or make it a two-day camping trip. In two to four hours, you reach a lone shepherds' hut, where two or three shepherds tend 200 to 300 sheep and goats from May to September. The trek starts from the west side of Baltit Fort. Follow the irrigation channel behind the fort for about half an hour. About five minutes past the headworks of the channel, there is a clear spring welling up from under the cliff on the left; this is a good place to fill your water bottles.

The next hour is steep going, up a rocky ravine to the end of the glacier, which you see below you on your right—a black mass of gravel and rocks that you may not immediately recognise for what it is. You then come out on a small patch of grass beside a clear stream. Five willow trees remain; the rest have been cut for firewood.

The last hour is much easier walking, along a clear path to the shepherds' hut, with good views of Ultar Peak (7,388 metres), which is still unclimbed, and Bubulimating (meaning 'Bubuli's peak'), a 1,000-metre sheer pinnacle of black granite. Bubulimating is named after an unfortunate Hunza princess named Bubuli. According to local legend, her demon husband, King Kiser of Tibet, dreamed that his homeland had been invaded in his absence and decided to return there, telling his wife that he would be back in Hunza when donkeys grew horns, millstones grew beards and rivers flowed uphill. Lest the princess get into trouble in his absence, he seated her on the granite spire with a 90-kilogramme bag of millet seed and a cockerel, telling her: 'Give him one grain a year. When the grain is gone, I shall return.' There she still sits, and you can hear her wailing during winter storms.

For another of King Kiser's jealous exploits, see page 128.

Ask permission from the shepherds if you wish to camp. This pasture belongs exclusively to the mir. One old shepherd remembers as a boy running down to Baltit Fort morning and evening with the milk. He can still run up in about 90 minutes.

Those with some climbing experience can continue up to the ridge for even better views. Rockfalls are a danger, though, so it is a good idea to hire a shepherd to show the safest paths.

On the return journey, if you have climbing experience and do not suffer from vertigo, you can take the topmost irrigation channel across the cliff face for about one kilometre and come out above Victoria Monument, with a panoramic view of Hunza, Nagar and Rakaposhi. Be careful not to damage the channel. Take some tennis shoes with you so you can walk comfortably in the water in the channel, as the retaining wall is fragile and dangerous.

From the KKH up Hasanabad glaciers (Muchu Har and Shishpar) to summer pastures: We have not done this trek (please send corrections and more information). Apparently, this can be either a hot day trip up to the combined snout of the Hasanabad glaciers or a strenuous three- to six-day hike along the glaciers to summer pastures. Take a Suzuki from Karimabad or Ganesh to the bridge across the Hasanabad River, three kilometres downriver (west) of Aliabad. Follow the trail up the east side of the stream from a point near the roadworks camp. There is a lunch spot and possible campsite after about three hours, past the snout and by a big boulder. Continue up to the shepherds' settlement of **Khudadate Harag** (*harag* meaning 'pasture' in Burushaski) and camp at about 2,400 metres.

The valley now divides. You can hike northeast up the Shishpar Glacier for one or two days along a difficult, eroded path, passing through several summer pastures to

Dudara Harag. Camp by the shepherds' huts and spend a rest day exploring the area, watching the shepherds work and taking in great views of Shishpar and Passu peaks and the glacier.

For an extremely difficult trek, you can return to Khudadate Harag and take the northwest branch up the **Muchu Har Glacier** and follow it up for a couple of days past some shepherds' settlements to **Shandar**. Camp with the shepherds if there are any. The way is not easy and there are fewer herds these days, as shepherds now have alternative sources of income arising from the KKH and tourism. (Information from Hermann Kreutzmann and Ashraf Aman.)

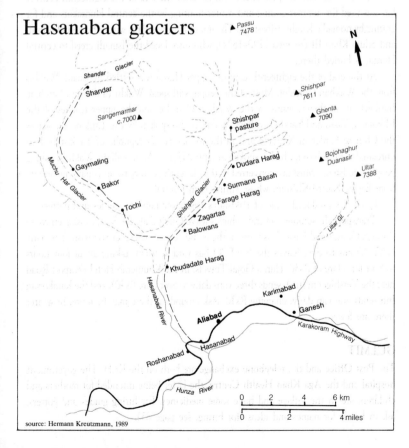

Hasanabad glaciers

source: Hermann Kreutzmann, 1989

UPPER HUNZA (GOJAL)

Upper Hunza—or Gojal, as the inhabitants call it—stretches from Shishkot Bridge to the Khunjerab Pass. The area offers two well-known treks: along the Batura Glacier and up the Shimshal Valley. There are also many good day walks in the area from Gulmit, the capital (about 35 kilometres up the KKH from Aliabad), Passu (a further 15 kilometres beyond Gulmit) and Sost, the Pakistani customs and immigration post (about 80 kilometres below the Chinese border, at Khunjerab Pass).

Upper Hunza had no permanent villages until the end of the eighteenth century but was used for summer grazing and winter hunting by the central Hunzakuts and for grazing by nomadic Kirghiz tribesmen. The mir of Hunza had his winter house in Gulmit, and Silum Khan III (reigned 1790–1824), who introduced the Ismaili creed to central Hunza, is buried there.

At the end of the eighteenth century, upper Hunza was settled by Ismaili Wakhis from the Wakhan Corridor. Most of the people still speak Wakhi (a dialect of archaic Iranian), as do their cousins in the Wakhan Corridor and the upper reaches of the Ishkoman, Yasin and Yarkhun valleys. Wakhi is also spoken by the Tajik people across the Chinese border in Xinjiang and in the former Soviet republic of Tajikistan. It is unrelated to Burushaski, which is spoken in central Hunza. Almost all the Wakhi-speaking peoples are Ismaili Muslims, converted in the eleventh century by an Ismaili missionary from Egypt, Nazir-i-Khisran, whose shrine is in Chitral.

Gojal has produced some of Pakistan's best mountaineers, guides and porters.

Transport: In summer, several vehicles leave Gilgit daily for Sost, passing en route through Gulmit and Passu. Take any of them and get out wherever you wish. The daily NATCO bus to Sost leaves the NATCO bus yard at 9 am, taking about four hours to Sost for a fare of Rs30. Hunza Gojal Travels, in the Khunjerab Hotel (Airport Road near the Vershigoom Inn), sends three vans daily to Sost (fare Rs40), and the Karakoram Inn sends one van daily, charging Rs30. Ask around, as there may be more. In winter there are fewer.

GULMIT

The **Post Office** and the **telephone exchange** are both on the KKH. The government **hospital** and the **Aga Khan Health Centre**, the latter being intended for mothers and children, are in the village and have some medicines. For hiring guides and porters, ask in hotels for names and ideas (for hiring, see page 83).

Accommodation: It is more fun to stay up in Gulmit village, 500 metres above the KKH, and get a sense of village life, but there are two new hotels on the highway. Hotel prices given below are for early 1992 and are meant to be a guideline for comparison between hotels. Prices rise proportionally, except when a hotel is renovated, in which case its prices jump.

Silk Route Lodge, on the KKH; tel 18 (s/d Rs350/450). Carpeted rooms, trying hard to please. Same management as Village Hotel. Camping allowed.

Hunza Alpine Motel, on the KKH; tel 6 (s/d Rs350/450). New, lacks atmosphere.

Tourist Cottage, on the KKH; tel 19 (d Rs80–150, dorm in traditional-style room Rs30). Good atmosphere, helpful for trekking information.

Village Hotel, in Gulmit village at the end of the polo ground; tel 12 (s/d Rs250/400). Owned by the Hunza prince Mirzada Shah Khan, a well-known guide from the 1950s and '60s. Some cheaper rooms, one charming local-style room upstairs, good trekking information, lovely garden. Camping allowed.

Marco Polo Inn, in Gulmit village; tel 7 (s/d Rs250/400). Owned by the prince Raja Bahadur Khan and built in his garden. Relaxed atmosphere, especially when the raja is there to tell stories. Local-style room in his house. Camping allowed.

NAPWD rest house, in Gulmit village beside the polo ground (d Rs60, book in Gilgit). Run down.

SHORT WALKS AROUND GULMIT

Map: Swiss Karakoram map, reliability fair; U502 NJ 43-14 (Baltit), reliability poor.
Open zone; easy to strenuous; maximum height optional; roughly March to November, depending on altitude.

The **Gulmit Museum**, full of traditional ethnic artefacts, is in a room of Raja Bahadur Khan's house, beside the Marco Polo Inn, and is well worth a visit, especially if the raja is there to show you around with his usual charm and enthusiasm. **Old Gulmit** is at the north end of the polo ground. Here you find the mir of Hunza's summer residence, which is no longer used, the old Ismaili mosque with carved woodwork, the Tomb of Silum Khan III, water mills and old houses.

Kamaris, Andra Fort and Gulmit Glacier: Follow the jeep road up from the polo ground and twist up for about an hour to the higher village of **Kamaris**, which offers fine views back to the jagged Passu spires. You can take a 30-minute detour northeast from Kamaris to visit the ruins of the 200-year-old **Andra Fort** (Andra Gelah), before continuing along the jeep road northwest for another hour to the end of the Gulmit Glacier.

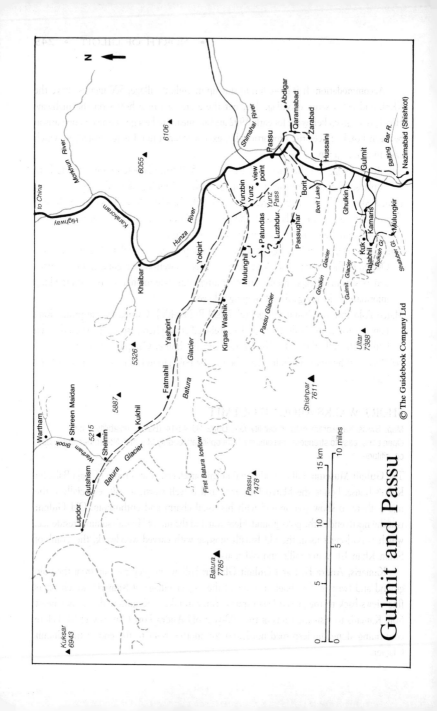

Gulmit and Passu

© The Guidebook Company Ltd

Two-day trek to summer pastures: A trail leads up the south side of the Gulmit Glacier in about two hours to the summer pastures at **Kuk** (meaning 'spring'), where you can camp. If you take a Gulmit guide, you can climb steeply south from here up to **Rajabhil** (*hil* or *hel* meaning 'pasture' in Wakhi), a summer pasture on the ridge between the Gulmit and Bulkish glaciers. Continue across the ridge and pass through the **Darwaza** (meaning 'door'), a remarkable opening in the mountain that leads over to the Bulkish Glacier. Descend to **Bulkishkuk**, a pasture where farmers leave the oxen (castrated bulls) for the summer to fatten. Cross the stream at the snout of the Bulkish Glacier, climb south up over the ridge to the Shatuber Glacier and descend to the pasture of **Mulungkir**, where there is a shepherds' hut. It takes the villagers about ten hours to get here from Gulmit. Allow two days for the normal trekker. (Information from Hermann Kreutzmann.)

Kamaris to Borit Lake: This takes about four hours from Gulmit. Another trail from Kamaris crosses the Gulmit Stream and joins the end of a jeep track at Ghulkin village. The jeep track links up with the KKH, while a footpath crosses the moraine-covered Ghulkin Glacier and climbs up to the small Borit Lake. To cross the glacier, take your bearings from a stone cairn on the south side and a dip in the lateral moraine on the north side. The crossing takes about an hour and is not difficult if you are used to glaciers. Otherwise, hire a boy in Ghulkin to show the way. You can stay at the Borit Hotel (Rs30 per bed) just above Borit Lake. From Borit Lake, the jeep road takes you in 30 minutes to **Borit Bala (Lower) Village**, from where a trail leads up the high lateral moraine on the south side of Passu Glacier to waterless summer pastures—a round trip of several hours. It is about a two-hour walk from Borit to **Passu** village (see short walks from Passu, page 250). Borit down the jeep track to **Hussaini** and the KKH is about an hour's walk.

Gulmit across Hunza River and down to Shishkot Bridge: This takes three hours and should be done only in cool weather. Cross the footbridge below the Hunza Alpine Motel and follow the path downriver, watching out for falling rock and debris. The river bed here is a wide gravelly plain made up of the debris left when the river was blocked in 1974 by a surging glacier down the Balting Bar. A lake formed stretching back to Passu, drowning a section of the KKH for three years and wiping out the first Chinese bridge. Walk through **Nazimabad** village to the new, Chinese-built Shishkot Bridge and hitchhike back to Gulmit.

PASSU

Passu, about 115 kilometres from the Chinese border, is a 150-year-old settlement at 2,540 metres. The village owns the grazing rights up the north side of the 56-kilometre-long Batura Glacier, so is able to support large herds of yaks, cattle, sheep and goats, but is less fortunate with its agricultural land. The Shimshal River flows into the Hunza just above the village and has always caused severe flooding and erosion in Passu. The entire old village, including its polo ground, gradually fell into the Hunza River, so half of the inhabitants migrated south or founded new settlements elsewhere.

A new AKRSP water channel from the Batura Glacier, completed in 1985, irrigates a large, formerly barren area above the village. This is the eighth attempt to harness the waters of the Batura, the other seven having been demolished by the glacier as it advanced or receded. For the time being, this new channel brings renewed prosperity to the remaining 61 households of Passu—witness the new school and *jamat khana* (community centre). But many of the village men still find jobs outside the village as drivers, factory workers, guides and porters, leaving the women at home to work double time, looking after the land and herds.

The only **telephone** is in the Passu Inn. There is a small **dispensary** but no Post Office or bank. You can sometimes rent sleeping bags and tents in the village, so ask around.

Guides and porters: Ask Ghulam Muhammad at the Passu Inn, who has a good map of Batura Glacier. We hired Qamar Jan and Akram, who were tough bargainers but good humoured, experienced and in possession of great singing voices. Read the section on hiring porters (page 83).

Accommodation: Hotel prices given below are for early 1992 and are meant to be a guideline for comparison between hotels. Prices rise proportionally, except when a hotel is renovated, in which case its prices jump.

Passu Inn, on the KKH; tel 1 (d Rs250, traditional family room sleeping six Rs300). Popular with hikers, good meeting place.

Shishper View, on the KKH two kilometres south of Passu (d Rs250).

Batura Inn, on the KKH a kilometre north of Passu, beside the old Chinese roadworkers' camp (d Rs100–150).

NAPWD rest house, opposite the Passu Inn (d Rs60; book in Gilgit, see page 170).

SHORT WALKS AROUND PASSU

Passu–Hussaini–Qaramabad–Passu: On this walk, which takes four or five hours from Hussaini, you cross the Hunza River on two hanging bridges. Hitchhike or take public transport down the KKH to Hussaini (the NATCO bus passes at about 7.30 am). Find your way down through Hussaini to the Hunza River, which is not easy, then cross the long swinging footbridge. Climb the sheer rock face along a well-built path for one hour to cultivated fields of barley and potatoes belonging to Hussaini villagers, who keep their animals here in winter.

Continue up past the last house of **Zarabad** and follow the irrigation channel through juniper bushes to the highest patch of green. Cross the ravine as high as possible and descend the other side to the pastures and cultivated fields of Qaramabad, which, though partly abandoned, belongs to Passu villagers. A well-used trail leads across barren land and down a gorge, back to the Hunza River. The suspension bridge is 200 metres long and in poor condition, with widely spaced planks—not for vertigo sufferers. Once across, you will find a good path that is cut into the cliff in places, as it follows the river upstream for about an hour, coming out onto the KKH about 40 minutes below Passu. (Information from Elisabeth Gardner.)

Qaramabad to Abdigar Ridge: Apparently, you can climb up from Qaramabad to the top of the ridge behind, known locally as Abdigar. This is an overnight trip offering stunning views of the Hunza River, the Passu Glacier and the Batura Massif. From Abdigar, you can continue to the Shimshal route by taking a pass to the Abdigar Glacier.

Yunz Pass across the ridge between Passu and Batura glaciers: This takes five or six hours round trip, with no water available most of the day. Start at the Passu Inn, head down the KKH and take the first trail right towards the Passu Glacier. Climb steeply up the lateral moraine on a good path, then along high cliffs. After an hour, you are high above the snout of the glacier and the new Passu Lake. A short, steep climb takes you to a plateau, with impressive views over the white, crevassed Passu Glacier. Follow the moraine for an easy 15 minutes, then turn right up a steep gully, finally emerging on a hot, dry, flat ridge, which leads in 45 minutes to the Yunz Pass, which is about two and a half hours from Passu. A 90-minute detour leads right (east), up to a viewpoint over the Hunza River.

Alternatively, you can follow the dry ridge west, climbing to **Patundas** for more magnificent views of the glacier and mountains. A short descent from Yunz Pass takes you to the deserted shepherds' huts at **Yunz**, which has magnificent views (the best of the whole trek) along the Batura Glacier to Batura Peak (7,785 metres). Batura, the 28th-highest peak in the world, was first climbed by the Germans in 1976. Each hut at Yunz has a hollowed stone outside to hold water, which had to be carried up from the glacier.

A steep path leads down the lateral moraine to the glacier and **Yunzbin**, the first camp of the Batura trek, a flat, sandy spot surrounded by wild roses and small shrubs. A new hut has been built here, but it is extremely hot in the afternoon, with no other shade except a patch under a small rock with room for two or three people. The only water is from a pool on the glacier, a few minutes walk from the campsite. From the top of the lateral moraine, there are magnificent evening views of the Batura Massif reflected in a glacier pool.

A clear animal trail leads both up and down the glacier (see below for the glacier trek). Day trippers follow down the path, which is flat at first, then drops steeply for 90 minutes to the terminal moraine—from which views extend to the Passu spires—and to the new AKRSP water channel, which you follow to the KKH. Three-quarters of the way down, below an enormous rock, there is a deep, clear pond, which is excellent for swimming. Do not contaminate the water channel, though, as it is the drinking supply for Passu. You can try hitchhiking back to Passu along the KKH. Alternatively, there is a so-called short cut back to Passu from halfway down the steep part of the descent from Yunz, but we were told it is long and hot.

Passu to Borit Lake: This takes two to three hours. Behind the Shishper View Hotel, two kilometres down the KKH, a path zigzags up, following the electricity poles, to a small pass with panoramic views back along the river to the Passu spires. The trail climbs up barren pastures to a dry irrigation channel along the top of the ridge above the Passu Glacier, with a view down to Passu Lake. (You can detour along this ridge as high as you like for extra views of the Batura Massif.) The trail to Borit drops down the other side of the ridge, passing through the ruins of old Borit village to the irrigated fields surrounding **Borit Bala (Lower) Village**, with its massive apricot trees. A jeep track from the KKH stops in the village; follow it down for 30 minutes to Borit Lake. You can stay at the Borit Hotel, beside a small, well-stocked shop. The lake is now very small but attractive in spite of its green colour.

For the walk from here to Gulmit, see short walks from Gulmit (page 247). It is about a 45-minute walk along the jeep road to the KKH at **Hussaini**. (Information from Elisabeth Gardner.)

BORIT LAKE UP TO PATUNDAS AND DOWN TO MULUNGHIL

Map: Swiss Karakoram map, reliability good; U502 NJ 43-14 (Baltit), reliability poor. Open zone; easy (except crossing glacier); minimum four days; maximum height 4,183 metres; late May to October.

Patundas is a summer pasture at 4,183 metres on the ridge between the Passu and Batura glaciers. It belongs to Ghulkin villagers, who occupy it from June to August. Do not attempt this hike unless you are already acclimatised. Hire Ghulkin porters (union rules: they own the pastures so also the porterage rights). The stages are very short, only two to three hours each, so it turns out to be quite expensive—but worthwhile.

Stage 1: Borit Lake to Passughar, two to three hours. Cross the hot, dry ridge to Passughar pasture, in the ablation valley on the south side of Passu Glacier. Carry plenty of water with you. You can camp by the two shepherds' huts at Passughar.

Stage 2: Across Passu Glacier to Luzhdur, two to three hours. Crossing the Passu Glacier is difficult. Do not attempt it alone; if you have no porters, hire a shepherd. Luzhdur is an unused pasture at 3,400 metres with three deserted huts. It is surrounded by juniper bushes and backed against the rock wall on the north side of Passu Glacier.

Stage 3: Luzhdur to Patundas, two to four hours. This is a climb gaining 800 metres in altitude to Patundas pasture, on top of the ridge between the Passu and Batura glaciers. The path up is steep but not difficult. The views are magnificent, but there is very little water, only a few drops from a crack in the rock wall. Three Ghulkin women live here with their children and about 900 sheep and goats until the end of August, when the water dries up. Most trekking groups take a rest day here and make the easy hike to the base camp of Passu Peak and back.

Stage 4: Patundas to Mulunghil. The way down to Mulunghil on the Batura Glacier is extremely steep, with terrific views along the glacier. Here you join the Batura Glacier trek (see below). (Information from Hermann Kreutzmann.)

BATURA GLACIER I

Map: Swiss Karakoram map, reliability good; U502 NJ 43-14 (Baltit), reliability fair.
Open zone; easy (except crossing glacier); five to ten days; maximum height 4,000 metres; mid-May to October.

Most of this trek is an easy stroll along a flower-filled gully between the lateral moraine of the Batura Glacier and the mountain. The only difficult part is crossing the glacier. The mountain views of Batura, Passu and Shishpar peaks are superb. The Passu women who spend the summer in the pastureland beside the glacier are friendly to female trekkers and speak some Urdu as well as their native Wakhi.

Passu porters are tough bargainers. They charge a fixed rate of ten days from Passu village to Gutshism and back, though you can easily cover these 70 kilometres in five or six days. Trips up the side valleys carry extra charges. Except for crossing the glacier, you do not need a guide. The Passu people can cross the glacier more or less anywhere and drive their herds across to summer pastures, but this does not mean it is easy. Unless you are experienced with Karakoram glaciers, you should not try it alone. Hire someone to show you across. If you are lucky, you can follow a guided trekking party across, but do not count on this.

Stage 1: Passu to Mulunghil or Kirgas Washik, four to seven hours. If you are fit, you can start the Batura trek by taking the more scenic, five- to six-hour route over the Yunz Pass to Yunzbin (see above). Send your porters directly to Yunzbin and join them there. If you are less fit, you should go with your porters and do the Yunz Pass on your return.

From Passu village to Yunzbin, follow the KKH for about four kilometres north, then turn west along the Passu irrigation channel to the snout of the Batura Glacier. You can hire a jeep or wagon in Passu to cover the first hour's walk along the KKH. From the glacier snout scramble up the terminal moraine, following a rough shepherds' track on the south side of the glacier for an hour or so. This is barren and stony ground, so it can be hot and strenuous going. At the top of the moraine, the path levels out and follows a dry gully between the southern lateral moraine and the mountain. There are a few wild roses and thorn bushes, along with some purple vetch and the odd succulent plant, as well as impressive views back to the jagged granite spires above Passu.

Yunzbin, a pay stage, is the traditional first night stop, 90 minutes to two hours from the irrigation channel (see description above). From Yunzbin, the Passu villagers take their herds of yaks, sheep and goats north across the glacier to the other side. It is the shortest crossing but not the most highly recommended. It is more scenic and cooler to continue along the greener southern side to Kirgas Washik and cross there.

Mulunghil, about one hour from Yunzbin along an easy path on the south side of the Batura Glacier, is a small summer pasture belonging to Hussaini village, with a couple of shepherds' huts occupied only from May to July—a flat area where you can camp and get water from a pool on the glacier.

Continue the easy walk, partly along the crest of the lateral moraine with good views down across the glacier to the Batura Massif and other peaks. The mountainside is dotted with juniper bushes, and the occasional willow nestles in the gully between the lateral moraine and the mountain. Wild roses, gooseberries, rhubarb, potentilla, rockroses, anemone and many other flowers grow on the moraine. You pass **Savsjewy Lake** and a couple more shepherds' huts at **Garben** before reaching **Kirgas Washik** (meaning 'eagle's nest'). The pair of shepherds' huts here, about two hours from Mulunghil, are deserted by August.

Stage 2: Mulunghil or Kirgas Washik to Yashpirt, three to six hours. The place to cross the glacier changes every year but is usually somewhere near Kirgas Washik. The crossing is difficult and dangerous for the uninitiated without a guide, but for those experienced with Karakoram glaciers it is relatively easy. We crossed about ten minutes' walk up from Kirgas Washik, where there is an excellent campsite beside a small stream but no shade. The first 30 minutes on the glacier take you over large, rough boulders, the next 30 minutes across relatively smooth but slippery white ice, with crevasses and glacier lakes. The next hour is over stones and rocks, all of which move as you step on them. You must pick your way along the ridges between the crevasses. Depending on where you arrive at the north side, it is about another hour's easy walking along the northern lateral moraine to Yashpirt.

Yashpirt (meaning 'horse pasture'), at 3,300 metres, is the main summer settlement for the Passu people, set a little way up the mountainside on a wide grassy slope surrounded by juniper forest, with a spectacular view down across the Batura Glacier to the Batura Massif. The First Batura Iceflow, a wide crevassed glacier, oozes down the north face of Batura, making a superb backdrop for the settlement. Avalanches thunder down Batura, and rocks rumble into crevasses on the glacier. In July a clear stream flows through the settlement, and a second stream fills a shallow lake below the village, which is warm enough for swimming by mid-morning.

Most of the 61 households in Passu village have a summer hut up at Yashpirt. Nowadays only a few of them are used. About ten women and their small children come up here in the middle of May with about 100 yaks and over 1,000 sheep and goats. The yaks—there are no donkeys or horses in Passu—are loaded with the quilts, housewares and food necessary for the summer. The women stay here until the beginning of August, when they move further up the glacier to the small settlements of Kukhil and Gutshism. They milk the animals, drive the herds up the mountain in the morning, round them up in the evening and make butter and cheese. The cheese (*qurut*) is dried on the roofs of the huts. Trekkers can usually buy milk, yogurt, buttermilk (*lassi*), cheese and tea from the shepherdesses. Chickens are not taken up for the summer, so eggs are not available. Organised trekking parties are expected to buy a goat and have a feast with dancing and singing, watched by the whole settlement.

If you are fit, Yashpirt to Gutshism and back makes a good day walk of six to eight hours. Alternatively, you can take it slowly in three stages.

Stage 3: Yashpirt to Kukhil, two to three hours. The route follows a shepherds' trail west through juniper and tamarisk woods. A few kilometres from Yashpirt, there is a well-watered flat area, where the Passu people, when there were more of them coming up to the summer pastures, used to grow barley.

Fatmahil, 90 minutes' easy walk upstream from Yashpirt, is a collection of half a dozen deserted shepherds' huts at the mouth of a side gully opposite the First Batura Iceflow. Stones washed down from the gully now cover the field in front of the huts.

A few willows and mountain poplars survive at the edge, and roses and juniper shrubs dot the hillside. There are now so few women in the summer pastures that Fatmahil is no longer used except by hunters and trekkers.

Fatmahil to Kukhil takes another one hour to 90 minutes, a lovely walk along a stream between the lateral moraine and the mountain. At one point an abandoned mill stands by the stream. The moraine is covered with purple vetch and a host of other flowers.

Kukhil, a small summer settlement with a few huts and a goat pen, is used in August and September. The mountains are covered in juniper and willow scrub, and there is a good campsite beside the stream. From the top of the lateral moraine you have excellent views up and down the Batura Glacier.

Stage 4: Kukhil to Gutshism, two to four hours. Most of the way the path follows a rock-filled stream past juniper, willow and ash and a myriad alpine flowers. About halfway between Kukhil and Gutshism is **Shelmin**, a wide field where the Wartham Brook flows down from the north. You can follow this stream up for two days through **Shireen Maidan** to **Wartham**, a pasture with no huts but superb views of the Batura Massif.

Gutshism, the last summer settlement up the Batura Glacier, has 13 shepherds' huts scattered round a goat pen near the stream. It is cold here at night, but from the top of the lateral moraine there are clear views of the Batura and Passu massifs in one direction and the Kuksar Range in the other.

The flower-filled ablation valley ends at **Lupdor**, two hours beyond Gutshism and about 20 kilometres from the snout of the glacier. From here on the only route is on the glacier. For those with mountaineering skills, there is a technical trek north from Lupdor over a 5,200-metre pass to the Chapursan Valley.

Stage 5: Return Gutshism to Yashpirt, a good place for a rest day.

Stage 6: Yashpirt to Yunzbin, five to six hours. For a change of scenery, you can continue all the way down the north side of the glacier and cross directly to Yunzbin. The first two hours to Yokpirt (meaning 'yak pasture') are beautiful, taking you through groves of willow, tamarisk, juniper, silver birch and wild rose bushes (as big as trees) and blue clumps of wild lavender. **Yokpirt**, with a deserted shepherds' hut beside a small lake, which is surrounded by trees but dry by August, would be a great campsite if it were not for the mosquitoes.

From Yokpirt, the next two hours are a hot and monotonous scramble along the lateral moraine. The glacier turns a corner here and scrapes against the mountain, so there is no easy valley to follow outside the lateral moraine. Crossing the glacier to

Yunzbin takes one to two hours, picking your way around pools and along the ridges between the crevasses. The glacier is completely covered in gravel and boulders, and the way is difficult to find without a guide.

Stage 7: Yunzbin to Passu, two to three hours by the direct route, or three to four hours by the recommended route, over the Yunz Pass to the Passu Glacier (see above). (Additional information from Elisabeth Gardner.)

BATURA GLACIER II

Map: Swiss Karakoram map, reliability good; U502 NJ 43-14 (Baltit), reliability fair.
Open zone; easy; three days; maximum height 4,000 metres; May to October.

This is a recommended trek for those who are fit. You need no tent, as you can sleep in shepherds' huts. Porters ask for four days' pay. For a description, see the Yunz Pass short walk from Passu and the trek up Batura Glacier above.

Day 1: Passu over the Yunz Pass to Kirgas Washik.

Day 2: Half day to Yashpirt, with an afternoon walk to Kukhil and back.

Day 3: Yashpirt back to Passu.

PASSU UP SHIMSHAL VALLEY

Map: Swiss Karakoram map, reliability good; U502 43-15 (Shimshal), reliability poor.
Restricted zone (in 1990, but permit is easy to get from police in Gilgit); easy to strenuous; three to four days one way; maximum height 3,100 metres; April to November (to Shimshal village only).

Remote and inaccessible, Shimshal was once a penal colony where the mir of Hunza exiled criminals and troublemakers. Shimshal village is a 45-kilometre walk up a harsh, deserted gorge bombarded by dangerous landslides. The 120 households of Shimshal—about 1,000 people, all Ismaili Muslims—are collected in three hamlets surrounded by terraced and irrigated land. The attractions for trekkers are the unspoiled seclusion of the valley, the many glaciers and the various exciting possibilities for the return trip.

The Shimshal people are building a road through the gorge, an AKRSP project that is advancing only a few kilometres each year. In 1990 they had completed about 15 kilometres—a miracle of village engineering requiring the blasting of a track across a sheer cliff face. A section of this was lost in a landslide in 1989.

There is no food for sale in Shimshal, so bring all your supplies with you. (Of course, if you offered enough money, the people would sell food to you, but this would leave them short.) About half of the people of Shimshal have tuberculosis.

Hire your guide and Shimshali porters in Passu. We recommend hiring a vehicle in Passu to take you to the end of the jeep road, thereby saving yourself a hot, tedious walk. The jeep road to Shimshal leaves the KKH about 1.5 kilometres north of the Batura Inn, crosses the Hunza River, wends across a wide, barren plain and enters the Shimshal Gorge. The locals take two days to walk in to Shimshal village, but we describe it in four stages. We have not been there, so please send corrections.

Stage 1: Passu to Dutt, four to five hours. Passu to Jurjur would take about five hours on foot, but the new jeep road now goes all the way, landslides permitting. **Jurjur** is a sandy beach beside the river, with a fresh spring and rock shelters at the base of the cliff where you can sleep. You will probably wish to continue straight to Dutt.

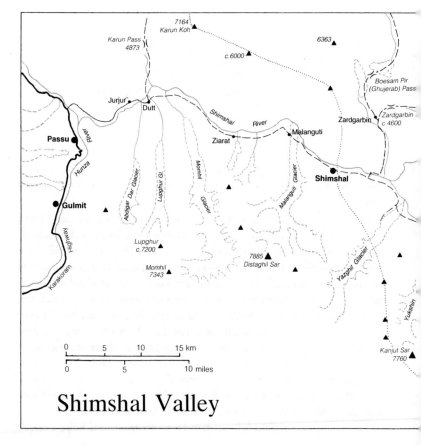

Shimshal Valley

Jurjur to Dutt (marked Pikut on most maps) takes three to five hours on foot. The new road ends about two kilometres (30 minutes' walk) before Dutt, riding five to ten metres above the river, with the cliff of the gorge towering a further 50 metres above. The rock formations are interesting, but there is no view out of the gorge. Two or three hours' walk from Jurjur, cross the Shimshal River on a foot bridge and continue on the easy path along the south side to Dutt, where the valley briefly opens out, making room for two small shepherds' huts. A tiny spring hides in some bushes 150 metres from the second hut towards the Shimshal River. You can cook and sleep in the huts.

Stage 2: Dutt to Ziarat, four to six hours. A long, hard, dry day. The last source

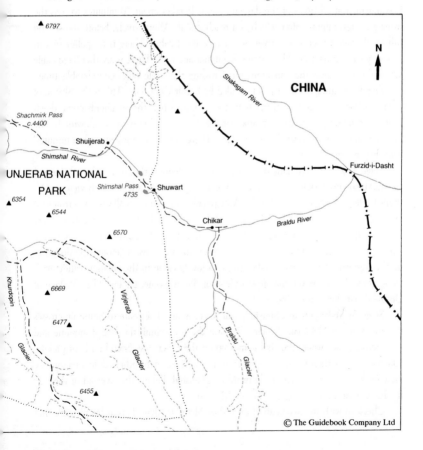

of water is the stream draining from the Momhil Glacier, about an hour from Dutt. There follows two hours of steep zigzagging up to the top of the gorge and 90 minutes back down across a sliding sandy slope to river level. Across from the top of the gorge are views up deep, unapproachable valleys leading to the high snows of **Karun Koh** (7,350 metres). Climb once again for half an hour up the cliff and down another sandy slope to river level.

Here you have a choice of routes, depending on the conditions. Sometimes it is possible to stay on the south bank, where you must dash along the river, running the gauntlet of stones falling from high on the notoriously dangerous cliff above. This stretch is bombarded at all times of the day and night. It takes about 20 minutes to pass the worst part, ten minutes after which you reach Ziarat. Alternatively, before the second hill climb, you can cross the river on a single fixed cable. There is no pulley or car, so you need your own shackle, harness, karabiner and rope. There is another fixed cable across the river after the dangerous bit. Crossing the cable takes considerable time.

Ziarat (meaning 'shrine') is surrounded by hundreds of flags. This is the Shrine of Shams, whose *urs* (death festival) is in the autumn when the shepherds come down from the summer pastures, give thanks for the summer and pray for a safe winter. The large pilgrims' hut at Ziarat sleeps about 50. There is a clear spring about ten minutes' walk beyond the shrine.

Stage 3: Ziarat to Malanguti, four to six hours. Follow the river's edge all the way to the **Malanguti Glacier,** crossing en route a couple of side streams with views up V-shaped valleys to white, pointed peaks. A shepherds' hut sits in a small pasture surrounded by wild roses on the west side of Malanguti Glacier. From the top of the moraine, there are magnificent views of **Distaghil Sar**—at 7,885 metres, the 20th-highest peak in the world, first climbed from the other side in 1960 by the Austrians. A detour four kilometres up the western lateral moraine takes you to a lovely camp in the ablation valley, with trees, grass, flowing water and superb views of the awesome, unclimbed north face of Distaghil Sar dominating the glacier.

Stage 4: Malanguti to Shimshal, four to six hours. The route to Shimshal crosses the snout of the Malanguti Glacier. To find the way, climb the lateral moraine and look across to see where the trail comes up on the other side. Spend an hour picking your way across—there is no path—and climb the moraine on the other side for a panoramic view back across the glacier and forward to Shimshal. Follow the river all of the way to the first Shimshal village, at about 3,100 metres.

Check in with the headman of Shimshal, Shambir Khan. It is at his pleasure that you stay in Shimshal. Though the arrival of democracy in the form of the Aga Khan Rural Support Programme is threatening Shambir Khan's traditional power, you still cannot move without his approval. Send back Passu porters, if you have any, and hire new Shimshali ones. Ashraf Aman recommends Rajab Shah and Muhabad Shah as reliable Shimshali guides.

The Khunjerab National Park begins at Shimshal village, east of which the Shimshal Valley opens out to wide, green pastures with shepherds' huts and herds of sheep, goats and yaks. Be careful not to disturb the wildlife. Apparently, snow leopard (Wakhi name *pes*) and wolf (*chapt*) are comparatively plentiful, and there are a few herds of bharal or blue sheep (*ramappo*) near the Shimshal Pass. Only a few of the endangered wild Tibetan ass (*kulan*) remain, and these are beyond the Shimshal Pass, near the junction of the Braldu and Shaksgam (locally known as the Mustagh) rivers.

SHIMSHAL VILLAGE TO SHIMSHAL PASS

Map: Swiss Karakoram map, reliability good; U502 43-15 (Shimshal), reliability poor.
Restricted zone; strenuous; four days; maximum height 4,735 metres; July to August.

This difficult path, sometimes 800 metres above the river, takes you to the Shimshal Pass, on the Central Asian watershed.

Stage 1: Shimshal village to Zardgarbin, three to five hours. This is a comparatively short day, but you climb from 3,100 metres to 3,800, and acclimatisation may be a problem. Camp in the first grazing grounds at Zardgarbin. Here the path divides, one track going north to the Ghujerab River (see below), the other east to the Shimshal Pass.

Stage 2: Zardgarbin to Maidur. This is a killer. You climb steeply on scree to the **Zardgarbin Pass**, at about 4,600 metres, then down on treacherous slopes to about 3,600 metres. After lunch, you go up again to about 4,400 metres to cross the **Shachmirk Pass** and down to about 3,600 metres. Camp at Maidur.

Stage 3: Maidur to Shuijerab. A comparatively gentle day takes you across barren plateaux, on which you may see ibex, to a good camping spot at the shepherds' settlement at Shuijerab.

Stage 4: Shuijerab over Shimshal Pass to Shuwart. At this point you are up in the open valley (*pamir* in Wakhi). You pass two lakes and finally reach the Shimshal Pass (4,735 metres). This overgrazed high pasture is worth all the difficulties in getting there. About 200 metres down toward China is Shuwart, a shepherds' settlement where the women of Shimshal tend about 1,000 yaks and 3,000 sheep and goats in July and August.

It is about 30 kilometres from the pass to **Furzid-i-Dasht** on the Shaksgam (Mustagh) River, which we think is the Chinese border, fixed in 1963, 40 kilometres west of the line shown on the U502 map. We have heard rumours of a tourist imprisoned by the Chinese for trespassing ('spying') without a permit or visa. For your own safety, do not go too far beyond Shuwart. (Information from Gordon Thomson and Christian Dupre.)

The Shimshal Pass route was the one taken by Hunza raiders to attack traders' caravans crossing the Karakoram Pass from Leh to Yarkhand. Lieutenant Francis Younghusband, the British spy exploring the passes across the Karakoram and Hindu Kush, was the first Westerner to visit the Shimshal Pass, in 1889. The Kirghiz showed him the way from the Chinese side, from which, he said, access was guarded by a well-positioned Hunza fort. He did not cross to Shimshal but returned down the Shaksgam River to explore the perimeter of Hunza and report on the Khunjerab and Mintaka passes.

At Khaian Aksur, a surprisingly fertile oasis a few days' journey downriver from the Shimshal Pass, Younghusband had his celebrated encounter with his Russian opposite number, Captain Grombtchevski. The two spies spent two amicable days together, inviting each other to dinner, drinking vodka and brandy, pouring over maps and discussing Anglo–Russian rivalry and the future of Asia. Grombtchevski took a photo of the meeting, in which the diminutive Younghusband (168 centimetres) is standing on a block to bring him up to the level of his 188-centimetre Russian counterpart.

There is a rumour that you can cross from the Shimshal Pass over the **Zhit Badav Pass** (about 5,300 metres) to the **Virjerab Glacier** and return to Shimshal village that way in three days, but we have not met anyone who has done it.

ONWARD OUT OF SHIMSHAL VALLEY

There are three possibilities for onward treks leaving the Shimshal Valley.

1. **Khurdopin Glacier to Khurdopin Pass and Snow Lake**. This is a difficult, technical trek requiring mountaineering skills. Shimshal village to Snow Lake and on down the Biafo Glacier to Askole takes ten to 12 days (see Philip Bartlett, *Alpine Journal* 1988/89).

2. **Over Shimshal Pass and up Braldu Glacier to Snow Lake**. Mike Searle, the only person we know with information on this trek, said it was a nightmare, the Braldu being the most awful glacier he had ever been on. The route is for mountaineers only with full mountaineering equipment. Apparently, Shimshal Pass to Askole is considered about 14 stages by the Passu porters, who say they know the way, and you should be able to do it in nine days. Shimshal Pass via the Braldu Glacier to Snow Lake, then

across the Hispar Pass and down to Nagar is considered 19 stages and should take you about 11 days. We suggest you try to find Shimshali porters with the help of Shambir Khan, the headman in Shimshal.

3. **Over Boesam Pir (Ghujerab) Pass to KKH**, described below.

SHIMSHAL OVER BOESAM PIR (GHUJERAB) PASS TO KKH
Map: Swiss Karakoram map, reliability good; U502 43-15 (Shimshal), reliability poor. Restricted zone; strenuous; six to eight days; maximum height about 5,090 metres; end of September only.

This is a tough trek traversing 70 kilometres through the heart of the Khunjerab National Park and coming out between Sost and Dih. It is possible only at the end of September, as you have to cross the Ghujerab River, which is in spate earlier in the season, about six times. Apparently, the name Boesam Pir is not recognised by the locals, and we do not know the popular name (send information please). Note that there are two places known as Dih, one on the Ghujerab River and the other (marked as Jun Kharchanai on the U502 map) on the Khunjerab River. The KKH, which follows the Khunjerab River, is not marked on the U502 map, which differs considerably from the Swiss Karakoram map.

Officially, the Khunjerab National Park is closed to trekking to avoid disturbing its Marco Polo sheep, an endangered species whose numbers are declining alarmingly, and whose last resort is the area near the Khunjerab Pass. This trek along the Ghujerab River is well publicised, but we suggest you avoid it in respect of the Marco Polo sheep. However, if you must go there, be aware of the fragile environment, make no noise, and do not allow your porters to wander off 'game spotting' or hunting. We recommend you take a local guide from Shimshal.

Stage 1: Shimshal to base of Boesam Pir Pass. From Shimshal take a path north, rising steeply for the first three to four hours, then levelling out a bit for about four kilometres. The trail joins the Zardgarbin River and follows it steeply to the top of a hill, where it forks. The right-hand trail leads further uphill to the Zardgarbin Pass and the Shimshal Pass. The left-hand path follows a flattish valley for about four kilometres to the base of the Boesam Pir (Ghujerab) Pass, where you can camp.

Stage 2: Over Boesam Pir Pass to Mandi Kushlag. Crossing the Boesam Pir Pass (5,090 metres) is steep but not difficult. There is a small lake and snowfield at the top. On the other side, follow the Drui Stream down to the shepherds' settlement of Mandi Kushlag and camp.

Stage 3: Mandi Kushlag to Chapchingal River. Pass the shepherds' settlement of **Hapdija** and descend to the junction with the Chapchingal River. Camp.

One path branches north from here, leading in 20 kilometres up the Chapchingal Valley, across the **Chapchingal Pass** (about 5,150 metres) and down the Kuksel Stream to the KKH, joining it a few kilometres below the Khunjerab Pass. Steve Razzetti of Karakoram Experience has led a group across, but we suggest that it is better not to go, thus leaving the Marco Polo sheep undisturbed.

Stages 4 to 6 (or 8): Chapchingal River to KKH. The alternative path leads west down the Ghujerab River, past some shepherds' settlements, for 40 kilometres—three to five days—to join the KKH between Dih and Sost. Do not try it without a local guide, as the river goes into a gorge at one point and you must climb up over the shoulder of the ridge to proceed. The river crossings are dangerous, requiring rope.

If you cannot get out down the gorge, there is a difficult alternative route south across the mountains to the **Morkhun River** and down to the KKH at Morkhun village, about eight kilometres south of Sost. (Information from Steve Reich, David Watt, Ashraf Aman, Musarat Wali Khan and Hermann Kreutzmann.)

MORKHUM OVER KARUN PASS TO DUTT
Map: Swiss Karakoram map, reliability good; U502 43-15 (Shimshal), U502 43-14 (Baltit), reliability poor.
Restricted zone; strenuous; two to three days; maximum height 4,873 metres; August to September.

This is the old route into Shimshal, a difficult trek across the Karun Pass. Hire a guide or porter at Morkhun, eight kilometres south of Sost. Walk up through the contiguous village of **Jamalabad** (old name Jukulgar) and turn east up the Morkhun Valley, following an irrigation channel, then the stream, which you cross twice on log bridges. After the second bridge, head steeply up onto a terrace to the winter settlement of **Abgerchi** (two to three hours), where there are the ruins of two forts, one Kirghiz and the other Wakhi (see Schomberg, *Unknown Karakoram*). Another couple of hours takes you up an indistinct path to a higher terrace, where eight women tend herds in the summer settlement of **Boiber**. They used to grow barley here on either side of the Boiber Stream, alternate sides on alternate years. At **Puryar**, two to three hours higher, is a deserted pasture, where the villagers leave their donkeys and oxen to fatten for the summer. (Information from Hermann Kreutzmann.)

From here it is a steep, slippery and dangerous climb up to the Karun Pass (4,873 metres) and then down to Dutt on the Shimshal River. Make sure before you start that the bridge before Dutt is passable. We have not met anyone who has taken this route.

SOST

The last village in Pakistan on the KKH is Sost, the Pakistani immigration and customs post. It stands at about 2,700 metres, 82 kilometres from the Chinese border and 35 kilometres north of Passu.

The **bank**, on the KKH opposite the Khunjerab View Hotel, accepts travellers' cheques in US dollars and sterling; it is open 9 am–2 pm and 3–6 pm. The **Post Office**, on the KKH near the north end of the settlement, is open 9 am–4.30 pm. The **telephone exchange**, above the KKH toward the south end of the village, is always open. The **hospital** is up the road to the old village, near the jamat khana.

Accommodation: The KKH is lined with new hotels, all built in a year with no planning and few facilities. Ranging from cheap to moderate, most are overpriced for what you get. There is no need to book; just walk along and find one. Hotel prices given below are for early 1992 and are meant to be a guideline for comparison between hotels. Prices rise proportionally, except when a hotel is renovated, in which case its prices jump.

Tourist Lodge, north end of the settlement, tel 9 (s/d Rs300/450). Popular with tour groups and overpriced—but a good place to look if trying to cadge a ride.

Khunjerab View, one kilometre down the KKH, at the south end of the settlement, below the old village; tel 12 (d Rs350, dorm Rs70 a bed). Doubles carpeted; dorm cold and dirty.

Hunza Dreamland, two kilometres down the KKH (d Rs350, dorm Rs50). Lovely view but difficult for those without transport.

Mountain Refuge (d Rs150–250, dorm Rs35–60). Popular, clean, good place to meet people and exchange information.

New Mountain Refuge, off the KKH and up the road to the old village (t Rs200, dorm Rs40).

Sarklin and Carawan (d Rs200). Both overpriced and ill-managed.

National, beside the customs post (d Rs100). Small, suspiciously popular with locals.

Pak-China (d/t Rs100/150).

Al Zaman (dorm Rs50). Seedy and unappetising.

Shahin (dorm Rs35). Bare and cold.

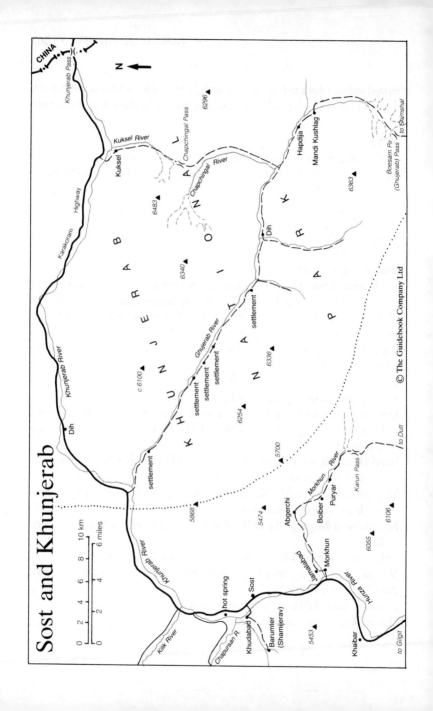

Sost and Khunjerab

SHORT WALKS AROUND SOST

Walk up the track to the **old village** above the KKH. Above the village is another example of determined village engineering, a AKRSP **water channel** that passes through a 400-metre tunnel. The roof of the tunnel is very high at the exit, as the villagers got the level wrong on their first attempt and had to dig down. You can follow the Sost Stream up for excellent views across the valley to the granite spires of Passu.

About seven kilometres upriver from Sost (about a kilometre before the petrol pump), some cairns mark a short path to the **hot spring** beside the river. The three pools are deep enough to lie in, and the continuous flow means you can wash without fouling the water for others. (Information from John King.)

Khudabad village, on the west bank of the Hunza River, is reached by a footbridge about 1.5 kilometres upriver from Sost. Turn right in the village and hike up for two to three hours, following the stream to where it forks, about six kilometres away. In the V between the two streams is the summer settlement of **Barumter** (Bardom Tir on the Swiss Karakoram map), meaning 'white pasture' in Burushaski. The settlement is also known as **Shamijerav**, meaning 'white water' in Wakhi. It is shared by two groups—Burushaski-speaking women from Khudabad and Wakhi-speaking men from Gulmit—who are separated by a low wall. (Information from Hermann Kreutzmann.)

CHAPURSAN VALLEY OVER CHILLINJI PASS
TO KARUMBAR VALLEY

Map: Swiss Karakoram map, reliability good; U502 43-15 (Baltit), reliability fair.
Restricted zone; strenuous; four days to Chillinji, about seven days to Boroghil; maximum height 5,291 metres; July to September.

The long, broad Chapursan Valley joins the Hunza River from the west, just above Sost. As in Gojal the people here speak Wakhi and are mostly Ismaili Muslims.

A jeep road goes up the valley for 35 kilometres to **Reshit**, where you can find porters. The wide, flat valley nourishes irrigated wheat fields, though in the mid-eighteenth century a flood covered much of the fertile land with a thick layer of clay and boulders. Legend says that the flood was caused by the saint Baba Ghundi, who came begging in the valley and received only some milk from an old woman. To punish the valley, Baba Ghundi sent the flood and mudslick, destroying everything except the old woman, her field and her hut—thus earning great respect for the rest of his life and deep veneration after his death. The valley is still littered with high mounds of flood debris, and pilgrims come from all over northern Pakistan and Wakhan to Baba Ghundi's shrine to pray and beg favours.

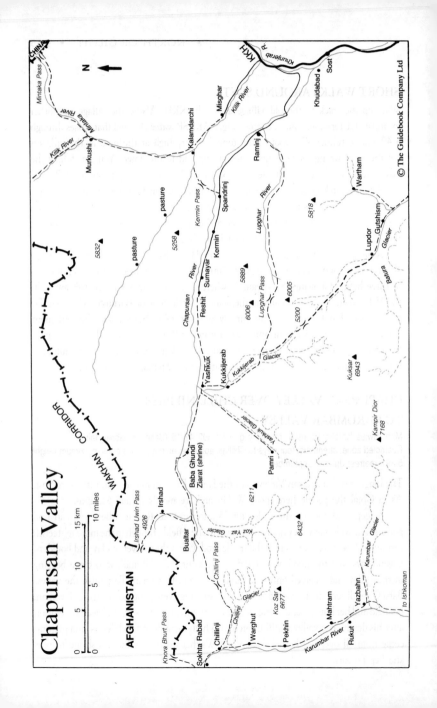

We have been only as far as Reshit—and that by helicopter—but apparently it is another 23 kilometres from there to the Shrine of Baba Ghundi, or 40 kilometres to the Chillinji Pass (5,291 metres).

At **Yashkuk**, a grassy oasis with thorn trees 11 kilometres above Reshit, you can spend the night and ford the deep stream of the Yashkuk and Kukkijerab glaciers in the early morning. There are several shepherds' summer settlements up the side of these glaciers, and apparently you can cross from the Kukkijerab Glacier over a technical 5,200-metre pass to the Batura Glacier, coming down to Lupdor. Alternatively, you can loop round across the Lupghar Pass and come back to the Chapursan Valley at Raminj.

A holy rock beside the road beyond Yashkuk shows the marks of hands, knees, toes and forehead. According to one of the many legends about Baba Ghundi, this is where he prayed. The rock is now a shrine and pilgrim resting place. Another holy rock along the way shows scratch marks, as if clawed by a hand, which are filled with an oily substance that never dries up.

The **Shrine of Baba Ghundi** is a small tomb of mud and stone enclosed by a high stone wall. According to R C F Schomberg, writing in *Between Oxus and Indus*, the shrine does not contain the saint's remains. A mound of old ibex horns is piled up at the gate, and inside there is a forest of poles bearing white flags left by pilgrims. There is also a pool of holy water that never overflows nor dries up.

The trail to Chillinji crosses to the north side of the Chapursan River, and about six kilometres further on a track branches north up the Irshad Stream to the **Irshad Uwin Pass** (4,926 metres) to the Wakhan (a closed zone). To the south, the **Koz Yaz Glacier** flows down off the white rampart of the northernmost tip of the Karakoram Mountains. You pass through a short gorge and emerge onto the grassy moraine of the **Chillinji Glacier**. Camp at **Bualtar**, a cave under a huge rock beside a stone sheep pen, at about 4,000 metres.

It is just possible from here to cross the Chillinji Pass, which is six kilometres away and a climb of 1,200 metres to the top, in one very long day with a 2 am start. From the top is a view of range upon range of mountains. The other side is a steep descent of nearly 2,000 metres on snow and scree to the **Karumbar Valley**, dividing the Karakoram from the Hindu Kush mountains. The traditional campsite is at **Chillinji**, a small cave near a sandy patch surrounded by birch scrub (see Tilman, *China to Chitral*).

The Karumbar River runs down through a narrow gorge for 55 kilometres to the end of the jeep road at **Imit** in the Ishkoman Valley. This route is passable only from September to May, when the water is low—even then it is desolate and difficult. This used to be the main route Hunza people took to Gilgit when their traditional enemies in Nagar controlled the route down the Hunza River.

The Karumbar Valley also provides an easy route to Chitral. Follow the Karumbar River up for 40 kilometres to the wide, grassy **Karumbar Pass** (4,188 metres) and cross to **Boroghil** in North-West Frontier Province (see page 348). The first eight kilometres is an easy, flat walk along the south bank to **Sokhta Rabad**, the traditional campsite on a grassy spot surrounded by willow and birch bushes. Across the river, a fairly well-defined path zigzags up steep slopes to the **Khora Bhurt Pass** to the Wakhan Corridor (a closed area); the pass was crossed by Francis Younghusband in 1891 (see Younghusband, *The Heart of a Continent*).

The track to Boroghil continues along the south side of the valley, along the edge of the **Chhateboi (Chashboi) Glacier**, which flows in from the south and completely fills the valley here. Crossing the glacier is difficult and takes about two hours, after which it is an easy walk along the Karumbar River for about seven kilometres to the campsite at **Shuinj**, where you cross the river. The last 13 kilometres to the top is up the broad, green valley past **Karumbar Lake**. There are a couple of stone circles at the top where you can shelter, but it is better to continue for 90 easy minutes down to **Margach**, the first summer village in Boroghil, which is occupied only in August (see page 348).

MISGHAR TO KILIK AND MINTAKA PASSES

Map: U502 43-14 (Baltit), reliability fair.
Restricted zone; strenuous; number of days optional; height optional; July to September.

Before the building of the Karakoram Highway, the Kilik and Mintaka passes were the main routes from Afghanistan and China to Hunza. They were not chosen for the KKH because they were thought too close to the Soviet Union.

The jeep road to Misghar (about 3,100 metres), where the army has a post, leaves the KKH about ten kilometres north of Sost. Six kilometres above Misghar, the long valley divides at **Kalamdarchi**, once the highest army post of the British Empire.

Kalamdarchi was also, in a manner of speaking, the *last* army post in British India, as the Union Jack continued to fly here four months after Independence. The post was under the command of Subadar Jamshed Khan, or 'Champagne Charlie' as he was known, who was the brother of the mir of Hunza and an ardent imperialist.

The path left leads through 30 kilometres of summer pastures to a dead end; the right branch reaches the Mintaka Pass, about 40 kilometres away. It passes first through a narrow gorge, then opens out to pastureland and passes several shepherds' summer settlements to **Murkushi**. Here the valley divides again, left for the **Kilik Pass**, and right for the **Mintaka Pass**, both leading to China. There is a cave shelter at the base of the Mintaka Pass.

KHUNJERAB NATIONAL PARK

Occupying 2,271 square kilometres from the Khunjerab Pass to Shimshal, the Khunjerab National Park begins 30 kilometres from Sost. It was established in 1975 in an attempt to save the Marco Polo sheep (*Ovis ammon poli*) from extinction and to preserve the other wildlife in the area: snow leopard, ibex, Tibetan wild ass, bharal, wolf, red fox, brown bear, cape hare and alpine weasel.

The park is currently closed to trekking to avoid disturbing the animals—especially the Marco Polo sheep, which survive only around the Khunjerab Pass. Their numbers are still declining alarmingly because of illegal hunting by influential Gilgit officials and Chinese. Tourists in cars are asked not to stop or walk in the park. Everyone stops at the top of the pass, and it is tempting to hike up one of the surrounding hills, but please resist the temptation. If the authorities can stop the illegal hunting, then there is hope that the Marco Polo sheep will become less shy, at which point walking in the park will be permissible.

The Tibetan wild ass is also endangered, their range now restricted to only the area east of the Shimshal Pass near the Chinese border. There are very few bears left, but snow leopard and wolf are comparatively plentiful. Lynx and wild dog may also live in the park, but no one has yet done a complete survey.

WEST OF GILGIT

The jeep road west of Gilgit leads to the Shandur Pass and Chitral, with side roads serving the valley kingdoms of Ishkoman and Yasin.

These two valleys are connected by easy, highly recommended treks with friendly, mostly Ismaili shepherds in the summer settlements and green pastureland right to the top of the passes.

South of the jeep road is a ridge of mountains separating the Gilgit and Indus valleys. Several footpaths lead across from one to the other through the wilds of Kohistan, which is not safe at the moment for trekking (see page 197). The other trails south from Singal, Gupis and Phundar cross to the Darel and Tangir valleys, but these are also too dangerous to explore without police support.

Further west, three safe treks lead south over the Dadarili, Bashkaro and Kachikhani passes to Swat (see pages 289, 291 and 292).

ISHKOMAN VALLEY

The Ishkoman Valley, running north to south to join the Gilgit Valley, divides the Karakoram Range from the Hindu Kush. Incorporated into Pakistan in 1972, Ishkoman was a vassel principality of Chitral in recent centuries, and the ex-raja of Ishkoman still lives at the capital, Chatorkhand. The valley is mostly Ismaili and is the home of an important Ismaili *pir* (religious leader) Sayyed Karim Ali Shah. Most people speak Khowar (the language of Chitral), Shina (the language of Gilgit) and Wakhi (the language of Wakhan).

Public jeeps leave Gilgit daily from the jeep stand in Punial Road. It is worthwhile booking the night before; women have priority for the front seat. It is about 100 kilometres to Chatorkhand and takes about six hours; you reach the Ishkoman Valley turnoff, after 68 kilometres, at Khanchi Bridge, a good jeep bridge across the Gilgit River. From Chatorkhand a public jeep goes most mornings up the east side of the Ishkoman River through Phakora to the road head at Imit. Occasional public jeeps go up the west side of the river through Ishkoman to the road head at Ghotulti. Alternatively, you can hire a jeep in Chatorkhand to take you to the beginning of your chosen trek.

Book the NAPWD **rest house** at Chatorkhand in Gilgit (see page 170). Chatorkhand also has a local hotel, or you can camp.

There are five possible treks from the Ishkoman Valley. A five- or six-day open-zone trek leads east from Chatorkhand or Phakora across the 4,600-metre **Naltar Pass** (for a description in the opposite direction, see page 209).

The 55-kilometre-long, restricted-zone trek to the **Chapursan Valley** (see page 265) begins at Imit and goes up the Karumbar River, through a difficult gorge not passable when the river is high in July and August, round the west side of Koz Sar (6,677 metres), to the **Chillinji Pass** (5,291 metres).

Another restricted-zone option from the top of the Karumbar River is to go northwest to the northernmost tip of Pakistan, skirting the border with the Wakhan Corridor of Afghanistan, and across the **Karumbar Pass** (4,343 metres) to Boroghil, at the top of the Yarkhun River (see page 348).

The treks connecting the Ishkoman and Yasin valleys are described in detail below. The **Ishkoman Pass** is well used by locals going to Darkot or upper Chitral (the latter of which is not open to foreigners without a permit), but the route is narrower, higher, less scenic and less populated than the **Asumbar Pass**. If you have time to do only one of these, we recommend the Asumbar.

ISHKOMAN OVER ASUMBAR PASS TO YASIN

Map: U502 NJ 43-14 (Baltit) and U502 NJ 43-13 (Mastuj), reliability mostly good.
Open zone; easy; four to five days; maximum height about 4,400 metres; July to October.

The Asumbar Pass—at about 4,400 metres, wide and gentle enough to be crossed on horseback—provides an easy, green trek with villages and summer settlements all along the way. From Phakora, cross the jeep bridge over the Ishkoman River to **Asumbar** village. Camp at 2,400 metres and arrange for porters and donkeys. Horses usually spend the summer up in the summer pastures and need to be booked in advance so that they can be brought down.

Stage 1: Asumbar to Chalinj, four hours. A well-made path follows the south bank of the Asumbar River, which tumbles over bright green boulders. For the first hour, you climb steeply through groves of willows and clumps of thorn and wild gooseberries, passing several small settlements surrounded by a few tiny fields. In the early morning, the path is in shadow, with cool air wafting from the stream. Higher up, the path is less steep, and it is shaded by silver birch, Himalayan pine, cedar and willow, with clumps of wild roses here and there.

After about two hours, a track leads toward the south and up to summer pastures. According to the U502 map, it continues over two passes, finally connecting with the

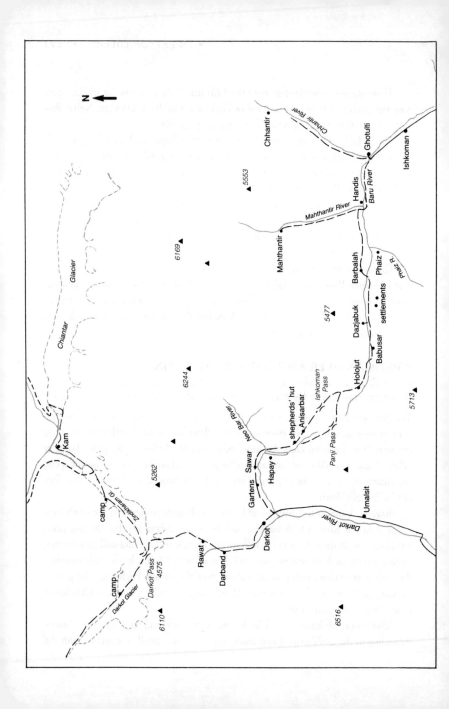

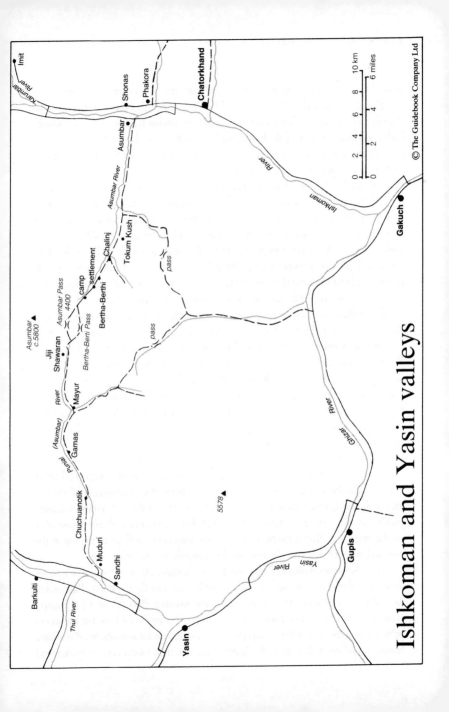

Ishkoman and Yasin valleys

main Asumbar Pass trek again at Mayur (we have not checked this ourselves).

The main path follows the Asumbar River. After another hour (three hours from Asumbar village) you reach the summer settlement of **Tokum Kush**, with fields of wheat, barley and maize, plenty of shade and good water. A further hour following the river through the woods takes you to Chalinj, a large summer settlement at 3,200 metres with a good spring on the edge of the wood.

The shepherds here are Ismaili Muslims from Shonas village, who come up from the end of May to the beginning of October. The women wear tall, quilted pillbox hats of flower-patterned material and long, gathered dresses over baggy trousers. They spend the summer in round houses constructed with dry-stone foundation walls and high-pointed roofs of birch poles covered in juniper branches, mud and pebbles. The smoke from the central fireplace oozes out through the chinks. Men take the animals up to the high pastures and collect firewood for the winter during the day, while the women and young children stay in the settlement and make butter in big copper churns.

Two valleys join here; a large side stream cascades down from the south to meet the main Asumbar River. A path follows this side stream up to the grazing grounds.

Stage 2: Chalinj to below Asumbar Pass, four hours. Follow the main Asumbar River northwest along an easy path that rises steadily for one and a half hours through silver birch and juniper trees to **Bertha-Berthi**, a small settlement of square stone houses with flat roofs populated by Gujar people from Asumbar village. It is too high here for the tall birch trees, so there are no high, pointed wooden roofs. An hour later you come to a second Gujar settlement of square stone houses, where you may be able to watch men making a type of cheese by boiling up huge pots of buttermilk outside over open fires. This is the last settlement before the pass. Beware of the dogs.

A final hour or so takes you to a huge meadow below the pass, with good water but no shade. Here at about 4,000 metres, grazing herds of yaks congregate at the top end of the field, where there is a natural salt lick. This is the last suitable campsite on the east side of the pass, and it is two to three hours from here to the next possibility on the other side. From Chalinj, it is five hours' continuous walking to the top of the pass and an hour down to the first suitable campsite on the other side.

Stage 3: Across Asumbar Pass, three hours minimum. There are two possible passes about two kilometres apart, separated by a rounded hill. The **Bertha-Berthi Pass** (4,410 metres) is the narrower one on the left, and the **Asumbar Pass** (about 4,400 metres) is on the right. An obvious path leads to the top of Bertha-Berthi Pass, but the snowy gully on the other side of this pass is steep and not suitable for animals. So, if you have horses or donkeys, follow the path almost to the top, then take a contour track round the central hill to the wider Asumbar Pass and cross there.

The view from either pass is magnificent, and for an even better panorama it is an easy climb to the top of the hill separating them. Back in the east, you can see the snowy mountains beyond the Ishkoman Valley separating it from the Hunza Valley. Ahead to the west, range after range of the Hindu Kush stretch as far as the eye can see, with Tirich Mir in the distance. A patch of permanent snow lies just below the top on the western side, beyond which are rolling pastures with knee-deep grass, gentians, edelweiss, geraniums and many other flowers, grazed by herds of horses and yaks (on the Ishkoman side, the pastures are grazed almost bare).

An hour below the pass is the first summer settlement of **Jiji Shawaran**, beside the river. According to the U502 map, the rivers on both sides of the pass are called Asumbar, but our Ishkoman porters called the river on the Yasin side the Punial. Cross the river at the settlement and continue down for about half an hour to a small lake, a perfect campsite at about 4,000 metres. It is six or seven hours' continuous walking from here down to the Yasin River, so you may want to go further down before camping. There is water and grazing all the way, so you can camp more or less anywhere.

Stages 4 and 5: Down to the Yasin River. This is an easy walk, following the river all the way through birch and juniper woods, and past settlements, down to permanent villages surrounded by fields of wheat, barley, maize and vegetables. At **Mayur** (about 3,560 metres) a big side stream comes down from the south. This is where the U502 map indicates an (unproven) alternative route (see above).

Cross the side stream on a bridge opposite Mayur settlement and follow the path across steep mountainside through shady woods. Below on the right, the river foams over green rocks and occasional red, purple and orange boulders. Finally you emerge from the woods at **Gamas** to find the first fields and permanent settlements, which are on both sides of the river. About an hour later, there is a good bridge across the river to wide, flat fields of wheat and barley at **Chuchuanotik**. From here to the Yasin River is a three- to four-hour easy walk—still hot in September, and very hot in summer, so best begun in the early morning. A good campsite is above the bridge on the south bank. (If trekking from Yasin to Ishkoman, this is the best place to camp the first night.)

Below the bridge, the path passes through fields in a wide bowl, then the valley narrows, and the path rides above the right bank through a long gully on the flank of the mountain, with willows down by the river. There are various possible campsites along by the river. They are building a jeep road up this valley, but we do not know how far it has progressed.

You join the Yasin River at the large village of **Sandhi**, seven kilometres north of

Yasin. Public jeeps leave Sandhi every morning for Yasin, Gupis and Gilgit. There is a bridge across the Yasin River halfway between Sandhi and Yasin town, from which a jeep road runs north up the Yasin River through Barkulti to Darkot. Another jeep road turns up the Thui Valley for 15 kilometres to the village of Nialthi and the beginning of the trek across the Thui Pass (see page 281).

ISHKOMAN OVER ISHKOMAN PASS TO DARKOT

Map: U502 NJ 43-14 (Baltit) and NJ 43-13 (Mastuj), reliability mostly good.
Open zone; easy to strenuous; three to four days; maximum height 4,587 metres; August (even at the end of which there is still plenty of snow).

Locals cross the Ishkoman Pass in two days, but we took three in 1988, even though we were fit and acclimatised. We crossed the pass in the opposite direction to what we describe here, so our reversed timings may be inaccurate.

In the Ishkoman Valley, the jeep road ends at **Ghotulti**, an attractive village set in groves of fruit trees, where we were welcomed by the sons of Hussain Ali and camped in their garden under falling apricots. Occasionally a public jeep from Chatorkhand comes to Ghotulti; otherwise you will need to hire one privately (bargain hard). Camp in Ghotulti and arrange porters or donkeys.

Stage 1: Ghotulti to Dazjabuk, five to eight hours. Two streams join at Ghotulti: the Chhantir, flowing down from the north (we have not explored this, but there are summer pastures there), and the Baru, flowing from the Ishkoman Pass in the west. Follow the Baru River; there are paths on both sides, but we took the south side on a good donkey path high above the stream. You cross a huge rockfall and continue to **Handis**. At about 3,000 metres, Handis is the highest winter village, surrounded by fields of barley but too high for fruit trees. It is completely deserted in August, when the families are further up the valley with the herds, returning in September to harvest the barley. From Handis, the view north up the Mahthantir Valley shows jagged peaks. Cross the river on a bridge and fill your water bottles, as there is no water for several hours along the path high above the north bank.

Phaiz, the first summer settlement, which was deserted when we passed through, is a collection of stone huts with pointed wooden roofs covered in juniper branches and mud. A steep path leads down to a bridge crossing to the main Phaiz settlement on the other side, at the mouth of the wide, green Phaiz Valley, which leads to more pastures and jagged peaks. The main Baru Valley is narrow and steep sided, so there is no view ahead.

Continue high on the north bank through birch, juniper and cedar trees to **Barbalah** (marked Galtir on the U502 map) at about 3,200 metres. Here, about three or four hours from Ghotulti, you have your first view up the valley. As two women trekking without men, we found the women here very friendly, perhaps making Barbalah a good place to camp if you want to take the trek more slowly and enjoy observing the shepherds' life. The women speak Shina and Khowar. They wear tall red, blue and green pill-box hats and bright clothes as they tend herds of cattle, sheep and goats.

Cross a bridge at Barbalah for a lovely walk high on the steep hillside along the south bank, undulating through juniper scrub with occasional cedar, pine and rowan trees and wild rose bushes. You pass a couple of settlements high above the path and, after about an hour, come down again to the river and a bridge to the settlement of Dazjabuk, a good campsite at about 3,300 metres. This would be a good place to rest and acclimatise for a day.

Stage 2: Dazjabuk to Holojut, three to five hours. The first hour is an easy walk along the river to **Babusar,** the last settlement at 3,400 metres, comprising seven shepherds' huts by a small lake. The women here make butter by shaking the milk in goat skins, so they are probably Gujars, though we did not think to ask.

Along the way are more possible campsites under the trees and beside the water— good places for a rest day. Then you begin climbing quite steeply up through birch forests and, in a couple of hours, gain nearly 500 metres, coming out above the tree-line to the wide meadow of Holojut. Herds of horses and cattle graze on the green floor of what must once have been a lake. Three foaming, white icefalls cascade off the surrounding mountains that wall in the pasture. There are no shepherds' huts here, but you will find a good spring and a stone fireplace sheltered by a large rock at the lower end, where you enter. Camp at about 3,900 metres.

Stage 3: Holojut across the Ishkoman Pass (4,587 metres). The climb northeast to the top is very steep—allow four to five hours to cover the almost 700 vertical metres to the top. It took us two and a quarter hours coming down (the path was not clear, but while on snow we found footprints to follow). Start early so you will be over the top before 10 am, when the snow starts to soften. The last kilometre to the top is a gentle approach across snowfields, but you are hemmed in, so there are no extensive views (there is a second pass, the Panji, marked on the U502 map, but we did not see it). You are now in Yasin territory.

On the Yasin side there is a wide, gentle snowfield and a small glacier. Keep to the right but not too close to the cliff, as there are rock falls. Rope up if the glacier is snow covered. In an hour or so, you can get down to the first clump of willow bushes beside a tiny spring, a sheltered campsite at about 3,900 metres, just above the Anisar

Bar (*bar* meaning river). Our Darkot porters called the site **Anisarbar**.

Stage 4: Anisarbar to Darkot, four to five hours. Walk down through sparse pastures with gentians and blue anemones, then into a barren gorge covered in loose shale, dropping about 300 metres to the first shepherds' settlement, a lone hut and goat shed (also called Anisarbar by our porters). A further hour brings you down to the junction of the Anisar Bar and Neo Bar rivers and the first big settlement at **Hapay**, six houses at about 3,500 metres, surrounded by barley fields and occupied for three months in the summer.

At last the view opens out, and you can see all the way down to Darkot and up the Neo Bar to more summer pastures. The walk down to Darkot takes two to three hours on a clear donkey path (keeping the river on your left) through **Sawar**, with its willow-lined street, and **Gartens**. Both of these are now permanent villages, since Darkot lost a considerable portion of its arable land in a recent landslide.

Darkot is a large village with a school and shop, situated at about 2,700 metres in a wide, fertile bowl at the northern end of the Yasin Valley. It is 35 kilometres down the jeep road to Yasin village, the capital of the valley, but when we were there the road was blocked and there were no jeeps. At **Umalsit**, a two-hour walk south, you are more likely to find transport.

Do not be tempted to cross the Darkot Pass to Boroghil unless you have already been to Chitral to get your permit from the deputy commissioner there (see page 302). Boroghil is a restricted zone, and the police and army posts at Boroghil watch all the routes. Besides, the pass is very steep on the south side so is best approached from the north.

For the history of this strategic pass, see below.

YASIN VALLEY

Like the Ishkoman Valley, the Yasin Valley (local name Warshigum) runs north to south, joining the Ghizar (upper Gilgit) Valley at Gupis. It lies to the east of Ishkoman, at an altitude of 2,100 to 2,750 metres. In its lower 60 kilometres, the valley is wide, flat and well watered, making it comparatively fertile, with irrigated fields on either side the river. There are no rocky defiles, so communication along the valley is easy, with roads on both sides of the river.

The people here speak the aboriginal language, Burushaski, as in Hunza, and the upper class also speak Khowar, as in Chitral. Yasin lies in the newly formed district of Ghizar, the name of the Gilgit Valley west of Gakuch, the district capital.

Until the twentieth century, Yasin was an important kingdom controlling the shortest and easiest route between the Oxus and Indus valleys. In the early centuries AD, it was the capital of the kingdom of Little Bolor, which ruled Gilgit. We know from the Chinese Tang Annals that, early in the eighth century, the Tibetans, who controlled Great Bolor (Baltistan), tried to gain access through Yasin to the Oxus Valley in order to join forces with the Arabs and attack China. With Chinese help, Yasin kept the Tibetans at bay until about 742, when the Tibetans persuaded the king of Yasin to marry a Tibetan princess and align himself with Tibet.

The Chinese retaliated by attacking in 747. With 10,000 troops, they crossed the Pamirs and defeated an equal force of Tibetans on the Wakhan side of the Boroghil Pass, then chased them across the Boroghil and Darkot passes. The Chinese then took Yasin and cut the birch-rope bridge across the Gilgit River at Gupis (which had taken a year to build), thus blocking the advance of Tibetan reinforcements coming from Gilgit, as the Gilgit River cannot be forded in summer and there is no route along its north bank. Chinese rule proved to be short lived, however, as a defeat in 751 near Tashkent at the hands of the Arabs lost them control of Central Asia.

There is no reliable historical record for a thousand years, until the Chinese returned in 1749. In the eighteenth and nineteenth centuries, the Kushwaqts, who ruled in Mastuj, controlled Yasin and, at times, Gilgit as well. The Ghizar Valley west of Yasin is wide and smooth (as is the Shandur Pass), making it easy for Mastuj to communicate with Yasin.

Yasin is famous as the place where George Hayward, a distinguished solitary explorer for the Royal Geographical Society, was murdered in 1870. Hayward was hoping to cross the Darkot Pass in his search for the source of the Oxus and was travelling without RGS sponsorship, as he had written a sensitive article in the Calcutta paper *The Pioneer*, describing Kashmiri soldiers' atrocities in Yasin a few years earlier, which included tossing babies in the air and cutting them in half as they fell. (The British needed the goodwill of the maharaja of Kashmir, so Hayward wrote a letter formally dissociating himself from the British government and the RGS.) He had set off completely at his own responsibility, without hope of rescue if he got into difficulties or retaliation if he were killed.

On July 13, Hayward rode into Yasin and was warmly greeted by Mir Wali, the prince of Yasin, whom he had met on an earlier visit. No one knows exactly what happened next, but it appears that Hayward quarrelled with Mir Wali, possibly over his route out of Yasin. It seems Mir Wali had been ordered by his suzerain, the Kushwaqt ruler in Mastuj, to detour Hayward via Mastuj to Boroghil, as Hayward was carrying desirable gifts and both Yasin and Mastuj were loath to see them leave their territory.

Hayward must have suspected something, for a few kilometres outside of Yasin town he carved his name on a rock with an arrow pointing north in the direction he was going. (The carving is still there; ask in Yasin town for directions to it.) At Darkot village, Mir Wali's men caught up with Hayward, who sat up all night to prevent a surprise attack. When, at dawn, he finally nodded off, he was swiftly overcome. The incident inflamed the Victorian imagination, and Henry Newbolt immortalised it in his emotional poem *He Fell Among Thieves*. Hayward is buried in Gilgit.

After this, the British, fearing a Russian advance over the Boroghil and Darkot passes, took an interest in the valley and opened its agency in Gilgit in 1877. Britain and Russia continued to jostle for control. Russian spies stood at the top of the Darkot Pass in 1890, peering down into Yasin, but retreated unseen. Five years later, the Pamir Boundary Commission crossed the Darkot Pass with 600 ponies to survey the frontier. The Russian threat subsided, and in the twentieth century Yasin became just another small kingdom ruled by a raja. It was absorbed by Pakistan in 1972.

Public jeeps leave Gilgit daily for Yasin. Catch the jeep at the jeep stand in Punial Road; it is worth booking the night before. The journey is 112 kilometres through Gakuch to Gupis, on the Ghizar River, where a side road branches north up the Yasin River for the remaining 25 kilometres to Yasin village. The journey from Gilgit takes about six hours, but when the new truck road is completed from Gilgit to Gupis it should be considerably quicker.

At about 2,650 metres, Yasin village is a sprawling settlement, whose centre consists of a couple of shops and a petrol pump at the edge of a polo ground. Basic **supplies**, such as sugar, tea, flour and potatoes, are available in Yasin, but you should plan to bring most of your supplies from Gilgit.

There is a good NAPWD **rest house** at Gupis and another at Yasin village in a large orchard. These cost Rs60 per night and are bookable only in Gilgit (see page 170). Otherwise, you can camp, but ask permission first and be prepared to pay a camping fee.

There are many short treks you can do within the valley. Though we have not done it, we recommend Draskin to Darkot over the **Ghamubar Pass**. This is a two- to three-day trek beginning at the junction of the Thui and Das rivers. Follow the Das River north to **Hakal** village and the summer settlements of **Chhelish** and **Shotikuto.** Loop around east over the Ghamubar Pass (4,432 metres) and down to **Darkot**, for a total of about 30 kilometres.

There are five possible treks out of the Yasin Valley. Heading east to Ishkoman, a four- to five-day trek over the **Asumbar Pass** (about 4,400 metres) begins at Sandhi village. A three- to four-day trek to Ishkoman from Darkot crosses the 4,587-metre **Ishkoman Pass** (for descriptions going the other direction, see pages 271 and 276).

The restricted-zone, six- to eight-day trek north from Yasin over the 4,575-metre **Darkot Pass** to Boroghil begins at Darkot and takes you to the top end of the Yarkhun River of Chitral, then down to Mastuj. This trek is best attempted from the other end, as we describe it (see page 341). This is because you must go first to Chitral town to get your permit from the deputy commissioner.

We describe below two treks west to the Yarkhun Valley, one over the **Thui Pass** and the other over the **Nazbar and Zagar passes**.

YASIN OVER THUI PASS TO YARKHUN VALLEY

Map: Japanese *Mountaineering Maps of the World* page 224 (Eastern Hindu Raj), reliability good; U502 NJ 43-13 (Mastuj), reliability mostly good.
Open zone; easy to strenuous; four to five days; maximum height 4,499 metres; July to October.

This is a scenic, moderately easy trek following one of the ancient trade routes. Thui Pass is just passable for a sturdy donkey, but the trek requires stamina and good health, as for three days you are above the highest shepherds' summer settlements. A local guide is recommended.

The Thui River joins the Yasin River ten kilometres north of Yasin town, and a jeep road follows the valley for 15 kilometres, ending at **Nialthi** village, at about 2,840 metres. From Yasin town, a public jeep leaves daily at 9 am for **Harpu**, four kilometres short of Nialthi. It costs Rs15 per person, but you can pay extra to be taken to the end of the road. Porters are available in Nialthi. In the villages of the Thui Valley, you can buy fruit and vegetables in season.

Stage 1: Nialthi to Ramach, four to five hours. From the end of the jeep road at Nialthi, follow the footpath for 15 minutes to a bridge across the Thui River. Cross the bridge and walk for one hour on the level through fields of wheat, barley and millet bordered with willow and poplar trees. Continue north for a second hour along the river through a barren stretch relieved by some thorn and willow bushes to **Mushk**, a summer settlement where villagers from Nialthi live for half of the year.

Lasht, the next summer village, 30 minutes further north, is a small settlement of a few square stone houses surrounded by some fields. Ask here about the condition of the bridges further upriver. If the bridge two hours away at Pastuji is in good repair, stay on the east side of the river; otherwise, cross just after Lasht and walk up the west bank, climbing gently. Birch woods clothe both banks, and waterfalls tumble in slow motion down gullies carved in the jagged mountains on either side of the narrow valley.

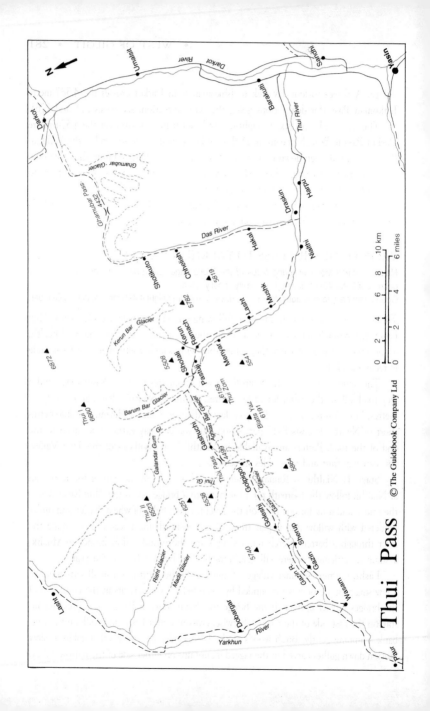

Thui Pass

© The Guidebook Company Ltd

At **Menyar**, one hour from Lasht on the west bank, a shepherds' shelter nestles under a huge sloping rock. Ramach, on the east bank 90 minutes from Lasht, is at about 3,000 metres and offers excellent campsites with fresh spring water in the birch woods on either side of the river.

Stage 2: Ramach to Gashuchi, four hours. Two valleys meet at Ramach, coming down on either side of a nameless 5,508-metre peak. The northeastern (right) valley leads up to the last summer settlement of **Kerun**, while the northwestern (left) valley comes down from the Thui Pass. **Pastuji**, half an hour up the northwestern valley, is a small settlement with a bridge across the river (broken in 1987). The best path follows the northern bank, but, if need be, you can take the rough, indistinct track on the southern side, crossing rolling scree for about one hour to **Shotali**, at the snout of the Aghost Bar (known locally as the Gashuchi) Glacier, where the stream called the Barum Bar flows in from the north. You can detour up the west side of the Barum Bar Glacier to see **Thui I Peak** (6,660 metres). Shotali (about 3,300 metres) is the last possible campsite with wood. If you go on to Gashuchi, your porters will collect firewood here and carry it.

Continuing west up the Aghost Bar Glacier, it is easiest to walk straight up the centre of the glacier, a comfortable stroll of three and a half hours from Shotali to Gashuchi (rope up if the crevasses are covered with snow). The donkey path follows the northern edge of the glacier, along the lateral moraine. A third of the way up, the Galandar Gum Glacier flows down from **Thui II Peak** (6,523 metres) in the north.

In September, Gashuchi makes a perfect campsite, with a small, sheltered, flat area beside the glacier large enough for two or three tents and conveniently near a patch of permanent snow and a clear, shallow pool. On the hillside above are a couple of shallow caves. The top of this hill is a rounded meadow, knee deep in flowers: geraniums, garlic, pinks, stonecrop and saxifrage. Snowcocks and ibex roam the higher pastures.

From the hill looking south, you see glaciers tumbling down the north face of **Thui Zom** (6,158 metres). A stream with a waterfall flows down the valley below Thui Pass to disappear under the Aghost Bar Glacier.

Stage 3: Gashuchi across Thui Pass to Goleshi, five to six hours. Do not follow the stream up to the Thui Pass. The better path is up the hill above the Gashuchi campsite for a spectacular 45-minute walk through flowers to the head of the valley. You then cross a small snowfield to the edge of a wide alluvial fan at the end of the valley. A clearly defined donkey path runs diagonally across the scree to the top of the Thui Pass (4,499 metres). It takes about two hours to reach the top of the pass from Gashuchi. The narrow ridge of the pass is covered in loose gravel and swept by biting winds. The views back down the Yasin side show a circle of pointed, rocky, 6,000-metre peaks touched with snow, with a wide green meadow on the rounded hill in the foreground and the Aghost Bar Glacier snaking down to the Thui Valley.

On the Chitral side, the view is blocked by a semi-circle of 5,000- to 6,000-metre peaks enclosing a glaciated bowl. The path is steeper on this side, falling straight down a bank of scree that would be difficult for a donkey. You can run down it in 20 minutes, but it would be a hard one-hour puff going up. From the bottom of the scree slope, follow the Thui Glacier (known locally as the Golpigol Glacier) down toward the south for one hour, scrambling across the boulders of the moraine. A rough route is marked by occasional cairns, but there is no path. Be sure to end up with the river on your right, as it is difficult to cross lower down.

Golpigol summer pastures lie in a narrow bowl at the bottom of the glacier, with Blatts Yaz towering in a 2,000-metre wall over the eastern end and the gleaming-white Gazin Glacier cascading steeply off its slopes. Herds of cattle and dzos graze in this bowl, surrounded by about ten rocky peaks, all between 5,000 and 6,200 metres high.

If crossing Thui Pass from Chitral to Yasin, Golpigol is the best place to spend the night; there is shelter and a good water supply but no shepherds' huts. Thui Pass is not visible from Golpigol. To reach it, turn north up the terminal moraine of Thui Glacier and then east over the pass (without a guide it may be difficult to find the way).

Continuing from Yasin towards the Yarkhun, the stretch from Golpigol to Goleshi is a two- to three-hour walk down the north side of the huge Gazin Glacier. You have to detour once out onto the glacier, but the rest is an easy ridge walk along the crest of the moraine, with views south across the Gazin Glacier to craggy mountains and east to the sharp pyramid of Thui Zom. The last stretch to Goleshi is along the wide, flat, stony pastures between the lateral moraine and the mountains, along a clearly defined path.

Goleshi, at about 3,400 metres, is a lone shepherds' hut and goat pen with a narrow campsite nestled under the lateral moraine and beside a clear stream. Climb to the top of the moraine for superb views east and west along the Gazin Glacier.

Stage 4: Goleshi to Wasam, three to four hours. This is an easy walk down the Gazin River to the Yarkhun River, past permanent villages of Ismaili Muslims. After one hour you come to **Mithar Panji**, another lone shepherds' hut and goat pen, after which the path passes through light brushwood scrub for one hour to a bridge across the Gazin River at **Sherup**. From here on down, paths run along both banks of the river. There is another bridge at **Gazin** village, an hour below Sherup. From Gazin to

Wasam on the south bank takes about 70 minutes, if the water is low enough to follow the river bed for part of the way—or a hot two hours, if you have to climb to the upper path across the scree. If following the path on the north side of the Gazin River, you will have to detour north up the Yarkhun River for about a kilometre to the bridge. The bridges across the Yarkhun are frequently washed out in the summer melt, so ask in each village about the condition of the bridges ahead.

At the northern end of the bridge at Wasam, the track rides about 20 metres above the river, with superb views east all the way up the Gazin Valley to the sharp point of Thui Zom in the distance. The road may be jeepable from here down to Mastuj, depending on the bridges. If on foot, it is a hot couple of hours from Wasam to **Paur** (pronounced Pawoor) and a further very hot three or four hours down to the main jeep bridge across the Yarkhun, just north of **Brep**, where you should be able to find a public jeep to take you the 20 kilometres down to Mastuj.

YASIN OVER NAZBAR AND ZAGAR PASSES TO YARKHUN VALLEY

Map: Japanese *Mountaineering Maps of the World* page 212 (Central Hindu Raj), reliability good; U502 NJ 43-13 (Mastuj), reliability mostly good.
Open zone; strenuous; maximum height 5,008 metres; August to September.

We have not done this trek and have very little information about it, as it seems to be rarely done (a full description would be welcome).

The trek begins a couple of kilometres north of Yasin village where the Nazbar (*bar* meaning 'stream') flows down to join the Yasin. The jeep road enters a short way into the Nazbar Valley to **Nazbardeh** village. Hugh Swift says it takes 'two short days from Yasin to reach the base of the pass, but the way to the last rocky stretch of scree leading to the pass is not straightforward, so take a local with you'.

The trek starts out with what seems to be an easy walk for about 18 kilometres along the Nazbar and through villages to the last settlement at **Shukan**. No more settlements are marked on the maps for the next nine kilometres to the top of the Nazbar Pass (4,977 metres) or for 13 kilometres the other side, down the Ano Gol and Bahushtaro Gol (*gol* meaning 'stream' in Khowar), until you reach **Haringal Shal**. It is 40 kilometres from Nazbardeh to Haringal Shal.

From Haringal Shal, follow the Bahushtaro Gol south for about five kilometres, down to **Dedero Shal** at the junction of the Zagaro Stream. (The rivers on either side of the Zagar Pass seems to be called the Zagaro.)

From here you have two options. The first is to continue south down the Bahushtaro Gol for about 20 kilometres to join the Ghizar River at **Shamran**, which is on the jeep road from the Shandur Pass to Gilgit, about five kilometres east of **Phundar**.

The second is to turn west up the Zagaro Stream for about seven uninhabited kilometres to the snow-covered, 5,008-metre Zagar An (*an* meaning 'pass' in Khowar). Continue down the other side about 14 kilometres across rolling pastureland, with occasional shepherds, until you meet the trail coming down from the Chamarkhan Pass. (We had a good look at this stretch through binoculars from the Chamarkhan Pass trail in mid-August 1988, and it appeared to be smooth, easy grassland leading to large snowfields

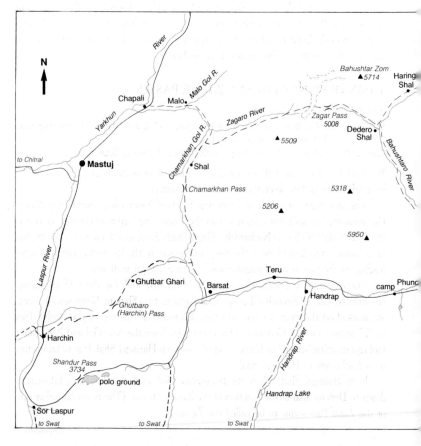

below the Zagar An.) Follow the right bank of the Zagaro Stream for the last seven kilometres down to the Yarkhun River settlement of **Chapali**, which is on the jeep road about 11 kilometres upriver from Mastuj. It is 33 kilometres from Haringal Shal to Chapali.

GHIZAR AND THE SHANDUR PASS

Ghizar, the name for the western end of the Gilgit Valley above Gakuch, is a new political district administered from Gakuch. The jeep road continues west from Gakuch, through Gupis and along the Ghizar (upper Gilgit) River for about 100 kilometres to the Shandur

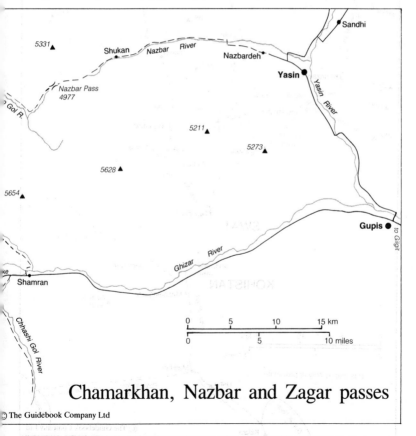

Chamarkhan, Nazbar and Zagar passes

© The Guidebook Company Ltd

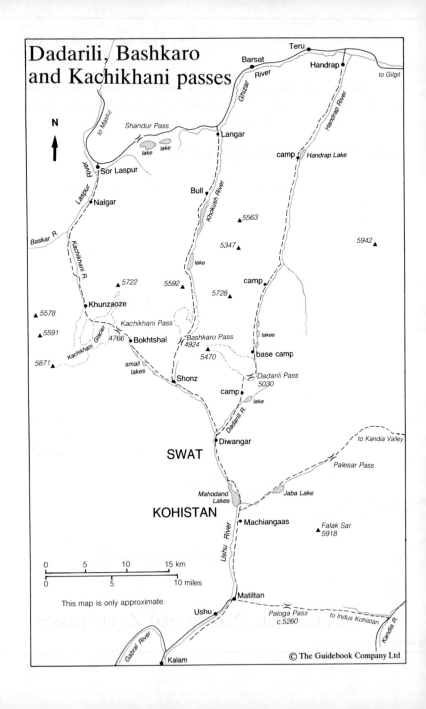

Dadarili, Bashkaro and Kachikhani passes

N

Teru
Barsat
Handrap
Ghizar River
to Gilgit

Shandur Pass
lake lake
Langar
camp Handrap Lake
Handrap River

Sor Laspur
to Mastuj
River
Laspur
Nalgar
Baskar R.
Bull
Knokush River
▲ 5563
5347 ▲
5942 ▲

Kachikhani R.
▲ 5722
5592 ▲
lake
5728 ▲
camp

▲ 5578
Khunzaoze
▲ 5591
Kachikhani Pass
Bashkaro Pass
lakes
4766 Bokhtshal
4924
base camp
5871 ▲
Kachikhani Glacier
5470
Dadarili Pass
5030
small lakes
Shonz
camp
lake

Dadarili R.
Diwangar
to Kandia Valley

SWAT
Palesar Pass

Mahodand Lakes
Jaba Lake

KOHISTAN
Machiangaas
Falak Sar
5918

Ushu River

0   5   10   15 km
0   5   10 miles
This map is only approximate.

Matiltan
Ushu
Paloga Pass
c.5260
to Indus Kohistan
Kandia R.

Gabral River
Kalam

© The Guidebook Company Ltd

Pass, then enters Chitral District in North-West Frontier Province.

Public jeeps leave Gakuch and Gupis almost daily for the top end of the Ghizar Valley, and very occasionally you may find a public jeep going to Mastuj in Chitral. You can usually rent a private jeep. We do not recommend walking along the jeep road, as it is too hot.

The best time to visit may be the end of June, when the annual **polo game** is played on the Shandur Pass between the teams of Gilgit and Chitral. Plenty of transport goes up to the pass at this time. You can camp on the crowded pass and watch the polo matches for a couple of days, while collecting information and making plans. About 12,000 people camped for the 1990 match.

The only treks we have done in Ghizar are the Chamarkhan and Shandur passes (see below), but there are various other possibilities.

Shamran, about 55 kilometres west of Gupis, is the starting point for a trek up the **Bahushtaro Gol**, taking you through summer pastures for about 20 kilometres and then either east over the **Nazbar Pass** to Yasin or west over the **Zagar Pass** to Mastuj in Chitral (see page 285).

Paths also lead south from Shamran up to villages and summer pastures along the **Chhashi Gol**. This area is never visited by tourists and would be interesting to explore as far as the watershed. Do not cross the pass into the Tangir Valley and the wilds of Kohistan, though, unless you have official protection (see warnings on pages 172 and 197).

Phundar, about five kilometres beyond Shamran, has a well-equipped NAPWD rest house (book in Gilgit, page 170) nicely situated on a ridge overlooking the Ghizar River on one side and a small lake on the other. A couple of kilometres beyond the rest house is a good campsite in a meadow beside the river, where you can swim, fish (buy a licence first for Rs10), rest and plan your next trek. From Phundar campsite, we walked south steeply up through a village to a small lake for a pleasant couple of hours with fine views up and down the Ghizar Valley.

HANDRAP OVER DADARILI PASS TO SWAT

Map: U502 NJ 43-13 (Mastuj), reliability mostly good; U502 NI 43-1 (Churrai), reliability very poor.

Open zone; strenuous; six days; maximum height about 5,030 metres; August to September.

About 15 kilometres up the jeep road from Phundar toward the Shandur Pass, Handrap (about 2,900 metres) is the start of a well-known but little-used trek to Swat over the

Dadarili Pass (about 5,030 metres). A jeep bridge crosses the Ghizar River to Handrap, where you can hire porters, but goes no further up the Handrap River.

Stage 1: Handrap village to Handrap Lake, three to four hours. These first 13 kilometres are very gentle. Follow the path up from the village, keeping the Handrap River on your left. There are very few people here—no fields or grazing and no villages above Handrap. Camp at Handrap Lake, which is surrounded by birch and juniper and is known for its excellent fishing.

Stage 2: Handrap Lake to Camp 2, six hours. Up a wide, easy valley with flowers and trees, this is pleasant walk straight toward a 5,728-metre peak, keeping the river on your left.

Stage 3: Camp 2 to Base Camp, four hours. The river is wide and open at the top end, spread out into three lakes. Camp just after the highest lake, on a small, sandy space big enough for two tents.

Stage 4: Across Dadarili Pass, about eight hours. Start at 5 am, as there are dangerous falling stones later in the day. Bear to the left, leaving the gorge on your right, and walk up across alternating patches of snow, ice and rock. The last 500 metres is a gentle climb on a snowfield. It takes four to five hours to reach the top. From the top you see a huge snow-filled depression five kilometres across. Descend steeply on scree for 300 metres to the snow and walk round the right-hand edge of the depression on the snow. Climb out of the depression and bear left. Walk down through a 25-metre-wide gully filled with snow, keeping on the left, with steep cliffs above. After two to three hours, you get down to a green, open area. Camp with a view down to a lake about 250 metres below.

Stage 5: Down to Mahodand Lake, six to seven hours. Start out with the river on your left, walking down through flowers on a clear trail. After 90 minutes, wade across the river to the left bank and follow it down to the first settlement, two to three hours from camp. About 90 minutes later you come to **Diwangar**, a shepherds' settlement at the junction of the Dadarili River and the river coming down from Kachikhani Pass. It is another two to three hours to Mahodand Lake (meaning 'fish lake'), keeping the river on your right all the way. Mahodand Lake is lovely—a fresh-water body amid wide meadows dotted with trees. You can camp anywhere, but beware of theft, as you are now in Swat Kohistan, and the locals have a bad reputation. Have a rest day here for fishing. (Information from Vaqar Zakaria.)

Stage 6: Mahodand Lake to the end of the jeep road, see the Kachikhani Pass trek (page 292).

HANDRAP TO SHANDUR PASS

Map: Japanese *Mountaineering Maps of the World* page 212 (Central Hindu Kush), reliability good; U502 NJ 43-13 (Mastuj), reliability mostly good.
Open zone; easy (jeepable over Shandur Pass); Shandur Pass open June to early November; Chamarkhan and Ghutbaro passes open July to October.

The jeep road west of Handrap leads, after five kilometres, to the large village of **Teru**, where there is a basic NAPWD rest house (book in Gilgit, see page 170). A tourist hotel is under construction in **Barsat** (3,300 metres), ten kilometres further west and the last village in the Ghizar Valley.

Barsat is the starting point for the two-day trek over the **Chamarkhan Pass** (4,344 metres) to Chapali on the Yarkhun River, from where you can jeep the 11 kilometres down to Mastuj (for a description going the other way, see page 339). If hiking from this end, you would need a shepherd to show the way, as the terrain is open, rolling pastures, with paths running in all directions, so that it is not at all clear which goes to the Chumarkhan Pass. The pass is ideal to ride over, and there are plenty of donkeys in Barsat (we saw no horses, but they are probably available if you are determined enough to find them). We paid Rs100 per day for each donkey, which we hired in Chapali in 1988. The owner came along to look after them at no extra charge.

Alternatively, you can go from Barsat across the **Ghutbaro (Harchin) Pass** to Harchin on the Laspur River in Chitral. This pass is higher than the Chamarkhan, and apparently it is very steep on the west side (we have met no one who has crossed it).

Between Barsat and the Shandur Pass, the Khokush River flows in from the south, leading to the **Bashkaro Pass** (4,924 metres) to Swat. Apparently there are several shepherds' summer settlements along the river and good fishing in a lake about ten kilometres up. The sides of the lake are so steep that you may wish you had a boat to cross it. Beyond the pass, you join the Kachikhani route at the summer settlement of Shonz.

The 3,734-metre **Shandur Pass**, about 12 hours from Gilgit by jeep, is blocked by snow from November to May. The top of the pass is flat, open summer pasture with two lakes, an ideal spot to camp—though no doubt less than pristine just after the polo match. You can walk up from Barsat on the Gilgit side, or from Sor Laspur on the Chitral side, and spend some easy, safe days camping, exploring and getting acclimatised. This is a popular route for jeep safaris and mountain bikers, so you will not be alone. There are shepherds' settlements throughout the pass.

Colonel William Lockhart, in 1885 the first European traveller across the pass, called it a plateau. This was the route taken by British soldiers on the march from Gilgit to relieve the siege of Chitral in April 1895. Determined Colonel James Kelly achieved the impossible by bringing his men and guns through the snow to surprise the Chitralis at their back door. The pass presented considerable difficulties, according to Lieutenant W Benyon, who was quoted by John Keay in *The Gilgit Game*:

> Here are some 250 men [other reports say 500] . . . working shoulder to shoulder . . . brought two mountain guns, with their carriages and supply of ammunition, across some 20 miles [30 kilometres] of deep soft snow, at the beginning of April, the worst time of the year. These men were also carrying their own rifles, greatcoats and 80 rounds of ammunition and wearing heavy sheepskin coats; they had slept for two nights in the snow and struggled from dawn to dark, sinking at every step to their waists.

The treks at the top end of Chitral district are best approached from Chitral town, as you need to go there first to get your permit from the deputy commissioner. Do not attempt to trek into Chitral without a permit, which could prejudice the authorities against trekkers coming after you. There are checkposts at all the strategic points.

SOR LASPUR OVER KACHIKHANI PASS TO SWAT

Map: U502 NI 43-1 (Churrai) and NJ 43-13 (Mastuj), reliability very poor.
Open zone; strenuous; six days; maximum height 4,766 metres; August to early September.

We have not done this well-known trek, and our information and map are unreliable. We believe the trek to be strenuous but straightforward. Chitrali porters are more amenable than the Kohistani men of upper Swat, so we suggest doing this trek from Chitral to Swat, rather than the other way, unless you are trekking with a reputable company that will make all of your arrangements. The disadvantage of doing the trek in this direction is that the first two days are very strenuous. Whereas upper Chitral is dry and barren, Swat is in the monsoon belt, with pine-covered hillsides and green pastures.

It is 22 kilometres from **Mastuj** to Sor Laspur, the end of the jeep track on the Chitral side. Take a public jeep from Chitral town to Mastuj (see page 306), but you may have to hire a private jeep for the remainder of the journey. Spend the night in the rest house in Sor Laspur or camp beside the stream at about 3,000 metres.

Stage 1: Sor Laspur to Baskar River, seven hours. Follow the Laspur River up for three to four hours, keeping the river on your right and passing through some small trees to **Nalgar**, the last permanent village, which is surrounded by trees and wheat fields. This is the best place for lunch. Continue up the Laspur River for a further three to four hours to the junction of the Kachikhani and Baskar rivers, which together form the Laspur 14 kilometres above Sor Laspur. Camp here by the stream, where there is a stone circle shelter for the porters.

Stage 2: Baskar River to Khunzaoze, six to eight hours. Follow the left-hand river, the Kachikhani, crossing it on a footbridge so that the river is on your left. Some hours later, cross back again on a footbridge where there is some greenery and a few bushes. For the next three hours the valley is stony and barren, until you reach Khunzaoze (meaning 'queen's place'), where there is a green spot surrounded by snowy mountains on all sides. Camp.

Stage 3: Across the Kachikhani Pass (4,766 metres), eight to nine hours. Start early to avoid the danger of falling rocks after 11 am. Walk up the stony lateral moraine with the glacier on your right. After four hours, move onto the glacier, which is stony for the first 30 minutes but then white and easier to the top. Keep to your left about a kilometre from the top to avoid an ice cliff on your right. At the top, you will find views of snow-covered mountains and the forests of Swat below. The south side of the pass is snowy and steep before it eases off, with several glaciers flowing down from various directions. Descend in two hours, passing below a dramatic icefall to **Bokhtshal**, a meadow with birch trees and flowers. Camp by clear stream full of trout at 3,840 metres.

Stage 4: Bokhtshal to Shonz, six to seven hours. Continue less steeply down, following the river through birch trees and past green grass and several lakes. Camp at Shonz, a large Gujar shepherds' settlement used in June and September. Beware of the Gujars, though, as these often problematic people sometimes steal. If shepherds are here, arrange sleeping places so that the porters encircle the trekkers, thereby protecting your belongings.

Stage 5: Shonz to Machiangaas, six to seven hours. A gentle walk down the green, wooded valley takes you past banks of orchids and gentians and herds of horses, cattle, buffalo, sheep and goats to **Mahodand Lake**. Continue to Machiangaas, a big pasture about five kilometres across and seven kilometres long. Camp anywhere. Pakistanis come here to collect medicinal herbs for pharmaceutical companies in Karachi.

Stage 6: Machiangaas to Palugah, four hours. This is an easy walk through forests of mature pine and deodar, past the first village and on to the end of the jeep road at Palugah. You can camp across a small stream near the forest or continue the ten kilometres to **Matiltan**, three hours' walk along the jeep road, which follows the stream down all of the way. Matiltan, at 2,442 metres, is set in fields of wheat, maize and potatoes and is shaded by large walnut trees. The village boasts views of the twin peaks of Bateen.

You should be able to get a jeep or minibus from here for the 40-minute ride down to Kalam 16 kilometres away. You can camp or stay at the Baghicha Hotel (Rs120 per double). (Information from Babu Muhammad.)

We do not describe any more trekking here, as the region is Kohistani and it is best to rely on a reputable trekking company to arrange porters and protection here. For information on Swat, see *Pakistan Handbook* by Isobel Shaw. See also the Dadarili Pass (page 289) and Kohistan (page 203).

CHITRAL

Chitral is an isolated, 320-kilometre-long valley in the northwestern corner of Pakistan. The Hindu Kush Range, dominated by Tirich Mir, separates it from Afghanistan and the Soviet Union on the west and north. It is divided from Hunza, Gilgit, Swat and Dir, on the east and south, by the lower Hindu Raj Mountains (a name, meaning 'Hindu rule', that is unpopular in Pakistan, where the range is simply called the Hindu Kush). Chitral offers several treks that are easier and greener than those in the Karakoram and Himalaya ranges further east. The Hindu Kush are lower and generally less jagged than the Karakoram, and in lower Chitral, which is just on the edge of the monsoon belt, the steep slopes are covered with trees to over 3,000 metres and the lower ridges are sometimes crowned with sparse pastures.

Further north, outside the monsoon belt, the valleys look more like the Northern Areas of Pakistan, with villages forming small irrigated oases along the rivers wherever water can be channelled to some flat piece of land. Even in the north, though, there are reasonably large areas of pasture at higher altitudes and on the passes.

From November to June, Chitral is cut off from the rest of Pakistan by snow-covered passes. The one tenuous lifeline with the rest of the country is the small Fokker Friendship plane that flies in from Peshawar on clear days. In summer the valley is accessible by jeep road across the 3,118-metre Lowari Pass from Dir in the south, and across the 3,734-metre Shandur Pass from Gilgit in the east. There is an easier route into Chitral from Afghanistan, along the Kunar River. This was closed for many years, but since 1990 it is unofficially open again for buses and trucks, though still closed to all foreigners.

Most confusingly, the river draining the Chitral Valley is not called the Chitral River. Instead, it has three names, rising as the Yarkhun in the northeast and becoming the Mastuj in central Chitral and the Kunar below Chitral town. It flows out of Chitral into Afghanistan to join the Kabul River at Jalalabad, by which circuitous route its waters eventually reach the plains of Peshawar and the Indus. The Chitral River is a small tributary that joins the Kunar at Chitral town.

The Chitral Valley is home to about a quarter of a million people, who show a strong influence from both Iran and Badakhshan, as well as the ancient civilisation along the Oxus River. Though ten languages are spoken in Chitral, about 85 percent of the people speak Khowar, the Kho people having lived originally along the Torikho River (*kho* still appears in many place names). These Khos are not related to the warlike Pathans in neighbouring Afghanistan to the west, nor to the wild Dir Kohistanis to the south. Many of them have blue eyes and are stunningly handsome.

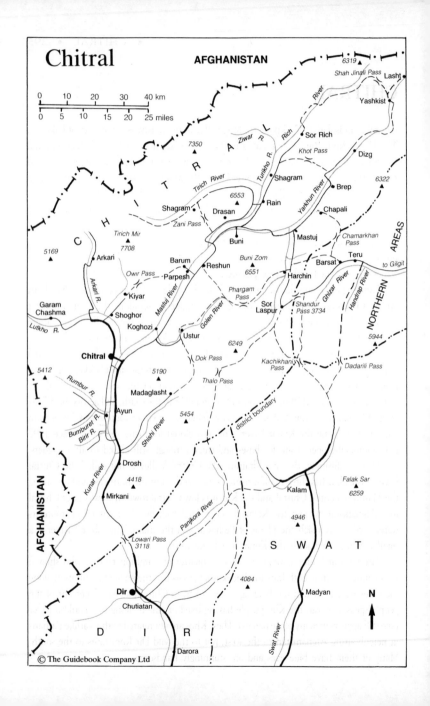

Most of the people of Chitral are Muslims, two-thirds being Sunni. The other third are Ismaili, followers of the Aga Khan, most of whom migrated from Wakhan and Badakhshan and are now concentrated in the Garam Chashma and Mastuj areas. About 3,000 non-Muslim Kalash people live in three valleys south of Chitral town, and a few thousand Gujar tribesmen (Sunnis) migrate up to summer pastures with their herds in summer.

Though not themselves traders, the Chitralis gained a good income by taxing trade through their territory. Passing through in 1906, Aurel Stein remarks in his book *Serindia* that they had 'far higher standards in comforts of life, manners, and methods of cultivation' than their neighbours. In the past ten years, the Gilgit region has developed more quickly than Chitral as a result of the Karakoram Highway, but nowhere in Chitral have we seen the dirt and poverty of Baltistan.

CHITRAL HISTORY

Chitral was always an important valley because it controlled the shortest and easiest route from China and Central Asia to the northwestern portion of the Indian subcontinent. This branch of the Silk Route ran from Kashgar to Tashkurgan, over the Wakhjir Pass and down the Oxus (Ab-i-Panja) River. Then it either crossed the Boroghil Pass (3,804 metres) and Darkot Pass to Yasin (see page 279) or followed the Yarkhun/Mastuj/Kunar River all of the way down through difficult gorges to the Lowari Pass, then over to Swat. According to Aurel Stein, writing in *Serindia*, another route avoided the gorges by coming round through Afghanistan and entering Chitral lower down by way of the Dorah (Garam Chashma) Pass to Garam Chashma and Chitral town. Yet another route stayed even longer in Afghanistan and came down the Bashgol Valley and across the Nawa Pass to Bajaur.

The route through Chitral rose and fell in popularity according to the stability of the area. In the centuries before and after Christ, China was powerful, and this was the great highway for trade to the Roman Empire. The area was peaceful as long as it was Buddhist, from about the first century BC to the eighth century.

From his diaries we know that Fa Xian, the Chinese Buddhist pilgrim, came across the Boroghil Pass in AD 403, but he had delayed at Kashgar for the great quinquennial assembly held in the spring and did not reach the Yarkhun River before the melting snows made the passage down to Mastuj too difficult. Instead, he crossed the Darkot Pass to Yasin, continuing south to the Darel Valley, down the Indus and over to Swat (see page 201).

The next Chinese Buddhist pilgrim whose diary survives was Song Yun, who also came from Kashgar but travelled further south in Afghanistan, through Badakhshan, and from there across the Mandal Pass and down the Bashgol Valley to the Kunar River. He entered Chitral coming up the Kunar in 519, then continued through Dir to Swat, where he spent the winter.

Xuan Zang, the most famous of the Chinese Buddhist pilgrims—who left his native Xi'an to spend 16 years, from 629 to 645, wandering round India—visited Swat both coming and going, following Song Yun's route. Xuan Zang left a long description of upper Chitral (see page 338).

Early in the eighth century, Tibet managed to gain control of Gilgit and Yasin and, in about 742, made successful overtures to Chitral. The Chinese retaliated in 747 by invading over the Boroghil and Darkot passes and capturing Yasin (see page 279). (It was also in 747 that the great Buddhist teacher—and tantric sorcerer—Padmasambhava was invited from Swat to Tibet to spread Buddhism.) The Chinese took Chitral in 750 but, the following year, suffered a crushing defeat near Tashkent at the hands of the Arabs. The Chinese lost control of the whole region—not to the Arabs, but to the Tibetans, who aligned themselves with Kashmir to keep the Arabs out. The Chinese had no influence over the area for the next 1,000 years.

The last Buddhist pilgrim to pass through was Wu Kong in 750. He crossed the Boroghil Pass, followed the Yarkhun down to Mastuj, then went across the Shandur Pass to Ghizar and south to upper Swat.

In about 1050, Nazir-i-Khisran, an Ismaili missionary from Egypt, arrived in Chitral. He had been sent by the Ismaili imam, who ruled the Fatimid Empire from Cairo, to convert the peoples of Persia and Afghanistan. He had remarkable success in Badakhshan and Wakhan, which have never waivered from the Ismaili creed. Nazir-i-Khisran's shrine is in Garam Chashma.

For the next few centuries, with the Arab expansion into Central Asia, the route through Chitral became increasingly dangerous and fell into disuse until the first quarter of the thirteenth century, when the Mongols under Ghengis Khan swept across Asia, eventually uniting all of China, Central Asia and most of Eastern Europe. For more than a century, the trade routes were open again, allowing travellers such as Marco Polo to pass from Italy to China. Marco Polo went by the Bashgol Valley route in about 1273, but he describes central Chitral and the Northern Areas from hearsay as 'noisy with kingdoms'.

As sea routes were developed by the Arabs for trade with China, the Central Asian route lost its vital importance. Again it fell into disuse until the beginning of the sixteenth century, when the Moghal emperors imposed two centuries of stability on the Indian subcontinent.

About this time, the Katur-Khushwaqt Dynasty rose to power in Chitral (*katur* being the title by which the strongest leader of the Kho was known). When Moghal power declined, the Chinese again controlled the area, invading over the Boroghil Pass in the mid-eighteenth century and taking Mastuj. The early-nineteenth-century map of Pakistan that hangs in our study shows as Chinese the entire west bank of the Indus down as far as Attock. The Katur-Khushwaqts paid tribute to China and kept relative peace in the valley.

In 1885, after rapid Russian expansion in Muslim Central Asia, the British began to survey the passes of the Hindu Kush. Fearful that the Russians might cross the Boroghil Pass and steal Chitral, they made an agreement with the Katur *mehtar* (ruler), Aman ul-Mulk, by which they paid him a generous subsidy to keep all Russians out. He kept the agreement and ruled with a firm hand until his death in 1892. There followed a murderous scrum for the throne, with five contenders holding it briefly in the course of the following three years. In 1895, the British attempted to keep the Russians out by backing one of the younger contenders, Shuja ul-Mulk (affectionately known as Sugar-and-Milk). A force led by Surgeon-Major George Robertson found itself besieged in Chitral Fort. The much-publicised relief of Chitral was effected after 48 days by a force of 500 men led by Colonel James Kelly, who achieved the impossible by carrying two mountain guns from Gilgit across the snowbound Shandur Pass in April (see page 291). A permanent garrison was then maintained in Chitral.

Sir Shuja ul-Mulk died in 1936 and was succeeded by Sir Nasir ul-Mulk. The last mehtar of Chitral, Saif ur Rahman, was killed in a plane crash on the Lowari Pass in 1954, and Pakistan took over the state administration. In 1969 Chitral became a district of the North-West Frontier Province and is now governed directly by Pakistan through the deputy commissioner in Chitral town.

The last mehtar's oldest son is in the Pakistani foreign service. The other ul-Mulk descendants are still important princes in the valley, owning many of the forts. Two descendants, Siraj and Maqsood ul-Mulk, run the trekking company Hindu Kush Trails.

CHITAL INFORMATION
WHEN TO GO

At some 1,475 metres, Chitral town is snowbound in winter but not too oppressively hot in summer. The annual rainfall is about 450 millimetres in Chitral town and 600 millimetres in Drosh, falling mostly from February to May. The best time to go is from April to October.

GETTING TO CHITRAL

By air: There are three flights daily scheduled from Peshawar to Chitral—at 7, 9.45 and 11 am. The flight takes 55 minutes and costs US$40 if booked overseas, or Rs375 one way (plus Rs10 airport tax) for foreigners if booked in Pakistan. Pakistanis get a subsidised flight costing Rs200 one way. On Saturdays a flight is scheduled from Islamabad to Chitral via Swat, leaving at 11.35 am and costing Rs595 for foreigners or Rs410 for Pakistanis (a flight this late in the day is unreliable, so it is better to fly from Peshawar).

PTDC reserves two priority seats on each flight for tourists. Apply to the PTDC office at Dean's Hotel in Peshawar, or Flashman's Hotel in Rawalpindi, and ask for a special booking for these reserved seats, thereby receiving a note of confirmation to take back to PIA. Book several days in advance, if possible on the earliest flight of the day, and be prepared for flight cancellations, especially during the monsoons rains from mid-July to mid-September. Try to sit on the left-hand side of the plane to see the remote tribal areas along the border of Afghanistan.

If your flight is cancelled, wait at the airport and try to get on a later plane. Be flexible. On our most recent trip, we waited round all morning, then got a refund and hired a private taxi in the airport car park to take us to Dir in six hours for Rs900. There we transferred to a public wagon to cross the Lowari Pass to Chitral.

Chitral Airport is a few kilometres north of Chitral town. Public Suzukis meet the plane and take you into town for about Rs5. These are crowded, and you need to be quick to get a seat. Pay extra to be taken to your chosen hotel. Private-jeep booking is Rs50.

By road: The most interesting way to Chitral that is open to foreigners is by road via the Malakand Pass, Dir and the Lowari Pass. Public buses, wagons and minibuses leave Peshawar daily for Dir, where you usually have to change before continuing over the Lowari Pass (open June to November) to Chitral. Check at your hotel in Peshawar for the latest information, but in 1992 buses for Dir, costing Rs30, left from the Government Transport Service (GTS) Bus Terminal opposite Dean's Hotel, with a second stop on the Grand Trunk Road near Hashnagri Gate. Minibuses for Chitral (known as Flying Coaches, costing Rs195 one way) left from the New Main (or General) Bus Stand (on the Grand Trunk Road about three kilometres east of the GTS Bus Terminal, near the old Haji camp).

As we go to press, only Afghanis and Chitralis can take a bus from the New Main Bus Stand on the Grand Trunk Road and travel through Mohmand tribal territory to cross the Nawa Pass into Afghanistan. This route joins the Kunar River at Chagha Serai and follows the west bank north for five hours, recrossing the Pakistani border at Arandu. The road crosses to the east bank for the last two hours to Chitral town. Ask round to learn the latest information.

In 1992 you could hire a whole minibus in Peshawar for Rs2,500, or a Datsun pickup or Suzuki van for Rs1,500. A taxi from the bazaar cost Rs900 to Dir or about Rs2,500 to Chitral, but it is sometimes impossible to cross the Lowari Pass in an ordinary car. You can also hire jeeps in Islamabad or Peshawar from PTDC or travel agents. The official rate is Rs6 per mile, plus a standard overnight charge and food for the driver. It is 227 miles (365 kilometres) from Peshawar to Chitral town via Lowari, and slightly further from Islamabad.

Swat to Chitral: From Mingora, in Swat, you can get to Chitral by bus or minibus, but you must change at Chakdara Bridge and wait for a vehicle coming through from Peshawar, which may already be full.

Chakdara Bridge across the Swat River: Have your identification handy, as there is a checkpost here. While you wait, take a moment to relive history. This crossing place on the Swat River was mentioned in the *Rigvada*, the world's oldest extant religious text, which was composed by the Aryans, who invaded the area in about 1700 BC. It is also mentioned in the *Mahabharata*, the epic Hindu story, and in Ptolemy's *Geographia*, circa AD 120. Alexander the Great crossed here in 327 BC, as did many other conquerers in later years. For a detailed description of the road, see *Pakistan Handbook* by Isobel Shaw.

Dir

Dir, naming both a district and a town, guards the route to the Lowari Pass, so you have to pass through it on the way to Chitral. You enter Dir District at Chakdara Bridge. At Timargarha, the first big town, a road leads west along the Bajaur River, through Mohmand tribal territory and the Nawa Pass, to Afghanistan (for Afghanis and Chitralis only). This was probably the route followed by Alexander the Great.

Until 1970, Dir was an semi-autonomous state ruled by a *nawab*, who did less for the welfare or development of his subjects than the rulers of Chitral or Swat. Few tourists have explored Dir District, though some are forced to spend the night in the old capital, Dir town. The people here are Kohistani. They—and their language—are of Dardic origin, and during Buddhist times (from the first century BC to about the eighth century AD) they lived on the plains of Panjkora and Swat. The Kohistanis were driven north in the fifteenth century by the expanding Pathan tribes to the south. At some point between the fifteenth and seventeenth centuries, they converted to Islam.

Few have a good word to say for the people of Dir. In the seventh century, the Buddhist pilgrim Xuan Zang called them 'inclined by nature to deceit'. Hugh Swift, author of *Trekking in Pakistan and India*, complained of stones thrown at him. As in all northern Pakistani towns, there are no women in sight; the difference here is that all males over the age of 15 parade in the bazaar carrying a rifle or Kalashnikov machine gun.

If stuck here, you can stay at the Al Manzar Hotel for Rs120 or at the government rest house, which is bookable for Rs60 at the PTDC in Dean's Hotel in Peshawar. Beware of theft. In general, women may feel more comfortable if they stay indoors—though Elisabeth Gardner, who contributed a great deal to this book, experienced no hassle at all even while travelling alone.

There are a couple of treks in Dir for intrepid explorers, but you are strongly advised to trek in this area only with the advice and permission of the deputy commissioner and the police—and then only with a reliable local guide. Note, too, that tourists have been robbed and raped in northern Swat along the Dir border.

Maps covering this area are restricted. The part of Dir covered by the U502 map NI 43-1 (Churrai) is wildly inaccurate, and even the Japanese *Mountaineering Maps of the World* leave a blank east of Dir town. However, Siraj ul-Mulk and his wife Ghazala, of Hindu Kush Trails, know this area. They have access to the necessary maps and have trekked across the **Thalo Pass** from Dir to Sor Laspur in the Shandur area. There is also an easy trek from the end of the jeep road up the **Panjkora Valley** to Kalam in Swat. Both treks pass through thick coniferous forest.

DIR TO CHITRAL

There are plenty of vehicles from Dir into Chitral, but they do not leave to a set schedule. In 1992 a wagon from Dir to Chitral town cost Rs75.

REGISTRATION AND PERMITS

In 1992 you also needed a permit from the Ministry of Tourism in Islamabad to trek in the areas of Chitral classified as either restricted or closed. Before you leave Islamabad, find out at the Ministry of Tourism the current status of the trek you plan to make (see page 59). The area is under revision, and some treks have recently changed from closed to restricted. Trekking in restricted or closed areas is an extremely expensive proposition, as in restricted zones you must have an official guide and cook with you, and in closed zones an official liaison officer as well. Just paying, feeding and clothing these for one week cost more than we normally spend in a whole summer.

Once in Chitral, you must register immediately with the police. You can do this daily 8 am–2 pm in summer (8.30 am–2.30 pm in winter) but only until noon on Thursday (closed Friday). Tell them everywhere you wish to visit, but you may want to word your list carefully, avoiding names that appear on the closed or restricted lists in the *Pakistan Trekking Rules and Regulations*. For example, you need not mention the Shah Jinali Pass, but just say that you want to trek from Sor Rich to Lasht. Similarly, there is no need to say Boroghil, but ask for the Zindikharam Glacier.

Ask the police if you need a permit from the deputy commissioner, who works the same hours as the police. The deputy commissioner changes each year, but he has the absolute power of yea or nay, so it is worth your while to be serious and charming with him. If he is interested in tourism, he is likely to give you whatever permit you wish.

Do not be tempted to trek in areas for which you do not have a permit. There are very few foreigners in Chitral—about 2,500 a year, most of whom stick to the Kalash valleys and the road to Gilgit—so your movements will be watched and reported. Do not do anything that may prejudice the authorities against tourists or make it difficult for those coming behind you to get permits. Never try to slip by a police checkpost without registering. You will be noticed, word will get back to the authorities, and the policeman responsible for letting you pass may lose his job.

The most difficult area for which to get permits is along the Afghan border. If you cannot get permission to trek there, be flexible and request a trek further away from the border, such as over the Owir, Zani, Thui, Lohigal or Dok passes, or the Kalash area (which, though it is right on the border, is such a tourist attraction that the authorities choose to keep it accessible). If all else fails, take a public jeep to Mastuj and head off across the Chumarkhan, Shandur or Kachikhani passes into Ghizar or Swat districts (where the trekking is unrestricted) and leave Chitral for another time.

In 1992 you needed a permit from the deputy commissioner to visit the Kalash valleys valid for seven days; you bought your permit from the police at the entrance to Bumburet and Rumbur for Rs50. A permit to see the Kalash dance is available in the valleys for Rs1,000. Ask at your hotel for the latest rules.

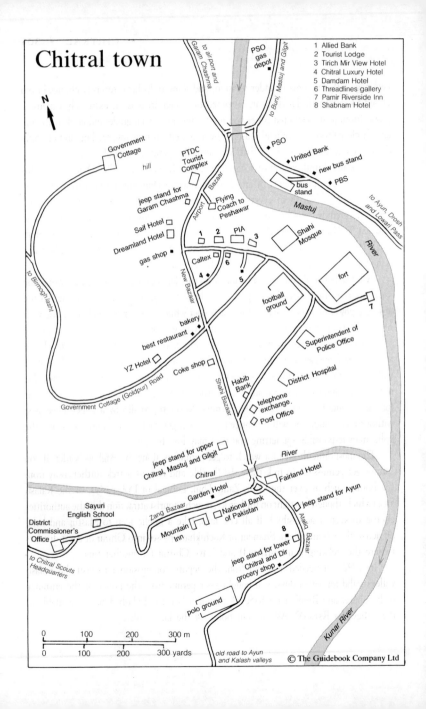

Chitral town

N

1 Allied Bank
2 Tourist Lodge
3 Tirich Mir View Hotel
4 Chitral Luxury Hotel
5 Damdam Hotel
6 Threadlines gallery
7 Pamir Riverside Inn
8 Shabnam Hotel

to air port and
Garam Chashma

to Buni, Mastuj and Gilgit

PSO gas depot

Government Cottage

hill

PTDC Tourist Complex

jeep stand for Garam Chashma

Saif Hotel

Dreamland Hotel

gas shop

PSO

United Bank

new bus stand

bus stand

PBS

to Ayun, Drosh and Lowari Pass

Airport Bazaar

Flying Coach to Peshawar

Mastuj

1 2 PIA 3

Shahi Mosque

Caltex

6

4

5

fort

River

football ground

New Bazaar

bakery

best restaurant

YZ Hotel

Coke shop

Superintendent of Police Office

District Hospital

Habib Bank

telephone exchange

Post Office

Shahi Bazaar

Government Cottage (Goldpur) Road

to Birmogh lasht

jeep stand for upper Chitral, Mastuj and Gilgit

River

Chitral

Fairland Hotel

jeep stand for Ayun

Sayuri English School

District Commissioner's Office

to Chitral Scouts Headquarters

Zang Bazaar

Garden Hotel

Mountain Inn

National Bank of Pakistan

8

jeep stand for lower Chitral and Dir

grocery shop

Ataliq Bazaar

polo ground

Kunar River

0   100   200   300 m

0   100   200   300 yards

old road to Ayun and Kalash valleys

© The Guidebook Company Ltd

CHITRAL TOWN

The **Tourist Information Centre** is in the PTDC Tourist Complex; tel 683. **Habib Bank** (open 9 am–1 pm, Monday to Thursday, and 9 am–12 pm, Saturday and Sunday), the **Post Office** (open 8 am–2 pm), the **telephone and telegraph office** (open 24 hours a day—the telephone code for Chitral is 0533), the **hospital** and the **police station** are on the road leading down to the fort.

You can find all basic supplies in the **bazaar**: rice, wheat flour, sugar, powdered milk, biscuits, honey, jams, tinned fruit and peas, potatoes, lentils (*dhaal*), onions and cornflakes. There is even a fair chance of finding instant coffee, Ovaltine, porridge oats, packet soups, sardines and tinned meat, but it would be safer to bring these last with you from Rawalpindi or Peshawar.

Bottled gas and **gas stoves** are available at the PSO station on the Mastuj road. A stove costs Rs250, and a small gas cylinder weighing 25 kilogrammes requires Rs1,150 as a deposit; refills cost Rs75. The best **restaurant** in town is on the corner of Government Cottage (Goldpur) Road, where about Rs10 buys a meal.

The **trekking agency** to contact here is Hindu Kush Trails, Mountain Inn, Chitral; tel (0533) 800, 781 and 581; fax c/o GPO Chitral 0533. The address in Islamabad is c/o Siraj ul-Mulk, PO Box 2039, Islamabad. This agency is run by the ul-Mulk family, who once ruled Chitral; the princes themselves act as guides. They are well connected throughout the valley, well organised, reliable and happy to give expert advice. If you do your own hiring, ask guides and porters for references and personal recommendations (see page 83).

Private jeeps are for hire in Chitral. Find out the going rate by asking round in your hotel before you start to bargain with the jeep driver.

Maps: Most of Chitral District is covered by the U502 sheets NJ 43-13 (Mastuj); NJ 43-14 (Baltit) and NI 43-1 (Churrai), but the section along the Afghan border, shown on NI 42-4 (Chitral) and NJ 42-16 (Tirich Mir), are restricted, so they are not sold to the general public. The Japanese *Mountaineering Maps of the World* cover almost all of the Hindu Kush but are difficult to find.

PUBLIC BUSES

There are five public bus and jeep stations in Chitral town.

For **lower Chitral** go to Ataliq Bazaar. The fare to Ayun is Rs7, to Bumburet and Rumbur Rs10, to Birir Rs15, to Drosh Rs16 and to Arandu on the Afghan border Rs23. There are two Government Transport Service (GTS) jeeps daily, at 5.30 am and 6.30 am, costing Rs80 to Dir, where you can catch a GTS bus to Peshawar for about Rs30.

For a **Flying Coach to Peshawar**, go to Airport Bazaar, almost opposite the Dreamland Hotel, down beside the fields. There are as many as four coaches per day, at 3 and 4 am and 3 and 4 pm. The journey takes about 12 hours (with a meal stop in Dir) and costs Rs195.

For **upper Chitral, Mastuj and Gilgit**, go to Shahi Bazaar. Sarhadada Jeep Stand is just below the small bridge on the left. About six jeeps leave daily for Mastuj, a six-hour journey costing Rs100. A private jeep to Gilgit costs about Rs5,000 and takes two days to cover the 406 kilometres over the Shandur Pass. Public jeeps go to the end of the road in every valley almost daily for a fixed fare. To Wasam in the Yarkhun Valley costs Rs140; to Porkhot in the Khot Valley Rs120; to Sor Rich in the Turikho (Rich) Valley Rs120; to Zundrangram in the Tirich Valley Rs120. Ask round at the jeep depot for details.

For **Garam Chashma**, go to Airport Bazaar at the PSO station opposite the PTDC Hotel. Jeeps leave every hour or so and cost Rs18 for the two-hour ride to Garam Chashma (32 kilometres). Sussoom takes four hours and costs Rs25; Arkari is five hours for Rs35. Ask about other destinations.

A **new bus stand** has been established on the other side of the river, opposite the mosque, but in 1992 no one was using it, as it was too far away and there was no shade.

Most public transport leaves in the very early morning, and prices are fixed. It is best to make your booking the night before.

Ordinary petrol is available in Chitral town and on the main Mastuj road near Buni.

ACCOMMODATION

Hotel prices given below are for early 1992 and are meant to be a guideline for comparison between hotels. Prices rise proportionally, except when a hotel is renovated, in which case its prices jump.

Mountain Inn, Ataliq Bazaar; tel (0533) 581, 781, 800; fax c/o GPO Chitral 0533 (s/d Rs350/450). The best in town—pleasant and peaceful, with a central garden and nice atmosphere. Hindu Kush Trails' office in front entrance. The owner, Haider Ali Shah, is the gentle, soft-spoken man tending the flowers.

PTDC Tourist Complex; tel (0533) 683 or book through PTDC Islamabad, tel 819384, 815653, 812957 (s/d Rs500/600). All rooms have a fan and are clean. Small, noisy garden along the road. Poor value.

Pamir Riverside Inn, on the river beside the fort; tel (0533) 525 (d Rs325). Double bungalows on the Kunar River bank. New, cool and quiet.

Dreamland, New (Kublisht) Bazaar; tel (0533) 615 (s/d Rs100–115/150–225). Rooms are clean, some upstairs ones are airy with a view. Helpful management and good value.

Tourist Lodge, Shahi Majid Road, beside PIA office; tel (0533) 652 (s/d Rs200/300). Restaurant with great view of Tirich Mir.

Tirich Mir View, beside PIA office; tel (0533) 571 (d Rs100). Best of the cheapies, with a splendid view, cool veranda and garden—but beware of bedbugs.

Fairland, by Chitral River bridge; tel (0533) 768 (s/d Rs120/150, charpoy on the veranda Rs30). Hangs over the Chitral River, so cool. Charpoy is good value.

Garden, on Chitral River, opposite Mountain Inn (s/d Rs60/100). Basic, but with a nice, quiet garden.

YZ, Government Cottage Road; tel (0533) 690 (s/d/t Rs30/50/70). Small central garden. Prices will jump when renovated.

Pakistan, Hospital Road (s/d Rs20/30–120). Basic.

Shabnam, Ataliq Bazaar (dorm Rs20, charpoy Rs10). Basic.

Damdam and Chitral Luxury, near PIA office (d Rs50). Basic and unappealing.

Saif, New (Kublisht) Bazaar (very basic charpoy Rs10, and good food for Rs15 per meal).

SHORT WALKS IN AND AROUND CHITRAL TOWN

A good warm-up trek from Chitral town is to **Birmoghlasht** (meaning 'plain of walnut trees'), the old summer palace above the governor's house, for panoramic views of the whole valley and Tirich Mir. Start at dawn, as it is a hot, unshaded two-hour climb up the jeep road past the radio mast and meteorological station. The old palace and polo ground are abandoned, and most of the walnut trees are gone, but Tirich Mir and the other Hindu Kush peaks, and the bird's-eye view down to Chitral town, are worth the climb. It is 15 kilometres by the jeep road, so cut straight up the ridge above the radio mast.

The jeep road dates from the 1930s when the *mehtar* (king) used to drive up in his Model T Ford (which, along with a Dodge, was carried in pieces across the Lowari Pass and assembled in Chitral). You can peer in the windows to see the '30s furniture, but everything is locked. The mehtar, Sir Shuja ul-Mulk, used to sit cross-legged on the veranda receiving petitioners, who bowed their way up the steep stairs between two rows of guards, under the amused gaze of the mehtar's 15 sons, who stood in attendance behind their father. The women's quarters behind are in ruins. There is an irrigation channel to feed the palace, but it is not always running, so take water with you. There is a spring about 30 minutes' walk north of the palace; follow the branch jeep road to find it.

The main jeep road continues a further three kilometres to the new **VIP Wildlife Preservation Bungalow** (do they mean hunting lodge?) on top of a hill. You can camp in the mature forest beyond the bungalow. There is a small, unreliable spring in the forest about 20 minutes' walk to the west—pay the *chowkidar* at the bungalow to show you where it is. The trail follows the crest of the ridge for 90 minutes to the highest point, from where you can branch west into the mountains or continue round the horseshoe ridge to come down again near Chitral Airport.

From Birmoghlasht, look south across the steep, narrow valley of the Chitral River (a small mountain stream that joins the Kunar River at Chitral town) to the other ruined summer palace of **Bronshal**, which is slightly higher and further upstream than Birmoghlasht. Little remains, but it makes a great hike from Chitral. You cannot get there from Birmoghlasht, but you can trace the access path on the other side of the valley.

To reach Bronshal, start from behind the deputy commissioner's office in Chitral and follow the Chitral River west for a short way, before branching left up a smaller stream. The first part is steep and hot to a shepherds' hut, then you join a contour path through the woods for the rest of the way. Up and back is too far for one day, but there is a good camping spot in the pine forest near the ruined summer palace. When the mehtar was in residence here, he used to come out at 9 am each day with his binoculars to view the *salaams* from his courtiers across the valley at Birmoghlasht.

Bronshal is the start of a trek over the hills to the Kalash valleys, and there are great morning walks along the ridge above the ruined palace. The only problem is finding the water sources.

The Chitral Gol was one of the royal hunting reserves of the mehtar, Sir Shuja ul-Mulk. Khush Ahmed ul-Mulk, one of his sons, says that it was alive with markhor, ibex and snow leopard 60 years ago. Yet in *Stones of Silence*, George Schaller describes wintering in the valley in 1974, depressed to find only a few markhor and one snow leopard.

SOUTH OF CHITRAL

KALASH VALLEYS

The prime attractions of Chitral are the Kalash valleys, the home of the non-Muslim Kafir Kalash (meaning 'black infidels') situated southwest of Chitral town between the Kunar River and the Afghan border. These valleys of Birir, Bumburet and Rumbur are on the edge of the monsoon belt, so the vegetation is dense, with giant walnut and fruit trees draped in grapevines overhanging swiftly flowing streams. Lush, green fields on the valley floor grow wheat, barley, vegetables and fodder, and the steep, 3,000-metre ridges between the valleys are clothed in evergreen forest right to the top.

To visit the Kalash you need a permit. Check with the Chitral police before leaving Chitral town if you can still buy this for Rs50 at the entrance to the valleys. If you are staying more than seven days, you need a permit from the deputy commissioner.

The Kalash have come to realise their value as an ethnic curiosity and are now rather commercialised. You can arrange for the Kalash women to dance if you buy another permit costing Rs1,000 (ask the police where to get it).

The 3,000 Kalash living in about 20 villages in the lower ends of Birir, Bumburet and Rumbur were once part of a much larger group living in neighbouring Afghanistan. The whole area was called Kafiristan, meaning 'land of the infidels', but in 1896 the Afghani Kafirs were forcibly converted to Islam and the name of their homeland changed to Nuristan (meaning 'country of light'). The Chitrali Kafir Kalash still follow their own religion, a mixture of animism and ancestor- and fire-worship, and have retained some of their original culture. They make offerings to several gods, each god protecting a different aspect of daily life: Surisan protects cattle; Goshedoi tends milk products; Praba looks after the fruit; Sajigor, the highest god, is in charge of everything.

Kalash women wear black woollen robes (*kalash* meaning 'black') tied at the waist by a black sash. They hang multiple strings of red beads around their necks and plait their hair into about five narrow braids, which stick out from under a magnificent headdress made of black material covered with rows of cowrie shells and assorted buttons and crowned with a large, tasselled pompom of reddish wool. The tailpiece of the headdress flows down the back and is reminiscent of women's headwear in Ladakh. Unlike Muslims, Kalash women do not observe *purdah*, though they expect payment if you photograph them. Kalash men wear ordinary *shalwar-kameez* and are indistinguishable from their Muslim neighbours.

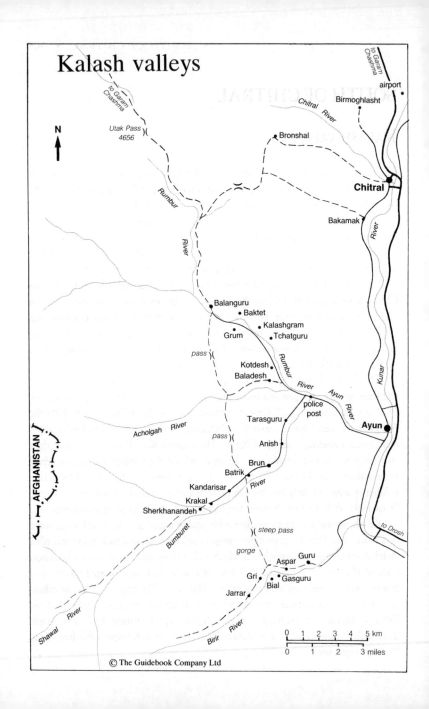

The Kalash valleys of Bumburet and Rumbur are about an hour's jeep drive from Chitral town. The third valley, Birir, is further south. The main road south of Chitral town, which is surfaced, follows the east bank of the Kunar River via Drosh to the Lowari Pass. Two bridges give access to the narrow jeep road that runs along the west bank. One of these is two kilometres above **Ayun**, the other seven kilometres below. Ayun, 16 kilometres from Chitral town, marks the turning to the three Kalash valleys.

Daily public jeeps go to all three valleys from Ataliq Bazaar for Rs10 or Rs15, or you can go to Ayun for Rs7 and change there. It is 10 kilometres from Ayun to the police check post at the beginning of the Ayun River, where you will be stopped. In 1992 you could buy your permit for the valleys here. Two valleys meet at the police post, the Bumburet from the south and the Rumbur from the north.

BUMBURET VALLEY

Bumburet, the largest and most commercialised of the three Kalash valleys, is about 15 kilometres long, with a jeep road running about 12 kilometres up from the police post to **Sherkhanandeh**, the first Muslim village beyond the Kalash area.

Brun, the main Kalash village of Bumburet, has several small hotels; the Kalash Hilton, the Kalash View and the Frontier all charge Rs40–80 per bed. You can buy a dance permit in Brun. In **Anish**, a village before Brun, the Benazir and Ansaf hotels cost Rs80–100 for a double, and the Benazir has a good campsite on the grounds. The Peace Hotel (Rs50 inside, Rs20 outside) at **Batrik**, beyond Brun, is the most popular with backpackers and has a comfortable campsite in the garden. Further up at **Krakal** is the Kalash Hotel. More hotels are being built.

Most of the Kalash villages are set back from the road with tightly packed houses stacked one above the other up the steep hillside. You see little of the Kalash way of life from a jeep, and tourism has spoiled most of the original charm, so the best way to explore the valleys is on foot. Female tourists who take the time to be friendly can wander slowly from village to village and sit with the women as they work on their wide, second-storey verandas, cooking, spinning and weaving in summer. You may be able to buy yogurt, butter and thick cakes of leavened bread filled with walnuts and cheese. Eggs are available from Muslim families who live in the Kalash villages (nearly half the households are now Muslim), but the Kalash themselves do not keep chickens, which they consider unclean.

Even if you do not go inside, you can examine the architecture of the carefully built houses, with their huge wooden beams alternating with layers of neatly jointed stones. The dry-stone work in Kalash is the best we have seen anywhere in Pakistan. The wooden temples in most villages have doors and pillars carved with entwined geometric designs and goat and horse heads. Go gently here, as some of the holy places can be visited only by men.

Menstruation huts, where Kalash women retire for a week of peace and quiet during menstruation and after childbirth, can be visited only by women. Do not go inside, though, as elaborate cleansing rituals are necessary before entering and after leaving.

In the woods near the villages you will stumble on Kalash graveyards—one of the most startling features of their culture. The dead are left in wooden coffins above ground. Many of the lids are left open to let the souls out, and the bones lie exposed to view. Some of the coffins are carved, and wealthier people stand wooden effigies beside the coffins. As many of these have been stolen, few are left in the Kalash area, but there are some good examples in the Peshawar Museum.

Exploring up the side valleys, you find irrigation channels that are miracles of simple engineering: wooden aqueducts supported on wooden poles fly across narrow gorges, and closely fitted dry-stone buttresses, resting on the smallest of projections, hold the channels in place across the often-vertical cliff walls to irrigate tiny clearings in the woods. Building these takes years of skilled labour, and maintaining them constant vigilance.

If you are lucky enough to visit the Kalash at one of their festival times (or buy a dance permit) you will see the women dance and sing, shuffling and stamping in a complicated series of circles and cartwheels, their arms round each other's waists, accompanied by the rhythmical beat of a large drum. The Kalash also play tin flutes (penny whistles), and you often hear the shrill notes floating across the pastures. The main festivals are the spring ceremony in mid-May, the harvest festival in late August, the autumn celebration to mark the walnut and grape harvest and the winter festival in December, which heralds the winter solstice. The exact dates change yearly. The dancing and singing is accompanied by feasting, the drinking of wine and the sacrifice of goats on smoke-blackened altars in the woods. We have never been to a festival but expect that they are pretty commercialised by now, with the possible exception of the winter solstice.

There are three possible treks from Bumburet. One option is to follow the Bumburet River up out of the Kalash area to the summer pastures along the **Shawal River**, where you can camp the night with the Muslim shepherds and spend a day watching the men milking and making butter and cheese. The other options are described in more detail below.

BUMBURET VALLEY TO BIRIR VALLEY

Map: none (the U502 map is restricted, and the Japanese *Mountaineering Maps of the World* map is inaccurate).
Restricted zone (seven-day permit available at entrance to valleys for Rs50); easy; five to eight hours; maximum height about 3,000 metres; April to October.

This trek takes you over the extremely steep, 3,000-metre ridge separating the Bumburet and Birir valleys. This is very hot in July and August, and even early or late in the season it is best to start at first light so you can climb the ridge while it is still in morning shadow. Only the very fit will get over in five hours. We met one couple who took 12 hours, having taken the wrong path.

Start at the Peace Hotel in **Batrik**, cross the Bumburet River on the footbridge, and follow the irrigation channel through terraced fields and groves of hollyoak (*Quercus ilex*) up into the gully. There is a confusing surfeit of paths; take the path up the central gully, even though the more obvious one branches off to the right. Keep to the left side of the gully. The last reliable water supply is the wooden aqueduct feeding the highest fields. From here on, the hollyoak trees give way to giant pine, fir and cedar.

The top of the ridge is very narrow—on the whole trek we saw nowhere flat enough to pitch a tent. On the Birir side, the first half-hour is an easy zigzag down. The path then enters a narrow, sheer-sided gorge (with slippery white stones underfoot), which twists and turns so that it is impossible to see back to the top of the pass. A number of side gorges join the main gorge, but the route down is fairly obvious.

Trekkers going from Birir to Bumburet should be sure to take the gully that has a huge, white cliff face on the right-hand side, from which white stones have recently fallen in a large rockfall. When you come out of the gorge on the way up, you still have an hour to climb to the pass (it looks deceptively near, but the trees on top are huge and look closer than they really are). The only source of water on the Birir side is about halfway down the gorge.

The gorge comes down to the Birir River at the village of **Gasguru**, about half an hour's walk upstream from **Guru**, the main village in the Birir Valley. At Guru there are several hotels and a government rest house, or you can camp. This is the best place to organise the Kalash dancing. Ask at the hotel how to buy a permit. You pay the Rs1,000 directly to the headman of Guru.

In 1987 the jeep road was washed out, and Guru was a two-hour walk in from the main Ayun road. Despite this barrier—and despite Birir being the least commercialised of the three Kalash valleys, being further from Chitral and more difficult to reach—the local people here have seen too many tourists.

BUMBURET VALLEY TO RUMBUR VALLEY

Map: Japanese *Mountaineering Maps of the World* page 272 (South of Chitral), reliability fair; the U502 map is restricted.
Restricted zone (seven-day permit available at entrance to valleys for Rs50); one to two days; maximum height optional to about 3,000 metres; April to October.

The third option from Bumburet is to hike to the Rumbur Valley. The easiest and most-recommended way is to walk along the jeep track the 15 kilometres from **Brun** to **Balanguru**, taking side trips into the various Kalash villages along the way.

The trek across the mountain tops is steep and takes two days as there is another valley in between. There are no villages along the way, though there are Muslim shepherds' summer huts. The two ridges you cross are each about 3,000 metres high, with views of neighbouring tree-clad ridges in all directions.

RUMBUR VALLEY

Although Rumbur is less altered by tourism than Bumburet, it is still very commercialised. Women here rarely dance for tourists and often turn away when being photographed. The jeep road runs seven kilometres north from the police check post along the river, past villages set back from the road, to **Balanguru**, the last and most important of the Kalash villages, about halfway up the valley. This is the home of Saifullah Jan, the only educated Kalash man, who speaks fluent English and acts as the spokesman for the Kalash. He has some legal training and fights to win government grants for the Kalash and for the protection of their timber and grazing rights. Ask his permission before camping. There are several basic hotels in Balanguru: the Rumbur Hotel and (another) Kalash Hilton both charge Rs50 for a double.

From the Rumbur Valley there are two possible treks: a steep but rewarding two-day trek across the hilltops to Chitral town, and a more ambitious and strenuous three-day trek across the 4,656-metre Utak Pass to Garam Chashma on the Lutkho River. The Utak Pass trek (which we have not done and will not describe) requires a permit, and a guide is recommended for both.

RUMBUR VALLEY TO CHITRAL TOWN

Map: Japanese *Mountaineering Maps of the World* page 273 (South of Chitral), reliability fair; the U502 map is restricted.
Restricted zone (seven-day permit available at entrance to valleys for Rs50); easy; two days; maximum height about 3,000 metres; April to October.

Stage 1: Balanguru to ridge top. Start from the end of the jeep road at Balanguru, cross the river on the footbridge, walk through the village and follow the beautifully constructed footpath with the river on your left. The path is supported on an immaculately fitted dry-stone buttress across the base of the cliff—as carefully built as an Inca path in Peru. After half an hour, by which time you are out of the Kalash area, you reach a small mosque with green wooden pillars. Turn east (right) up a small side stream, which leads up to the Kalash summer pastures.

Follow the stream for about an hour, passing under several superb wooden aqueducts that fly high across the gorge, to where two streams join. The sides of the valley are extremely steep and covered in a dense growth of trees and shrubs. High up on the left are some Kalash summer huts surrounded by small fields of maize and apple trees festooned with grapevines. The path zigzags straight up through the undergrowth, rising high above the stream, and leads after half an hour to some shepherds' huts hidden in a forest of truly enormous pine and cedar trees, some with trunks over two metres in diameter. As there is no flat ground anywhere, the shepherds' huts are cut into the hillside, the back wall formed by the earth. The shepherds stay here from June to October.

Above the huts, the path continues through thick forest, following a narrow irrigation channel that brings water to a patch of maize and vegetables in a clearing. As it is easy to get utterly lost in the forest, those who have come this far alone are advised to hire a shepherd to show the way to the top of the ridge, about 90 minutes' climb above the huts. At the point where two streams join, follow the right-hand stream up. When that stream divides, again take the right-hand stream. Be sure to fill your water bottle at the spring that feeds the second stream, as there is no water for the final, steep hour to the top.

The top of the ridge is gently rounded pastureland just above the tree-line, with *artemisia*, wild gooseberries and herds of goats. From here you can see down a ravine into the Kunar Valley to the east; in the other directions higher, tree-covered ridges hide the ridges and mountains beyond.

Follow the ridge top north and take a contour goat path round the east side of a nameless 4,205-metre, rounded mountain to the top of the higher ridge that overlooks Chitral. Here you are rewarded with the snow-covered summit of Tirich Mir rising above the intervening hills, and far to the east Buni Zom rests on the horizon. Camping is a problem: on top of the ridge there is no water, while half an hour lower down there is water but no flat land. We opted for water and the roof of a goat shelter, which was just large enough for our tent. Male trekkers could probably share a shepherds' hut with the Muslim herders who tend the animals on the Kunar side from June to October.

Stage 2: Ridge to Chitral town. The path to Chitral is along the top of the ridge. You can either cut down the first ridge and end up at the village of **Bakamak**, above the Afghan refugee camp on the Kunar River, or continue on a contour to the second ridge, nearer Chitral town, and go down from there to Chitral. You also have the option of going one ridge further north, beyond which is the precipitous **Bronshal** gully, which leads steeply down past the old summer palace of the mehtar of Chitral. The palace is a good place to camp (see page 308).

JUGHOR VALLEY

Just south of Chitral town, on the east side of the Kunar River, the Jughor Gol River flows down from snowy peaks. You can do an easy two- to three-day trek up and back, or continue on a strenuous trek over either the **Domukh Pass** to Karas or the **Madaglasht Pass** to Madaglasht, both in the Shishi Valley. There is also a pass leading over to **Koghozi**, and a fourth pass goes to the **Roghilli Valley**, coming down to Uzghor in the Golen Valley. We have not been over any of these, and the Japanese *Mountaineering Maps of the World* pages 272 and 273 (South of Chitral), the only map available, is too inaccurate to be really useful. The best time to go is from July to September.

The Jughor Gol joins the Kunar River at Jughor village, a couple of kilometres down the main road from the old jeep bridge below Chitral. Try in Jughor to hire a local shepherd who knows the best crossing places. The shepherds build some bridges in early July when they go up with their herds; otherwise you must ford the waist-deep stream about 15 times. Carry sneakers to wade in.

Paths follow both banks on the lower stretch. High above the southern bank, an impressive water channel built in the 1960s cuts across a precipice. You pass through a narrow gorge, crossing the stream many times, and come after about 90 minutes to the first village, which is surrounded by fields. Another 90 minutes' walk takes you to the last permanently inhabited farm at **Kokel**, high above the river and surrounded by enormous walnut trees. Ask permission to camp on grass in the orchard.

In July, shepherds take their herds up to higher pastures, from where you can reach the passes. If you go, please send information. (Information from Elisabeth Gardner.)

SHISHI VALLEY

The Shishi Valley, which joins the Kunar River from the east 40 kilometres south of Chitral town and three kilometres north of Drosh, is just inside the monsoon belt and gets about 600 millimetres of rainfall a year. It was once thickly forested, but the new road up the valley enables timber contractors to truck the timber out. With no adequate government control, deforestation and erosion are resulting from indiscriminate felling. The official figure for trees cut in Chitral each year is 600,000, but the true figure must be twice that.

Madaglasht (*lasht* meaning 'flat place'), at the head of the Shishi Valley, is a prosperous Ismaili village of 40 households living in square houses built of massive pine beams. The villagers, who speak Farsi (Persian), migrated here in the last century from Badakhshan, in Wakhan, to make guns and lead ammunition for Aman ul-Mulk, the mehtar of Chitral (ruled 1852–92).

Madaglasht is easily accessible by public transport from Chitral town, with a change at Drosh. **Public buses** and jeeps leave Chitral for Drosh every 15 minutes from the lower Chitral station in Ataliq Bazaar. The distance is 44 kilometres and the fare Rs16. Vehicles leave Drosh daily for Madaglasht, a distance of 43 kilometres, and cost Rs30. The turning for Madaglasht is five kilometres north of Drosh.

You can also trek to Madaglasht directly from Chitral up the **Jughor Valley**, at the head of which there is a choice of two routes, either left across the **Madaglasht Pass** to Madaglasht, or right across the **Domukh Pass**, which leads down to Karas, 15 kilometres downriver from Madaglasht.

SHISHI VALLEY TO GOLEN AND LASPUR VALLEYS

Map: U502 NI 43-1 (Churrai) and NJ 43-13 (Mastuj), reliability fair; Japanese *Mountaineering Maps of the World* page 269 (Tirich Mir and Buni Zom) and page 273 (South of Chitral), reliability fair.

Restricted zone (permit required from deputy commissioner of Chitral); strenuous; four to six days; maximum height 5,056 metres; July to September.

This trek takes you from the Shishi Valley over the Lohigal or Dok pass to the Golen Valley, with the option of continuing over the Phargam Pass to the Laspur Valley.

Spend a night in Madaglasht village to arrange porters, as the men usually work in the fields until 6 pm. There is a good campsite about ten minutes above the village beside the trout hatchery. Ask permission before camping.

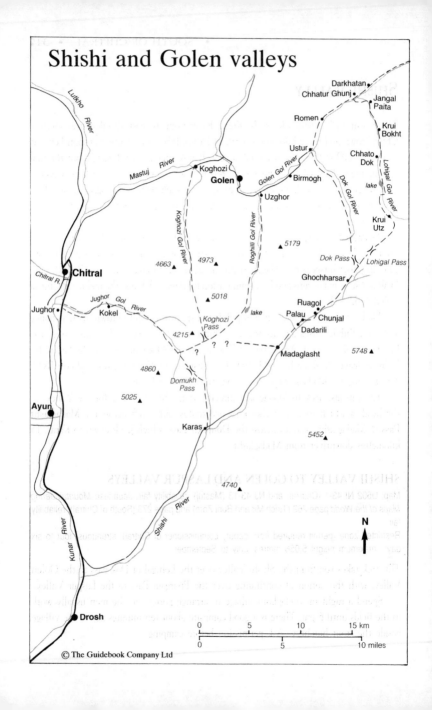

Shishi and Golen valleys

Lukho River

Mastuj River

Koghozi
Golen

Darkhatan
Chhatur Ghunj
Jangal
Paita
Krui
Bokht
Romen
Ustur
Chhato
Dok
Golen Gol River
Birmogh
Lohigal Gol River
Uzghor

Koghozi Gol River

Roghilli Gol River

Dok Gol River

Krui
Utz

▲ 5179

4663 ▲

4973 ▲

Chitral R.
Chitral

Jughor

Jughor Gol River

Kokel

▲ 5018

lake

Dok Pass

Lohigal Pass

Ghochharsar

Ruagol
Palau
Chunjal
Dadarili

5748 ▲

4215 ▲
Koghozi Pass

? ?
? ?

Madaglasht

4860 ▲

Domukh Pass

5025 ▲

Ayun

Karas

5452 ▲

Shishi River

4740 ▲

N

Kunar River

Drosh

| 0 | 5 | 10 | 15 km |

| 0 | 5 | 10 miles |

© The Guidebook Company Ltd

Stage 1: Madaglasht to Ghochharsar, five to seven hours. Keeping the river on your right, follow it up through farmland for two hours to **Dadarili**, a flat pasture and good possible campsite by the river. Another half-hour takes you to **Palau**, where you walk through the crumbling walls that enclosed the Chitral Scouts' camp in British times. The scouts used to heliograph to the British base at Drosh from the top of the hill to the north of the camp. In the 1920s, this became a British ski resort. The map of the hill still hangs in the officers' mess in Drosh, showing the nursery slopes (with a bonneted nanny pushing a pram) and the intermediate and advanced slopes—all of which are easy by today's standards.

For the next hour you walk through sparse pine forest with some cedar and larch past **Chunjal** to Ruagol, two summer settlements occupied by Gujar herders, who are paid by the villagers along the Shishi Valley to take the herds to the mountains and make butter and cheese. To make cheese (called *panek*) the Gujars boil up the milk until it condenses into a soft curd, then wrap the curd in birch bark and leave it in the stream for several months, weighed down with stones.

Ruagol, consisting of ten huts and various goat pens in the last patch of woods below the tree-line, is occupied from mid-May to the end of September. It is the last possible campsite before Ghochharsar. The shepherds take two hours to walk from Madaglasht to Ruagol, but it took us three and a half hours.

From Ruagol to the next shepherds' settlement at Ghochharsar is a steep, hot, two-hour climb above the tree-line, with no water within reach. Leave the stream and follow a clear animal trail up a ridge, with the river below on your right, then cross an overgrazed pasture and several steep-sided, eroded ravines. A shale scree leads into a steep, rocky gorge, where you face a difficult climb on a ledge across a cliff face, with a waterfall thundering beside you; if you slip, you fall about 15 metres. The square stone huts of Ghochharsar are across a log bridge a few hundred metres above the waterfall. The most sheltered campsite is along the river in the valley above the settlement; the more exposed campsite, in the pasture below the settlement, has spring water and a magnificent view down the Shishi Valley.

Stage 2: Ghochharsar across Lohigal Pass to Krui Utz, five to eight hours. On the U502 map, the Dok An (*an* meaning 'pass' in Kowari) and the Lohigal An have been transposed. To confuse matters further, the locals call the Lohigal the Ghochharsar An.

It is two to three hours to the top of the pass, walking mostly on patches of snow in July. Between the snow patches, keep the stream on your right. From near the top, you can turn north across the Dok Pass (labelled Lohigal An on the U502 map) and down the Dok Valley to **Ustur** in the Golen Valley.

From the top of the 4,377-metre Lohigal Pass (labelled Dok An on the U502 map) you descend down easy snow into the Lohigal Valley, which is guarded on the south by Ghochharsar Peak (6,249 metres). Below the snow-line, lush pastures full of flowers—including edelweiss and orchids—are the summer home of herds of horses, donkeys, cattle, sheep and goats. There are several good campsites along the river, but your porters will want to continue to the first Gujar settlement of Krui Utz (meaning 'red spring') for the night.

Stage 3: Krui Utz to the junction of the Lohigal and Golen rivers, four to five hours. Follow the left bank down for 45 minutes to a log bridge by a large rock, where you cross to the right bank. About 90 minutes from Krui Utz, a turquoise lake lies just above the Gujar settlement of **Chhato Dok**, which consists of three stone huts with a magnificent view north to Buni Zom (6,551 metres). **Krui Bokht** (meaning 'red stone'), an hour further north, has three huts sheltering under a large red rock, below which sparse juniper and pine trees pave the way to **Jangal Paita**, a large Gujar settlement in the pine forest about three hours from Krui Utz.

At the junction of the Lohigal and Golen rivers, there are several settlements of Gujar herders set around a large marshy pasture fringed by willow trees. You can camp by fresh springs on the south bank of the Golen River, or cross on a bridge to **Chhatur Ghunj** and an excellent campsite. We moved upstream to **Darkhatan** (meaning 'wooden house') on the north bank, where there are two Gujar huts surrounded by fenced hay fields, showing what the whole valley would look like if it were not so overgrazed. Chickens and eggs are available here. Camp in the poplar trees beside a silted irrigation channel.

Stage 4, easy option: Darkhatan down to the Chitral-to-Mastuj road, eight hours. From the junction at Darkhatan, it is an easy three- to four-hour walk down the green Golen Valley through **Romen** to **Ustur**, the highest permanent village and the end of the jeep road. **Birmogh** (meaning 'walnut'), the next village surrounded by huge walnut trees, is about 45 minutes' walk downriver from Ustur and the first place you are likely to find a jeep. Public jeeps leave early most mornings for Chitral; the fare is Rs25. Or you can walk all the way down to the main Chitral-to-Mastuj road in about three hours, following the jeep road through an impressive gorge. You come out about one kilometre upriver of **Koghozi.** There is frequent public transport on the main road, but it is often full.

Stage 4, strenuous option: Darkhatan up to Phargam Pass, three to five hours. Keep the river on your right all the way, walking first through sparse juniper and birch trees to **Dungari Kuru** (meaning 'potato patch'), two Gujar huts surrounded by a field of potatoes opposite the mouth of the Shachioko River, which joins the Golen from the southeast. **Dukadaki** (meaning 'mound'), about a kilometre upriver, is a Gujar hut surrounded by fenced hay fields. It is named after the giant heaps of gravel sitting in the middle of the stony river bed.

From here a track leads steeply up to the 4,601-metre **Shakuh Pass** and a two-day walk to **Reshun** on the Chitral-to-Mastuj road.

Shiak, on the Golen River, an hour's walk up from Dukadaki through overgrazed scrubland, consists of a group of Gujar huts opposite the mouth of the Shiak River. **Chakoli Bokht**, meaning 'white or cracked stone' and named after the huge white stones that have fallen off the cliff above, is the highest shepherds' settlement in the valley, comprising three huts occupied from July to September. There is a campsite for about three tents down by the river beside a spring, but, if you wish to cross the Phargam

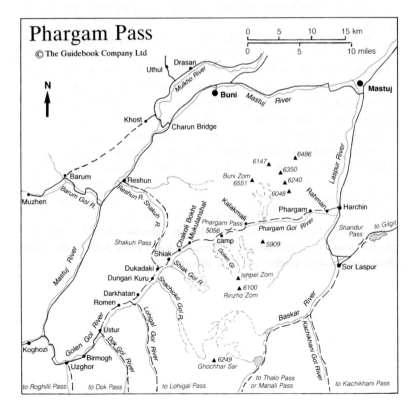

Phargam Pass

© The Guidebook Company Ltd

Pass the next day, you should continue for another hour and camp at about 4,000 metres on the last possible patch of green at **Mukulanshal**, below the pass. There are no shepherds' huts here, but there is fresh spring water and a good view down the valley.

Stage 5: Across the Phargam Pass, seven to ten hours, including five or six difficult hours to the top of the 5,056-metre pass. The first hour to the base of the pass is a relatively easy scramble across huge boulders. There is no path. Continue steeply up over huge moving boulders towards the Golen Glacier. Do not follow the Golen Glacier, but fork left instead and climb on hands and feet up the right side of the giant scree for a couple of hours. You need a guide to show you the path that leads from above the scree, in about three hours, to the top of the Phargam Pass.

About an hour before the pass is a ring of stones known as the King's Camp. This is a possible campsite but very cold, so if you plan to use it you need a tent for your porters.

At the top is an enormous corniche of snow—find your way through beside a large rock. On the other side is a large, snowy basin surrounded by pointed peaks. Slither down steep snowfields for about three kilometres to a muddy patch about five metres across. This is the only possible campsite, about two hours from the top. From just beyond this is a view down into the Phargam Gol Valley, where you should find a footpath that leads steeply down in 90 minutes to the river and **Kalakmali**, a nice campsite in a big field with flowers, willow bushes and some rudimentary stonewall shelters.

Stage 6: Kalakmali to Rahman and the Shandur-to-Mastuj Road, four to six hours. Follow the left bank of the Phargam River through barren, uninhabited land—at first along a path, then across huge, moving boulders to a large side stream with waist-deep water. A second side stream sometime later is less deep. Then the valley opens out for the friendly, fertile villages of **Phargam** and Rahman and the beginning of the jeep road leading down to the Laspur River opposite **Harchin**, where you can catch a public jeep down to Mastuj or up to Sor Laspur. (Information from Chakoli Bokht to the Laspur River from Elisabeth Gardner and Babu Muhammad.)

NORTH OF CHITRAL

GARAM CHASHMA ROAD

A paved road heads northwest up the Lutkho River to Garam Chashma (meaning 'hot spring') 32 kilometres away, a two-hour journey costing Rs18 in the public jeeps that leave frequently from the PSO Station opposite the PTDC Hotel in Airport Bazaar. Gobor, the last village before Afghanistan, can be reached in four hours for Rs35. You need a permit to travel beyond Gobor.

Garam Chashma sports a good hotel, the Injigan (tel 14; s/d Rs350/450), boasting an 'exclusive hot swimming pool'. Or you can stay at the government rest house (d Rs60; book through the deputy commissioner in Chitral) or at one of the cheap Afghan hotels (about Rs25 per night, with meals for Rs15), some with hot water piped from the hot springs. In the public baths above the village (Rs5 entry) the water is too hot for comfort.

The **Shrine of Nazir-i-Khisran**, an Ismaili missionary sent from Egypt in about 1050, is on the island in the river at Garam Chashma. Nazir-i-Khisran converted Badakhshan—including the Wakhis, the Tajiks and other tribes—to the Ismaili creed.

Trekking beyond Gobor across the **Dorah Pass** (4,510 metres) into Afghanistan is forbidden. This was the main trade route for the past 2,000 years and was heavily used during the Afghan war by the mujahedin, who crossed to Garam Chashma to collect the American arms available there and trade their drugs and lapis lazuli from the nearby mines in Afghanistan.

The **Utak Pass** (4,693 or 4,953 metres, depending on the source—no maps are available to the public) leads south from Garam Chashma to the Rumbur Valley in the Kalash area for a three- to four-day trek. This is a closed zone, and the police post prevents you from crossing the river without a permit.

Halfway between Chitral and Garam Chashma, side roads lead north up the Karimabad (or Ozher) River for 15 kilometres to Sussoom (two hours), and up the Arkari River for 40 kilometres as far as Owerdeh (or Ower) village (five hours).

From **Sussoom** at the top of the Karimabad River, it is a two-day open trek across the easy, green and picturesque **Owir Pass** (4,338 metres) to Barum in the Owir Valley. We describe this trek going in the opposite direction (see below).

The narrow **Arkari Valley**, skirting the west side of Tirich Mir and populated by Ismailis, offers four treks (see *Moutaineering Maps of the World* pages 268 and 248). From

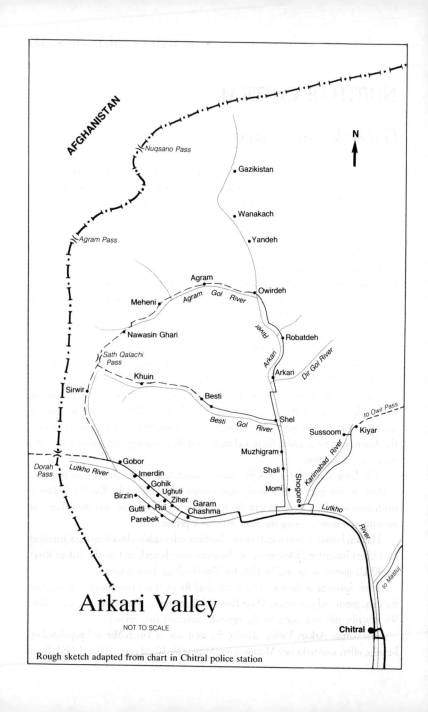

AFGHANISTAN

Nuqsano Pass

Gazikistan

Agram Pass

Wanakach

Yandeh

Agram

Owirdeh

Meheni

Agram Gol River

River

Nawasin Ghari

Robatdeh

Arkari River

Sath Qalachi
Pass

Arkari

Dir Gol River

Khuin

Sirwir

Besti

Shel

to Owir Pass

Besti Gol River

Sussoom

Kiyar

Muzhigram

Dorah
Pass

Gobor

Lutkho River

Shali

Shogore

Karimabad River

Imerdin

Gohik

Momi

Ughuti

Birzin

Ziher

Lutkho

Gutti

Rui

Garam
Chashma

River

Parebek

to Mastuj

Arkari Valley

NOT TO SCALE

Chitral

Rough sketch adapted from chart in Chitral police station

Arkari village you can trek east up the **Dir Gol** (*gol* meaning 'river' or 'valley'), with fine views of the Dir Glacier and the forepeaks of Tirich Mir and other peaks rising to between 5,000 and 7,000 metres. From the end of the jeep road at Owerdeh (or Ower), you can continue north along the river for at least another 20 kilometres through three shepherds' settlements and eventually up to the **Noqsano Pass** (5,246 metres) into Afghanistan.

Perhaps the nicest treks in the area lead west from Owerdeh, up the Agram Valley (no maps available to the public) for three or four easy hours to the summer settlement of **Agram** (3,170 metres), which is surrounded by wheat and barley fields and offers splendid views east to Tirich Mir. Thirty minutes later you reach wide pastures full of orchids and primulas, with a perfect campsite beside a spring in a willow wood.

Meheni, 90 easy minutes further up the Agram, is the next summer settlement, surrounded by more barley fields. Meheni is followed an hour later by a good campsite at **Nawasin Ghari**, at 3,450 metres. **Sath Qalachi An** (meaning 'seven hands pass') is a seven-hour climb from Nawasin Ghari, with views of Tirich Mir from the top. We were there in June, when there was too much snow to cross the pass, but Major Khush Ahmed ul-Mulk has trekked it and says that, beyond the pass, you can turn east and continue back down the Besti Gol for three or four hours to the shepherds' settlement at **Khuin**. A couple more hours bring you down to **Besti** village and the end of the jeep road leading back to the Arkari Valley. Like the Chitral Gol, the Besti Gol was a royal hunting reserve famous for its ibex 60 years ago.

Alternatively, the track south from Sath Qalachi An leads in three hours to the shepherds' huts at **Sirwir**, from where it is another couple of hours to the Lutkho Valley above Gobor. There is a police check post in Gobor.

MASTUJ ROAD

The second road north from Chitral town follows the Mastuj River northeast to Mastuj, and from there jogs south then east across the Shandur Pass to Gilgit in the Northern Areas. Jeep roads lead up the side valleys of Golen to the southeast and Barum, Turikho and Yarkhun to the north.

The Golen River joins the Mastuj River about a kilometre upstream from **Koghozi**, about 22 kilometres northeast of Chitral town. A jeep road follows the valley up to the last permanent village at **Ustur**. You can catch a **public jeep** most mornings from the upper Chitral bus station in Shahi Bazaar at least as far as **Birmogh**, four kilometres short of Ustur. The cost is Rs25.

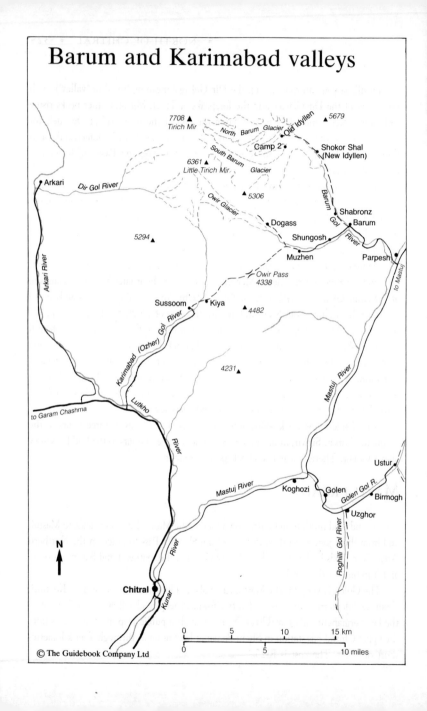

Barum and Karimabad valleys

7708 ▲
Tirich Mir

▲ 5679

North Barum Glacier

Old Idyllen

South Barum Glacier

Camp 2

Shokor Shal
(New Idyllen)

6361 ▲
Little Tirich Mir

▲ 5306

Owir Glacier

Arkari

Dir Gol River

Barum Gol

Shabronz
Barum

Dogass

Shungosh

Arkari River

5294 ▲

Muzhen

Parpesh

to Mastuj

Owir Pass
4338

Sussoom

Kiya

▲ 4482

Karimabad (Ozher) Gol River

4231 ▲

Lutkho

to Garam Chashma

River

Mastuj River

Ustur

Mastuj River

Koghozi

Golen

Golen Gol R.

Birmogh

Uzghor

River

Roghilli Gol River

N

Chitral

Kunar

0   5   10   15 km

0   5   10 miles

© The Guidebook Company Ltd

From Ustur you can trek northeast in four or five days across the **Phargam Pass** to Sor Laspur. Or you can head southeast across either the **Dok Pass** or the **Lohigol Pass** to Madaglasht. We describe these treks in the opposite direction (see page 317).

BARUM VALLEY OVER OWIR PASS TO KARIMABAD VALLEY

Map: *Mountaineering Maps of the World* page 268 (Tirich Mir and Buni Zom), reliability fair; the U502 map is restricted.
Open zone; easy to strenuous; three to ten days; maximum height optional; possible July to October but best in August and early September.

This can be an energetic, three-day crossing of the Owir Pass (4,338 metres), southwest of Barum village, with superb views of the mountains Tirich Mir and Buni Zom, or it can be extended to include ten days' gentle exploration of the Barum and Owir glaciers, which flow down from Tirich Mir. You can also trek northeast from Barum village across the hills to Khost.

Stage 1: Chitral to Barum, four hours by jeep. The main jeep road up the Chitral Valley follows the east bank of the Mastuj River. At the confluence of the Barum and Mastuj rivers, about 45 kilometres above Chitral town and four kilometres below Reshun, a narrow jeep bridge crosses the Mastuj River to **Parpesh**, a small village on the west bank, perched on a flat shelf out of sight of the Chitral-to-Mastuj road. The narrow jeep track climbs steeply round difficult hairpin bends for seven kilometres to Barum village.

If all of the bridges are in place, the jeep track continues a further seven kilometres through Shungosh to Muzhen. **Public jeeps** go most days from Chitral to Barum for Rs50; otherwise take any jeep up the Chitral Valley, get off at the bridge at Parpesh, and walk three hours to Barum. You can hire porters and donkeys in either Parpesh or Barum. Camp beside the river at about 2,500 metres.

Stage 2: Barum to above Muzhen, three hours. The jeep road climbs steeply for four kilometres from Barum to Shungosh, up barren, eroded mud cliffs with white salts leeching out in crusty streaks. A forest of poplars has been planted along the top of the cliffs in an effort to prevent further erosion. **Shungosh**, placed on a large, fertile shelf above the cliffs, is a prosperous village with a polo ground and hospitable Sunni Muslims.

Muzhen (pronounced 'Mujen'), a gentle three-kilometre stroll above Shungosh, is the end of the jeep road. Follow the track above Muzhen through fields of barley; there are several good, grassy campsites by the stream, with birch trees for shade. All of the wood is protected, so there is none for a fire except what you can buy from the villagers.

Isolated farms are scattered up the mountainside to above 3,200 metres. In winter the snow is a metre deep, and the animals are kept indoors for several months.

Stage 3: Muzhen to just below top of Owir Pass, three hours. The hills above Muzhen are wide, flower-filled pastures criss-crossed by many paths. It is not clear which path leads to the pass, but you just wander on up. The long, flat ridge at the top offers magnificent late-evening and early-morning views of Tirich Mir, Buni Zom and ridge after ridge of hills disappearing into Afghanistan.

You cannot see Tirich Mir from the lowest point of the pass, where the path crosses, but a five-minute walk either north or south brings it into view. A 20-minute walk north along the ridge gives superb views from the top of a hillock.

It is best to camp on the Barum side, so you can enjoy the sunrise behind Buni Zom and the morning light at the top of the pass, but it is worthwhile climbing all the way to the top before returning to find a campsite. Several small springs ooze out of the hillside, so it is easy to find a good, grassy site, with fresh water but no shade. Collect dried dung for fuel. If the weather is good, plan to spend two to three hours wandering along the ridge enjoying the views. Even in September there are still patches of snow on the pass, so it may be difficult earlier in the season. Be properly equipped, as it is extremely cold at night at this altitude. And, as the winds can be very fierce, anchor your tent to large stones.

Stage 4: Owir Pass to Kiyar, three hours. For the first half-hour on the Kiyar side, you descend steeply across slabs of loose, sliding slate to wide pastures with fresh water and many possible campsites. To descend to Kiyar, follow the obvious path on the left flank of the valley down through pastureland. This is an easy walk along a contour, crossing several streams, with excellent views up the valley to Tirich Mir. Kiyar is not the highest village, but it is the end of the jeep track.

Sussoom, the next village below Kiyar and the most important in the valley, is connected to Chitral by daily public jeep. From Sussoom to the Chitral-to-Garam Chashma road takes 90 minutes by jeep down the very narrow, steep-sided Karimabad Valley. (This valley was recently renamed after Prince Karim, the Aga Khan, by the local Ismaili population. The valley used to be called Ozher—pronounced 'Ojer'—but in Chitral they tell jokes about the supposed stupidity of Ozher people, much like Irish jokes in England, Polish jokes in the United States and Belgian jokes in France.) The left side of the valley is a dramatic slate cliff, its layers pitched to vertical. The resulting towers of slate look like windowless skyscrapers.

You can start the trek with side trips up to the **Barum** and **Owir glaciers**.

Day 1: Barum village to New Idyllen, four to five hours. From Barum follow the

Barum River north for one hour to green and fertile **Shabronz**, the last village. Then walk a further 30 minutes along a dramatic water channel on a narrow path with a steep drop. The last three hours involves a slippery scramble across scree, along the eastern edge of the Barum Glacier, to New Idyllen (or Shokor Shal), a summer pasture in the ablation valley surrounded by willow, birch and juniper trees. There are good views southeast to the Hindu Raj and west to Little Tirich Mir. This was base camp for the Norwegian expedition that made the first ascent of Tirich Mir in 1950 and named the site (see Naess and others,*Tirich Mir, the Norwegian Himalaya Expedition*). Camp at about 3,300 metres.

Day 2: New Idyllen to Old Idyllen, three to five hours. Follow the ablation stream up for about two kilometres to where the ablation valley divides. One branch goes northeast, along the river and up a slaty valley; another goes north up a narrow, steep cleft; a third branch goes northwest along the **Marmano Shal**, following the glacier, which at this point turns westward and becomes the North Barum Glacier, consisting of a series of steep icefalls running down from Tirich Mir. From either side, steep tributary glaciers flow down to the main glacier. Cross the North Barum Glacier to the ridge dividing the North and South Barum glaciers. Here at about 3,900 metres, on a triangle between the two moraines and the mountain, is Old Idyllen, the Norwegian 1949 reconnaissaance camp. It is a dusty site, with some shade under willow shrubs, a good water supply and superb views.

Day 3: Explore the ridge between North and South Barum glaciers. Norwegian Camp 2, at about 4,300 metres, has excellent views of Tirich Mir and all its subsidiary peaks. Camp at Old Idyllen.

Day 4: Old Idyllen to Shabronz, five hours. Camp in Shabronz village, which is shaded and pleasant at 2,700 metres.

Day 5: Shabronz to Dogaas at the base of the Owir Glacier, five to six hours. Walk up through farmland to Muzhen, then turn northwest up the Owir River—an easy contour walk along waterways up a wide valley. Camp at about 3,300 metres in a grassy meadow by a clear stream, at the base of the Owir Glacier, where there are superb views.

Day 6: Optional side trip up the Owir Glacier, five hours. A hard trudge over rough scree and rubble for a not-very-distinguished view from the top. Return to Dogaas for the night.

Day 7: Dogaas to below Owir Pass, five hours. Return down the Owir River to Muzhen, then continue from Stage 3 above. (Information on the Barum and Owir glaciers from Hans van Hoeflaken.)

TURIKHO, TIRICH AND RICH VALLEYS

The green and fertile Turikho Valley, about 100 kilometres long, wends south from the Afghan border to join the valley of the Mastuj River about 65 kilometres northeast of Chitral town. It gives access to magnificent trekking west into the heart of Chitral, close to the highest mountains of the Hindu Kush. East of Turikho, the Khot and Shah Jinali passes lead over to the Yarkhun Valley.

The lower Turikho Valley is known as Mulkho, the middle section is called Turikho, and the upper part is called the Rich Valley.

Two roads lead into the valley. The older, slower route leaves the Mastuj road immediately after Charun Bridge, which carries the jeep road from the south bank to the north bank of the Mastuj River just upstream of the junction of the Turikho and Mastuj rivers. This leads to **Mulkho**, the lower Turikho Valley. The new, faster road to the upper Turikho and Rich valleys leaves the Mastuj road about 12 kilometres further up, just opposite Buni, the capital of central Chitral.

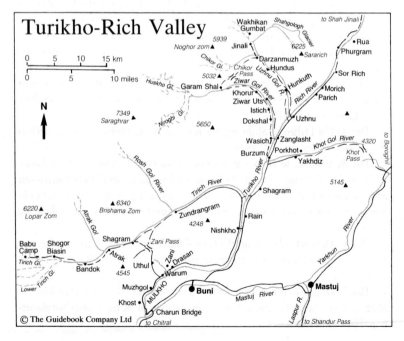

Oddly, Buni, the largest town in upper Chitral, is not marked on any map, though it is mentioned in books about the seige of Chitral in 1895. The town is across on the south side of the Mastuj River, but it is accessible by a jeep bridge. It is the government headquarters for upper Chitral and has government rest houses and some local hotels.

MULKHO OVER ZANI PASS TO TIRICH VALLEY

Map: U502 NJ 43-13 (Mastuj), reliability good; *Mountaineering Maps of the World* page 248 (High Hindu Kush), reliability fair.

Restricted zone; easy; maximum height 3,886 metres; roughly mid-April to mid-October, depending on altitude.

The Zani Pass is at the top of the long, steep-sided ridge separating the Mulkho (lower Turikho) and Tirich rivers. In a private jeep you can get from Chitral town to the top of the pass in one day—provided that the jeep is powerful enough to make the grade. If you are already acclimatised, you can camp beside a small ridge-top lake near the end of the jeep track, about two kilometres southwest of the pass, for magnificent morning and evening views of Tirich Mir and Saraghrar Mountain to the west and north and Buni Zom to the southeast. The pass also makes a good one-day side trip en route from Chitral to Mastuj. If travelling by public jeep, you will probably have to start trekking at Warum and spend the first night at Uthul.

To reach the Zani Pass, take the main Chitral-to-Mastuj road for about 70 kilometres from Chitral to Charun Bridge, which crosses the Mastuj River. On the north bank of the Mastuj River turn left (west) towards Khost and the Mulkho River. Cross the Mulkho on a narrow bridge in the impressive **Nisa Gorge**, where the road is cut on a ledge in the sheer cliff face. This was a favourite point for ambushing invaders of Chitral, but Colonel James Kelly, having crossed the Shandur Pass to rescue Surgeon-Major General Robertson during the siege of Chitral in 1895, managed to fight his way through in a brilliant little battle.

Khost, on the west bank, is a wide, fertile stretch of irrigated land dotted with scattered villages. These are connected by steep, narrow jeep roads, offering ideal walks with great views and friendly people. The Khost polo team is famous for having some of the best players in Chitral. You can walk from Khost to Barum across the hills.

Follow the northwest bank up for 15 kilometres through **Muzhgol** to **Warum** (Warinjun on the U502 map). **Public jeeps** leave Chitral town daily for the Mulkho-Turikho Valley, costing Rs50 to Warum. You can also catch jeeps from Buni.

At Warum, a jeep track heads northwest (opposite a sign to Mulkho Police Station) and winds up through irrigated fields for five kilometres to **Uthul**, a permanent village at about 3,000 metres and the last village below the pass. Only occasionally do public jeeps go up to Uthul. The irrigated land ends immediately above Uthul, where the jeep track becomes very steep, zigzagging up across the bare hillside for a further three kilometres to the top. If climbing this on foot, it is a very hot two and a half hours in full sun from Uthul to the top.

The top of the pass is wide, rolling and bare, with easy, flat walks for many kilometres along the crest of the ridge, which runs northeast to southwest. The jeep road follows the ridge southwest for about two kilometres to the headworks of an irrigation channel that takes water from the lake on top of the ridge down to the villages in the Tirich Valley. The best views are from the highest point on the ridge, which is southwest of the pass, from where you see Tirich Mir and Saraghrar on one side and Buni Zom on the other.

A footpath descends steeply to the Tirich River and continues all the way southwest to the head of the Tirich Valley.

TIRICH VALLEY TO TIRICH MIR

Map: *Mountaineering Maps of the World* page 248 (High Hindu Kush), reliability good; U502 NJ 43-13 (Mastuj), reliability good; U502 NJ 42-16, for west of Bandok, is restricted. Restricted zone (requiring a permit from Islamabad and from the deputy commissioner of Chitral); strenuous; four to seven days; maximum height 4,700 metres; July to September.

This is a scenic trek across the Zani Pass (see above) and up the Tirich Valley, with superb views of Tirich Mir. We have not been there and would be grateful for more information. You can get a **public jeep** from Chitral to the road head at Zundrangram in the Tirich Valley, a 12-hour journey of about 120 kilometres, costing Rs120. It is more fun, though, to enter the valley on foot across the Zani Pass.

Zani Pass to Shagram or Atrak, two to three hours. The descent from the top of the pass to Shagram on the Tirich River is steep (note that there is another Shagram on the Turikho River). You can camp in the green pastures of Shagram or continue southwest upriver for another few hours to the shepherds' summer settlement of Atrak. The Atrak Gol, flowing in from the north, leads to the Atrak Glacier and may make interesting trekking.

Bandok is the last summer pasture, a few kilometres from Atrak. At 3,400 metres, it is an ideal campsite in a meadow surrounded by birch trees. From here it is four hours' steep climb up along the river to the end of the Tirich Glacier, then along the side of the glacier on a difficult track to **Shogor Biasin** (4,100 metres). From this spot, opposite where the Lower Tirich Glacier joins the Tirich Glacier, there is a magnificent view of Tirich Mir up the Lower Tirich Glacier.

Continue up the Tirich Glacier about five hours to **Babu Camp**, the advanced base camp at 4,700 metres. From here you can see the mountains Ghul-Lasht Zom, Aspe Sufaid, Noshaq and Ishtor-a-Nal, but not Tirich Mir.

Return by the same route to Shagram, then, instead of crossing the Zani Pass, continue on down the Tirich River through several villages for another three hours, to the end of the jeep track at Zundrangram. Just above Zundrangram, the Rosh River, flowing in from the north, may make interesting trekking for about 14 kilometres up to the Rosh Glacier. (Information up the Tirich Valley from Ashraf Aman.)

UPPER TURIKHO VALLEY

The upper Turikho Valley is best reached by the new jeep road leaving the Chitral-to-Mastuj road opposite Buni. **Public jeeps** run most days, if the road is open, from Chitral to **Morich**, at the head of the Turikho-Rich valley, for Rs120. Alternatively, you can take a jeep for Rs50 from Chitral to Buni, from where you can catch one of the daily jeeps for another Rs50 to Morich. Or you can hire a private jeep in Buni for about Rs1,800 to the end of the jeep road.

The new road climbs over the barren ridge dividing the Mastuj and Turikho rivers, then follows the east bank of the Turikho up through green villages all the way to the head of the valley. A jeep bridge connects the old and new roads at **Nishkho**. Cross here to reach the Tirich Valley, which is jeepable as far as Zundrangram (see above). Below the confluence of Tirich and Turikho rivers is **Rain**, with its polo field and local restaurant. Here a Buddhist stupa about three metres high, dating from about the eighth century, is carved in outline on a rock beside the road. Just above the confluence, a footbridge also gives access to the Tirich Valley.

Shagram, about seven kilometres north of Rain, is the most important village in this part of the valley, boasting an AKRSP rest house and a local prince.

The **Khot Valley**, entering from the east a few kilometres above Shagram, leads over the **Khot Pass** (4,320 metres) to the Yarkhun Valley. A jeep road runs about five kilometres up the valley to **Porkhot**. Daily **public jeeps** run from Chitral to Porkhot for Rs120, taking eight to nine hours. Here you can find porters to lead you up through the summer pastures and over the Khot Pass in two days. According to Hugh Swift, you have views back (west) to the high Hindu Kush and ahead to the rugged spires of the Hindu Raj. On the Yarkhun side, the path descends steeply, following a ridge down to **Dizg** and the jeep road to Mastuj (see page 341).

The bridge across the mouth of the Khot River at **Burzum** is often washed out, so you may have to walk from here up the Turikho-Rich River. There are foot bridges across the Turikho-Rich at Burzum, Zanglasht and Uzhnu.

The **Ziwar Valley** drops down from the northwest to join the Turikho about four kilometres north of the Khot Valley, opposite Zanglasht. We have not been up there, but according to Fosco Moraini in *Where Four Mountains Meet* (1959) the first day up is through a difficult gorge decorated with numerous rock carvings, to the first camp at **Ziwar Uts**, at 2,580 metres. Above this the going is easier, along a valley hemmed in by sharp, reddish peaks and spurs past a superb waterfall and a grove of ancient cypress trees. The valley turns west, and you have your first view of Saraghrar (7,349 metres), 'a high peak rising above a steep glacier-covered massif, with black rocky spurs and buttresses lower down'. It is 12 hours from Ziwar Uts to **Garam Shal** (3,100 metres), 'a sloping plateau, perched above the valley . . . an enchanting spot: an oasis of grass and shrubbery, with birches and willows and budding flowers'—and stone circles for shelter (this was once a permanent village). Carved on a rock is a hunter who, with bow drawn, is about to let his arrow fly at a group of ibex. This is base camp for Saraghrar and various other 6,000- to 7,000-metre peaks.

Hindu Kush Trails leads treks in this valley. According to Maqsood ul-Mulk, it makes a superb round to go up the Uzhnu Gol, across the **Chikor Pass** and down the Ziwar Gol (see below).

The Turikho River becomes the **Rich River** north of the Ziwar tributary. The jeep road, still following the east bank, passes through green villages, which are pleasantly cool at about 2,300 metres. Ahead you can see the sharp peak of Sararich Zom (6,225 metres).

The **Uzhnu Valley**, next to enter from the northwest, is the starting point for the Chikor Pass, as described by Maqsood ul-Mulk (see also Trevor Braham, *Himalayan Odyssey*). A footbridge crosses the Rich below the confluence to give access to the Uzhnu Valley, and the track climbs steadily, following the west bank through green pastures, with fine views of Sararich Zom Peak on your right. Camp after about six hours in a birch wood, near shepherds' huts at **Hunkuth**. Another six hours takes you up through more pastures to the shepherds' settlement at **Hundus** (or Unduz) for the second night. It then takes about four hours to **Darzanmuzh**, where the Chikor Gol, flowing down from the Chikor Glacier, joins the Uzhnu. Camp.

You can detour on up the Uzhnu River to **Wakhikan Gumba**, at about 3,300 metres, where there are Wakhi graves. The area used to be grazed by the herds of shepherds from the Wakhan, until the passes were blocked by ice. A scramble up steep moraine leads to the junction of the Chutidum and Kotgaz glaciers, where there is a stony base camp with a view opposite to towering Noghor Zom (5,939 metres).

It is not clear which is the best approach to the **Chikor Pass** (please send information). The views from the top, at about 4,575 metres, are said to be magnificent. You can see ten peaks higher than 6,000 metres—all of the high Hindu Kush to the west, Buni Zom and Awi to the south and Thui Zom to the east. It takes about eight hours from Darzanmuzh over the pass to **Garam Shal** on the Ziwar River (see above).

Hindu Kush Trails describes the descent in three days (with no mention of the rock carvings seen by Moraini). First you face five hot hours down the west bank to **Khorur**, where there are trees, spring water and deserted shepherds' huts surrounded by grass. The second day takes you in six hours over rocky terrain past a waterfall to a hot spring and good camp at **Istich**. The third day takes six hours, through the permanent village of **Dokshal**, and then down a good track to **Wasich** on the Turikho River.

The Rich Valley continues northeast through **Parich** to **Morich**, where on a rock beside the road there are engravings of ibex and a modern jeep. Public jeeps stop here, but you can force a private jeep on through **Sor Rich** and **Dokan** and most of the way to **Phurgram**, seven or eight hours by private jeep from Chitral town. **Rua**, the last permanent village, is a couple of kilometres beyond Phurgram. There is good camping at all of the villages mentioned above. We recommend that you hire porters at Rua, as these villagers have the grazing and wood-cutting rights on the Shah Jinali Pass and know the route well.

RICH VALLEY OVER SHAH JINALI PASS TO YARKHUN VALLEY

Map: U502 NJ 43-13 (Mastuj), reliability good; Mountaineering Maps of the World page 236 (Eastern Hindu Kush), reliability good.
Restricted zone (permit required from Islamabad and from the deputy commissioner in Chitral); easy; four days; maximum height 4,259 metres; July to September.

Stage 1: Rua to Dhershal, five to seven hours. The first two hours are hot and barren, across stones and scree along the west bank of the Rich River. Ahead to the north is the mountain wall 6,000 metres high, blocking the way to Afghanistan. After about 90 minutes, cross to the east bank and continue on hot black stones past a small, inconspicuous spring of clear water. **Moghlang**, a shepherds' hut about two hours from Rua, sits at about 3,000 metres, surrounded by birch and willow trees in the fork of the Rahozon and Shah Jinali streams. This is sometimes used as the first camp. There are fine views from here back down the main valley and west up a side valley to Chhutidum Zom (6,442 metres).

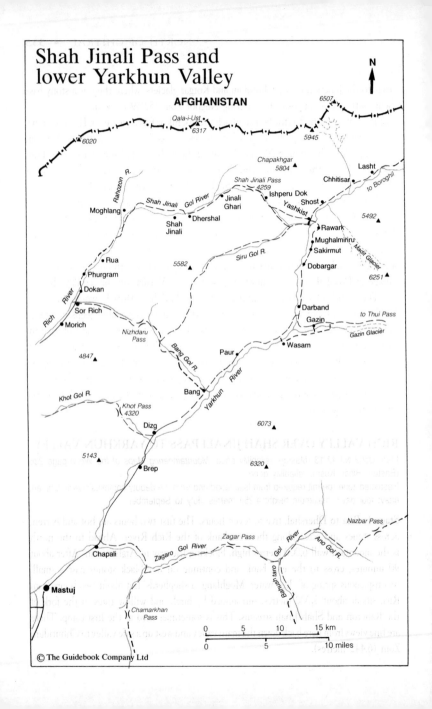

Shah Jinali Pass and lower Yarkhun Valley

AFGHANISTAN

N

6507

Qala-i-Ust
6317
5945

6020

Chapakhgar
5804

Lasht

Chhitisar

to Boroghil

Shah Jinali Pass
4259

Rahozon R.

Shah Jinali Gol River

Jinali
Ghari

Ishperu Dok

Yashkist

Shost

Moghlang

Dhershal

Shah
Jinali

5492

Rawark

Mughalmiriru

Madil Glacier

Sakirmut

Rua

5582

Siru Gol R.

Dobargar

6251

Phurgram

Rich River

Dokan

Sor Rich

Darband

Morich

Nizhdaru
Pass

Bang Gol R.

Gazin

to Thui Pass

Gazin Glacier

4847

Paur

Wasam

Yarkhun River

Khot Gol R.

Bang

Khot Pass
4320

Dizg

6073

5143

6320

Brep

Nazbar Pass

Zagar Pass

Ano Gol R.

Chapali

Zagaro Gol River

Bahushtaro Gol River

Mastuj

Chamarkhan
Pass

0   5   10   15 km

0   5   10 miles

© The Guidebook Company Ltd

Opposite Moghlang, turn east up the Shah Jinali River, following the south bank. Fill your water bottles at one of two side streams surrounded by willow bushes, then enter a small gorge. Here the path on the south side had slipped away in 1989, so we crossed to the north side on the resulting bridge of rocks and followed a vertiginous path across many loose screes for two hours, with the river below us on the right. Climb steadily to a grassy shoulder where the valley begins to open out; the slopes are tinged green with *artemisia* and fringed by juniper bushes.

Four to five hours from Rua you should be opposite **Shah Jinali**, a summer settlement on the south bank, with grazing cattle (but no shepherds in July 1989) in green fields surrounded by willow and birch trees. There is usually a bridge across the river here, but it is not obvious from the path. If you have the time, this would be an excellent spot for a rest day to acclimatise. We continued for another hour along the north bank to a plank bridge, crossing to the south side and Dhershal, a shepherds' settlement with huts set in a flat pasture surrounded by birch trees, about ten minutes' climb above the Shah Jinali River. We camped here at about 3,350 metres, with fine views back down the valley—the best campsite of the whole trip.

Stage 2: Dhershal to Jinali Ghari, three to four hours. This is a beautiful walk through knee-high grass and flowers (geranium, willow herb) and across plenty of side streams surrounded by groves of willows, with the Shah Jinali River well below you on your left. After about 90 minutes, drop down to the stream and follow the stony bed past clumps of blue anemonies and delphiniums. The path turns north, and you leave the main stream and climb up a green hillside, following a side stream and heading east to Jinali Ghari, a deserted shepherds' settlement with three stone circles beside a clear stream fringed by a few willow bushes. For some reason, the villagers of the Rich Valley were not using these pastures in 1989. Camp at about 3,700 metres.

Stage 3: Jinali Ghari across Shah Jinali Pass to Ishperu Dok, four to six hours. Climb east above the campsite, keeping the stream on your left, through knee-high geraniums and wild onions (*Allium*) with good views north to the snowy dome of Qala-i-Ust (6,317 metres) and the mountain wall separating you from Afghanistan and the Oxus (Ab-i-Panja) River.

After about 90 minutes, cross the stream and follow its very gentle rise for a couple of kilometres through overgrazed pastures. The herds of horses, cattle, goats and sheep here are from the Yarkhun Valley, having stolen across the pass to use these pastures. Just before the top is a wide, flat meadow—the 'king's polo ground' that gives the pass its name. You can camp here beside a clear spring and surrounded by edelweiss and other flowers, if you have tents and food for your porters, but they prefer to go down to Ishperu Dok. The top is wide and flat, with several small lakes on either side. It was raining when we were there, so we cannot describe the view. Keep an eye out for Himalayan Vultures.

It is about 75 minutes down to Ishperu Dok along a clear goat track, with views north to the granite spires of Chapakhgar (5,804 metres), the mountain scarred by the black, rubble-strewn glacier running off it. The surrounding hillsides are overgrazed and contoured by goat paths. Ishperu Dok is a comparatively large settlement (seven families in 1989, with lots of children) of herders who come up for the three summer months with animals from the villages in the Yarkhun Valley. The men guard the herds, and the women milk mornings and evenings, making butter every few days inside the huts, using large earthenware pots. Female trekkers are welcome in the huts to photograph. We watched the boys play a sophisticated game with sticks and stones, but it was too complicated for us to work out the rules. Camp below the settlement at about 3,900 metres.

Stage 4: Ishperu Dok to Yashkist, three to five hours, depending on the condition of the path. You drop 800 vertical metres down to the Yarkhun River. The normal path follows the Ishperu Dok Stream, crossing it several times on bridges. In 1989, however, the path had been wiped out by landslides, so we detoured up the mountainside for two difficult hours. Ask in Ishperu Dok about the condition of the track and hire a shepherd to guide you if it sounds difficult.

For the trek along the Yarkhun River, see page 341.

MASTUJ AND BEYOND

Mastuj, at about 2,400 metres, was once the capital of a principality. Sometimes, like today, it was part of Chitral, and at other times it formed a separate unit with Yasin. Xuan Zang, the famous Buddhist pilgrim who journeyed from Xi'an to India in 629, gave a long description of Mastuj in his journal, though he did not visit it himself. He writes: 'All kinds of crops are grown, pulse and wheat . . . and grapes in abundance.' He describes the mining of luminary orpiment (trisulphide of arsenic, used as a yellow dye and artists' pigment), which is still mined today, and he adds: 'The climate is cold; the manners of the people are lively and impetuous, their nature upright . . . They are narrow in their views and only moderately industrious . . . and mostly wear woollen garments.' The king and his subjects were Buddhist, not over regulated by ceremony but sincere in their faith. There were two monasteries housing a small number of monks.

Mastuj is also mentioned in the Tang Annals of the eighth century as a cold country producing 'five cereals, wine and pomegranates. During the winter people live in caves. The inhabitants of this kingdom have always assisted the Little Po-lu [Gilgit] in spying out the middle kingdom [China].' The annals say that the Arabs made repeated approaches to the chief of Mastuj early in the eighth century but were always refused. In recognition, the Chinese emperor Xuan Zung (not to be confused, of course, with the pilgrim Xuan Zang) sent envoys in 720 to invest the chief with the title of king. The Chinese also extended their support to other small territories from Kashmir to Samarkand that were threatened by the Arabs. Clearly, Mastuj was distinct from Chitral at this time.

After the Chinese left there were no records for 1,000 years, until their return in the eighteenth century. In 1913 the British gave Mastuj to the Katur ruler of Chitral and Yasin, Sir Shuja ul-Mulk, who passed it on to his son Khushwaqt ul-Mulk, who still owns the fort and connected properties. The people of Mastuj, from Reshun to Shandur and Boroghil, are almost all Ismaili.

MASTUJ INFORMATION

Mastuj is smaller than Buni but has a **Post Office, dispensary** and about 25 shops selling all basic supplies. There is a local **hotel** in the bazaar, and several **rest houses**, if you can get permission to stay in them. To stay in Mastuj Fort you must book in advance with Hindu Kush Trails, Mountain Inn, Chitral town.

Public jeeps run daily from Chitral town, taking six hours to Mastuj and costing Rs100. From Mastuj one jeep road heads south for the Shandur Pass, and a second jeep road leads north up the Yarkhun River, crossing on a new bridge at Brep, and continuing to Dizg in summer and to Lasht in winter, when the rivers are low.

From the Yarkhun Valley you can trek west across the Khot and Shah Jinali passes to the Turikho-Rich River or east across the Chamarkhan, Zagar and Thui passes to Gilgit District. There are no side roads off the Yarkhun Road.

MASTUJ OVER CHAMARKHAN PASS TO GILGIT VALLEY

Map: U502 NJ 43-13 (Mastuj), reliability good; *Mountaineering Maps of the World* page 212 (Central Hindu Raj), reliability good; see sketch map of Nazbar and Zagar passes in Gilgit section (pages 286–7).
Open zone; easy; two days; maximum height 4,344 metres; June to October.

This is the shortest trek between the Chitral and Gilgit valleys. It is an easy walk, though rather steep on the Chitral side, with a height gain of 1,700 metres, so you need to be acclimatised before you set out. The pass is surrounded by barren hills, all lower than 5,400 metres, with no glaciers in sight. The friendly Gujar nomads on either side of the pass tend herds of dzos, goats, sheep and donkeys.

The trek starts at **Chapali**, a large village at 2,650 metres surrounded by trees and fields on the alluvial fan of the Zagaro River, which joins the Yarkhun ten kilometres north of Mastuj. There are **public jeeps** daily from Mastuj to Chapali, or you can rent a private one for about Rs200. Porters, donkeys and horses are available in Chapali.

Stage 1: Chapali to Shal, four to six hours. Follow the village path up through orchards and fields with the river on your left for 20 minutes, then cross on a log bridge to the north bank and continue for one and a half hours to **Malo**, a stone shelter by a hay field where the Malo River flows in from the north. Wade across the Malo River and take the right-hand valley. Cross a second side stream (fill your water bottle) and keep the main river on your right, as you climb steadily through birch and willow trees then across a long scree above the river. After another hour there is a suitable campsite for one tent beside the river in a clump of birch trees. Climb steadily, then drop to cross the Zagaro River on a birch-log bridge, and take the right-hand valley following the Chamarkhan River. Climb steeply on a clear donkey path up slopes covered in *artemisia* and the occasional juniper tree.

Alternatives: To the east are inviting views up the Zagaro Valley. A contour path across rolling pastures high above the river on the south side looks like the easiest approach to the **Zagar Pass** (5,008 metres), from which a path leads to the **Nazbar Pass** (4,977 metres) and follows the Nazbar River down to Yasin. From Chapali to Yasin by this route is 73 kilometres, which would take five or six days. Alternatively, between the Zagar and Nazbar passes a path leads south down the **Bahushtaro Gol** River to join the Ghizar (upper Gilgit) River at Shamran (see page 285).

The path to the Chamarkhan Pass crosses a side stream about three hours' walk from Chapali, with a possible campsite on the other side, beside a rock with stone wall shelters but no clean water. It is best to climb for another hour to Shal, a Gujar summer hut by a clear stream at about 3,200 metres, with magnificent views back down the valley.

Stage 2: Across the Chamarkhan Pass to Barsat, six to eight hours. It is a steady climb of three to four hours from Shal to the top of the pass. The flowers are superb—dense clumps of purple thyme, pin cushions of tiny, prickly pink flowers, mauve geraniums, yellow buttercups, honey suckle and various primulas and potentilas. The top is a long, rolling, stony pasture covered with patches of grass and clover grazed by large herds of dzos. The path, marked by cairns at intervals, meanders for nearly three kilometres across the pass.

From the top to Barsat takes three to four hours. There are many paths and side valleys, but keep descending steadily with the main river on your right. There are several good campsites near the river; if you are not in a hurry, you can camp and gently explore up here for several days. A further option is the path that leads west across the **Ghutbaro (Harchin) Pass** to Harchin. To avoid getting lost, it is wise to take a porter or a guide or to ask a shepherd for directions.

Barsat, at 3,300 metres, is a cultivated area rather than a village—the houses are spread over the valley, each surrounded by fields. There is no shop. The police post is a couple of tents beside the bridge carrying the jeep road from the Shandur Pass. The police can point out the natural carbonated spring nearby—about 500 metres up the Barsat River on the west bank, accessible by jeep—for some fizzy mineral water smelling of sulphur.

A few jeeps cross the Shandur Pass, mostly tour companies on jeep safaris, but with luck and patience you may be able to pick up a **public jeep**. It is 51 kilometres across the pass to Mastuj and about 12 kilometres in the other direction to Teru, which stretches for two kilometres along the jeep road and boasts a rest house, Post Office and one shop. There are a few private jeeps for hire in Barsat and Teru; a private jeep to Gilgit costs Rs1,000–2,000. Bargain hard.

YARKHUN VALLEY OVER DARKOT PASS OR KARUMBAR PASS

Map: U502 NJ 43-13 (Mastuj) and NJ 43-14 (Baltit), reliability good. *Mountaineering Maps of the World* page 224 (Eastern Hindu Raj), reliability good; see Shah Jinali Pass map on page 336 for the lower Yarkhun Valley.
Restricted zone (requiring a permit from the Ministry of Tourism and the deputy commissioner of Chitral); strenuous; seven to eight days; maximum height 4,575 metres; July to September.

The Yarkhun River north of Mastuj follows a wide valley with villages and cultivation by every side stream. There is occasional **public transport** from Mastuj up the valley at least as far as **Dizg** in summer, or you can hire a private jeep for Rs500-600, which takes about three hours to Dizg. In winter you can drive further up the valley, how far depending on the volume of water in the side streams. A daunting sign at Brep reads 'Boroghil 120 kilometres'. Hire porters in Dizg, though not many are available. Sometimes you can hire horses and donkeys.

From Dizg a steep path leads west up the side valley to the **Khot Pass** (*khot* meaning 'cloud'), which rises to 4,320 metres between peaks about 5,000 metres high. The path goes down to the Turikho Valley, in which the jeep road begins at Porkhot (see page 333). The mountains to the east of the river rise in an impenetrable knot to over 6,300 metres.

Stage 1: Dizg to Paur (pronounced 'Pow-er'), five hours. Walk up the winter jeep road for about three hours through several village oases to **Bang**, and continue for about two hours to Paur, a good place to camp at about 2,650 metres. The stretches between villages are hot and barren. Look for intricate carving and painting around the doors in the villages; the designs still show the acanthus and lotus flowers of classical Buddhist art.

From Bang a track leads up through summer pastures and across the **Nizhdaru Pass** to the Rich Valley.

Stage 2: Paur to Dobargar, six to eight hours. Ask about the state of the bridges.

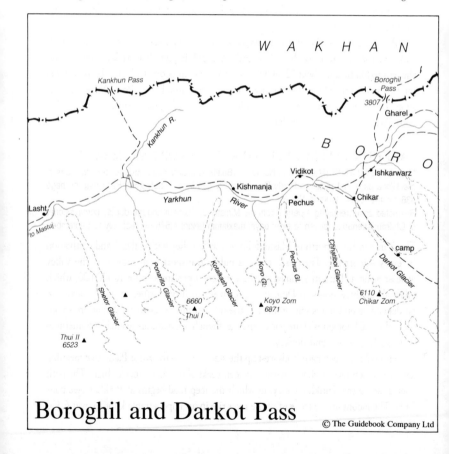

Boroghil and Darkot Pass

© The Guidebook Company Ltd

If the bridge at Darband is usable you can walk there in about four and a half hours from Paur. Otherwise you have to cross the river at **Wasam** and detour via the fertile fields of **Gazin** around the mouth of the Gazin River, in which case you are unlikely to reach Dobargar in one day. There are magnificent views up the Gazin Valley to Thui Peak at its head. (For a description of the trek from Yasin across the Thui Pass to Gazin, see page 281.)

At **Darband** the valley narrows, making it a natural point of defence in earlier times against invasion from the Wakhan; there used to be a watch tower on either side of the river here. The walking is hot in this stretch, but for the last eight kilometres (two

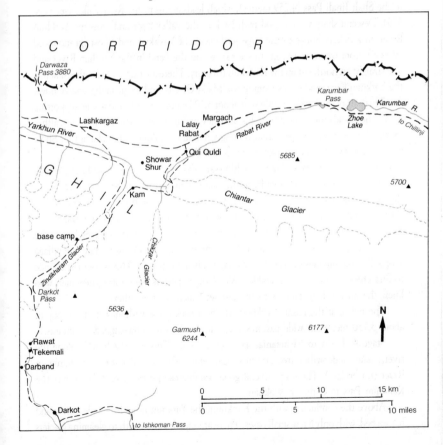

hours) to Dobargar the valley opens out again, with several possible campsites along the river. The last two kilometres to Dobargar involve scrambling across a landslide of boulders and mud. Dobargar is a large settlement surrounded by fields of potatoes, peas, lentils, millet, barley, wheat and poppies. From Gazin village to Dobargar takes five hours.

Stage 3: Dobargar to Lasht, five to seven hours. The first hour past the villages of **Sakirmut** and **Mughalmiriru** is flat and very hot. It is worthwhile taking an hour to detour steeply up to **Rawark**, a few houses set in steep, green fields, with friendly villagers and a magnificent view down the Yarkhun River and up the gully opposite to the **Shah Jinali Pass** (4,259 metres), which leads across to the Rich Valley (see page 335). Descend sharply on a good path back to the valley floor and cross the Yarkhun River on a rickety bridge to the large settlements of **Yashkist** and **Shost** (pronounced 'Shuist'), from where you begin to see east round the bend in the Yarkhun River and also straight on northeast up the Kankhun tributary. There are fine views southeast across the Yarkhun River and up a stream to the Madit Glacier and its gleaming, snowy ridge.

This part of the Yarkhun Valley, at about 3,100 metres, is wide and fertile, supporting many households surrounded by fields of barley and lucerne. There are lots of healthy-looking horses and more than enough hungry mosquitoes. Aurel Stein claims that Shost was the capital of Yarkhun (see Stein, *Serindia*).

The winter jeep track climbs to **Chhitisar**, which is contiguous with Lasht, a large village of 40 houses set in a wide, fertile plain. This was an important settlement in the eighth century but was later abandoned, only to be resettled again at the end of the nineteenth century, when the British pacified the area. Lasht boasts a Chitral Scouts fort, police post, new primary school and three-bed medical dispensary (the last in the valley) and a large storehouse that in 1989 contained American wheat. The one village shop sells basic supplies such as rice, tea, sugar, oil and kerosene. This is your last chance to find chickens, eggs and vegetables. We changed porters here, hiring new men who knew the area well to take us to the last settlement in the valley.

The police at the Lasht checkpost will turn back those without permits. Camp at about 3,150 metres in wide pastures with views across to snow-capped mountains.

Stage 4: Lasht to Kishmanja, six to eight hours. This is a lovely walk along the river, passing under willow trees and crossing several thigh-deep tributaries of the Kankhun River (no bridges). There are several good possible campsites. A path leads over the Kankhun Pass to Sanin in Wakhan.

Above the confluence with the Kankhun, the Yarkhun flows in a wide, sandy and barren bed, with only a few small oases. There are superb views south to gleaming glaciers flowing off Thui I (6,660 metres), a wedge-shaped peak reminiscent of the Matterhorn, and Koyo Zom (6,871 metres). The July-to-August path climbs 100–200 metres up and down the mountainside about three times to avoid the river. When the water is lower, the path follows the river. Kishmanja is one large house occupied by 17 people and surrounded by about six hectares of wheat, barley, peas and tobacco. A flat, green space in front is large enough for camping, and fresh water is five minutes away.

Kishmanja marks the beginning of the Boroghil region, which stretches up to the Karumbar Pass. About 1,000 people live in Boroghil, many of whom have Mongolian features, having migrated from Wakhan. Wakhi is the main language. About 125 school-age children live in the region, without access to school or medical facilities. Some 80 percent of the people are opium addicts. You may well see Pathan traders riding up the valley.

Stage 5: Kishmanja to Ishkarwarz. After half an hour you have a magnificent view south to the 6,872-metre Koyo Zom and, a little later, the impressive Pechus Glacier flowing off of it. Climb up a good path to **Vidinkot**, seven houses at about 3,500 metres, some 300 metres above the valley floor. Across the river is **Pechus**, which is named for its hot spring. Beyond Vidinkot you get your first view of the convoluted and crevassed Chhatiboi Glacier, which ends in a great wall of ice jutting into the Yarkhun. Just after the glacier, a bridge crosses to the south bank.

To avoid the gorge on the Yarkhun, climb southeast up the hill, keep left (east) where the path forks (the right fork leads directly to **Chikar** and the Darkot Pass), and cross pastures and irrigated fields high above the gorge to an enormous, lonely house, which is marked on the U502 map. The track follows a high contour to Ishkarwarz, where there is a Scouts post and a border police post to guard the Boroghil Pass (3,807 metres). The pass stretches in a wide, grassy sweep to the north. Do not be tempted to slip across the border into the Wakhan Corridor, but ask the police for permission to go to the top for a look. Camp at about 3,500 metres with the Scouts or further up the hill by the shepherds' hut. Howling dogs are a nuisance.

The **Boroghil Pass**, the shortest, easiest route from Central Asia to the Indian Subcontinent, was an important trade route and line of invasion. Chinese pilgrims of the fifth to seventh century describe the pass in detail, and from the Tang Annals we know that the Tibetans crossed the Darkot and Boroghil passes with 10,000 men in August 747 to do battle with the Chinese general Xian Zhi just the other side of the Boroghil in Wakhan. The Chinese defeated the Tibetans, chasing them back across the passes and invading Yasin and Gilgit with 3,000 soldiers (see page 279). Many explorers and adventurers of the nineteenth and twentieth century have come this way, among them Lord Curzon (*Pamirs and the Source of the Oxus*, 1896, and *Leaves from a Viceroy's Note-book*), Aurel Stein (*Serindia, Desert Cathay*, 1912, and *Innermost Asia*), T G Longstaff (*Byways in the Hindu Kush*), R C F Schomberg (*Between the Oxus and the Indus* and *Kafirs and Glaciers*) and Wilfred Thesiger (*The Last Nomad*).

From Ishkarwarz you have three options: You can (1) turn south and go through Chikar directly to the Darkot Pass, (2) continue east up the Yarkhun to Karumbar Lake and the Karumbar Pass (4,188 metres) and on to the Ishkoman Valley or (3) follow the Yarkhun up for a day, then turn south up the Zindikharam Glacier to the Darkot Pass.

ALTERNATIVE 1: DIRECTLY TO DARKOT PASS

Stage 6: Ishkarwarz to Darkot Base Camp, three and a half hours. The path rises through undulating pastures to **Chikar**, the last settlement until Rawat, 20 kilometres away across the pass. Take porters from Chikar who know the way across the pass. Two and a half hours of easy walking along an excellent path on the side of the valley—with first the river, then the glacier on your right—takes you to the first of three possible campsites surrounded by a stone wall. The best site is the third one, at about 4,100 metres (or 100 metres above the glacier) about one hour further on, because it is flatter, more sheltered and nearer water.

Stage 7: Darkot Base Camp across Darkot Pass to Darkot, six to eight hours. Walk for half an hour on the lateral moraine of the glacier, then walk up the middle of the wide, flat Darkot Glacier, crossing crevasses and streams for an easy two hours to the pass—a flat, circular pancake at 4,575 metres that takes about half an hour to cross. In all directions are views of granite peaks interspersed with glaciers. A glaciated ridge 200 metres high separates you from the Zindikharam Glacier, so you cannot look down the Zindikharam to Lalay Rabat, at the top end of the Boroghil region. (Information from Ishkarwarz to Darkot Pass from Elisabeth Gardner.)

The descent is much steeper on the Darkot side, and the glacier is wet and slippery in the morning sun (crampons are recommended for the porters). Keep to the right going down off the glacier and, in the first bowl below the snout, cross to the left bank and join a well-made path that zigzags steeply down to the bottom of the valley. One hour below the top is a tiny campsite with two stone circles and room for one small tent beside a stream.

At about 4,000 metres you pass an engraved boulder, just above the path, with an eighth- to ninth-century stupa and a Tibetan inscription giving the name of its donor. Later carvings show a horse and rider, a mountain sheep and Arabic inscriptions reading

'Ya Allah madad', the Ismaili greeting, and 'Shah Kushwaqt', naming the Mastuj ruling family. About two hours from the top, you pass a small hot spring, which has room for one small tent right beside it, and a stone shelter.

A further hour on a distinct mule trail takes you to the settlements of **Rawat** and **Tekemali**, altogether about ten houses in a picturesque bowl scattered with evergreens, where Darkot people spend six months of the year growing barley, hay and a little wheat. The women here wear high pill-box hats and speak Burushaski. Their houses have stone bases and high, pointed wooden roofs covered with juniper branches and mud. There are several excellent campsites along the stream, at about 3,050 metres, looking across to the white glaciated ridge of Lamokor Mountain, which guards the gorge down to Darkot. Looking back to the Darkot Pass, you see the great, rough tongue of the Bulronashko Glacier, which pours down the mountain to the west of the hot spring.

Continuing from Rawat to Darkot (two hours), you cross the river to the right bank and go down through the narrow gorge of **Darband**, which shows remnants of a defensive wall recalling the history of the pass as a main line of invasion. At Darkot, the wide valley is filled with rich fields and fruit trees (see page 278).

ALTERNATIVE 2: KARUMBAR PASS
Map: U502 NJ 43-14 (Baltit), reliability good; *Mountaineering Maps of the World* page 208 (Koh-i-Chiantar), reliability good.

Stage 6: Ishkarwarz to Lalay Rabat (spelled Lale Ribat on the U502 map), six to eight hours. This is a lovely walk through rolling pasture along the north bank of the Yarkhun. We accepted rides on a herd of passing yaks; riding all day was slow but fun. Horses are also available. Cross the bridge below the police post (the first bridge across the Yarkhun) and follow a clear path past the wide, green valley sweeping up to the Boroghil Pass. Cross rolling, overgrazed pasture on the flank of the hills, far above the river. Every few hours you come to huge, lone huts or clusters of huts (almost all of which are marked on the U502 map) surrounded by fields of barley and spinach.

Gharel, two hours from Ishkarwarz, is the winter home of Yar Muhammad, known as Yoriq ('Alas, poor Yorick!'), the second-most-important man in Boroghil, who spends August in the summer pastures at Margach. An hour later you pass the path leading up to Darwaza Pass (*darwaza* meaning 'door'), the 3,880-metre entry to the Wakhan Corridor. A further two hours brings you to **Lashkargaz**, which consists of seven houses scattered over the plain and is the winter home of Mirza Raffa, the leader of the Boroghil people, who spends the summer higher up the valley. The next couple of hours offer wide views over the broad, green valley, across the Yarkhun and up the white expanses of the Zindikharam Glacier to the Darkot Pass (see below). **Showar Shur**, with its little fort, shelters down by the river. This is where Mirza Raffa spends September with his herds.

Turn northwest up the Rabat River to **Lalay Rabat** (two to three hours from Lashkargaz), the August camp of Mirza Raffa, five stone huts and some goat pens with a fantastic view south to the Darkot Pass and northwest to the Karumbar Pass. Mirza Raffa migrated to Boroghil from Wakhan in 1949, and his people built Lalay Rabat at that time. They are Ismaili and pray that one day the Aga Khan's development projects will reach them. Their first hopes are for a school, medical help to cope with their opium addiction, training in livestock protection and management, and an improvement to the track up from Lasht.

Camp at about 4,000 metres.

Stage 7: Lalay Rabat to Karumbar Pass, three hours. This is an easy day trip, up and back along wide, smooth pastures grazed by herds of yaks, horses, goats and sheep. (We hired horses and rode up in two hours). After 20 minutes you pass the four huts of **Margach** (pronounced 'Margetch') summer settlement and, just before the pass, deserted Rabat settlement, comprising two roofless stone shelters. Wilfred Thesiger, who was here in 1952, writes of 'the same sense of space and cleanness' he had known in the deserts of Arabia. The top of the pass, at 4,188 metres, is flat and marshy, with russet-coloured pools draining into a small lake on the Chitral side and the large Zhoe Lake on the Ishkoman side. A couple of stone circles offer shelter in the green hollow on top. A glaciated ridge of mountains forms a 5,700-metre wall hemming in the pass on the south, with shimmering ice tumbling in steps down towards the pass. The northern wall, its bare, grey-green slopes warmed by the sun, rises to the same height.

For the trek down the Karumbar River to Ishkoman, or over the Chillinji Pass to Chapursan, see page 265.

ALTERNATIVE 3: ZINDIKHARAM GLACIER OVER DARKOT PASS

You can reach the Zindikharam Glacier directly from Ishkarwarz along the south side of the Yarkhun River in about five hours, but if you have time it is more fun to spend a couple of days exploring the Rabat Valley and visiting the Karumbar Pass first. We hired yaks and a guide in Qui Quldi (Kirgiz for 'the place where sheep are lost'—misspelled Qiu Quldi on the U502 map), which is the summer settlement for people and herds from Chikar. Rustam is a recommended yak wallah and guide who knows his way across the pass. Darkot has the shop nearest to the Boroghil area, so you should not have much difficulty finding porters eager to go there and use their wages to buy rubber boots, horseshoes, buckets and clothes.

Stage 6: Qui Quldi to Kam, four hours at yak speed. There is no bridge across the Yarkhun, which is born out of the Chiantar Glacier at 3,650 metres above sea-level. Descend from Qui Quldi (no path) to the wide, stony river bed, which you follow up to the terminal moraine of the Chiantar Glacier. Scramble across the moraine (90 minutes), wade the fierce lateral stream, descend the left bank of the Yarkhun, and wade the thigh-deep Chikzar River (no problem on a yak). Then climb up the ungrazed hillside, knee-deep in grass and flowers, to **Kam**, a shepherds' stone circle beside a dense patch of willow bushes, with clear views up the Rabat Valley opposite and, to the east, along the Chiantar Glacier. Unless you are very strong and determined, we recommend camping here at about 3,750 metres.

Stage 7: Kam to Darkot Pass Base Camp beside the Zindikharam Glacier, four to five hours at yak speed. Keep the Zindikharam River well below you on your right, and follow a faint, intermittent path for two hours to the snout of the glacier, where the river roars out of a cave of black ice. Climb steeply east up the difficult glacial moraine and down onto the glacier (one hour). Head on a long diagonal across the smooth ice, stepping over tiny crevasses, to the western edge of the glacier, where the first side glacier enters. There is an excellent, small campsite in the ablation valley below a green mountain slope, with good rock shelters for porters and fodder for yaks. Camp at about 4,200 metres.

Stage 8: Base Camp to Rawat, five to seven hours. Leave early so you are off the snow before 10 am, when it starts to soften. Rope up and beware of hidden crevasses. An easy couple of hours up the wide, smooth ice takes you to the top of the pass, at about 4,620 metres. Striated glaciers flow off the surrounding peaks. A distinctive black triangular rock rises like a beacon from the sweeping snowy curve marking the top. On the other side you look down to a wide bowl of snow, with the Darkot Glacier sliding off to the northwest.

Imagine for a moment an army of 10,000 Tibetans crossing here in 747 to confront the Chinese on the other side of the Boroghil Pass. Picture their defeated remnants straggling back to Yasin, pursued by 3,000 Chinese. Consider the Russian spies standing here in 1891, peering down into Yasin. Finally, spare a thought for the Pamir Boundary Commission four years later, which struggled down the Zindikharam Glacier with 600 ponies, many of which fell into the crevasses.

A gentle descent takes you down to join the Chikar-to-Darkot route described above.

APPENDICES

Appendix 1

DISEASES YOU MAY ENCOUNTER
AND HOW TO AVOID THEM

by Dr John Shephard MD

Water-borne and faecally spread diseases include the following.

Cholera. Still one of the most-feared diseases in the developing world, cholera produces painless, profuse, watery diarrhoea and is associated with vomiting in the severe form. If supportive treatment in the form of oral rehydration therapy (ORT) is not given, the patient suffers circulatory shock and dehydration. Kidney failure may follow, with a high risk of mortality.

Hepatitis A. The sufferer feels unwell, with nausea, vomiting, diarrhoea, appetite loss, headaches and malaise. After one or two weeks, the sufferer becomes jaundiced but begins to feel better; the appetite returns. The jaundice passes, and the majority of cases resolve themselves within three to six weeks.

Enteropathic E coli. This produces diseases including an illness indistinguishable from severe cholera, diarrhoea of varying severity and an illness similar to shigella dysentery.

Salmonellosis. Salmonella gastroenteritis is most commonly picked up from dairy products and undercooked meats. It causes diarrhoea. Typhoid and paratyphoid fever usually develop only where there is poor hygiene and overcrowding. These diseases can last for four weeks; symptoms include fever, cough, sore throat and constipation followed by diarrhoea and rash. Complications include pneumonia, meningitis and urinary tract infections.

Shigella. This is an acute intestinal infection causing diarrhoea with severe cramping stomach pains, nausea and vomiting. It gets better by itself.

Reiter's syndrome. This can follow gastro-intestinal infection with shigella or salmonella. It comprises a triad of symptoms: arthritis, urethritis and conjunctivitis. There is a very high incidence of long-term complications and recurrences.

Amoebiasis. This is spread by water, food and person-to-person contact. Incubation is variable from a few days to months. The germ causes a colitis with mild intermittent diarrhoea and abdominal discomfort, progressing to bloody diarrhoea with mucus. Complications are rare.

Giardiasis. This is spread by water and person-to-person contact. Caused by the parasite *Giardia lamblia*, this is a disease of the intestine that appears as diarrhoea, nausea, lack of appetite, abdominal distension and discomfort. In prolonged cases, weight loss can be marked even in previously healthy adults. The cysts infest most of the water in Pakistan but can be killed by iodine or boiling or can be filtered out with a Katadyne filter or any filter with a maximum pore size of .5 microns.

Other unwelcome potential residents in your body include various intestinal worms transmitted in uncooked food and from faeces, both human and animal.

If you get any sort of diarrhoea, it is essential not to become dehydrated, so you must take an oral rehydration therapy (ORT) such as Dioralyte, which is readily available in Pakistan.

Avoiding all these diseases is simple and easy. Scrupulous attention to water purification and personal hygiene is all that is required. The following may help:

Purify all drinking water either by the method described on pages 77–8 or by boiling for 10 minutes. Do not even think of trying what the locals drink. They are immune to it; you very definitely are not. Draw water from above your campsite, and ensure that you do not pollute water courses yourself.

Prepare latrines whenever you make camp, ensuring that they are well away from water sources and from the campsite itself. Cover after each use.

Wash your hands before touching food or utensils. Ensure that your cook, if you have one, understands the principles of good hygiene and the vagaries of the Western digestive tract. If you have to pay extra to stay healthy, so be it—it is money well spent.

Keep food covered at all times. Flies are one of the vectors of all the diseases listed above.

Do not wander round campsites in bare feet. Wear sandals or shoes at all times.

Avoid camping in areas where pollution is obvious. Find areas that are open, well ventilated and off the beaten track.

FURTHER READING

Expedition Medicine, published by the Expedition Advisory Centre, Royal Geographical Society, 1 Kensington Gore, London.

First Aid Manual, published by the British Red Cross Society and St John's Ambulance.

For medical books, products and advice, contact: Masta at the London School of Hygiene and Tropical Medicine, Keppel Street, London WC1; and Nomad Travel Pharmacy at 4 Potters Road, New Barnet, Herts. EN5 5HW.

Appendix 2

SELECTED TRAVEL AND TREKKING AGENCIES

IN PAKISTAN

Adventure Tours Pakistan, PO Box 1780, Islamabad; tel 852505; telex 54484 TOURS PK. Run by Ashraf Aman from Hunza, the first Pakistani to climb K2, this company is reliable and good value.

Walji's Adventure Pakistan, PO Box 1088, Islamabad; tel 823963, 812151, 828324/ 6; telex 5769 and 5836 WALJI PK; cable WALJIS; fax (92 51) 823109. This is the biggest travel agent in Pakistan, with local offices in Lahore, Karachi, Peshawar and Gilgit and international offices in the United States, Germany, France, Japan and Switzerland. They have reliable, experienced guides—expensive, but good reputation.

Karakoram Treks and Tours, Razia Sharif Plaza, Blue Area, Islamabad; tel 829120; telex 54480 MIRZA PK; cable BALTORO. With branch offices in Skardu, where they own the Yurt and Yak Serai, and in Gilgit on Airport Road. The owner, Nasir Abbas Mirza, is a Skardu man and very reliable. This was the first trekking agency to open in Pakistan.

Nazir Sabir Expeditions, PO Box 1442, Islamabad; tel 853672, 252580, 252553; telex 5811 NAIBA PK; fax (92 51) 250293. Nazir Sabir from Hunza was the second Pakistani to climb K2. He is an experienced and reliable mountaineer, and his company specialises in mountaineering expeditions.

Himalayan Trekking, PO Box, 1769 Rawalpindi; tel 63014; telex 5576 TTISM PK; cable HIMALAYA. Skardu office, PO Box 621; tel (0575) 280; Cable BAT. Owned by Muhammad Ali Chengezi, a reliable guide and specialist in the Baltistan region.

Horizon Travel, 47 School Road, F-7/1, Islamabad; tel 813815; fax (92 51) 821275. The owner, Kaiser Hayat, is well connected and specialises in taking his clients to dinner in private houses to meet interesting people.

Expedition Pakistan, 16 Saeed Plaza, Blue Area, Islamabad; tel 814360/1, 811301/2; telex 5537 PT PK; fax (051) 811457, 824319. A subsidiary of Travelwide Services, with people who are knowledgeable and full of ideas. They supply equipment and food for expeditions and deliver it to base camp. Expensive, but send for the catalogue to see what is offered.

Baltistan Tours, PO Box 604, Satellite Town, Skardu, Northern Areas; tel (0575) 626. Specialising in Baltistan.

Mountain Movers, Airport Road, Gilgit; tel (0572) 2967; fax (92 572) 2525. Owner Musarat Wali Khan is well connected and reliable, an expert on the Gilgit and Hunza areas and a specialist in rafting and kayaking.

Adventure Center (Pvt) Ltd, PO Box 516, Gilgit; tel (0572) 2409; fax (92 572) 2409. Owner Ikram Beg runs the best bookshop in Gilgit (G M Beg bookstall) and is an experienced guide. This is a small company, specialising in the Gilgit and Hunza areas.

Himalaya Nature Tours, Gujal House, Riaz Road, Khomer, Gilgit; or Silk Route Lodge, Gulmit; tel (0572) 2617; fax (92 51) 824245. This company is owned by Mirzada Shah Khan, an interesting prince from upper Hunza and well-known guide of the 1950s.

Hunza Tours & Treks, PO Box 38, Rawalpindi; tel 420530, 421463, 844190; telex 54499 HUNZA PK; fax (92 51) 584566 Att 781. Owned by Abbas Khan.

Pamir Tours, PO Box 545, Gilgit; tel (0572) 3939; fax (92 572) 2525. Owned by Zia Ullah Baig.

Hindu Kush Trails, PO Box 2059, Islamabad; Chitral office, Mountain Inn, Chitral; tel (0533) 800, 781 or 581; fax c/o GPO Chitral 0533. Run by the ex-royal family of Chitral, this company is very well connected and a specialist in the Hindu Kush.

OVERSEAS

Karakoram Experience Ltd, Trekkers Lodge, 32 Lake Road, Keswick, Cumbria, CA12 5DQ, England; tel (07687) 73966/72268; telex 64206 CUMEXP G; fax (07687) 71121. Six years' experience in the area makes it reliable, with excellent overseas guides and good Pakistani ground staff.

Sherpa, 131A Heston Road, Hounslow, Middlesex TW5 ORD, England; tel (081) 577 2717/7187; fax (081) 572 9788.

Mountain Travel Ltd (ExplorAsia), 13 Chapter St, London SWIP 4NY, England; tel (071) 630 7102; telex 266774 EXPLOR G; fax (071) 630 0355.

Explore, Explore Worldwide Ltd, 1 Frederick St, Aldershot, Hants GU11 1LQ, England; tel (0252) 319448; telex 858954 EXPLOR G; fax (0252) 343170.

Exodus, All Saints' Passage, 100 Wandsworth High St, London SW18 4LE, England; tel (081) 870 0151; telex 8951700 EXODUS G; fax (081) 871 9731.

Allibert, Agence Chapareillan, route de Grenoble, 38530 Chapareillan, France; tel 76 45 2226; telex 308 711 F Allibert; fax 76 45 2728. Or 39 rue du chemin Vert, 75011 Paris, France; tel (1) 48 06 1661. Well organised; leads some excellent treks.

Club Aventure, 122 rue d'Assas, 75006 Paris, France; tel (1) 46 34 2260; telex 202 227 CLUBAVT.

Himalaya Trekking, Constant Erzeijstraat 49, 3523 Vt Utrecht, Netherlands; tel (030) 871420.

Appendix 3

URDU GLOSSARY

Urdu is the national language of Pakistan. It is the mother tongue of only nine percent of the population, but the majority of Pakistanis who have been to school can speak some Urdu. Developed as the lingua franca in the camps of armies invading from the north, Urdu is a mixture of Persian, Arabic and various local languages. It is very similar to Hindi, the lingua franca of northern India, except that Urdu is written in Arabic script and Hindi uses Sanscrit script.

All nouns are either masculine or feminine, and the adjective agrees with the noun. Most masculine nouns end with -a; most feminine nouns end with -i. Both masculine and feminine nouns usually end with -e in the plural.

Verb endings differ if it is a man or a woman speaking. In the present tense, a man ends his verbs with -a, a woman ends hers with -i (for example, 'I go' is 'Meyn jata hun' for men and 'Meyn jati hun' for women). One well-known British officer who learned all his Urdu from his mistress always spoke as if he were a woman, much to the amusement of his troops.

1	ek	11	gyara
1 1/2	dehr	12	bara
2	doh	13	tera
2 1/2	dhai	14	chawda
3	teen	15	pundra
4	char	20	beess
5	paanch	25	pacheess*
6	chay	30	teess
7	saat	40	chaleess
8	aath	50	pachaass*
9	naw	100	ek saw
10	dus	1,000	ek hazaar
		100,000	ek lakh
		10 million (=100 lakh)	ek crore

*It is easy to confuse pacheess (25) with pachaass (50).

greeting (Peace be with you)	Salaam alay kum
reply (With you also be peace)	Waalay kum as Salaam
How are you?	Aapka (or tumhara) kia hal heh?
I am well	Teekh heh or teekh takh (colloquial)
What is your name?	Aapka (or tumhara) naam kya heh?
Do you speak English?	Kya aap ungrezi boltay heyn?
I am English/American/French	Meyn ungrez/amrikan/fransisi hoon
I don't know	Moojhay pata (or malum) naheen
I don't understand	Moojhay sumej naheen a-reha (m) rehi (f)
thank you	shukria
good bye	khoodha haafis
yes	jihaan, haanji or haan
no	naheen (na'en)
I	meyn
you (familiar)	tum
you (polite)	aap
he, she, it, they (nearby)	yeyh
he, she, it, they (further away)	voh
we	hum
you (plural)	aap
they	voh log
this	yeyh
that	voh
my	mera (m) or meri (f)
your (familiar)	tumhara/tumhari
your (polite & pl)	aapka/aapki
his, her, its (near)	iska/iski
his, her, its (far)	uska/uski
our	hamara/hamari
their (nearby)	inka/inki
their (far)	unka/unki
food	khaana
meat	ghosht
beef	gai ka ghosht (or burra ghosht)

cow	gai	porter	kooli
chicken	murghi	man	admi
goat meat	bukri ki ghosht	woman	aurut
goat	bukri	mother	amma *or* ammi
mutton	behr ka ghosht	people	lowg
sheep	behr	boy	lerka
horse	gora	girl	lerki
donkey	gudda	boy baby	bucha
		girl baby	buchi
apple	seb	son	beta
apricot	khubani	daughter	beti
bread	roti, naan, chapati		
barley	jau	bed	pulang
cabbage	gobi	bedding	bister
cauliflower	p(h)ool gobi	blanket	kambal
cheese	cheez	candle	mom butti
egg	unda	lamp	butti
fish	muchli	curtain	purda
fruit	phul	electricity	bijli
grapes	ungur	fan	punkha
lentils	dhaal	home	ghur
onions	piaz	house	mekaan
potato	aalu	pillow	takya
rice	chavel	room	kamra
salt	namak	sheet	chaarder
spinach	palak	string bed	charpai (paya = *leg*,
sugar	cheeni	(charpoy)	charpai = *four legs*)
tomato	temater		
vegetable	subzi		
walnut	akhrout	bridge	pull
wheat	gundum	firewood	lakhri *or* jilani ki lakhri
wheat flour	atta	flower	p(h)ool
yogurt	duhi	grass	ghaas
buttermilk	lassi	mountain	pahar
milk	dudh	path	rasta
tea	chai	rain	barish
water	pani	river	daria
water (clean)	saaf pani	road	sarak

snow	barf	expensive	manga
spring	cheshma	good/OK	achaa
sun	dhub	very good	behut achaa
tree	darakht	absolutely right	bilkul teek
village	gaon	well done/good	shabash
		OK/correct	teek heyh
today	aaj	big	burra (m)
tomorrow	kul (plus verb in future tense)*		burri (f)
		a lot/much/plenty	buhat
yesterday	kul (plus verb in past tense)*	all	sub
		small	chota/choti
day before yesterday	persun*	a little	thora/thori
day after tomorrow	persun*	only	sirif
		hot	guram
		cold	thanda/thandi
		new	naya/nayi
		old	purana/purani
morning	subah	clean	saaf
evening	shaam	dirty	ganda
day	din	full	bhura hua
week	hufta	empty	khali
month	mehina	enough/stop	baas
year	sal	not enough/few	kum
hour	ghuntay	near	nazdeek
time	vakht	far	dur
o'clock	bujay (literally 'ring' of the bell)	ahead	aag-ay
		behind	peechay
What time is it?	Kya vakht heh? or Kitnay bujay heh?	above	uper
		below	neetchay
		inside	under
three o'clock	teen bujay	outside	baher
three hours	teen ghuntay	here	idher
quickly/early	jaldi		(or yehaan)
early morning	subah sa-ver-ray	there	udher
late	der		(or vehaan)
after this/next	is kay bad	from	say
very	behut	to	ko

*Pakistanis often mix up 'yesterday' and 'tomorrow' in English.

difficult	mushkil
closed	bund
white	sufaid
black	kala/kali
red	lal
blue	nila/nili
yellow	pila/pili
green	hara/hari
ready	tay-yar
Is it ready?	Tay-yar heh?
who?	kawn?
how?	kesay?
which direction?	kiss turaf?
Which way to Chitral?	Chitral kiss turaf heh?
which house?	kawnsa ghur?
whose?	kiska/kiski?
what?	kya?
when?	kub?
where?	kehaan?
how much?	kitna? (kitnay *plural*)
How much is this/that?	Yeyh/Voh kitnay ka heh?
	Yeyh/Voh kitnay pesson ka heh?
What is this/that?	Yeyh/Voh kya heh?
Is the bridge good?	Kya pull sai (*or* achaa) heh?
Is the bridge broken?	Kya pull tutahua heh?
How far is it?	Kitna dur heh?
Can you find ___ in Baltit?	Kya ___ Baltit may milta hey?
Where is Ali?	Ali kehan heh?
When will he return?	Voh kub vaapis aa-engay?
What work do you do?	Aap kya kaam kertay heyn?
What work can you do?	Aap kya kaam ker-suktay heyn?

Can you do it?	Kya aapka ker suk-engay?
I can do it	Meyn ker sukta hoon (m)
	Meyn ker sukti hoon (f)
Can I do it?	Kya meyn ker sukta hoon? (m)
	Kya meyn ker sukti hoon? (f)
I want/need ____	Mujhay ___ chahiay
I am coming	Meyn aa-reha hoon (m)
	Meyn aa-rehi hoon (f)
You come here	Aap ither ana (or Aap ither ao)
I will come back	Meyn vaapis aata (or aati) hoon
I will return tomorrow	Meyn kul vapis aa-unga (or ungi)
Come back tomorrow	Aap kul vapis ana (or ao)
I am able to come	Meyn aa-sukta (or sukti) hoon
I cannot come	Meyn naheen aa-sukta (or sukti) hoon
I go	Meyn jaata (or jaati) hoon
I go back	Meyn vapis ja-reha (or rehi) hoon
You go back	Aap vapis jana (or jao)
I will do it	Meyn kerta (or kerti) hoon
I work	Meyn kaam kerta (or kerti) hoon
You do the work	Aap kaam kerna (or kero)
I give you Rs100	Meyn apko eek saw rupay day-reha (or rehi) hoon
You give me ____	Aap ____ mujhay dena
I eat food	Meyn khana kharta (or kharti) hoon
You eat food	Aap khana khao
I drink water	Meyn pani peeta (or peeti) hoon
for me	mera leeyay (m) meri leeyay (f)
for you	aap kay leeyay (polite)
	or tumhareh leeyay (familiar)
and	awr
or	ya

Appendix 4

BALTI GLOSSARY

by Nasra and Nasir Abbas Mirza

Balti is archaic Tibetan. It is spoken throughout Baltistan.

1	chik	20	nee shew
2	nyis	30	sum shew
3	sum	40	nee shew nyis
4	zhi	50	graf shew
5	gra (*roll the r in your throat*)	60	nee shew sum
6	trook	70	rdhun shew
7	rdhun	80	nee shew zhi
8	rget	90	rgu shew
9	rgu	100	rgya
10	shew	1000	stong chik

greeting	As salaam alay kum
reply	Waalay kum es salaam
How are you?	Yang chinay yud?
Are you well?	Yang chinay yud?
I am well	Nga liachmo yud
What is your name?	Ya ree mintakhpo cheein?
Do you speak Urdu?	Ya la Urdu skad ungay ta?
I am English/American	Ngla Angrez/Amreekan in
I don't know	Ngla stakhpa met
I don't understand	Ngla ngozin met
thank you	azhu
good bye	hoodai phagring
yes	in
no	met

food	zaan
meat	sha
beef	ba sha

cow	bang	teenage girl	nachungmo
chicken	biango		
rooster	biafo	bridge	zamba
goat	rawak	firewood	shing
goat meat	ra sha	mountain	brak
sheep	loo	path	lam
mutton	loo sha	peak	ri
horse	rtha	rain	charpa
donkey	bongbu	river	gyamso
		road	lam
apricots	paring	snow	khaa
bread	kurba	spring	chumik
cheese	chaka *and* purus	sun	neema
fish	nya	tree	stakjee
fish meat	nya sha	valley	lungma
grapes	rgun	village	drong
lentils	strunjun		
maize	hachul cha	today	dering
onions	tzung	tomorrow	haskay
potato	aalu	yesterday	gunday
rice	bras	day before yesterday	karchak
salt	paiyu	day after tomorrow	snangla
sugar	kara		
walnut	starga	morning	dyokpa
wheat	krow	evening	guntak
wheat flour	bakh pei	day	neemala
yogurt	lopi onga	month	lza
milk	onga	year	lokor
tea	cha	hour	genta
water	chu	What time is it?	Wakh po chi
water (drinking)	zangspa chu		sung set?
		three o'clock	baja sum
man	mee	three hours	genta sum
woman	bustring	quickly	shokhmo
boy	pru	early morning	dyok pika
girl	bongno	late	guray

after this/next	shulpo
very	ishin
expensive	rinchan
good	liakhmo
very good	ishin liakhmo
well done/good	liakhmo
OK/correct	liakhmo
big	chogo
a lot/much/plenty	ishin
all	gangma
small	tzuntzay
a little	tzuntzay
only	chiksa
hot	tso
cold	drakhmo
new	serpa
old	sningma
clean	dasay
dirty	kamlok
difficult	kish kish
white	karpo
black	nakpo
red	marpo
blue	sgnunpo
yellow	serpo
green	sgnunpo
Which way to Skardu?	Skardu gay lampo la gwin?
how much?	tsaam tsay?
How much is this/that?	Rinpo tsaam tsay?
What is this/that?	Doo dhin?

Is the bridge good?	Zambo drolay yut ta?
Is the bridge broken?	Zambo chaksay yut ta?
How far is it?	Tzaam tzee thaghring yut ta?
Where is Ali?	Ali gar yut?
When will he return?	Lok se naam ongmin?
What work do you do?	Yang chee las bith?
Can you do it?	Yang la diu bya ya ne ta?
Is it ready?	Chatakh yota?
It is ready	Chatakh yoth
I come	Ngla ongut
You come	Ya ong (or kya-ong)
I will come back	Ngla loksay ongut
I will return tomorrow	Ngla haskay loksay ongut
Come back tomorrow	Kya-ong haskay loksay ong
I go	Ngla gwit
I go back	Ngla loksay gwit
You go back	Kya-ong loksay song
I give you Rs100	Ngla kya ong la hmul rgya mee nit
silver (= money)	hmul
I eat food	Ngla zit
You eat food	Kya zit
I drink	Ngla tungit
for me	nala
for you	kya-ong la

Appendix 5

BURUSHASKI GLOSSARY (HUNZA DIALECT)

by Parveen and Ashraf Aman

Burushaski is an aboriginal language unrelated to any other, now spoken only in Hunza, Nagar and Yasin (with different dialects and accents in each). Formerly, it was spoken all over the Gilgit-Hunza region. It is complicated by having four classes of nouns: human masculine, human feminine, nonhuman animate and inanimate.

1	han	20	alter
2	atta	30	alter torumo
3	usko	40	alto alter
4	walto	50	alto alter torumo
5	zthundo	60	iski alter
6	mishindo	70	iski alter torumo
7	thelo	80	walti alter
8	althambo	90	walti alter torumo
9	huncho	100	tha
10	torumo	1,000	saas

greeting	Beemei ban *or familiar singular* Bemei ba
reply	Shuwa ban *or* Shuwa ba
How are you?	Beemei ban?
Are you well?	Shuwa ban?
I am well	Shuwa ba
What is your name?	Besen quik bila?
Do you speak Urdu/English?	Urdu/Angrezi écha? *or* Urdu/Angrezi bash hei baa?
I am English/American	Jay Angrez/Amreekan ba
I don't know	Ar leel api
I don't understand	Akay ya ba *or* Asulo apal jila
thank you	ju mar *or* mar ju (ju gor *singular*)
good bye	yeshua
yes	awa (*or* shuwa, *literally* OK *or* good)
no	ya *or* beeya

I want	jar awar ji	cauliflower	gobi
		cheese	kurut
I	jay	egg	tingan
you	un	fish	tumo
he/she	in	fruit	pamul
we	may	grapes	graying
you	ma	lentils	cha
they	oo	maize	makai
this/that	gussay/issay	onions	gashu
		pear	paysho
my	ja	potato	alu
your	unay	rice	buras
his/her (nearby)	keenay/kinmo	salt	bayu
his/her (further away)	eenay/inmo	spinach	palak
our	mee	sugar	shukur
their (nearby)	kuway	tomato	balogan
their (further away)	uway	vegetable	hoi
		walnut	tili
food	shapeek	wheat	gur
meat	chap	wheat flour	gur ye dagowang
beef	chap	yogurt	domanum
cow	buwa		mamu
chicken	gar ka mutz		
goat	tseer		
goat meat	tseeray chap	buttermilk	diltar
sheep	belees	milk	mamu
horse	hagur	tea	chai
		water	tsil
		water (clean)	sisi num tsil
apples	balt		
apricots	gzoo		
barley	hari	man	heer
barley flour	hari ye	woman	goos
	dagowang	boy	hiles
bread	shapeek or	girl	dusseen
	tooltopo		
		bridge	bash
cabbage	kaguming	firewood	grasheel

flower	askoor	very	but
grass	shirga	expensive	kaimat *or*
mountain	chish		taanum
path	gun	good	shuwa
rain	haralt	very good	but shuwa
river	sinda	well done/good	but shuwa
road	gun	OK/correct	shuwa
snow	gay	big	ooyum
spring	bul	a lot/much/plenty	but
sun	sa	all	ooyon
tree	tum	small	jot
village	giram	a little	kumon
		only	seerup
today	koolto		
tomorrow	gimalay	hot	geroorum
yesterday	suboor	cold	chagoorum
day before yesterday	yargun tsing	new	tosh
day after tomorrow	heepulto	old	men
		clean	safar
morning	tsor deemo	dirty	terkish
evening	sasat toomo	full	iyon
day	guntz	empty	push
week	altaang mutz *or*	enough/stop	bos
	hufta	not enough/few	bos api
month	hisa	near	aseer
year	yol	far	matan
hour	genta	ahead	yar
time	ken	behind	ilgi
o'clock	garoom	above	yatay
What time is it?	Berum garibi?	below	yaray
three o'clock	iski garibi	inside	ulo
three hours	iski genta	outside	holay
quickly	tsor	here	kolay
early	tsor	there	elay
early morning	tsor deemo tsor	difficult	abash
late	karano	blocked	bun
after this/next	itsoo watay	shut	tum

white	burum	What work can you do?	Besan duro etish gomai ba?
black	mutum	Can you do it?	Gutay eechuma? or Eetish gomai ba?
red	bardum		
blue	shikum		
yellow	shikerk	I can do it	Eetish aamaya ba
green	joot shikum		
ready	tayar		
Is it ready?	Tayar biya? or Tayar bila?	I come	Jay daium
		You come	Undu koma
who?	men/amin?	I will come back	Jay zgu chum
how?	bela tay?	I will return tomorrow	Jee malay zgu chum
which direction?	ami tali?		
Which way to Baltit?	Baltitar ami tali?	Come back tomorrow	Jee malu zgu
which house?	ami tha?	I am able to come	Jee jush aamaya ba
whose?	menay?		
what?	besan?	I cannot come	Jee jush aya maya ba
when?	beshal?		
where?	amulo?	I go	Jee nicha ba
how much?	beruman?	I go back	Jee par maya ba
		You go back	Par manay
How much is this/that?	Berumanar bi/bila?	I will do it	Jee eecham
		You do it	Un eh
What is this/that?	Bisan bi/bila?	I work	Ja duro eecha ba
Is the bridge good?	Bash shuwa bia?	You do the work	Un duro eh
Is the bridge broken?	Bash takay ee mani bi?	I give you Rs100	Jay tha rupia gucham
How far is it?	Beruman matan bi?	You give me	Un jo
Can you get vegetables?	Hoi demergur sha bana? or Hoi bitsana?	I eat food	Ja shapeek cheecha ba
		You eat food	Un eh shapeek cheecha
		I drink water	Ja tsil mia ba
Where is Ali?	Ali amulo bai?		
When will he return?	Beshalar guchi?	for me	ja ganay
What work do you do?	Besan duro echa?	for you	un eh ganay

Appendix 6

KHOWAR GLOSSARY

by the ul-Mulk family

Khowar is the main language of Chitral and is also spoken in Ghizar (the upper Gilgit Valley) and Yasin. It is an Indo-European language. To form the plural, add -an to the singular.

1	ee	20	bishir
2	ju	30	bishir josh
3	troi	40	jubishir
4	chor	50	jubishir josh
5	ponj	60	troibishir
6	chhoi	70	troibishir josh
7	sut	80	chorbishir
8	osht	90	chorbishir josh
9	nyoh	100	shor
10	josh	1,000	hazar

greeting (Peace be with you)	Salaam alay kum
reply (With you also be peace)	Waalay kum es salaam
How are you?	Kicha assus?
Are you well?	Jam assussa?
I am well	Jam assum
What is your name?	Ta nam kyargh?
Do you speak Urdu/English?	Urdu/Ungrezi janissa?
I am English/American	Awa Ungrez/American
I don't know	Hush no koman
I don't understand	Hush no koman
thank you	meherbani or shukria
good bye	khuda yar
yes	ji or jam
no	noh
I want	mash ki mau

I	awa
you	thu
he/she (nearby)	hes
he/she (far away)	hasa
we	ispa
you	pisa
they	hatet *or* het
this/that	haya/hes
my	ma
your	ta
his/her (nearby)	horo
his/her (far away)	hatogho
our	ispa
their (nearby)	hetan
their (far away)	hatetan
food	shapik
meat	pushur
beef	leshiri
cow	leshu
chicken	gahak
goat	pai
goat meat	pai-iri
sheep	kelli
mutton	kell-iri
horse	istor (*after Astor, where they came from*)
apples	palogh
apricots	juli
barley	siri
barley flour	siri peshiru
bread	shapik
cabbage	bund gobi *or* kalam (*kale*)
cauliflower	phul gobi
cheese (soft)	pangir
cheese (hard)	kilal

cheese (salty)	abada
egg	ayukun
fish	matsi
fruit	méwa (maywa)
grapes	drurch
lentils	dhaal
maize	joari
onions	treshtu
pear	tong
potato	alu
rice	gringh
salt	trup
spinach	palak
sugar	shokor
tomato	petingal
vegetable	shakh
walnut	birmogh
wheat	gomb
wheat flour	gomb peshiru
yogurt	macheer
buttermilk	shethu
milk	cheer
tea	chai
water	ooghr
water (drinking)	pazgah ooghr
porter	bardoyu
man	mosh
woman	kimeri
boy	dakh
girl	kumuru
son	zhaw
daughter	zhur

bridge	ser
firewood	dhar
grass (hay)	jush
grass (fresh)	gaaz
footprints in snow	shuk
mountain	zom
path	pawn
rain	boshik
river	darya
road	sarak
snow	heem
spring	utz
stream	gol
sun	yor
tree	kaan
village	deh
today	hannun
tomorrow	pinga chhui
yesterday	dosh
day before yesterday	ohtili
day after tomorrow	pingga
morning	chuchi
evening	shaam
day	anus
week	hufta
month (moon)	maas
year	sal
hour	genta
time	wakht
o'clock	buja
What time is it?	Kya wakht?
three o'clock	troi buja
three hours	troi genta

quickly	tez *or* shau
early	rareshti
early morning	chuchi rareshti
late	gur
after this/next	hamo ghar achi
very	boh
expensive	rkimati
good	jam jam
very good	boh jam
well done/good	jam aru *or* shabash
OK/correct	sahi *or* hosk (*honest*)
big	yut
a lot/much/plenty	boh
all	suf
small	serk
a little	pukh
only	serif
hot	petch
cold	ooshak
new	nogh
old	zaru (*man or animal*)
	paranu (*inanimate*)
clean	pazgah
dirty	nazgusti
full	tip
empty	khali
enough/stop	bas
not enough/few	kum
near	shoi
far	dudheri
ahead	prushti

behind	achi
above	sora
below	bula
inside	undrayni
outside	bayri
here	hayera
there	hera
difficult	gyran
closed	bund
white	ishperu
black	shah
red	krui
blue	och *or* sowz
green	sowz *or* och
yellow	zech
ready	taiyar
Is it ready?	Taiyar hoya?
It is ready	Taiyar hoy
who?	kaa?
how?	kicha?
which direction?	ki wash ki?
Which way to Chitral?	Chitral kiwashki sher?
which house?	ki dur?
whose?	kus?
what?	kiagh?
when?	dust?
where?	kura?
how much?	kanduri?
How much is this/that?	Haya kanduri/ hes kanduri?
What is this/that?	Haya kiagh/ hes kiagh?

Is the bridge good?	Ser jam shéra?
Is the bridge broken?	Ser chitti shéra?
How far is it?	Kanduri dudéri sher?
Can you get vegetables?	Shakh len boya?
Where is Ali?	Ali kura asur?
When will he return?	Kya wakht achi goi?
What work do you do?	Kya kurum kosan?
What work can you do?	Kya kurum koriko bos?
Can you do it?	Koriko bosa?
I can do it	Awa koriko bom
I come	Awa geeko
You come	Ghay
I will come back	Awa achi bom
I will return tomorrow	Awa chuchi achi bom
Come back tomorrow	Chuchi achi ghay
I am able to come	Awa geeko bom
I cannot come	Awa geeko no bom
I go	Awa biman
I go back	Awa achi biman
You go back	Tu achi bogha
I will do it	Awa korom
You do it	Tu koray
I work	Awa korom koman
You do the work	Tu korom koray
I give you Rs100	Shor rupea doman
You give me	Tu maten det
I eat food	Awa shapeek zhee boman
You eat food	Shapeek zhee beh
I drink water	Awa ooghr piman
for me	maten
for you	taten

Appendix 7

DOWN-COUNTRY HOTELS AND TRAVEL INFORMATION

Quoted hotel prices are for one night in a double room in early 1992. They are meant to be a guideline for comparison between hotels. Prices rise proportionally, except when a hotel is renovated, in which case its prices jump. Hotels are listed from expensive to cheap.

KARACHI
INTERNATIONAL STANDARD AND EXPENSIVE: Rs2,500–5,000
Sheraton, Club Road; tel 521021; telex 25255 ASHER PK.

Holiday Inn, Abdullah Haroon Road; tel 522011; telex 28035, 25466 HIK Pk.

Pearl Continental, Dr Zia-ud-din Ahmed Road; tel 515021; telex 23617, 24713 PEARL Pk.

Avari Towers Ramada Renaissance, Fatima Jinnah Road; tel 525216; telex 24400 AVARI Pk. The tallest building in Pakistan. Excellent Japanese restaurant.

Taj Mahal, Shahrah-e-Faisal; tel 520211; telex 24267 TAJ Pk.

MODERATE: Rs600–2,000
Midway House, Star Gate Road, near airport; tel 480371; telex 25860 MHL Pk. The usual in-transit hotel.

Beach Luxury, Maulvi Tamiz-ud-din Khan Road; tel 551031. Excellent seafood restaurant in garden.

Metropole, Club Road; tel 512051; telex 24329 METRO Pk. Oldest hotel in town.

Mehran, Shahrah-e-Faisal; tel 515061; telex 23616 MHK Pk.

Airport, Star Gate Road, near airport; tel 480141/5.

GOOD VALUE: Rs300–1,000
The best-value moderate and cheaper hotels are in Saddar Bazaar along and between Daud Pota Road and Raja Ghazanfar Ali Road. It is easy to walk from one to the other until you find one to your liking. Try:

Sarawan, Raja Ghazanfar Ali Road, Saddar Bazaar; tel 525121/5; telex 25584 BLOCK Pk; fax 21-510278 (Rs330). All facilities, best value in town, but usually full.

Jabees, Abdullah Haroon Road; tel 512011.

Gulf, Daud Pota Road; tel 515831/5, 525146/9.
Reliance, Daud Pota Road; tel 510036, 521921.
Sarah, Parr Street; tel 527160/2.
United, Daud Pota Road; tel 515010/4.
Chiltan, National City, Ocean, Al-Mashriq and many more in Saddar Bazaar.

INEXPENSIVE: Rs80–300

These recommended cheapies supply a room with bath—hot water in winter but no airconditioning in summer. We list only a few; there are many others worth trying in Saddar Bazaar, around Cantonment Station, in Boulton Market and along Shedi Village Road in Lee Market.

Al-Salatin, Daud Pota Road, Saddar; tel 516362, 527368.
Ambassador, Daud Pota Road, Saddar; tel 514820, 514200.
Shalimar, Daud Pota Road, Saddar; tel 529491, 527671.
Chandni, Daud Pota Road, Saddar; tel 511487, 529467.
De Paris, Mir Karamali Talpur Road, Saddar; tel 524411/3.
International, Sheikh Chand Street, Saddar; tel 211089.
Al-Farooq, Summerset Street, Saddar; tel 511031/2.
Royal, II Chundrigar Toad, near Habib Plaza; tel 211089.
Sunshine, Cantonment Station; tel 512316.

HOSTELS

Amin House Youth Hostel, 2 Maulvi Tamiz-ud-din Khan Road (Rs25).
YMCA, Strachen Road opposite Governor's House; tel 516927, 613022 (Rs80).
YWCA, M A Jinnah Road; tel 71662. Recommended for women travelling alone.
Salvation Army, Frere Road behind Empress Market; tel 74262 (Rs40). Dorm only.
Railway Retiring Rooms, Karachi City and Karachi Cantonment Stations (Rs75). For those with a valid railway ticket.

ISLAMABAD

EXPENSIVE: Rs2,500–4,000

Holiday Inn, Aga Khan Road, F-5/1; tel 826121/35; telex 5470, 5612 HISSD Pk; fax 92 51 820648.
Islamabad Hotel, Municipal Road, G-6/2; telex 5643 IHI Pk; fax 92 51 820763.

MODERATE: Rs600–2,000

Ambassador, Khyaban-e-Suhrawardy; tel 824011/5. Big bathtubs, clean, good value.
Shehrazad, Super Market; tel 822295/6, 823519. Central location.

The three hotels in Shakarparian Park near Rawal Dam listed below are on the main bus line halfway between Islamabad and Rawalpindi. They are quiet and make a good choice for bird-watchers, walkers and horse-riders. However, they are remote, so there is no choice of restaurant.

Lake View Motel; tel 821025, 821057. No view of the lake, comfortable, clean, AC, small restaurant.

Dreamland Motel; tel 814381/5. Central AC. Rooms are small but clean with nice bathrooms. Mosquitoes may be a problem.

Pak Tures Motel; tel 824503, 813116. Further from Rawal Dam and slightly cheaper.

REST HOUSES: Rs500–1,500

There are about 40 rest houses scattered throughout Islamabad offering four to ten rooms, usually with AC. On the whole they are good value and comfortable. Drive around and look for the rest house signs. We have visited (and can recommend) Accommodators Two. We include some other addresses and phone numbers; many others are listed in the *Hotel Guide*.

Accommodators Two, House 9, Street 36, F7/1; tel 817320, 818478. Six rooms, clean and with helpful management.

Decent Accommodators, House 2, Street 15, F7/2; tel 815275, 815335.

Best Accommodators, House 6, Street 54, F7/4; tel 815840.

Capital Inn, House 18, Street 4, E6/3; tel 815546.

Decent Lodge, House 261A, Street 22, E7; tel 825536, 818668.

Delux Accommodators, House 12, Street 18, F7/2; tel 814718, 813577.

Host, Block 3A Markaz F/8; tel 858119, 856621.

Lodgings, 41A College Road, F7/2; tel 812973.

CHEAPER HOTELS: Rs200–650

We have not checked any of the following. Please send information if you find a good cheapy in Islamabad.

Blue Star, 1, I & T Centre, G8/4; tel 852810, 852717.

Capital Inn, G/8 Markaz; tel 857357, 858157.

Dream Land, 2, Street 54, G9/4; tel 858101/2.

Sitara, 3C, Sitara Market, G7 Markaz; tel 819953.

There is a **camping ground** opposite Aabpara Market, near Rose and Jasmine Garden. The charge is Rs10 per day, plus a parking fee of Rs5 for a car and Rs10 for a wagon or truck. Platforms fitted with electricity and water supply cost Rs5 per day. Kitchen, washroom and toilet facilities are provided.

OTHER INFORMATION
Most offices are open 9 am–12.30 pm and 1.30–4 pm.
Tourism Division, Ministry of Tourism, College Road, Jinnah Market, F-7/2; tel 820856.
Pakistan Tourism Development Corporation (PTDC) Head Office, House 2, Street 61, F 7/4, Islamabad.
PTDC hotel bookings, contact PTDC Motel Head Office, Block B-4, Markaz F-7 (Jinnah Market), Bhitai Road, Islamabad.
Telegraph and telephone office, behind Holiday Inn F-5. Never closes.
General Post Office, Post Office Road, G-6/2; tel 825957. Open 8 am–2 pm.
Pakistan International Airlines (PIA), Nazim-ud-din Road, Blue Area; tel 8225031.
Passport Office, Aabpara Market, near National Bank; tel 826837.
Foreigner's Registration Office, Ayub Market, F-8.

RAWALPINDI
EXPENSIVE: RS2,500–3,500
Pearl Continental, the Mall; tel 66011/21; telex 5736 PEARL Pk; fax 63927.
Shalimar, off the Mall; tel 62901/21; telex 5764 SHLMR Pk.

MODERATE: RS500–1,500
Flashman's, PTDC, The Mall; tel 581480/8. Colonial style bungalows, central, all facilities, good meeting place.
Kashmirwala's, 2 The Mall; tel 583186/9. Large block hotel with no character but good food.
Gatmell's, Jail Road, near Army House; tel 581648, 582388. Quiet, large rooms, excellent value, storage facilities for expeditions.
Pine, 251 Iftikhar Janjua Road, behind Pearl Continental; tel 63660, 68017/8. Small rooms but quiet. Bargain hard.
The big hotels along Murree Road near Liaquat Chowk tend to be noisy and overpriced. The Park, National City, Shangrila, Sandhills, Potohar and Marhaba (there are many more) are all around Rs500–800 for a double.

Rawal and United, off Murree Road near Committee Chowk, are quieter but slightly more expensive.

CHEAPER: RS300–800

There are dozens in this price range along Murree Road and Liaquat Road and around Saddar and Raja bazaars.

New Kamran, Kashmir Road, Saddar Bazaar; tel 582040. Slightly quieter and good value.

Asia, off Murree Road near Committee Chowk; tel 70898. Quiet, big rooms.

Queen and Al Farooq, off Murree Road near Committee Chowk, are both large, quiet hotels off the main road.

Al-Hayat, Murree Road, Liaquat Chowk; tel 70979, 554880. Popular with backpackers but noisy. This is the cheapest we checked out.

INEXPENSIVE: RS80–300

The cheap hotels by the railway station are often full, and many will not accept foreigners. Good alternatives are:

Railway Retiring Rooms, Rawalpindi City Station (s/d Rs40/75). Bring your own bedding.

Youth Hostel, 25 Gulistan Colony near Ayub Park. Too remote.

YWCA, 64A Satellite Town. Women only. A bit run down, but cheap and safe.

OTHER INFORMATION

Most offices are open 9 am–12.30 pm and 1.30–4 pm.

Punjab Tourist Information Centre, 44 Mall Plaza, Mall Road; tel 64824, 65824.

Tourist Information Centre, PTDC, Flashman's Hotel, The Mall; tel 581480/4.

PIA, the Mall; tel 67011, 66231.

American Express, Murree Road; tel 65617. Open 9 am–1 pm.

General Post Office, Kashmir Road; tel 65691. Open 8 am–2 pm.

Telegraph and telephone office, The Mall; tel 65854, 65809. Open 24 hours.

Foreigner's Registration Office, Rashid Minhas Road, Civil Lines; tel 63866.

Passport Office, 6th Road, Satellite Town; tel 848051.

PESHAWAR

INTERNATIONAL CLASS: 2,000–4,000

Pearl Continental, Khyber Road; tel 76361/9; telex 52309 PEARL Pk; fax 76465. All facilities.

MODERATE: RS400–1,500

Dean's, Islamia Road; tel 76483/4, 79781/3. PTDC-run but poorly managed. Old-style building with verandas, a pretty garden and some charm.

Green's, Saddar Road; tel 73603, 74304. Clean, pleasant, round a courtyard.

Galaxie, by jail bridge; tel 212172/4. Large and conveniently situated.

Habib, Shoiba Bazaar, near Khyber Bazaar; tel 210787, 219316. Well situated in old town, with helpful management. Good value and reasonably clean. Also offers good cheap rooms without AC. Popular with foreigners.

INEXPENSIVE: RS20–100

Khyber, Main Saddar Road (beside Green's); tel 73688. Offers doubles and dorm. Popular with tourists but overpriced and with bedbugs in the dorm.

Salatin, Cinema Road; tel 210279, 213770. Good food.

Kamran, Khyber Bazaar; tel 210145. Round a courtyard. Dirty.

National, inside Kabuli Gate, Jangimala, in a small side street off Qissa Khawani; tel 212491 (d/t Rs20/30). In an old house along a canal, with a central court. Restaurants in the street outside. Best value.

Three Star, Amin and Zabeel Palace, side by side on the GT Road near the bus station, have cheapish non-airconditioned doubles and moderately priced AC rooms, but they are noisy, and few foreigners stay there.

There are other cheap hotels in Saddar Road, Chowk Fawara, Namak Mandi, Cinema Road and along the Grand Trunk Road. In summer some hotels let you sleep outside for Rs10–15 per bed. Ask at PTDC for the new location of the **campground**. Other options include:

Youth Hostel, Peshawar University. Remote.

YMCA Hostel, near Peshawar University. Equally remote.

Railway Retiring Rooms, Peshawar Cantonment Station. For those with a valid ticket.

RESTAURANTS

Peshawar is famous for its street stalls, especially in Shoiba Bazaar for Afghani food and in Namak Mandi for *karai* (fried meat with onions, tomatoes and spices). Also try the fish stalls out on the road to Charsadda in Sardaryab, on the left side of the road. Salatin's, on Cinema Road (tel 210279, 213770), is one of Peshawar's best cheap indoor restaurants and is famous for its Pathan atmosphere.

OTHER INFORMATION

Tourist Information Centre, PTDC, Dean's Hotel; tel 79781/3, 76481.

Peshawar Museum (one of the best in Pakistan); tel 72252, 74452.

Passport Office, Gunner Road; tel 78931.

General Post Office and banks are in Saddar Bazaar. Open 8 am–2 pm.

Telephone and telegraph office, on The Mall. Open 24 hours.

Permits for the Khyber Pass from the Home Secretariat on Police Road.

SWAT: SAIDU SHARIF AND MINGORA
MODERATE: RS500–2,000

Swat Serena, Saidu Sharif; tel (0536) 4212, 4604. Or book through Serena, Karachi; tel 537506/9; telex SERENA Pk; fax 530397. International standard, with good food and service in old colonial style. Highest recommendation.

Pameer, Grand Trunk Road, Mingora; tel (0536) 4926, 4306; fax (0536) 4301. In centre of town. Less expensive but lacks charm.

Royal Palace, Aqba, Saidu Sharif; tel (0536) 5497. Overpriced.

CHEAPER: RS80–300

There are about 30 middle-range and cheap hotels in Mingora along the Grand Trunk Road, Madyan Road and around Green Chowk. The real cheapies do not accept foreigners.

Udyana, Grand Trunk Road, Mingora; tel 5076.

Abasind, New Madyan Road, Mingora; tel 2122.

Holiday, Makan Bagh, Saidu Sharif Road; tel 4443.

SWAT: MARGHAZAR

Green's Marghazar, White Palace, Marghazar; tel 5474. The converted summer palace of the first wali of Swat. Well positioned at the end of the valley, ten kilometres from Saidu Sharif.

SWAT: MALAM JABBA

A 50-room hotel was built here in 1988. It is now owned by Avari but had not opened by 1991. There is one ski run, to which access may be a problem in winter. In summer there is pony trekking and mini-golf.

SWAT: MIANDAM

At 1,800 metres, Miandam is the best place to spend your first night in Swat in summer. Camping is allowed and recommended. There are six hotels, all moderate in price.

PTDC Motel; tel 10. Or book through PTDC Islamabad; tel 819384, 815653. Well positioned, with a lovely garden and helpful staff. If all the rooms are full, you can take a spare bed outside and sleep under the trees in the garden. The best run of the PTDC hotels.

Pameer Guest House. Book through Pameer Hotel Mingora (see above).Overpriced.

Green Peaks; tel 11, slightly cheaper.

Karashma (tel 4), Nizara (tel 5) and Bright Star are slightly cheaper.

SWAT: MADYAN

Priced between Rs150 and Rs600, in descending order:

Madyan; tel 2. Or book through (0536) 4599. Right on the river.

River Palace, near bridge; tel 42.

Tourist; tel 90.

Mountain View; tel 7.

Nisar; tel 4, 41.

Shalimar, Imran, Gulf, Sarfaraz, al Farooq, Inayat and others.

SWAT: KALAM

All between Rs150 and Rs700, in descending order:

PTDC Motel; tel 14. Or book through PTDC Islamabad; tel 819384, 815653. Nice position with a good garden.

Mindona Inn; beside the rapids. Recommended.

Khyber. Worth checking out.

Falaksir; tel 10. Good position.

Sangam (tel 15), Heaven Breeze (tel 16), Khyber, King's Valley, Taj Mahal, Shangrilla, Kalam, Falk Naz, Qayyum, Khalid, Mehran are all slightly cheaper.

SWAT INFORMATION

Tourist Information Centre is in the Swat Serena Hotel; tel 5007.

Banks are open 9 am–1 pm, Monday to Thursday, 9 am–12 pm, Saturday and Sunday.

Post Office is open 8 am–2 pm.

Telephone and telegraph office is open 24 hours; the dialing code for Swat is 0536.

Appendix 8

TREKKING BIBLIOGRAPHY

Band, G, *Road to Rakaposhi* (Hodder & Stoughton, London, 1955). Cambridge expedition to Rakaposhi in 1954; exploration of treks from Chalt.

Banks, M E B, *Rakaposhi* (Secker & Warburg, London, 1959). Attempt of Rakaposhi in 1956 and first ascent in 1958.

Barker, R, *The Last Blue Mountain* (Chatto & Windus, London, 1959). Ill-fated Oxford expedition to Haramosh in 1957.

Barrett, R L and K, *The Himalayan Letters of Gypsy Davy and Lady Ba* (Heffers, Cambridge, 1927). Classic account of travels in Ladakh and Baltistan.

Barry, J, *K2 Savage Mountain, Savage Summer* (Oxford Illustrated Press, Oxford, 1987). Harrowing account of the disasterous summer of 1986, when 13 people died on K2.

Barth, F, *Indus and Swat Kohistan: An Ethnographic Survey* (in *Studies Honouring the Centennial of University Ethnographic Museum, Oslo, 1857–1957*, Vol 3).

Bates, R and H, *Five Miles High* (Dodd, Mead & Company, New York, 1939). Describes the 1938 American expedition to K2.

Bechtold, F (trans. Tyndale, H E G), *Nanga Parbat Adventure* (John Murray, London, 1935). German tragedy on Nanga Parbat.

Biddulph, J, *Tribes of the Hindoo Koosh* (Calcutta, 1880; reprint Karachi, 1977). Dry account by the first political agent to Gilgit.

Bonatti, W, *On the Heights* (Rupert Hart-Davis, London, 1964). Autobiography including Gasherbrum IV in 1958.

Bonnington, C J S, *Everest Years: A Climbers Life* (Hodder & Stoughton, London, 1986). Autobiography including Ogre.

Braham, T, *Himalayan Odyssey* (Allen & Unwin, London, 1974). Autobiographical account of 30 years of trekking and climbing in India and Pakistan.

Brown, J, *The Hard Years* (Gollanz, London, 1974). Autobiography including first ascent of Mustagh Tower.

Buhl, H, *Nanga Parbat Pilgrimage* (Hodder & Stoughton, London, 1981). Reprint of the classic autobiography of the climber who first conquered Nanga Parbat—solo and without oxygen—in 1953.

Caroe, O, *The Pathans* (Macmillan, London, 1958; reprint Oxford University Press, Karachi, 1975). Scholarly but readable history from 550 BC to 1957.

Child, G, *Thin Air* (Patrick Stephens, London, 1988). Expedition to Lobsang Spire, Broad Peak and Gasherbrum IV. Prize-winning bestseller.

Churchill, W, *My Early Life* (Butterworth, London, 1930; reprint Fontana, London, 1959). Exuberant tales of life as a young officer in the North-West Frontier.

Clark, J, *Hunza—Lost Kingdom of the Himalayas* (reprint Indus Publications, Karachi, 1980). Account of an American geologist who worked in Hunza for 20 months in 1950–51.

Clinch, N, *A Walk in the Sky* (The Mountaineers, New York, 1982). First ascent of Gasherbrum I (Hidden Peak).

Cockerill, G K, *Report on Various Reconnaissances in Chitral Territory, 1893–5* (Simla, 1896).

Conway, W M, *Climbing and Exploration in the Karakoram–Himalayas* (Fisher Unwin, London, 1894). Exploration of Hispar, Biafo and Baltoro glaciers in 1892.

Curran, J, *K2: Triumph and Tragedy* (Grafton Books, London, 1989). The tragic summer of 1986, when 13 died on K2.

Curzon, G N, *Leaves from a Viceroy's Note-book* (Macmillan, London, 1926).

——*Pamirs and the Source of the Oxus* (Geographical Journal, London, 1898). Accounts from the viceroy of India.

Diemberger, K, *Summits and Secrets* (Allen & Unwin, London, 1971). Includes Broad Peak, Chogolisa and Tirich Mir.

——*The Endless Knot: K2—Mountain of Dreams and Destiny* (Grafton Books, London, 1991). Tragedy on K2 in 1986, when Kurt's companion, Julie Tulis, was one of the 13 to die.

Duncan, E, *Breaking the Curfew—A Political Journey Through Pakistan* (Michael Joseph, London, 1989). Penetrating insight into what makes Pakistan tick.

Durand, A, *The Making of a Frontier: Five Years' Experience and Adventures in Gilgit, Hunza, Nagar, Chitral and the Eastern Hindu Kush* (London, 1899).

Dyhrenfurth, G O (ed), et al, *Dämon Himalaya: Internationalen Karakorum Expedition 1934* (Benno Schwabe, Basle, 1935). Expedition to Gasherbrum I; first ascent of Baltoro Kangri and east peak of Sia Kangri.

——*To the Third Pole: The History of the High Himalaya* (T Werner Laurie, London, 1955). The best account of Karakoram exploration and climbing up to 1955.

Fairley, J, *The Lion River* (Allen Lane, London, 1975). Good account of the Indus River from source to mouth.

Fanshawe, A, *Coming Through* (Hodder and Stoughton, London, 1990). Three expeditions including a traverse of Chogolisa.

Field, H, *An Anthropological Reconnaissance in West Pakistan* (Peabody Museum, Cambridge, 1959). Good collection of early anthropological material in Pakistan.

Filippi, F de (ed), *Karakoram and Western Himalaya 1909* (Constable, London, 1912). Duke of Abruzzi's expedition to Baltoro Glacier.

Fleming, P, *News from Tartary* (Johnathan Cape, London, 1936; reprint Futura, London, 1980). From Beijing to Srinagar with Ella Maillart in 1935. Describes Mintaka Pass, Hunza and Gilgit.

Greig, A, *Summit Fever* (Hutchinson, London). Expedition to Muztagh Tower.

Harris, J, *Much Sounding of Bugles: The Siege of Chitral, 1895* (reprint Karachi, 1975).

Hedin, S, *Trans-Himalaya* (Macmillan, London, 3 vols 1909–13). Great Swedish antiquarian travels in the Himalaya.

Herrligkoffer, K M, *Nanga Parbat—the Killer Mountain* (Knopf, New York, 1954). Describes the tragedies of Nanga Parbat and the first successful ascent.

Hoeflaken, H van, *Hiking Around Islamabad* (Asian Study Group, Islamabad, 1988).

Hopkirk, P, *The Great Game: On Secret Service in High Asia* (John Murray, London, 1990). Britain versus Russia—the struggle for Central Asia from 1810 to 1907. Gripping reading.

Houston, C H, and Bates, R H, *K2—the Savage Mountain* (McGraw Hill, New York, 1954). American attempt on K2 in 1953.

James, L, *With the Chitral Relief Force* (Calcutta, 1895).

Jettmar, K (ed), *Cultures of the Hindu Kush* (Franz Steiner Verlag, Wiesbaden, 1974). Selected papers from Hindu Kush cultural conference in Moesgard in 1970.

——*Bolor & Dardistan* (Lok Virsa, Institute of Folk Heritage, Islamabad, 1980). Interesting academic history of Gilgit and Baltistan.

——*Rock Carvings and Inscriptions in the Northern Areas of Pakistan* (Lok Virsa, Institute of Folk Heritage, Islamabad, 1984). Describes the petroglyphs along the Indus, Gilgit and Hunza rivers.

——*Between Gandhara and the Silk Roads—Rock Carvings along the Karakoram Highway* (Lok Virsa, Institute of Folk Heritage, exhibition catalogue, Islamabad, 1991).

Keay, J, *When Men and Mountains Meet* (John Murray, London, 1977). Readable stories of the exploration of the Karakoram and western Himalaya between 1820 and 1875.

——*The Gilgit Game* (John Murray, London, 1979). British and Russian agents play hide-and-seek in northern Pakistan from 1865 to 1895.

King, J, *Karakoram Highway, the Road to China* (Lonely Planet, Melbourne, 1989). Excellent guide to the KKH.

Kipling, R, *Kim* (Macmillan, London, 1899). There are many reprints of this classic novel of the Great Game.

Knight, E F, *Where Three Empires Meet* (Longman, London, 1893; reprint Indus

Publications, Karachi, 1973). Travels in Ladakh and Kashmir, and the British invasion of Gilgit and Hunza in 1891.

Kreutzmann, H, *Hunza Ländliche Entwicklung im Karakoram* (Dietrich Reimer Verlag, Berlin, 1989). Doctoral thesis on Hunza—in German and not translated.

Lamb, C, *Waiting for Allah* (Hamish Hamilton, London, 1991; reprint Penguin, London, 1992; pirate copies available in Pakistan). Outspoken account of life and politics in Pakistan by a young *Financial Times* correspondent, who was asked to leave.

Leitner, G W, *The Languages and Races of Dardistan* (Lahore, 1877). An academic work by an early ethnographer and linguist.

——*Dardistan in 1866, 1886 and 1893* (Woking, 1894; reprint New Delhi, 1978; reprint Karachi, 1985).

Lockhart, W, *Confidential Report of the Gilgit Mission, 1885–6* (London, 1889).

Longstaff, T G, *This My Voyage* (John Murray, London, 1950). Travels in northern Pakistan.

——*Byways in the Hindu Kush* (John Murray, London).

Lorimer, D L R, *The Burushaski Language* (Instituttet for Sammenlignende Kulturforskning, Serie B: Skrifter XXIX-1-3, Oslo, 1935).

——*Folk Tales of Hunza* (reprint Lok Virsa, Institute of Folk Heritage, Islamabad). Original stories collected in 1923–24 and published in 1934.

Lorimer, E O, *Language Hunting in the Karakoram* (London, 1938; reprint Indus Publications, Karachi, 1989). Fresh, lively account of life in Hunza in 1934 by Dr Lorimer's wife.

——*The Road to Hunza* (Geographical Magazine, III/4)

Loude, J-Y, *Kalash: Les derniers infidèles de l'Hindu Kush* (Berger-Levrault, Paris, 1980). Study of the Kafir Kalash.

Maillart, E, *Forbidden Journey* (Hienemann, London, 1937). Journey from Beijing to Srinagar with Peter Fleming in 1935. Entered Hunza across Mintaka Pass.

Maraini, F, *Karakoram: The Ascent of Gasherbrum IV* (Hutchinson, London, 1961). Italian expeditions in 1958 and 1959; describes first ascents of K2 and Gasherbrum IV. Well written, with good historical and ethnographical detail.

——*Where Four Worlds Meet* (Hamish Hamilton, London, 1964). First ascent of Mt Saraghrar in Chitral. Interesting discussion of the Kafir Kalash.

Mason, K, *Abode of Snow: A History of Himalayan Exploration and Mountaineering* (R Hart-Davis, London, 1955; reprint Diadem, London, 1987).

Masson, C, *Narrative of Various Journeys in Baluchistan, Afghanistan, and the Punjab 1826–1838* (London, 1842; reprint Oxford University Press, Karachi, 1974). Fascinating early journey through what is now Pakistan.

Mehra P, *The Younghusband Expedition: An Interpretation* (Asia Publishing House, Bombay, 1968).

Messner, R, *K2, Mountain of Mountains* (Kaye & Ward, London, 1981).

——*Solo Nanga Parbat* (Kaye & Ward, London, 1980).

Meyer, K, *How to Shit in the Woods* (Ten Speed Press, Berkeley, 1989). Excellent guide on how not to pollute.

Miller, C, *Khyber, British India's Northwest Frontier* (MacDonald and Jane's, London, 1977). History of the Khyber region.

Miller, K, *Continents in Collision* (Philip, London, 1982). Royal Geographical Society scientific expedition to the Karakorams.

Mons, B, *High Road to Hunza: An Account of the Author's Journey to Hunza in Kashmir* (Faber & Faber, London, 1958).

Moorcroft, W, *Travels in the Himalayan Provinces of Hindustan and the Panjab* (London, 1841).

Moorhouse, G, *To the Frontier* (Holt, Rinehart and Winston, New York, 1985). A journey round Pakistan with a description of people and places.

Murphy, D, *Where the Indus Is Young* (John Murray, London, 1977). Diary of an eccentric Irishwoman who spent a winter walking in Baltistan with her six-year-old daughter. Vivid descriptions.

——*Full Tilt* (John Murray, London, 1965). Bicycling from Ireland to India via Pakistan's Northern Areas. Full of encounters and insights.

Naess, A and others (trans. Sölvi and Richard Bateson) *Tirich Mir: The Norwegian Himalaya Expedition* (Hodder and Stoughton, London, 1952). The first ascent of Tirich Mir, written by the expedition members.

Naipaul, V S, *Among the Believers* (Deutsch, London, 1981). Travels in Iran, Pakistan and Indonesia, comparing Islamic peoples.

Neve, A, *The Tourist's Guide to Kashmir, Skardoo etc* (Civil and Military Gazette, Lahore, 1945). Great stage-by-stage description of travel in the last days of British rule. Tantalising list of maps then available.

Newby, E, *A Short Walk in the Hindu Kush* (Pan, London, 1981). Side-splitting account of hiking in Afghanistan's Panjshir Valley.

Patey, T, *One Man's Mountain* (Gollancz, London, 1971). Includes Muztagh Tower and Rakaposhi.

Pennell, T L, *Among the Wild Tribes of the Afghan Frontier* (London, 1909; reprint Oxford University Press, Karachi, 1975). Story of the life of a British missionary doctor in Bannu, NWFP.

Polo, Marco, *Travels* (in Latin, 1485; Travels Retold, Penguin, London, 1958).

Polunin, O, and Stainton, A, *Flowers of the Himalaya* (Oxford University Press, London, Delhi and Karachi, 1987). The best flower book for the Himalaya and Karakoram regions.

Reeves, R, *Passage to Peshawar* (Simon and Schuster, New York, 1984). Excellent analysis of present-day Pakistan.

Roberts, T J, *The Mammals of Pakistan* (Ernest Benn, London, 1977). Description with drawings of 158 species found in Pakistan.

——*The Birds of Pakistan*, Vols I and II (Oxford University Press, Karachi, 1991). The complete bird guide.

Robertson, G S, *The Kafirs of the Hindu Kush* (Lawrence and Bullen, London, 1896; reprint Oxford University Press, Karachi, 1974). The classic survey of the Kafir Kalash.

——*Chitral, the Story of a Minor Siege* (London, 1898).

Roch, A, *Karakoram-Himalaya, Sommets de 7000 metres* (Victor Attinger, Paris, 1935). International expedition to Gasherbrum I, Sia Kangri and Baltoro Kangri, with filmstar and film crew. Great descriptions. Not translated.

Rowell, G, *In the Throne Room of the Mountain Gods* (Sierra Club, San Francisco,1977; new edition with colour photos 1986). American 1975 expedition to K2. Superb description of history and people of Baltoro region and candid view of what expedition life is really like.

Saunders, V, *Elusive Summits* (Hodder & Stoughton, London, 1990). Attempts Conway's Ogre (Baintha Brakk) on the Biafo Glacier; Bojohaghur Duanasir in Hunza and Rimo in India—and succeeds on Spantik in Nagar.

Schaller, G B, *Stones of Silence* (Viking, New York, 1980). Exciting reading of Schaller's wildlife survey of 1972–75 in Chitral, Hunza and Baltistan (Baltoro Glacier).

Schofield, V, *Every Rock, Every Hill: The Plain Tale of the North-West Frontier and Afghanistan* (Century, London, 1984).

Schomberg, R C, *Between Oxus and Indus* (Martin Hopkinson, London, 1935; reprint Karachi, 1980).

——*Kafirs and Glaciers: Travels in Chitral* (Martin Hopkinson, London, 1938). Exploring northern Pakistan.

——*Unknown Karakoram* (Martin Hopkinson, London, 1936). Expedition to Shimshal in 1934.

Seaver, G, *Francis Younghusband: Explorer and Mystic* (John Murray, London, 1952). Biography.

Shaw, I, *Pakistan Handbook* (John Murray, London, 1989). Complete guide to Pakistan.

Shaw R B, *Visits to High Tartary, Yarkand and Kashgar, and Return Journey over the Karakoram Pass* (London, 1871). The first Westerner to reach Kashgar.

Shipton, E, *Blank on the Map* (reprint in *The Six Mountain-Travel Books*, Diadem, London, 1985). Exploring and mapping the central Karakoram, north of the Baltoro Glacier, in 1937.

——*Upon that Mountain* (reprint in *The Six Mountain-Travel Books*, Diadem, London, 1985). The last chapter describes the Hispar Glacier and Snow Lake in 1939.

——*That Untravelled World* (Hodder & Stoughton, London, 1969). Well-written autobiography by one of Britain's most famous explorers.

Shor, J and F, *At World's End in Hunza* (*National Geographic Magazine*, No 104, 1953).

Singer, A, *Lords of the Khyber* (Faber & Faber, London, 1984). Yet another history of the Pathan-British encounter in the NWFP.

Staley, J, *Words for My Brother* (Oxford University Press, Karachi, 1982). Extensive travel in Chitral, Gilgit and Hunza; alternately interesting and irritating.

——*Economy and Society in the High Mountains of Northern Pakistan* (Modern Asian Studies 3, 1969).

Stein, A, *Ancient Khotan* (Clarendon Press, Oxford, 1907; reprint Cosmo Publications, New Delhi, 1980). Stein's journey through Gilgit and Hunza and over the Mintaka Pass into China in 1900. Detailed academic report, exploring history and archaeology. Fascinating reading.

——*Serindia*, Vol I (Clarendon Press, Oxford, 1921). Detailed academic report of Stein's explorations through Swat, Dir and Chitral and across the Boroghil Pass into China in 1906. He traces the routes of Chinese Buddhist pilgrims and of Marco Polo and discusses history and archaeology.

——*Innermost Asia*, Vol I (Clarendon Press, Oxford, 1928; reprint Cosmo Publications, New Delhi, 1981). Stein's journey in 1913 through Chilas, Darel, Tangir and Yasin and over the Darkot and Boroghil passes to Kashgar.

——*On Alexander's Track to the Indus* (Macmillan, London, 1929).

——*Ruins of Desert Cathay* (Macmillan, London, 1912; reprint Indus Publications, Karachi, 1975). Personal account of Stein's Serindia trip. In two volumes.

——*On Central Asian Tracks* (Macmillan, London, 1933). Personal narrative of Stein's three expeditions through northern Pakistan and into western China.

——*Sand-buried Ruins of Khotan* (Fisher Unwin, London, 1903). Personal narrative of a journey of archaeological and geographical exploration in Chinese Turkestan.

Stephens, I, *Horned Moon* (Chatto and Windus, London, 1953). An early post-independence journey through Pakistan, Kashmir and Afghanistan.

——*Politics and Apricots (Hunza and Nagir)* (*The Geographical Magazine*, No 25, 1953).

Swift, H, *Trekking in Pakistan and India* (Hodder and Stoughton, London, 1990). Excellent trekking guide.

Tasker, J, *Savage Arena* (Methuen, London, 1987).

Thesiger, W, *The Last Nomad, Visions of a Nomad* (Collins, London, 1987). Long walks in remote valleys; disappointing on route description, but interesting observations and people.

——*Desert, Marsh and Mountain* (Collins, London, 1979).

Thomson, H C, *The Chitral Campaign* (London, 1895).

Tilman, H M, *Two Mountains and a River* (Cambridge University Press, Cambridge, 1948; reprint in *The Seven Mountain-Travel Books*, Diadem, London, 1983). An attempt by Eric Shipton and Tilman to climb Rakaposhi and Mustagh Ata.

——*China to Chitral* (Cambridge University Press, Cambridge, 1951). Last two chapters describe the Mintaka and Chillinji passes in 1948.

Trench, C C, *The Frontier Scouts* (Cape, London, 1985). Includes an account of the Gilgit Scouts and the events of 1947.

Vigne, G T, *Travels in Kashmir, Ladak, Iskardo [Skardu], etc* (London, 1842). By the first European to explore Skardu and the Baltoro Glacier.

Visser-Hooft, J, *Among the Kara-Koram Glaciers in 1925* (Arnold, London, 1926). Dutch lady travels with her husband, Dr P C Visser—the first Westerners to visit Batura and Shimshal.

Walker, W W, *Paddling the Frontier* (Walji's Travel, Islamabad, 1989). A guide to whitewater rafting and canoeing in northern Pakistan.

Workman, F B and W H, *In the Ice World of Himalaya* (Fisher Unwin, London, 1901). Exploring Skoro Pass, Biafo Glacier and Snow Lake.

——*The Call of the Snowy Hispar* (Constable, London, 1910).

——*Two Summers in the Ice-Wilds of Eastern Karakoram* (Fisher Unwin, London, 1917). Early exploration of the Himalaya-Karakoram.

Younghusband, F E, *Heart of a Continent* (London, 1896; reprint John Murray, London, 1986). A British agent who travelled across China and all round northern Pakistan and India, collecting information.

——*Wonder of the Himalaya* (John Murray, London, 1924).

——*The Light of Experience: A Review of Some Men and Events of My Time* (Constable, London, 1927). Younghusband became very religious in later life.

Younghusband, G J and F E, *The Relief of Chitral* (London, 1895; reprint English Book House, Lahore, 1980). A contemporary account of the relief of Chitral in 1895, by two famous brothers.

Appendix 9

EXPEDITIONS IN NORTHERN PAKISTAN TO 1957

Year	Leader	Main results	Source
1835	Vigne	Deosai, Skardu, Panmah, Baltoro gls	*Travels in Kashmir . . .*
1850	Schlagintweit	explored Nanga Parbat	AJ XXXIII
1856	Schlagintweit	Baltoro	PRGS 1, JRGS XXVII , XXVIII
1856	Godwin-Austen	Panmah, Baltoro gls	*Where Men & Mountains Meet*
1870	Hayward	Gilgit, Yasin	*Where Men & Mountains Meet*
1874	Biddulph	Hindu Kush, Boroghil Pass	*Where Men & Mountains Meet*
1876/8	Biddulph	Hunza, Shandur Pass, Chitral	*Where Men & Mountains Meet*
1883	MacNair	Chitral, Shandur Pass, Gilgit	*Where Men & Mountains Meet*
1885	Lockhart	Gilgit, Yasin, Chitral, Kafiristan	*Where Men & Mountains Meet*
1887	Younghusband	E (Old) Mustagh Pass	*Heart of a Continent*
1889	Younghusband	Saltoro, Hunza, Shimshal, Chitral	*Heart of a Continent*
1892	Conway	Hispar, Biafo, Baltoro gls	AJ XVI
1895	Mummery	explored S & W sides of Nanga Parbat	AJ XVIII
1899	Bullock-Workman	Biafo, Snow Lake	AJ IXX & XX
1902	Eckenstein	Baltoro, K2 to 6,700m	*Six mois dans l'Himalaya*
1902-3	Bullock-Workman	Chogo Lungma Gl	AJ XXII
1903	Feber & Honigmann	E Mustagh Pass, Baltoro	Bol CAI 1906
1908	Bullock-Workman	Hispar Gl	AJ XXIII, *Call of the Snowy Hispar*
1909	Duke of Abruzzi	Baltoro, Concordia, Chogolisa to 7,500m	AJ XXV
——	Longstaff	Saltoro Pass, Siachen Gl	GJ June 1910
1911-2	Bullock-Workman	Baltoro, Siachen	AJ XXXII
1913	Kellas	Diamer face of Nanga Parbat	GJ II 1917
1925	Visser	Hunza, Batura, Shimshal	GJ Dec 1926
1926	Mason	Shaksgam, Shimshal	GJ Apr 1927, *Abode of Snow*
1927	Montagnier	Ghujerab, Shimshal	GJ LXXII
1929	duke of Spoleto	Baltoro, Mustagh & Sarpo Lago passes	GJ May 1930
1932	Merkl	S side of Nanga Parbat	AJ XLIV
1933	Gregory & Auden	Biafo Gl	HJ VI
1934	Merkl	N side of Nanga Parbat	HJ VII
——	Dyhrenfurth	Baltoro, Baltoro Kangri, Sia Kangri	Alpes Feb & Mar and books
1936	de Ségogne	Baltoro, Hidden Peak to 6,800m	*Alpinisme* 1936, Montagne 1937
1937	Wien	N side of Nanga Parbat	HJ 1938
——	Shipton & Tilman	N side of K2, Braldu, Snow Lake	GJ Apr 1938, AJ 1938, HJ *Blank on the Map*
1938	Bauer	Nanga Parbat to 7,250m	AJ 1939, HJ XI

——	Houston	Baltoro, K2 to 7,900m	AAJ 1939, AJ 1939, HJ XI
——	Secord & Vyvyan	Rakaposhi to 6,860m	HJ XI, AJ 1939
——	Waller	Masherbrum to 7,620m	AJ 1938, HJ XI 1939
1939	Wiessner	Baltoro, K2 to 8,300m	AAJ 1940
——	Shipton	Hispar, Biafo, Panmah gls	GJ June 1940 & *Upon that Mountain*
——	Aufschnaiter	Nanga Parbat, Diamer face to 6,100m	HJ 1947 & *Seven Years in Tibet*
1943	Schomberg	Hispar, Nushik Pass, Chogo Lungma	AJ 1947
1945	Schomberg	E Mustagh Pass	HJ 1950
1947	Gyr & Kappeler	explored Rakaposhi & Haramosh	BW IV
——	Shipton & Tilman	Rakaposhi and Chalt	*Two Mountains and a River*
1950	Crace & Marsh	Shimshal	BW VI
1953	Herligkoffer	Buhl climbs Nanga Parbat	*Nanga Parbat Story*
——	Houston	K2, Windy Gap, Skoro Pass	MM 1954
——	Desio	attempt on K2	*La conquista del K2*
——	(American)	attempt on K2	AJ 1954
1954	Desio	K2 first ascent	AJ Vol 1954, 1955
——	Tissières	Rakaposhi attempt from SW	MW 1955, AJ 1955 &1956
——	Herligkoffer	attempt on Broad Peak	*Deutsche am Broad Peak*
1955	Conway	Masherbrum to 7,000m	AJ 1956, NZAJ 1956
——	Sander	Chogo Lungma Gl, Spantik	BW XI
——	Imanishi	Hispar, Biafo, Baltoro	HJ 1958
——	Francis	Hushe Valley	*Appalachia* 1955
——	Desio	geographic exploration of Karakoram	*Scarpone* 5221/55
1956	Banks & MacInnes	Rakaposhi to 7,160m	AAJ 1957, AJ May 1957
——	Hartog	Mustagh Tower	AJ 1956
——	Magnone	Mustagh Tower	GHM Annals 1956, Montagne 1956
——	Moravec	Gasherbrum II, Sia Kangri	BW 1958
——	Greenald	Biafo–Hispar gls	AAJ 1957, AJ 1959
——	Tyndale-Biscoe	Barpu and Kukuar gls, Nagar	HJ 1957, NZHJ 1957
1957	Schmuck	Broad Peak, Chogolisa to 7,400m	BW XII, *Broad Peak*
——	Gregory	Distaghil Sar to 6,700m	HJ 1958, Alpes 1958
——	Shipton	Siachen	AJ 1958, HJ XXI
——	Walmsley	Masherbrum to 7,710m	AJ 1958, AAJ 1958, HJ 1958
——	Streather	Haramosh to 6,300m	AAJ 1958, *Last Blue Mountain*

AJ = *Alpine Journal*, AAJ = *American Alpine Journal*, Alpes = *Les Alpes*, Alpinisme = quarterly of the Groupe de Haute Montagne (Paris), *Appalachia* = bulletin of the Appalachian Mountain Club (Boston), Bol CAI = *Bollettino del Club Alpino Italiano*, BW = *Berge der Welt* (*Mountains of the World*) , GHM = Groupe de Haute Montagne, GJ = *Geographical Journal*, HJ = *Himalayan Journal*, JRGS = *Journal of the Royal Geographical Society*, MM = *Montagnes du Monde*, MW = *Mountain World*, Montagne = *La Montagne*, NZAJ = *New Zealand Alpine Journal*, PRGS = *Periodical of the Royal Geographical Society*, RGS = Royal Geographical Society, *Scarpone* = a climbing magazine

Appendix 10

ARTICLES ON THE KARAKORAM, THE HINDU KUSH AND NANGA PARBAT IN ALPINE JOURNAL, 1955–89

To the Monk's Head on Rakaposhi, by R R E Chorley, 1955
Struggle for Rakaposhi, by M E B Banks, 1956
The Climbing of the Muztagh Tower, by J M Hartog, 1956
The Second Attempt on Masherbrum, by L R Hewitt, 1956
The Ascent of Rakaposhi, by F R Brooke, 1958
Masherbrum 1957, by J Walmsley, 1958
The Imperial College Karakoram Expedition, 1957 (Siachen and K12), by E E Shipton, 1958
The First Ascent of Haramosh, by H Roiss, 1959
The Italian Expedition to Gasherbrum IV, by F Maraini, 1956
The First Ascent of Chogolisa, by T Kuwabara, 1959
Snow Lake, 1956, by D H Greenland, 1959
The Army Mountaineering Association Expedition, 1959, by H R A Streather, 1960
The Batura Muztagh Expedition, 1959, by J I Edwards, 1960
A Roman Flag on Saraghrar Peak, by F Moraini, 1960
The Polish Expedition to the Hindu Kush, 1960, by B Chwascinski, 1961
Distaghil Sar, by W Stefan, 1961
Ascent of Trivor, by C W F Noyce, 1961
The Ascent of Masherbrum, by T F Hornbein, 1962
The Royal Air Force Karakoram Expedition, 1961, by A J M Smyth, 1962 (with map of Aling Gl)
Two Journeys in Swat Kohistan, by E J E Mills, 1962 (with map)
Swat and Indus Kohistan, by T Braham, 1963 (with map)
Khinyang Chhish, 1962, by P J Horniblow, 1963
The Ascent of Saltoro Kangri, by T Shidei, 1964
Communications on the Pakistan–British Karakoram Expedition, 1962, by J A E Hasell, 1964
More Climbs in Swat, by R J Isherwood, 1965
The First Ascent of Momhil Sar, by R Pischinger, 1965
The Scottish Hindu Kush Expedition, 1965, by J Wedderburn, 1966
Son Climbs from the Upper Tirich Glacier, by K Diemberger, 1966
The Exploration of the Hindu Kush, by B Chwascinski, 1966
German Chitral Expedition, 1965, by S Rausch, 1966
A Panorama of the Hindu Kush, by G Gruber, 1967
Journey to the Blue Valley, by P Newby, 1967
Shingeik Zom, the Smoking Mountain, by I Trübswetter, 1967
A Reconnaissance into North-east Chitral, by G Grubber, 1968

A Visit to the Chiantar Glacier Region, Eastern Hindu Kush, 1967, by A Linsbauer, 1968
Tirich Mir 1969, by H Day, 1970 (with map)
The Ascent of K6, by E Koblmüller, 1971 (with map)
North West Karakoram, by T Braham, 1971 (with map)
Two Expeditions to Malubiting, by A Kus & P von Grzycki, 1971 (with map)
Noshaq on Skis, by U Schwabe, 1972
British Central Hindu Kush Expedition 1971, by R Scott, 1972 (with map of Shkurigal Valley)
The Battle for Kinyang Chhish, by A Kus, 1972
Malubiting, Snowpeak above Desert Valleys, by H Schindlbacher, 1973
Chitral 1971, by W Stefan, 1973
Kaghan 1972, by W Stefan, 1973
Noshaq in Winter, by A Zawada, 1974
Hindu Kush, Alpine Style, by P D Boardman, 1974
Spanish Expedition Hindu Kush 1973, by J M Montfort, 1974
Sia Kangri (7,422m) 1974 Diary, by W Stefan, 1975
Shispare Climbed: Polish-German Expedition 1974, by J Kurczab, 1975
Trango Tower, by J V Anthoine, 1976
Trango Conclusion, by J V Antoine, 1977
Skhawr 1975 (Hindu Kush), by M Bala, 1977
Mountains of the Thui Gol, by D Broadhead, 1977
Victory and Tragedy on Broad Peak, by K Glasek, 1977
A Summer in Gilgit (1975) Part 1, by R Collister, 1977 (with map)
A Summer in Gilgit (1975) Part 2, by R Collister, 1978 (with map)
The British Ogre Expedition 1977, by J V Antoine, 1978
A Hundred Days in the Himalaya 1977 Latok II, by P Nunn, 1978
Spanish Expedition to Saraghrar 1977, by R Bramona, 1978
Polish K2 Expedition, by J Kurczab, 1978
1978 American K2 Expedition, by H Adams Carter, 1979
Wakhan 1977, by L Griffin, 1979
The Ascent of Thui II, by N P Tritton, 1979 (with map)
Anglo-Polish Hindu Kush Expedition 1977, by M Brniak, 1979
First Ascent of Pruppoo-Brukh (c7,000), Japanese Railway Workers, 1979
Buni Zom, by R Isherwood, 1980
Chilean Karakoram Expedition 1979 (Gasherbrum II), by G Oyarzún, 1980
Rakaposhi from the North, by S Kodama, 1981
British Conway's Ogre Expedition 1977, by A V Saunders, 1981
British 1980 Expedition to Baltoro Kangri, by B Hall, 1981
British West Karakoram Expedition 1981, by J Nixon, 1982 (with map of Thaime Chish)
Kanjut Sar West Face, by M Fujii, 1983
Oropolitics, by J Sircar, 1984 (with map of eastern Karakoram)

Broad Peak, by K Palmowska, 1984
Under the Spell of K2 and Gasherbrum, by K Diemberger, 1984
The East Pillar of Nanga Parbat, by K Herligkoffer, 1984 (with map)
A Sortie on Broad Peak, by K Diemberger, 1985
Broad Peak Climbed in One Day, by K Wielicki, 1985
Autumn in Shimshal and Naltar, by S Venables, 1985 (with map of Malanguti Glacier and Naltar)
Second Ascent of the Mustagh Tower, by M Duff, 1985
Bojohagar, by M Fowler, 1985
Siachen Indo-British Expedition 1985, by S Venables & D Wilkinson, 1986 (with map)
The Eastern Karakoram, by Kapadia, 1986
Scottish Gasherbrum III Expedition, by D Rubens, 1986 (with map)
Excursions and Climbs from the Karakoram Highway, by D Scott, 1986
Sosbun Glacier Region, by L Griffin, 1986
Alpine Club Karakoram Meet August 1985, by B Murphy, 1986
Walking Conway's Great White Roof, the First Traverse of Chogolisa, by A Fanshawe, 1987
The Golden Pillar, by A V Saunders, 1988
Karakoram Lessons, by R Payne, 1988
Crossing the Kurdopin, by Philip Bartlett, 1988
Expedition Style, by T Braham, 1988
On Trekking, by John Owen, 1988
Ups and Downs on Kunyang Kish, by Andy Wingfield, 1989

The *American Alpine Journal, Geographical Journal, Mountain World, Mountain, High* and many other mountain and trekking magazines have similarly impressive lists of interesting and informative articles.

Appendix 11

PAKISTAN'S HIGHEST MOUNTAINS

Most mountains have several peaks, some of which are merely numbered instead of named. In Pakistan there are five peaks over 8,000 metres, 29 over 7,500 metres and 108 over 7,000 metres.

Rank and name	Height m (ft)	Range	World rank
1. K2	8,611 (28,268)	Karakoram	2
2. Nanga Parbat	8,125 (26,656)	Himalaya	9
3. Gasherbrum I (Hidden)	8,068 (26,470)	Karakoram	11
4. Broad Peak	8,047 (26,444)	Karakoram	12
5. Gasherbrum II	8,035 (26,362)	Karakoram	14
6. Gasherbrum III	7,952 (26,087)	Karakoram	15
7. Gasherbrum IV	7,925 (26,014)	Karakoram	17
8. Distaghil Sar	7,885 (25,869)	Karakoram	20
9. Kunyang Chhish	7,852 (25,761)	Karakoram	22
10. Masherbrum NE	7,821 (25,660)	Karakoram	24
11. Rakaposhi (Domani)	7,788 (25,550)	Karakoram	27
12. Batura I	7,785 (25,541)	Karakoram	28
13. Kanjut Sar	7,760 (25,460)	Karakoram	29
14. Saltoro Kangri I	7,742 (25,400)	Karakoram	33
15. Trivor	7,720 (25,330)	Karakoram	36
16. Tirich Mir	7,708 (25,287)	Hindu Kush	41
17. Chogolisa I	7,654 (25,111)	Karakoram	46
18. Shispare (Batura)	7,619 (24,970)	Karakoram	49
19. Skyang Kangri	7,544 (24,750)	Karakoram	58
20. Pumari Chhish W	7,492 (24,580)	Karakoram	67
21. Noshaq	7,492 (24,580)	Hindu Kush	68
22. Tirich Mir NW	7,487 (24,563)	Hindu Kush	69
23. K12	7,468 (24,500)	Karakoram	73
24. Teram Kangri	7,463 (24,485)	Karakoram	74
25. Malubiting W	7,452 (24,448)	Karakoram	76

26. Sia Kangri	7,422 (24,350)	Karakoram	79
27. Skil Brum	7,420 (24,344)	Karakoram	80
28. Teram Kangri II	7,406 (24,298)	Karakoram	82
29. Haramosh	7,406 (24,298)	Karakoram	84
30. Istoro Nal	7,403 (24,288)	Hindu Kush	85
31. Mount Ghent	7,400 (24,278)	Karakoram	86
32. Yukshin Gardan	7,400 (24,278)	Karakoram	87
33. Ultar I	7,388 (24,239)	Karakoram	88
34. Teram Kangri III	7,381 (24,216)	Karakoram	90
35. Sherpi Kangri	7,380 (24,212)	Karakoram	91
36. Karun Koh	7,350 (24,114)	Karakoram	100
37. Momhil Sar	7,342 (24,088)	Karakoram	103
38. Saraghrar Peak I	7,338 (24,075)	Hindu Kush	104
39. Bajohagur-Duanasir	7,329 (24,145)	Karakoram	106
40. Gasherbrum V	7,321 (24,019)	Karakoram	107
41. Baltoro Kangri I	7,312 (23,989)	Karakoram	113
42. Urdok Peak I	7,300 (23,950)	Karakoram	114

Appendix 12

METRES TO FEET CONVERSION TABLE

metres	feet	metres	feet
3,300	10,827	6,100	20,013
3,400	11,155	6,200	20,342
3,500	11,483	6,300	20,670
3,600	11,811	6,400	20,998
3,700	12,139	6,500	21,326
3,800	12,467	6,600	21,654
3,900	12,795	6,700	21,982
4,000	13,124	6,800	22,310
4,100	13,452	6,900	22,638
4,200	13,780	7,000	22,966
4,300	14,108	7,100	23,294
4,400	14,436	7,200	23,622
4,500	14,764	7,300	23,951
4,600	15,092	7,400	24,279
4,700	15,420	7,500	24,607
4,800	15,748	7,600	24,935
4,900	16,076	7,700	25,263
5,000	16,404	7,800	25,591
5,100	16,733	7,900	25,919
5,200	17,061	8,000	26,247
5,300	17,389	8,100	26,575
5,400	17,717	8,200	26,903
5,500	18,045	8,300	27,231
5,600	18,373	8,400	27,560
5,700	18,701	8,500	27,888
5,800	19,029	8,600	28,216
5,900	19,357	8,700	28,544
6,000	19,685	8,800	28,872

INDEX

Page numbers in italics indicate maps. Those in bold face are main descriptions.